Sovereign Forces

SOVEREIGN FORCES

*Everyday Challenges to Environmental Governance
in Latin America*

John-Andrew McNeish

berghahn
NEW YORK • OXFORD
www.berghahnbooks.com

First published in 2021 by
Berghahn Books
www.berghahnbooks.com

© 2021 John-Andrew McNeish

Library of Congress Cataloging-in-Publication Data

Names: McNeish, John-Andrew, author.
Title: Sovereign forces : everyday challenges to environmental governance in Latin America /
John-Andrew McNeish.
Description: New York, N.Y. : Berghahn Books, 2021. | Includes bibliographical references
and index.
Identifiers: LCCN 2020051926 (print) | LCCN 2020051927 (ebook) |
ISBN 9781800731080 (hardback) | ISBN 9781800731097 (ebook)
Subjects: LCSH: Environmental policy—Latin America. | Natural resources—Latin
America—Management. | Mineral industries—Government policy—Latin America. |
Energy industries—Government policy—Latin America.
Classification: LCC HD9502.L32 M37 2021 (print) | LCC HD9502.L32 (ebook) |
DDC 333.7098—dc23
LC record available at https://lccn.loc.gov/2020051926
LC ebook record available at https://lccn.loc.gov/2020051927

British Library Cataloguing in Publication Data

A catalogue record for this book is available from the British Library

ISBN 978-1-80073-108-0 hardback
ISBN 978-1-80073-109-7 ebook

CONTENTS

FIGURES

ACKNOWLEDGEMENTS

At its end, it will be clear that this book is not a momentary reflection. It is a patchwork of different moments, intertwined ideas, debates and experiences stretching across borders, cultures, peoples and distances. Spanning over twenty years of my work and experience, I have a lot of people to thank and acknowledge. Their lives, their minds, their hospitality, their friendship and their support are what made this book possible at all. In this light, there is no single author.

In Bolivia, Guatemala and Colombia, there have been threats and challenges, but also enormous warmth and generosity from individuals and communities who could easily have ignored or felt threatened by my presence. More often than not, I have been taken in as though I was a member of the family. This was frequently by people who had little material wealth to share, and who had every reason because of their history and experience to suspect the presence of a pale-faced European. They nonetheless opened their doors and let me past the threshold of their homes, practices, imaginations, hopes and opinions. Don Vicente, this started with you in Santuario de Quillacas.

There are of course individuals (not all of whom I can mention here) who stand out in the course of these many years, some of them because of their humanity and others because of their wonderful mentality. Certainly, this book and the case study research to which it refers would not have been possible without the specific assistance and inspiration of Hector Jaime Vinasco and Renso Parra Garcia. Your dedication to your communities and the protection of the natural world on which we all rely is both astounding and truly inspirational. Arturo Matute, you and your family sum up the warmth and generosity of the latino family.

I have also been lucky enough to be able to work with the best in the business in social anthropology and international research. The past projects on which this book builds have combined wonderful scholars from both home and abroad. My close collaborators in past project design and research include Owen Logan, Axel Borchgrevink, Iselin Strønen, Cecilie Ødegaard, Indra Overland, Espen Leifsen, Einar Braathen, Maria Therese Gustafsson, Almut

Schilling Vacaflor, Rikard Lalander and Maria Guzman Gallegos. Together we have also had the pleasure of working with great Latin American-based scholars such as Fernanda Wanderley, Ivonne Farah, Don Sawyer, Maria Victoria Canino, Viviana Weitzer, Luis Sanchez Vasquez, Virgilio Reyes, Catalina Vallejo and Gabriel Rojas. I also feel lucky to have worked with my academic heroes: Rachel Sieder, Bret Gustafson, Suzana Sawyer, Anna Zalik, Fernando Coronil and Arturo Escobar. All of you have had a formative impact on my work, even when we have had cause to disagree.

Other recent academic experiences have also had an impact. I would not have started writing this book had it not been for the possibility to find calm as a visiting scholar from 2017 to 2018 at the Centre for Iberian and Latin American Studies (CILAS), University of California at San Diego (UCSD). Nancy Postero and David Mares were great hosts during my sabbatical year, and the imprint of my discussions with other visitors to the Centre and colleagues in the Indigenous Resource Politics group at UCSD are visible in the following pages. Nancy, I am stoked to be writing with you now.

Acknowledgement must also made of the support of my colleagues and students at the Norwegian University of Life Sciences (NMBU). The teaching and supervision of postgraduate students continues to be one of the most inspiring parts of my job. It is also a space for connections between ideas and fields that otherwise would never meet. I also recognize the value of my colleagues at the department and in particular the intellectual exchanges hosted by the Rights and Power in Development (RAPID) research cluster. Projects and publications are born out of these interactions. An expression of thanks to the University and the Norwegian Research Council (NFR) is also in order, given the amount of financing and flexibility they have granted to my research efforts over the years.

Anne, Isabella and Alex, words nearly fail me in expressing the deep gratitude I have to you as my family. You have suffered at times from my absence and my absent-minded or otherwise preoccupied presence when at home. None of what can be found in these pages would be possible, or mean anything, without you and your enduring love. You are my driving force. You are my *peace* of mind. . .

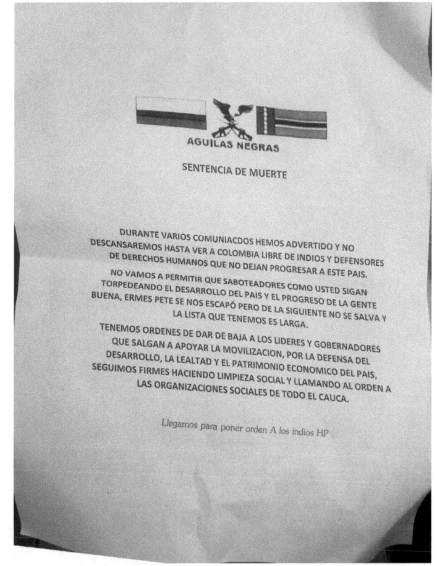

Figure 0.1 Death threat, 2016. Photo by Hector Jaime Vinasco. Published with permission

Introduction

SOVEREIGNTY MATTERS

An email marked urgent arrived in my inbox in December 2016. Given that messages sent to academics are rarely marked urgent, this mail stood out amongst the list of other emails from students and colleagues. It had been sent with a red flag from someone I barely knew in Colombia. I had met Hector Jaime Vinasco[1] some months before at a research conference in Santa Cruz, Bolivia, but he was not an academic. Hector Jaime, as I had learned in Santa Cruz, is a community leader from one of Colombia's indigenous communities in the Chocó region.[2] He had participated with surprising oratory skills in the event in Santa Cruz along with another colleague to publicly highlight the campaign he and his people had been involved in throughout his life. Hector Jaime's eloquent presentation contained a series of important insights, but also a positioning on self-determination I had not heard stated so directly by indigenous leaders I had met before. 'We are the state', Hector Jaime announced. 'When the Colombian state arrives to negotiate with us our claims of ownership to land and resources, we respond that "we are the state in this land, not you".'

The community had earlier elected Hector Jaime governor of the indigenous reserve. Having completed his period of service in that role, he had moved with the community's agreement into the role of heading a committee focused on local environmental challenges. This was connected to an effort to confront the extractive interests of private corporations and the Colombian state within their territory. Hector Jaime was involved in a campaign aimed at the defence of his community's land from encroachment by large-scale mining and other commercial interests. This was the continuation of a long history of struggle in which, despite the formal title given to the reserve in the mid-1500s, it had been necessary to constantly innovate institutional and political action in order to defend their territory. While Hector Jaime's territory had a history and tradition of small-scale artisanal mining, his community feared the consequences that large-scale mining and oil and gas exploration could have on the local environment. The community was well aware of the experience of other communities in Colombia and elsewhere, in which extractive activities had directly damaged and restricted the local water supply, as well as further restricting their sustainable use of the land for small-scale agriculture, hunting and fishing. Hector Jaime's email related to this historical context, but its urgency was caused by more recent and vital events.

Hector Jaime was trying to make contact because he now feared for his life. He had received an anonymous telephone message stating that an assassin (*sicario*) had been hired by a BACRIM (criminal band) organization[3] to kill him and his immediate family within the coming days and weeks. A letter posted through his door further suggested that the order related to the work he and his fellow community members were doing to block mining and other extractive activities entering their legal territory. The letter from the BACRIM organization placed this in its own twisted moral terms of social cleansing (*limpieza social*). The letter states: 'We are not going to permit saboteurs like you to continue torpedoing the development of the country and the progress of good people.' It continues by stating 'we have orders to bring down those leaders and governors who support mobilization, for the defence of development, loyalty and economic patrimony of the country.' Hector Jaime's email pleaded for assistance to push, by signature campaign, post and telephone, the national police and authorities to take this threat to his life seriously by providing protection and investigating the case. This is not exactly what happened.

Hector Jaime and his family continue to live in fear despite the email campaign started by colleagues from around the world. Direct protection by the state was not granted, but as a result of outside pressure, Hector Jaime was offered a bulletproof vest and the national police increased patrols of the area. A formal investigation to identify the source of the death threat was also started. Reflecting more recently on this moment, Hector Jaime – who graciously provided consent for its recount – is quick to point out that this threat was not only one to his person, but also to his community and to their way of life.

I start with this story not only to emotively grab attention, but also to immediately exemplify the key analytic intention of the volume, i.e. to insist that sovereignty is a vital matter. Sovereignty is a matter that is directly implicated in questions of land, territory and energy development, and a matter that persists as one of life and death for people in Latin American and further afield. It plays a key role in making the material (natural resources and their human value) political.

In recent decades, globalization and the dominance of the market economy made it appear that the importance of the state and, with it, of sovereignty was on the wane. Commodity markets – the sale of primary exports or raw materials – no longer appeared for many to be dictated by the interests of individual states and resource availability. They seemed largely controlled and guided by the operation of stock markets, trading algorithms, corporations and shareholder interests. At least this was the case until price fluctuations in the price of oil, coal, other minerals and basic materials, and the knock-on effects on the prices of food and other essential goods would intermittently remind us all of the facts. States not only continued to regulate for the market, but through the setting of tariffs, rents and prices via bilateral agreements or through negotiating bodies such as the Organization of the Petroleum Exporting Countries (OPEC) have continued to hold significant sway over the economy.

As I write this chapter, the price of oil in the US has fallen below zero for this first time in history (Ambrose 2020), and the oil economy in Norway, where I live, is under serious stress because of the fall in international prices. It was only an ideological sleight of hand that created the impression that it was the market that mattered, and not the state – or the state's sovereign claims on territory and resources. This magic of the market has evidently been significantly dispelled in recent years and not only because of the instability of the international markets and fluctuations of prices.

As Piketty (2020) has newly reminded us, markets, profits and capital are all historical constructs that depend on choices, and these choices are expressed as ideological assertions. In recent years, it is clear from the election of an increasing number of populist right-wing leaders – who formally denounce liberal globalists – that the magic of globalization and the market, and the role of the state is being reworked. A new ideological sleight of the hand is taking place to put a new – and very troubling – emphasis on the state and sovereignty, whilst also protecting business. New policies for immigration, border control and the relaxation of environmental regulations, as well as political decisions such as Brexit and the 'building of the wall' on the US-Mexican border, are all evidence of this. The COVID-19 pandemic has also had an impact, enabling states to express their sovereignty over land and territory in new ways, such as mandating curfews and the electronic surveillance of citizens as possible carriers of the virus.

Sovereignty is an issue that evidently still matters at the global scale. However, as this book makes clear, it is also important to draw attention to the persisting importance of sovereignty at other scales and of its empirical implication in concrete decisions regarding the direction of development, livelihood, and opportunities of individuals and their communities. Indeed, as I will stress in the following pages, sovereignty is significantly implicated in the vital matter of national, regional and local decisions regarding the ownership, use, protection and management of natural resources.

In this regard, Hector Jaime's story is not an exceptional event. His experience is but a drop in the ocean of a myriad of histories of indigenous, peasant and pastoralist communities that have been threatened in their struggles to defend their culture, autonomy and territories. These struggles are to some extent well known from earlier anthropological texts and the publicity of international work towards the establishment of conventions to recognize and defend indigenous rights.[4] The coverage made by the media and environmentalists of high-profile clashes over land and resources (e.g. Standing Rock and the Dakota Access Pipeline in the United States; the Alberta tar-sands in Canada; the Belo Monte Dam in Brazil; the Chevron case in Ecuador; Yanacocha and Peru; Garzweiler in Germany; Repparfjordan in Norway, etc.) have also raised public awareness that the environment remains a focus of severely opposing opinions. However, what has not been given so much attention is the fact that there are signs that the pace and severity of these clashes have newly escalated.

The assassination of people in similar positions to Hector Jaime has become an all too regular occurrence in multiple locations around the world. In its 2019 report, the international human rights organization Global Witness highlighted that on average, more than three land defenders (civil society leaders, human rights activists, indigenous and peasant leaders, etc.) were killed every week in 2018 ('Enemies of the State?' 2019). As the report states, these attacks were driven by destructive industries such as mining, logging and agribusiness. It also reveals in detail how countless more people were threatened, arrested or thrown in jail for daring to oppose the governments or companies seeking to profit from their land. Concerned about the rising trend of violence towards land defenders, *The Guardian* newspaper in the United Kingdom has launched a database together with Global Witness in an attempt to accurately record and map what they view to be a murder epidemic. Within these figures, the 'post-conflict' violence in Colombia stands out – it ranks third after the Philippines and Brazil. Despite the signing of a peace accord in 2016 with the main guerrilla organization (FARC-EP) FARC-EU, in the intervening years until May 2019, a total of 837 activists were killed in Colombia (Le Billon, Roa-Garcia and López-Granada 2020). The Washington Office of Latin America (WOLA) has been closely following this rise in the assassinations of civil society leaders, including a list of names of the dead in its monthly human rights updates on Colombia

(Sànchez-Garzoli 2017). These killings have occurred in a context in which the victims have denounced the increasing presence of armed actors in their community or territory.

Recent paramilitary and criminal actions are also tied to significant efforts to expand interests over a wider spectrum of resource extraction, i.e. timber, mining and oil and gas extraction (Grave Aumento de Asesinatos de Quienes Defienden los Derechos Humanos en Colombia 2017). Paramilitary interests in extractive projects are driven by the possibility of profits from extortion and protection rackets, from the direct control of mining operations, from the whitewashing of money through legitimate business (a long-time strategy of the cartels) as well as deals made with mining and oil companies interested in bumping up security in the face of increasing tension and conflict with local communities. In the recent COVID-19 pandemic, media reports suggest that paramilitary and related criminal organizations (BACRIM) exploited the lockdown as a means to further locate and target their victims (Parkin Daniels 2020). This also unfortunately coincides with the Colombian government's own efforts to put in place 'online' consultations as a means to speed up the extractive licensing process during the pandemic.

By placing an emphasis on sovereignty, this book seeks to study the lesser-known backstory to resource contestations in Latin America – some more violent than others – and to demonstrate their positioning within more extensive histories. In doing so, I revisit previous writing linking Latin America's economic development to the exploitation of natural resources – and return to a lesser-known literature underlining the operation and importance of subnational claims to sovereignty, territory and resources. A new connection is made here between the complex dynamics of conflict and contestation of resource extraction in Bolivia, Guatemala and Colombia. It will become evident that the politics of resource use in these three countries inherits and differently reformulates largely forgotten but still influential histories of colonization, state-formation, racism and social exclusion. It is this ongoing history in which the formation of claims to sovereignty are not formulated by states alone, but also by the dynamic interaction between states, communities and private actors in connection with international interests and pressures that I mean to characterize and capture in this book. Differing understandings of access to territory and natural resources and the expansion and governance of extractive activities are also emphasized here as an important catalyst and cause for contrasting expressions of sovereignty.

Sovereign Forces aims to provide new and necessary insights into the causes, dynamics and necessary governance responses to socio-environmental contestation of natural resource extraction and related energy developments in Latin America. It does so by emphasizing the political nature of resource extraction and energy production, and the analytic value of the concept of *resource sovereignty*. Resource sovereignty is a compound concept that my colleagues and I have proposed in earlier work (McNeish 2017; McNeish, Borchgrevink and Logan 2015a; McNeish and Logan 2012), but that I intend to further detail and clarify in this volume. Put simply, resource sovereignty is a hybrid concept that recognizes the manner in which different social sectors bracket material interests and social claims together to form political claims for land and territory. As we will see in the following pages, claims of popular sovereignty often directly challenge those of the state and market, and in doing so can be generative of conflict and contestation, but also of proposals for necessary transformation and cooperation.

Emphasizing the way in which popular expressions of sovereignty interact with dominant expressions of state and corporate sovereignty, the book captures the way in which people at both the centre and the margins of states in Latin America relate to questions of energy and resource extraction. The book reveals anew the surprising centrality of indigenous and peasant peoples – often considered marginalized populations – in legitimately answering key questions regarding resource use, extraction and energy development in Latin American countries. As such, a critical view of resource politics and environmental governance in the region highlights an analytic and practical need to reinstate a substantive consideration of their claims to sovereignty in the present. By drawing attention to histories of grievance and contrasting epistemologies and ontologies, the argument developed here for resource sovereignty importantly contrasts and expands beyond earlier catch-all explanations of the 'resource curse', and importantly questions persistently dominant institutionalist and rational choice assumptions in the resource politics and environmental governance literature.

These points will be given further foundation in this introductory chapter, before the book's central chapters qualitatively and empirically expand these themes. The book explores and argues in favour of the 'everyday' value of combining empirical insight regarding resource sovereignty with a critical institutional perspective regarding environmental governance in the region. There is, as I will demonstrate in the final chapters of the book, a crucial value to resource sovereignty beyond the analytical.

Resource Extraction and Contested Sovereignty in Latin America

I do not want to lose the reader because of unnecessary detail. A short introduction to the region's history is provided here in order to demonstrate a key premise of the book you now read. This premise being that national sovereignty and the trajectory of development in Latin America has been largely defined by a competition to discover, exploit and create wealth from resource extraction. To be clear, the legacy of Latin America's colonial experience and economic reliance on the extraction and export of natural resources has left a marked imprint on the political and social formation of the region. The greatly abridged history that follows serves to establish the wider political background of later chapters and my contention that expressions of sovereignty have long been contested beyond the boundaries of state and government.

Multiple authors writing about Latin America's history – from the Spanish conquest to the present day – recognize the key role that natural resources have played in drawing Latin America into the dynamics and influence of globalization and have contributed to the region's economic, political and social transformation. Eduardo Galeano is perhaps one of Latin America's best-known writers for having summed up the foundations of this story in his now classic political economic analysis of the region's development: *Open Veins of Latin America: Five Centuries of the Pillage of a Continent* (1997). Gold and silver, cacao and cotton, rubber and coffee, fruit, hides and wool, petroleum, iron, nickel, manganese, copper, aluminium ore, nitrates and tin – these are the veins Galeano traces through the body of the entire continent, from the Rio Grande to the Caribbean, and all the way to their open ends where they empty into the coffers in the United States and Europe. Whilst it would be misleading to suggest that Latin American history corresponds entirely to a story of extraction, it is nonetheless striking how many of the key moments in the region and the development of its states correspond with attempts to directly exploit or remotely control its rich natural resource base for political and economic gain. I also acknowledge that forms of governance in other colonized regions of the world were at times also crudely extractive (Hansen and Stepputat 2001).

The story of the fifteenth-century Spanish conquest and its relationship to an Iberian hunger for wealth and fortune – as much as territory and souls – has been repeated in countless popular accounts and moral tales. This story contains many well-known episodes and tropes. It starts with the landfall of Columbus on a small island in the Bahamas in search of new trade routes for the Spanish Crown and the subsequent discovery of natives wearing jewellery of hammered gold and tales of an island made of gold. Following this encounter, the rest of Columbus' five-month voyage became a restless quest not of geographical exploration, but for golden treasure across the islands now known today as Cuba, Haiti and the Dominican Republic (Markham 2019). Although Columbus never discovered what he was looking for during this or his subsequent three voyages, edited versions of his account were widely read across Europe in the sixteenth century. Later explorers and *conquistadores* (conquerers) would be significantly motivated by these accounts. This would lead to the betrayal of the Aztecs by Hernàn Cortez. It would lead to Pizarro's ransom of Atahualpa in exchange for a room full of gold. Inspiring popular writing the Spanish obsession with the promise of gold and wealth would lead to multiple doomed expeditions in both the colonial and republican periods to search for the lost city of El Dorado (where the native chief was reputed to be covered from head to toe in gold dust). A similar disastrous fate would await British Coronel Percy Faucett's 1925 search for the Lost City of Z (Grann 2009).

The colonial period also included the Spanish enslavement of the local population to work in the great silver mine of Potosí, the world's largest industrial complex in the sixteenth century. The unprocessed silver shipped from Latin American to Europe between 1503 and 1660 totalled 16 million kilograms, three times the European reserves of the time (Hickel 2015). Similar exploitation would occur in the Portuguese colonization and establishment of mines and plantations in the territory of Brazil. A new labour force was sourced from Africa as up to 8 million of the indigenous population succumbed to disease and the inhumane conditions of the mines and plantations (Blackburn 1997). African slaves mainly from West Africa would in turn die in the hundreds of thousands as they were packed into the holds of ships like sardines and fed to the extractive endeavours and plantations of the New World.

Other lesser well-known, but equally important developmental moments in Latin American history are also strongly tied to natural resources and their politics. The Indian rebellions of the late eighteenth century and the nineteenth century (including the Wars of Independence (1808–33)) occurred as a reaction to the injustices of the colonial system and a desire for political and rights at their centre (Stavig, Schmidt and Walker 2008). However, claims for freedom from colonial rule were not without connection to natural resources and the desires that encircled them. As in the American Wars of Independence, ambitions of resource exploitation and the lifting of restrictions on the trade of commodities also played a key role in igniting discontent and eventual armed action. Rebellion and revolution were inspired not only by a desire for human freedom, but also by the brokerage of entrance into market networks and the increased freedom of colonial elites to trade. Indeed, many of the leaders of these events were military officers, but they were also prominent traders, entrepreneurs, business and plantation owners. Striking cases in point are Tupac Amaru and Tupac Katari, who led large-scale Indian rebellions on either side of the Peruvian and Bolivian border in the late 1700s (Stern 1987). Both of these figures are now celebrated by the Aymara and Quechua populations as heroes who fought the white man and had considerable military success until their eventual capture and capital punishment. Bolivia even has a telecommunications satellite named after Tupac Katari. Less well known in the present day is that Amaru and

Katari were also traders who, albeit frustrated by the limits to profits caused by the regulations of the Spanish colonial economy of Alto Peru, operated and became surprisingly successful with the colonial economic system.

The destinies of postrevolutionary republican governments were also tied in different ways to a new politics of land (private titling), plantation economies and the up-swing and down-swing of international commodity prices. Throughout the end of the nineteenth and early twentieth centuries, political fortunes would be won and lost on the basis of the boom and bust of markets for sugar, bananas, rubber, silver, tin, gold, oil, guano (nitrogen fertilizer) and timber. Indeed, both the internal machinations of national political elites and investors and of international regional competition in Latin American circled to a large degree around efforts to capture and control these raw materials. Wars would be fought in this period to secure territories where natural resources vital to national development and prosperity were to be found. These wars would both target and make use of indigenous peoples.

In the 1870s, the Argentinean military launched a military campaign, commonly referred to as *the conquest of the desert*, to establish dominance over Patagonia, its lands and its indigenous peoples (over 1,000 Mapuche were slaughtered and over 15,000 were displaced from their homeland). From 1879 to 1884, Bolivia, Peru and Chile entered into military conflict over access to and control of the Atacama Desert, a region rich in copper and mineral nitrate (important in the manufacture of explosives). The War of the Pacific ended with Chile and Peru agreeing on the division of territory and Bolivia losing its historical land access to the sea, which is still an issue of political tension to this day. Between 1932 and 1935, Bolivia and Paraguay carried out a military campaign against each other to secure oil resources in the Gran Chaco. Whilst little known outside of Latin America, the campaign is known as one of the bloodiest of the twentieth century in which the fighting was centred in the midst of the region's dry, hot and thorn-ridden expanse (Chesterton 2017). The horrors of the war would leave an indelible mark on the national consciousness of the populations of both sides. In Paraguay, it would force the political and legal recognition of the Guarani people (making their language a national language alongside Spanish), who had been a key source of manpower and knowledge, in an otherwise racist and authoritarian state. In Bolivia, the experience of the Chaco War would lead directly to a new relationship between the indigenous majority and the state, and the reformulation of political alliances necessary to spark the later Nationalist Revolution of 1952 (Young 2017).

The Chaco War was also a campaign where clear lines were not only redrawn between two states, but where the vicious competition between oil companies and alliances between the state and corporate sectors were revealed. Indeed, the origins of the war are commonly attributed at least in part to a conflict between Royal Dutch Shell (backing Paraguay) and Standard Oil (supporting Bolivia) in a bid to wrest control over oil resources in the Andean foothills of the Chaco from each other. Both corporations provided the opposing countries with financing for military armaments, including heavy machine guns and planes that had been developed for use on the European battlefields of the First World War. Throughout the late nineteenth and early twentieth centuries, there would be a series of other notable occasions in which foreign interests, both state and corporate, would intervene in regional affairs in order to guarantee investments. Although the Spanish and the Portuguese lost their foothold in the region, other European corporations and powers were heavily invested in extractive activities in the region as well as the construction of necessary supporting infrastructure such as railways, roads and ports. Significant reaction to European meddling in Latin American affairs would come not only from regional governments themselves, but also in the guise of the determination of the United States to rid the New World of the Old.

The Monroe Doctrine coined in 1850 in the inauguration speech of President James Monroe would be understood by the end of the nineteenth century as one of the most defining decisions of US foreign policy. The stated objective of the Monroe Doctrine was to free the newly independent colonies of Latin America from European intervention and so that the US could exert its own influence undisturbed. Monroe's message proclaimed anticolonial principles, yet it rapidly became the myth and means for subsequent generations of politicians to pursue expansionist foreign policies (Sexton 2012). In 1898, President Theodore Roosevelt would importantly re-interpret the Monroe Doctrine to provide justification for the US intervention in the remaining Spanish colony of Cuba. Following its show of force in Cuba, Spain ceded the Philippines, Puerto Rico and Guam to the United States. The United States also established Cuba and Hawaii as its protectorates in this period. The Spanish-American War marked the end of the Spanish colonies in the Americas and the new assertion of the United States to intervene in Latin America in cases of 'flagrant and chronic wrongdoing by a Latin American Nation'. This was also referred to as the *Big Stick ideology* because of Roosevelt's advice to 'speak low and carry a big stick'.[5] Although sparking outrage from Latin American governments and statesmen, President Roosevelt's corollary would become the grounding definition of US policy towards 'its backyard' for many years to come, and of its self-appointed role as the 'hemispheric policeman'.

In the early twentieth century Roosevelt's big stick policy took the form of 'gunboat diplomacy', in which concerns with the internal workings of independent states in the Pacific and the Americas would result in the appearance of American naval ships in a conspicuous show of force and influence. Such demonstrations of force also led to the development and use of the US marines in a series of contexts considered essential to American interests, and all with resource-related importance (Cuba, Panama, Honduras, Nicaragua, Mexico and the Dominican Republic). These interventions under Roosevelt ended with the withdrawal of troops from Haiti in 1934. These military actions are often referred to as the Banana Wars in reference to the support given by the US government to the operations of the United Fruit Company in Central America (Tucker 2002). However, it is important to note that these interventions also included wider resource and strategic concerns (such as the securing of coaling stations in key Pacific and Central American ports, intervention in the Mexican Revolution to ensure continued US investment in oil production and the securing of access to the Panama Canal).

The Monroe Doctrine was officially repealed when Roosevelt left office, but its logics and intentions to a large degree remained a basic tenet of US foreign policy and action towards Latin America through the mid- to late twentieth century. Indeed, new arguments and practical application would become particularly evident with the start of the Cold War. Reacting not only to the rising political power and influence of communism, but also the Soviet Union's increasing access to economic resources in the region, the US government sanctioned a series of covert intelligence operations to turn the tide in its strategic favour. From the late 1940s through to the fall of the Berlin Wall in 1989, the US government used the Central Intelligence Agency (CIA) and other parts of its intelligence services to intervene and influence the dynamics of Latin American electoral campaigns and processes. Funding and training were given to opposition groups not only to strengthen the foundation of democratic election campaigns, but where necessary to remove their political opposition by force. The failed CIA efforts to support an invasion of Cuba by opposition forces at the Bay of Pigs in 1961 and to topple Fidel Castro were part of these plans. More successfully, a series of political alliances were formed with the political right in Latin America. Support was given by the United States to secretive campaigns not only to politically destroy the political left wing, but also to remove its presence entirely. The result was a series of counter-insurgency campaigns the length and breadth of Latin America to remove perceived dangerous elements and to secure US natural resource interests. The reformist and left-leaning governments of Jacobo Arbenz in Guatemala in 1952 and Salvador Allende in 1970 are two notable instances where US support forced political transformation became visible due to the terrible loss of life and ensuing records of human rights abuse.

These progressive governments, in line with the Mexican (1910–20) and Cuban Revolutions (1953–59) before them, had promised significant land reform and the fair distribution of profits from economic activities to all citizens. Right-wing governments, military leaders and political parties coordinated with the United States and with each other to hunt for left-wing sympathizers, many of them academics and union leaders. This resulted in the establishment of Plan Condór in South America and Operation Charly in Central America (both involving targeted assassinations, acts of symbolic violence and the use of torture). It also resulted in the capture and killing of the famed Argentine guerrilla leader Che Guevara in the foothills of the Bolivian Andes in 1967 (he had been in Bolivia to foment a revolution amongst peasant farmers and miners) (Anderson 2010). Although indigenous communities were persecuted in some instances by the leftist insurgents because of their lack of ideological purity (e.g. Guatemala), in general the armed struggles of the left in this period relied heavily on the cultural inspiration and manpower of marginalized communities (Young 2019). Left-wing guerrilla operations continued (the Colombian National Liberation Army ELN being the longest, i.e. 1964 to the present day), but counter-insurgency actions orchestrated with North American military and financial assistance effectively removed (other than in Cuba) the chances of the Latin American left to gain a lasting foothold in government throughout the years of the Cold War. Largely as a result of this, right-wing military government would remain the norm in Latin America until the early 1990s.

Parallel to its counter-insurgency efforts, the United States also employed the more 'softly spoken' strategy of securing its material and ideological interests in Latin America through the provision of development assistance (Field 2014). The Alliance for Progress launched by a newly elected President John F. Kennedy in 1961 proposed 'to complete the revolution of the Americas, to build a hemisphere where all men can hope for a suitable standard of living and all can live out their lives in dignity and in freedom'.[6] The revolution that Kennedy spoke of here was of course a countermove to the possibility of Communist transformation. Progress in the form of investment was guided towards countries that distanced themselves clearly from Soviet interests, or heavy state regulation of US corporate investment in the region. Because of the programme, economic assistance to Latin America nearly tripled between the fiscal year 1960 and the fiscal year 1961. Between 1962 and 1967, the United States supplied $1.4 billion per year to Latin America. However, as regional critics at the time noted, the amount of aid did not equal the net transfer of resources and development from the region. Latin American countries still had to pay off their debt to the United States and other First World countries. In addition, profits from the investments usually returned to the United States, with this frequently exceeding new investment. The US Richard Nixon government in 1968 would result in the significant reduction of US development funding to Latin America. However, under Nixon, new funding would be released to US involvement in Latin America due to the identification of a new developmental and existential threat emanating from the region.

In 1972, the Nixon administration signed into US law the War on Drugs. US concerns regarding drug use were initially focused on domestic consumption, drug-related crime and the rising level of narcotics abuse by American soldiers taking part in the Vietnam War. However, the rapid rise in the organized trafficking of drugs from Andean countries and of the Colombian Medellin Cartel in particular would draw US attention, money and political influence back to its 'backyard'. Launched in 2000, Plan Colombia would prove to be one of the most expensive efforts to coordinate the eradication of coca cultivation in Latin America (Rosen 2014). By the time of its end in 2015, the US had spent $9.94 billion of combined foreign aid, military spending (71% of the total) and diplomatic resources to curb the expansion of the drug trade in Colombia. Started under the conservative Pastrana government in 1999, Plan Colombia was hailed as a resounding success by the Colombian and US governments. They cite its military results in significantly reducing the numbers of armed guerrilla forces in the country. However, whilst contributing to a reduction in the growth of the FARC-EP[7] and ELN[8] guerrilla organizations and therefore contributing to the conditions of the recent peace deal, international and domestic analysts have demonstrated that it failed drastically in its goal of eradicating the drug trade (Alpert 2016). Indeed, Plan Colombia is directly connected to a series of human rights abuses in the country. Until their formal disbanding in 2005, paramilitary organizations that had been allowed to flourish under Plan Colombia carried out a series of political assassinations and massacres – often of indigenous, peasant and Afro-descendant communities resistant to their cause.

Whilst Plan Colombia has wound down and the War on Drugs is increasingly discredited in its claims of success, the certification process established as a mechanism through which the US aims to generate political leverage in Latin America continues. Enacted by Congress in 1986, the certification process continues to demand tougher counter-narcotic measures, including aerial fumigation by governments of producer countries (Alsema 2019). Countries failing the US-defined measures face mandatory sanctions, including the withdrawal of foreign assistance not directly related to counter-narcotic programmes and US opposition to any loans those countries had sought from multilateral development banks. The administration may also waive sanctions against a country that is not fully certified if it determines that doing so is in the 'vital national interests' of the United States. For the affected countries (Colombia, Peru and Bolivia), the certification process represented the clear continuation of US intervention and influence in regional development.

International invention through structural adjustment policies originated due to a set of global disasters during the late 1970s: this included the international oil and debt crisis, but also the hyperinflation experienced by Latin American governments in the early 1980s. From the mid-1980s and into the 1990s, the World Bank and the International Monetary Fund (IMF) introduced a series of conditions to international loans designed to rein in the runaway economies of the region. Commonly including a policy package aged at streamlining government spending and institutions, and the privatization of previously nationalized industries (which were deemed as insufficiently profitable), many governments in the region became beholden as never before to the expectations of the international community. Although countries were encouraged to demonstrate their 'ownership' of responsible economic management through the production of Poverty Reduction Strategy Papers (PRSPs), critics claimed that the imposition of strict market-friendly 'neoliberal' guidelines and limits to the contents of these policy documents curtailed national and regional sovereignty. Critics also highlighted the significant direct impacts of these economic changes on different vulnerable populations. Whilst Bolivia would, for example, be heralded for its efforts at structural adjustment (led by the then World Bank economist/ now Earth Institute's Jeffrey Sachs) in response to the hyperinflation caused by falling tin prices in the mid-1980s, its social costs would be severe.

The World Bank's requirements led to a significant reduction of public sector employment and the privatization and shrinkage of state-owned oil and mining operations. Thousands of tin-miners were made redundant, as were other public sector employees. Left without employment or access to land, some 500,000 people migrated from the highlands to the lowlands in search of alternative sources of income (McNeish 2006). As the 1990s unfolded, it also became evident that for many of the economically displaced, there was often no employment to be found other than in the informal economy. Itinerant street hawking, smuggling or illegal coca production grew significantly in these years. The direct effects of certification and structural adjustment would together form the background to the left-leaning and nationalist backlash that would sweep across Latin America in the late 1990s and early 2000s. The boom in international commodity prices that would simultaneously occur in this period would also encourage the rejection of neoliberalism in a number of Latin American countries.

Grievance and Greed

The role of natural resources as a catalyst for economic and political development and the expression of competing sovereignties in Latin America is immediately evident in the abbreviated history given above. There are moments too when it becomes clear that it is not only the usual suspects (national and international political and economic elites) but also less powerful social actors that make their imprint – or are made to make their imprint – on the character and trajectory of both national and regional development. Despite their clear enslavement, exploitation, marginalization and targeted eradication, indigenous and peasant peoples return throughout Latin American history as figures that help to define it as protagonists in state-formation.

This is an observation that has previously been made by a series of authors working on the history and ethnography of the region. Key texts in this regard include Erik Wolf's classic text *Europe and the People without History* (1982). Writing with a focus on the Americas, Wolf takes aim at the earlier anthropological portrayal of non-European cultures and peoples as being isolated and static entities before the advent of European colonialism and imperialism. Ironically referring to a preconquest people 'without history', Wolf demonstrates that these societies possessed perpetually changing societies and were active participants in the creation of new cultural and social forms emerging in the context of regional commercial empires. Drawing on Marxian concepts and a vivid consideration for the importance of history as a means to both create and erase knowledge, Wolf traces the effects and conditions in Europe and the rest of the 'known world' beginning in 1400 CE that allowed capitalism to emerge as the dominant ideology of the modern era. In this process, Wolf shows us how indigenous peoples were written out of history, but despite this would continue to influence its direction through their protagonism.

Influenced by other revisionist historians of the state (e.g. Corrigan and Sayer 1985) and following Wolf, multiple other writers have contributed to a turn in history and anthropology focused on 'everyday state formation' (Scott 1987; Nugent 1993, 1997; Mallon 1995; Migdal and White 2013). As the historian Alan Knight has observed, 'there can be no high politics without a good deal of low politics' (quoted in Joseph and Nugent 1994: 9). In Knight's revisionist analysis of the Mexican Revolution, it is observed that state formation not only takes place in extraordinary events of rebellion and violence, but over much longer time periods and through much more mundane actions of life and interaction. While standard historical accounts emphasize either the role of peasants and peasant rebellions or that of state formation, these historical and ethnographic works document in detail the state's day-to-day engagement with grassroots society by examining popular cultures and forms of the state simultaneously and in relation to one another.

A series of texts in historical anthropology (Nugent 1993, 1997; Larsen and Harris 1995) and sometimes ethnographic fiction (Taussig 1997) overturn assumptions regarding the automatic oppositional role of indigenous and peasant peoples, demonstrating their protagonism in state-building and the colonial and postcolonial mercantile economy. They also confound assumptions regarding the political origins of key events in history as resulting from confrontations only of territory and class, pointing instead to the deeper roots of indigenous struggles for land and justice that lead up to these events, such as in the case of the Nationalist Revolution in Bolivia in 1952 (Gotkowitz 2008). Uncomfortable though it might be to those of us inspired by debates on alternative development ideas and indigenous eco-philosophies (e.g. *buen vivir* (the good life), decolonialism, post-extractivism and the pluriverse), ethnographies of political dynamics in the recent past also demonstrate peasant and indigenous peoples engagement – and at times self-contradiction – in attempting to define the state.[9] Postero (2017), for example, demonstrates how the democratic cultural revolution promised by Evo Morales – Bolivia's first self-ascribed indigenous President – to reject neoliberalism and inaugurate a new decolonized society acted instead to consolidate power for a few and to reinforce the country's historic extractivist economic model. As I will describe later in this volume, this contradiction has also played a role in the fall of Morales from power at the end of 2019.

The role of peasant and indigenous peoples as protagonists in state-formation and resource politics is then already well documented in history, ethnography and the anthropological history of Latin America. However, it is much less well recognized within the economic modelling and analysis of political change and resource politics in the region. This is not to suggest that political science ignores the importance of ethnic politics in the region entirely (e.g. van Cott 2000, 2007; Sieder, Schjolden and Angell 2011; Nem Singh and Bourgain 2013; Sieder 2017). There is nonetheless a notable gap between historical and ethnographic accounts and efforts within politics and economics to conduct a large-scale quantitative study and theorization of the wider relationship between natural resource exploitation, politics and conflict. This is especially the case in the literature that focuses on the potential of natural resource exploitation to cause conflict, to restrict or damage economic growth, and a series of negative effects on democratic practice.

The term *resource curse* – first used by Auty (1993) to discuss the common mineral-based economies – is now applied in a vast field of both academic and policy-oriented work to describe how countries rich in natural resources are unable to use that wealth to boost their economies, and how counterintuitively these countries in general have lower economic growth and development outcomes than countries without an abundance of natural resources. Originally the resource curse was used to refer to a broad range of economy types reliant on non-renewable and renewable resources (timber, coca, oil and diamonds). However, as the debate surrounding the resource curse has developed, it is notable that non-renewable resource types vital to the global economy have captured a particular focus and influence in policy circles, i.e. hydrocarbons (oil, gas and minerals) (Ross 2012). In the studies and policy discussions regarding the resource curse, a large number of terms have been employed in an attempt to account for the complicated state of affairs faced by resource-rich countries in the Global South: intractable conflicts, new wars, resource wars, complex political emergencies, conflict trap, resource securitization, petro-violence and blood diamonds (Kaplan 1994; Kaldor 1999; Collier and Hoeffler 2005; Watts 2008).

The consensus built between these different terminologies and theories is that an abundance of natural resources is frequently at the root of violent conflict. As a result, general acceptance has been made of the existence of what Karl (1997) – on the basis of study of the political economy of Venezuelan oil – termed a *paradox of plenty*, i.e. that the vast majority of conflict-prone and war-ravaged states in the Global South, including those having recently emerged from violent conflict, are extractive economies that are endowed with strategic natural and mineral resources, yet cannot avert declining into debilitating violence and war. Equally puzzling for many scholars has been the observation that while these states contribute essential inputs to the global economy, they largely remain underdeveloped and politically unstable.

With these observations in mind, a growing body of academic work has considered the problems and possibilities of managing these resources. Growing awareness has also been made of the limitations of earlier analytical frameworks and the persisting importance of other extractive economies, particularly in an era in which climate change is driving a search for alternative energy sources (Rosser 2006; Wennmann 2007). Whilst recent writers support the general consensus of scholarship that natural abundance is associated with various negative development outcomes, this also comes with the important critical addition that this evidence is by no means conclusive (Binningsbø, de Soysa and Gleditch 2007; Stiglitz 2007; Theisen 2008). This is particularly the case when other geographies than Africa, such as Latin America, are taken into consideration (Dunning 2008). Criticism is also made of the language and measurements of some scholars, i.e. overly restrictive tools are used to define key concepts such as conflict, war and violence (Omeje 2008; Sambanis 2004). The ambivalence between causality and reality is highlighted: the ecology of civil war is determined by a host of factors rather than only resource capture (Ross 2004). In this expanding literature on resource governance, issues of power and grievance have also notably returned to the fore and water and land (and forest areas in particular) are recognized as central resources in ongoing conflicts. However, although new approaches to the resource curse have adopted important new insights from contextual, historical and political ecological study (e.g. Kahl 2006; Williams and Le Billon 2017), it remains noticeable that the resource curse literature has withheld some bias in terms of its top-down reading of the forces at work in state-building and the causality of resource contestation.

It was as a contribution of constructive critique to the debates on the resource curse that my colleagues and I first employed the term *resource sovereignty* (McNeish and Logan 2012). In *Flammable Societies*,[10] we acknowledged the clear tendencies for natural resources to act as a catalyst for conflict and rent-seeking (the competition and siphoning-off of profits made by states and companies in commodity-focused industries). However, our research on resource politics and energy development also indicated that some further qualification was needed.

Our research on the relationship between indicators of poverty and oil and energy governance across Latin America, North America, Africa, Europe and the former Soviet Union coincided with other critical analysts in questioning the claims of the more or less straightforward correlation between resource wealth and violence made by earlier authors (Rosser 2006). We also coincided with critiques that suggested that resource curse scholars had been too reductionist in positing a deterministic relationship between natural abundance, various pathologies (irrational behaviour and greed of elites, rent-seeking by social groups, and weak institutions) and negative development outcomes (poor economic performance, civil war and authoritarianism). Collier and Hoeffler's (2004) determination that greed counts for more than grievance as a determinant of resource conflict gave insufficient attention to issues of ideology, history and political feasibility.[11] As such, from our perspective, they did not sufficiently account for the role of social forces and external political and economic environments in dynamically shaping development outcomes.

Conclusions that a resource curse occurred largely depended on the generalization of findings from macropolitical and economic study of exceptional cases, i.e. East African countries in the midst of civil war. Explanations for the links between natural resources and conflict had largely failed to adequately account for the role of social forces formed over time, or external political and economic pressures in shaping outcomes (Ross 2004). In line with others (Omeje 2008; Steven and Dietsche 2008), we also argued, on the basis of the qualitative research we were conducting in Latin America and elsewhere, that there was a need to pay attention to the historical particularities of contexts under study. The examination of varied histories of socioeconomic development made it obvious that states function in a variety of forms in relation to natural resources and otherwise. Indeed, they function not only on the basis of internal political and social dynamics, but also in response to international commerce and to the geopolitical interests of other states (Ross 2012). Recognizing the incomplete nature of colonial governance, projects of state formation and the fluctuating influence of globalization, it was evident that notions of state, market and law are frequently different in postcolonial states compared to those of the European or North American ideal. As such, it was also evident that judgements of *stable, fragile* and *failed* in recent political science and economic analysis – even when not defined by political and morally laden criteria, but scientific criteria and variables – were of limited value as analytic tools to understand and address the underlying dynamics of resource conflict.

Resource sovereignty was coined by my colleagues in reaction to our reading of the gaps in the resource curse literature, and the rational choice orientation of 'resource curse' theorists in particular. It was not intended to echo the formulaic legal use of the term by the United Nations (UN) (1962) to refer to states' 'permanent sovereignty over natural resources'. It was also not meant to stay within the limits of an understanding of *resource nationalism* (Young 2017). Rather, it was meant to draw attention to the need for a more historically and anthropologically situated understanding of the relationship between sovereignty and resources (Sawyer and Terrance Gomez 2012). A link was made here with the recent theoretical turn and empirically driven observations of anthropologists and other social scientists regarding the operation of differing languages of *stateness* (nationhood and legality) and the significance of their interaction for resource politics (Blom Hansen and Stepputat 2001, 2006). Instead of a singular notion of sovereignty, from this perspective, competing languages of stateness and legality compete and interact over time to define the state and basis of governance through varied dialectics of struggle, i.e. the power of the state is far from simply constituted at singular events. Blom Hansen and Stepputat importantly suggest that sovereignty is understood from this perspective as a 'tentative and always emergent form of authority grounded in violence that is performed and designed to generate loyalty, fear and legitimacy from the neighbourhood to the summit of the state' (2001: 297). This is clearly not the classic idea of sovereignty of 'supreme authority within a territory', but rather an understanding of the distributed nature of sovereignty produced in everyday encounters with power. Hansen and Stepputat (2001) show how in postcolonial states as disparate as Guatemala, Pakistan, Peru, India and Ecuador, the authority of the state is particularly challenged from the local as well as the global, and how growing demands to confer rights and recognition to ever more citizens, organizations and institutions reveal a persistent myth of the state as a source of social order and an embodiment of popular sovereignty.

Sovereignty can therefore be observed to be both a politics of keeping the state at bay and as a statement of state power itself. Different attitudes towards territory and the exploitation of natural resources form an important part of this conversation and act to define ideas of social justice such as 'our oil belongs to the people' or 'this land is our land' (Coronil 1997; Apter 2005; Gledhill 2008). Resource wealth brings to the fore issues of political and social identity under the state and ultimately the ideological orientations and identity of the state itself. It also becomes evident as the perspective moves away from a restricted understanding of governance (only focused on state institutions) that categories of geopolitical and national sovereignty overlap with informal and imminent sovereignties.

It is within this field of political interaction that processes of natural resource exploitation further expose the jagged conjunctions of different conceptions of sovereignty (McNeish and Logan 2012: 24). Not escaping sovereign rule in every case, local people imitate, appropriate and adapt to histories of state domination through the employment of what authors differentially term 'languages of stateness' (Blom Hansen and Stepputat 2001), 'vernacular state-craft' (Colloredo-Mansfeld 2009) and 'choreographies of governance' (Swyngendouw 2005; Lund 2006). Importantly, these languages of the state need to be seen as being expressed at different scales. Resource sovereignty, as we have expressed it, does not separate, but rather aims to concurrently capture the great games of states and corporations for economic power and energy security and the histories of everyday needs, desires and expressed identities of local populations, and the physical properties of resources themselves (McNeish 2017: 1136). Here political economy's concerns with the history and impact of globalization (the presence of state structures and their questioning by local populations) are married with political ecology's efforts to recognize the dual epistemological and biophysical value of resources. Resource sovereignty as we have expressed it recognizes claims for territory, identity and capital are intertwined. Conflicts over land and resources are understood from this perspective as conjoined economic and ontological conflicts regarding the equivalence of knowledge and value.

In *Contested Powers* (McNeish, Borchgrevink and Logan 2015b),[12] it was made evident that resource sovereignty was a relevant analytic lens not only to interpret Latin America's history of non-renewable resource extraction, but to also study and more fully understand recent trends in its politics and energy development. Indeed, following the boom in commodities prices and the clear connections formed by new left governments between their post-neoliberal nationalist ambitions and the profits of expanding industries for non-renewable and renewable energy resources, it was evident that this perspective could be more relevant than ever.

For close to a decade – between the late 1990s and the late 2000s – Latin America appeared to be re-emerging as one of the powerhouses of economic and social development.[13] In this period, a steady increase in international commodity prices led to a continent-wide push to open new frontiers of resource exploration and extraction (McNeish, Borchgrevink and Logan 2015). Foreign direct investment (FDI) in many countries (e.g. Peru, Panama, Guatemala and Colombia) in the region increasingly focused on the extractive sector (Tissot 2012). In parallel to the extractives boom, another development also occurred in domestic energy consumption as the general level of wealth and wages in the region grew. Indeed, the growing foreign and domestic demand for raw materials and energy stimulated in Latin America an average GDP growth rate of between 4% and 5% in the years 2003–12 (Altamonte, Correa and Stumpo 2012: 7). Socio-economic conditions throughout the region improved in this period. With rising levels of wealth and middle-class consumption, the internal industrial and private demand for energy and in particular fossil fuels (diesel and petroleum) for transport also rapidly expanded (Tissot 2012: 6). However, unmatched expectations amongst the majority of Latin Americans regarding the benefits of resource wealth, and observations and strong feelings that in actual practice too much resource wealth was being siphoned off by foreign and regional elite interests, led to a disillusionment with neoliberal market-based macroeconomics and the election of a wave of new left governments throughout the region.

In the 2000s, new left governments (often referred to as resource national-ist – see e.g. Veltmayer and Petras 2014) expanded and – for a time – convinc-ingly used the windfall of extractive industries as a tool to stimulate national development, project geopolitical influence and replace market liberalization policies adopted in the previous decade. In the words of leaders in Venezuela, Ecuador, Bolivia, Argentina and Brazil, the booming extractive economies provided opportunities for a new post-neoliberal economy in which oil, mineral and energy wealth could be democratically *sown* like seed amongst the population (Clark 2010). New developments were also starting to take hold in the renewable energy sector, with governments throughout the region providing their direct and indirect backing for large-scale hydroelectric, bio-fuel, thermal and wind power projects, and the massive expansion of related infrastructure and electricity distribution networks. With the growing global concerns over climate change and momentum in Europe towards electric vehicles, some governments in the region (Chile, Argentina and Bolivia) saw the opportunity to move towards the establishment of industrial extraction of 'green' rare earth materials such as lithium, which is used in new battery technologies.

As our research for *Contested Powers* demonstrated, resource sovereignty was an important inroad not only to the study of these new resource-nationalist (Veltamayer and Petras 2014) governments and activities, but to also high-light their contention by rivals at different levels. Our work on cases of energy development stretching throughout the region and on related mo-ments of protest and conflict demonstrated that despite their rhetoric, new left governments repeated many of the exclusions and prejudices of earlier governments. Indeed, it was evident that there was little more than words that separated new left governments from those in other countries remaining on the political right when it came to the practice of economic development, a continued reliance on extractive practice that was damaging to both the environment and human wellbeing, and the expression of prejudices and violence towards indigenous and peasant peoples and other social groups that questioned the extractive model and sovereignty of the state. It also became clear in cases of major confrontation over wind and hydro-electric development in Mexico and Brazil that renewable energy was in itself no panacea for ending the social conflicts over energy issues. Many of the same problems and cleavages described for oil and gas extraction were also seen to surround renewable energy production in Latin America and elsewhere.

Sovereign Forces continues the exploration of Latin American resource extraction and energy development. Moreover, it further deepens the empirical and theoretical basis of resource sovereignty as an important analytical device to reveal, tease apart and explain recent development dynamics. In this book, we will see that competing expressions of sovereignty not only persist as the basis of severe and sometimes violent contention, but are to large degree also responsible for the troubles and downfall of left-wing leaders and the apparent resilience and current resurgence of the political right. Indeed, as we will see, resource extraction and related activities continue to fuel these political contestations at multiple scales.

Importantly, the book further evidences the role of 'everyday politics' in the region's resource politics and environmental governance. Whereas the earlier work of my colleagues and I was suggestive of the need to integrate an awareness of the everyday into both the theory and practice of environmental governance, in this book I go further by detailing the essential role that indigenous and peasant peoples have in this current process. I also make clear why this is particularly important at this moment in time.

New expressions of indigenous and popular sovereignty are being powerfully expressed by local communities the length and breadth of Latin America (Postero and Fabricant 2019). This is occurring not only because of the growing formalization of rights, a rhetoric of decolonialization, discussions of *buen vivir* (the good life) or a new culture of consultation between the community, the state and the corporate sector; rather, as the following chapters will detail, it is happening as a proactive reaction to the lack of substance of these same discussions and de jure protections, and the continued experience of structural racism and physical violence. This is intensified when people who speak out against expanding extractive development are assassinated and protests are quelled by security forces, when governments allow or encourage millions of hectares of tropical forests to burn during times of emergency (Beaulieu 2020), when nature conservation becomes an excuse for securitization and displacement (Bocarejo and Ojeda 2015), when rivers and other vital water sources are dammed and contaminated (Vidal 2017), and when climate change is recognized, but little action is taken, forcing thousands to migrate (Markham 2019). Through digital resources and expanding solidarity networks, indigenous and peasant communities and their supporters are made aware that these dynamics are not regional phenomena. The exploitation of the natural environment essential to the livelihood indigenous and peasant peoples has sped up everywhere. Resources and sovereignty are also contested everywhere. With this, new attempts to rethink and restate the bounds and essentials of legitimate sovereignty, to restate the state and the legal, are made to contest those of the government and the market. This book further pushes this subterranean political world to the surface – i.e. in order for environmental governance to have value in Latin America, it needs to substantively address the everyday features of resource sovereignty. These are features that are still as much about grievance as they are about the problematics of greed (i.e. rent-seeking). They are features that have potential not only for conflict, but also for peace.

Peace-Building with Bricolage?

It will be evident that this book draws on a broad range of disciplinary orientations and social theory to interpret qualitative empirical observations. This is a reflection of a rather eclectic experience as a social anthropologist carrying out research and teaching in the field of global environment and development studies. It is also a requirement of reading the complex relationship between sovereignty and natural resources. I argue that such a subject requires a high degree of inter-disciplinarity. I suggest that the purposeful collision of different frames of analysis and methods, whilst not without its challenges (including the navigation of interpretive and philosophical contradictions), can enable new insight and interpretation.

My positioning vis-à-vis a series of crisscrossing debates in social anthropology, political economy and political ecology will become evident in the discussions made in the following chapters. It should also become evident that whilst I respect disciplinary ambitions, I see the greater value of these fields of study at their edges or when they overlap and come into contact with each other. I will largely allow these dialectic interchanges to unfold throughout the book, but for the reader's orientation I will flag here a limited number of interdisciplinary waypoints.

I am interested in this text to demonstrate the value of resource sovereignty to both the analysis of resource conflicts and to the theorization of legitimate environmental governance and peacebuilding. I suggest here that in order to do so, certain contrasting schools of academic literature have to talk together more than others. In this book, these literatures include those on the history and anthropology (and historical anthropology) of everyday state-building in Latin America initially explored above. Importantly, they also include an exploration of the idea(s) of indigeneity, political ontology and the comparative legal and political science of sovereignty. Interested to establish the applied political implications of resource sovereignty, emphasis has also been given to the fields of resource politics, environmental governance and the anthropology of energy. These are literatures that deal with many of the same concerns and issues but operate with different frames and scales of analysis (McNeish, Borchgrevink and Logan 2015b). Indeed, in searching to apply resource sovereignty to the study of conflict and concrete outcomes for peace, I have been interested in the final chapters of this book in exploring a critical dialogue between critical institutionalism and resource sovereignty. This dialectic is not prescriptive but does provide important signposts that are of significance to environmental governance and, by extension, to environmental peacebuilding. It is important to note that my engagement with these literatures reflects my experience as an *engaged* political anthropologist (Bringa and Bendixen 2018) and their notable role in, and impact on, significant international and national development policy environments.

Conca and Dabelko (2002) formally introduced the term 'environmental peace-making' (now more commonly referred to as 'environmental peacebuilding') to describe the contributions of environmental initiatives to peace. The concept is now used to refer to 'all forms of cooperation on environmental issues between distinct social groups, which aim at and/or achieve creating less violent and more peaceful relations between these groups' (Ide 2019). With its emphasis on cooperation, the growing environmental peacebuilding literature contrasts with a wider neo-Malthusian literature that reductively places an emphasis on the link between environmental scarcity, risk and conflict (Homer-Dixon 1994; Hendrix and Salehyan 2012; Nel and Righarts 2008). Writers oriented towards environmental peacebuilding have demonstrated, for example, that, even in arid environments, interactions over international water resources are more likely to be cooperative (Wolf et al. 2003). Some posit that climate change-induced changes to water resources are unlikely to result in armed conflict (Bernauer and Siegfried 2012; de Stefano et al. 2017). Others go even further and claim that environmental issues like natural disasters may lead to a decrease in civil war risk (Slettebak 2012), provide opportunities to push along peace talks (e.g. Gaillard, Clave and Kelman 2008; Kreutz 2012), strengthen support for political leaders (Olson and Gawronski 2010), produce cooperation between conflicting parties (Endfield, Tejado and O'Hara 2004), and temporarily decrease crime rates and increase altruism (Lemieux 2014). Seeking to study conflict and produce opportunities for peace, environmental peacebuilding pursues initiatives to improve the environmental situation, prevent or mitigate environmental-related conflicts, create or sustain dialogues between conflict parties, or promote the conditions for sustainable development and durable peace (Carius and Dabelko 2004; Conca, Carius and Dabelko 2005; Ide 2019).

From early on in the development of the environmental peace-building field, there have been calls for a systematic, comparative and interdisciplinary assessment of its scholarship and practice (e.g. Carius 2007). However, there has been little development of a systematic approach and the tendency to showcase intervention success stories has overshadowed empirical research on the influence of baseline conflict and environmental conditions. Little research has considered the roles of two kinds of mechanisms within environmental peacebuilding: feedback between potential changes in the environment, conflict and peace conditions, and feedback across scales of intervention, i.e. top-down and bottom-up. In a review of the existing literature, Ide (2019) found no evidence of environmental peacebuilding leading to positive peace. Ide (2020) importantly observes that there is a potential 'dark side' to environmental peacebuilding when its focus is too narrowly set on achieving outcomes and when it fails to take explicit consideration of the driving mechanisms of conflict.

Interestingly there are parallels between these observations of gaps in the environmental peace-building literature and those regarding scholarship on environmental governance. As a field of study, environmental governance grew out of the acknowledgement within political science and economics of the role of institutions in grouping different actors together and in steering their action (Evans 2012: 46). As Rydin (2010: 96–97) writes: 'Institutions bind actors together into arrangements and patterns of behaviour that exhibit strong path dependencies . . . actors learn to behave in accordance with institutional norms and this reinforces certain behaviour.' Mainstream institutional governance emphasized that collective action is possible if it makes rational sense to do so. It was broadly optimistic about the possibility of identifying basic principles underlying effective institutions and assisting people to use these principles to 'design' institutional arrangements through a conscious and rational process. From this perspective, epitomized by the Nobel Prize-winning work of Ostrom (1990, 2005), the role of institutional governance is to provide information and assurance about the behaviour of others, to offer incentives to behave in accordance with the collective good and to monitor opportunistic behaviour. Over time, Ostrom's work inspired other analysts to adopt 'new institutionalist' approaches to the study and set-up of governance models. As in the 'resource curse' school of study, there was the introduction of ever more complex and varied sets of variables that are seen to affect the incentives and actions of actors under diverse governance systems.

Arguing that we 'should stop striving for simple answers to solve complex problems' and a move to 'polycentrism', Ostrom's Institutional Analysis and Development Framework (IAD) was developed to contain the most general set of variables an institutional analyst may want to use to examine institutional settings (biophysical conditions, attributes of community, rules in use), but also recognized the need to respond to different resource contexts and regimes. Ostrom's sensitivity to complex institutional settings is widely recognized for its role in dismantling earlier assumptions about the 'tragedy of the commons' (Hardin 1968). Aiming to demonstrate that government and wider institutional decision-making is not only a matter of individual behaviour, March and Olson (1984) coined the term 'new institutionalism' to emphasize that decisions are shaped to a large degree by pre-established rules and procedures through which institutions respond to real-life issues. New institutional analysis emphasizes the importance of institutional diagnostics in its search for the optimization of the design and legitimacy of environmental governance. Here 'design principles' are weighed up and the extent to which institutions influence the course of human affairs in a variety of social settings (causality), institutional performance and design are considered in depth (Young 1997).

The overall strength of the mainstream and new institutionalist school have been their theoretical and empirical demonstration that the management of common property through collective action is possible, that there are certain conditions that facilitate this, and that people govern resources through a range of formal and institutional forms (Cleaver 2012). However, despite claims of these frameworks relevance for higher scales of governance, they have been criticized for a narrow focus on local institutions and apolitical explanations of social-environmental interactions (Robbins 2004; Chotray 2007). Recent revisions from within these paradigms have started to take account of the complexities of context (Acheson 2006; Berkes 2007), the discordance of politics (Poteete 2009), and the unpredictable interaction between social and ecological processes (McGinnis 2010). However, the core assumptions, form and level of analysis of these paradigms remain intact. Critique is increasingly made of persisting rational actor assumptions regarding the direct relationship between well-designed community level institutions on the one hand and well-managed forest and improved livelihoods on the other. Citing Scott (1999), Cleaver highlights that in its focus on planning and design, legibility and codification, and the engineering of 'good governance' arrangements, mainstream institutionalism incorporates features of high modernism. As such, she claims that its modernist project of designing institutions (and systems) for natural resource management is partially doomed to failure (Cleaver 2012: 172)

As a recent development in the field of environmental governance, critical institutionalism claims to differ from earlier schools because the starting point is a broad focus on the interactions between the natural and social worlds rather than a narrower concern with predicting and improving the outcomes of particular institutional processes (Cleaver 2012: 13). In contrast with earlier approaches, critical institutionalism suggests that institutions managing natural resources are only rarely explicitly designed for such purposes and that their multifunctionalism renders them ambiguous, dynamic and only partially amenable to deliberate crafting (Cleaver 2012: 13). Critical institutionalists adopt a 'thicker' model of human agency (Cleaver 2012: 15). For them, strategic livelihood choices (about the use of resources) are critically influenced by social concerns, by psychological preferences, and by culturally and historically shaped ideas about the 'the right way of doing things'. In building her case for critical institutionalism, Cleaver (2012) draws on the work of Douglas (1987) and her use of the concept of *intellectual bricolage*.[14] Douglas extends the use of the term to refer to institutional thinking and to illustrate how the construction of institutions and decisions to act are rarely made on the basis of rational choice. Instead, she suggests, 'institutions do the thinking' on behalf of people, and institutions are constructed through a process of bricolage-gathering and applying analogies and styles of thought that are already part of existing institutions (Cleaver 2000: 380). *Bricolage* in this sense is furthermore acknowledged by Cleaver to be an 'authoritative process, shaped by relations of power' (Cleaver 2012: 49). Here the configuration of societal resources shapes the 'institutional stock' from which institutions can be assembled, and the choice of instruments and mechanisms that can be applied. In emphasizing that invented institutions are shaped by past arrangements and relationships of authority, Cleaver recognizes that she repeats a perspective already well captured in earlier political economy (Cleaver 2012: 194).

I suggest in this volume that in looking for the causes of conflict and the basis for peaceful and legitimate governance, environmental peace-building and environmental governance share a common cause. They share an interest in the possibilities for cooperation and legitimacy but lack context-specific 'everyday' detail as to what produces dispute and agreement. They also tend to be rather blinkered in their radius of study, assuming that environmental disagreements can be explained within the environmental field. Recognizing both the value and limitations of these approaches, I posit here that critical institutionalism, and its conceptualization of institutional bricolage, provides insight that is significant in terms of moving their understanding towards a more grounded and 'critical realist' perspective (Bhaskar 1975; Archer 1982, 1995; Porpora 2015; Vandenberghe 2015). Indeed, as I will detail in the penultimate and concluding chapters, their intended significance for delivering legitimacy and peace can be enhanced by further adding the idea of resource sovereignty into the mix.

More Than the Sum of Its Parts

Sovereign Forces is not written as an ethnography, which is the focus of much anthropological writing. It is a book about instances of natural resource contestation, and the value of the idea of resource sovereignty to their interpretation and improved attention in environmental governance. As such, the book intends to contribute to a literature on environmental politics. It does make use of ethnographic elements, but a fair judgement could be that it does this in a somewhat fragmented and cursory way. The use of ethnographic fragments has been both a necessity and an intentional choice. On the one hand, the book is not the product of a singular research project; it is the result of piecing together different fragments of time and qualitative research experience[15] stretching over multiple field visits and over twenty years (from 1996 to 2017). This is the reason for its particular focus on events and processes in Bolivia, Colombia and Guatemala – all sites of earlier research. It is also the reason for the book's particular emphasis on resource, energy and development politics in indigenous and peasant communities, which is the focus of much of this social research.

Written on the basis of fragments of time and research, the empirical details are admittedly not always as well defined as they could be. A traditional ethnography would undoubtedly give more space to detail the lives of individuals, their commentary of events and the intricacy of local everyday interactions. Indeed, as will become evident in the following pages, my observations are sometimes not the result of what I was looking for, but rather what occurred around edges of my research focus at that time. They are sometimes the result – as described later in the volume – of what I saw out of the corner of my eye, by mistake, because other information was not forthcoming or because events required other priorities at that time. In this regard, I am trying to make analytic value out of what some reviewers might term *a patchwork*. At the same time, I intend the book to purposefully be read as *more than the sum of its parts*. Indeed, coinciding with this, some anthropologists have recently launched a manifesto supporting such a patchwork approach to ethnography (Günel, Varma and Watanabe 2020). Although not the product of a single piece of research, as I have made clear above, the book interrogates issues and forces of vital social concern. In this regard, its fragmented nature is a strength.

By drawing together different ethnographic moments and locations, I am able to demonstrate that the issue of resource contestation – and the analytic frame of resource sovereignty – has widespread and long-lasting significance. In this regard, the book has a lot in common with what some authors refer to as multisited or *global ethnography* (Scott 1998; Buroway 2000; Tsing 2004; Ferguson 2006; Ongh 2006). These global ethnographic texts demonstrate the possibilities of detailing what is happening in local settings without losing sight of the fall and rise of ideas, processes and positions, or shifts in the organization and reach of capitalism. The local and the global are seen here as mutually constitutive, and steps are taken to avoid common pitfalls of other analytic tools that 'dominate', 'silence', 'objectify' and 'normalize' the experience and knowledge of others. In this book, the specificities of resource politics in Bolivia, Colombia and Guatemala are carefully considered, but so too are common dynamics that tie these places, peoples and political economies together. This is not the account of what happened in one isolated location, but, as the individual chapters make clear, what has happened and continues to take place in multiple locations throughout Latin America. The links I make between my own research experience and existing theoretical debates are intended to reinforce this even further. Lengthy sections of litera-ture review might frustrate some readers, but they play an important role in anchoring arguments, making connections and introducing some readers to new approaches. Each chapter is intended to reveal different characteristics of resource sovereignty, but also to build towards a common comparative conclusion.

In Chapter 1, 'Sovereignty within and beyond the State', I detail the significance of two major events in Bolivian politics: the *gasolinazo* (the backlash resulting from the ending of fuel subsidies) and the TIPNIS protests (a massive social response to the government's decision to build a road and open an area of the tropical lowlands to extractive interests). I suggest in this chapter that these events are not only telling of persisting tensions in Bolivian politics, but are also indicative of the complex nature of sovereignty in the country. Both events are also used as a springboard to a discussion of the close relationship that exists between the politics of natural resources, territory and sovereign claims within and beyond the state in Latin America. As such, the chapter provides an expanded discussion of the complex history and meaning of sovereignty in general, and of its particular significance in the politics of natural resources and the people involved in these especially Bolivian dynamics. The evident contestation of sovereignty from beyond and below the state is shown to contribute significantly to state institutional and national identity formation over time. The *gasolinazo* and TIPNIS events are also shown to reveal the centrality of territory and resources in this dynamic, and the political volatility it can cause – including the fall of a government.

In Chapter 2, 'Resource Politics at the Margins', I further explore the links between resource governance and contrasting visions and political definitions of sovereignty. In contrast to the preceding chapter, I demonstrate that resource politics is not limited to large-scale reactions and contestation of national policy, but a dynamic in which local actors effectively influence state and regional positions through their everyday engagement from the margins (the informal and illegal economy, the limits of national territory, and the socially excluded). As such, the chapter seeks to deepen an understanding of the multiscalar and contested nature of sovereignty and of the actively contrasting perspectives of resources and territory. It does this through empirical focus on local practices of smuggling (of fuel and natural resources) along the Bolivian (with Chile and Peru) and Guatemalan (with Mexico) borders, and an expanding panorama of militancy focused on the terms and impacts of environmental resource exploitation. The chapter also contains a further discussion and critique of the existing literature on resource politics and the resource curse. It demonstrates that these characterizations of resource politics are not wrong but are insufficient in their avoidance of competing claims of territorial and resource sovereignty that come from both below the level and from the margins of the nation-state.

In Chapter 3, 'Contesting Extraction and Sovereignty in Colombia and Guatemala', I explore in depth the intertwined politics of sovereignty and natural resources in two case studies. Whilst earlier chapters demonstrate the way in which popular sovereignty can be constituted at different scales of protest and confrontation with the state, or through efforts to circumvent state authority over territory and resources, I demonstrate here that other expressions of popular sovereignty also exist. In contrast to other global contexts in which indigenous and peasant peoples have learned the 'art of not being governed', popular sovereignty in Latin America and expressions of resource sovereignty are not only made through confrontation or avoidance. In Latin America, new political and legal spaces are not only granted to local communities but are – despite the risks of violence – actively shaped by community engagement with state entities. Indigenous and peasant communities, together with representative social movements and civil society organizations, draw on existing legal and political institutions and mechanisms in their efforts to secure a formal response to sovereign claims. Strategies of engagement with state legal and political institutions often take place concurrently with efforts to reaffirm distinct cultural and social identities, other meanings and values, and protest and strategies of circumvention. In the light of these empirical contexts, the chapter also contains an important discussion of the complex nature and meaning of indigeneity.

In Chapter 4, 'Citizens of Lithium and Salt', I emphasize that claims and contests for resource sovereignty are not only generated by economic and material claims, but often concurrently result from differing perspectives of the value and significance of the landscape, and of the possible impacts of resource development. In this chapter, I demonstrate that this is true not only of fossil fuels, but also of resources that despite their 'green' credentials result in similar social and environmental impacts to what are traditionally considered to be non-renewable resources. Charting the establishment of a nascent lithium industry in Salar de Uyuni, Bolivia and its contested significance, I evidence the manner in which material claims are embedded in long-established cultural and moral relationships with the landscape. Although similar concerns with economic gain and employment are expressed by local people, the chapter highlights through its focus on the politics of the establishment of lithium production in the Highlands of Bolivia that contrasting foundations for knowledge and ontology, and changing political pacts and alliances result in dynamic expressions of resource sovereignty. It is made evident that local people, communities, the Bolivian state and private sector interests are locked into a wider discussion and negotiation of sovereignty. I suggest this is not only serious in the sense of the dynamics of tensions and contestation at the local level, but evidently of much wider impacts, which are seen here as playing a further role in the dramatic dynamics surrounding the recent departure of President Morales from office. I also show that contestation should not be understood as the marking-out of completely contrasting ontological positions. Whereas distinct positions, ideas and beliefs can be identified, these frequently overlap and periodically align with each other as claims regarding sovereignty develop through history, and individuals and their communities encounter contradictions, threats and the need to compromise.

In Chapter 5, 'No Negotiation with a Gun to Your Head?', I return to the normative claim made at the start of this book, i.e. that resource sovereignty matters for peace and governance. The chapter starts with an account of the legal judgment that found in favour of the protection of the land rights of the Embera Chamí community of the Cañamomo Lomaprieta in western Colombia. I suggest that the case provides a further important insight into the complex relationship between claims for resource sovereignty and mechanisms for environmental governance. The case underlines the fact that sovereignty is already an issue navigated by current governance and law, but without full acceptance, or in cynical denial of the seriousness and historical basis of the issue. It also highlights that states can in some instances share histories of collusion and the direct enabling of the illegal circumvention and abuse of these rights. I also detail the links between the case, other similar cases and the wider politics of prior consultation. Further description of the politics of prior consultation expands the background to the Embera Chamí case and places into high relief the contradictory and problematic manner in which sovereignty is treated by Latin American states. In particular, it reveals a technocratic avoidance of certain features of contested sovereignty that require attention if environmental governance is to deliver on its aims. An exploration of the politics of prior consultation is also used as a segue to a necessary reflection on environmental governance as an academic field. I demonstrate that there is a clear correspondence to be formed between my concern with and argument for resource sovereignty with the current critical institutionalist turn. I argue that resources and sovereignty should be understood both as a catalyst for conflict but also as a signpost for environmental peacebuilding, i.e. indicators towards the logics and resolution of disagreements regarding territory and resources.

In the concluding chapter, 'Making Use of Sovereign Forces?', I pull together the strands of reasoning and evidence that form the foundations of the conclusions of the book. As such, the chapter re-emphasizes the significance of popular sovereignty in the context of Latin American history and contemporary politics. I underline the role of resource sovereignty as a means to more accurately detail the dynamics of resource conflict in the region. I also conclude with a further reflection on the role of resource sovereignty in governance and *local-level* peacebuilding, and of its contribution to a critical institutionalist perspective. The chapter also takes a last look at the significance of resource sovereignty within a context of current political, legal and intellectual dynamics. These dynamics suggest a more eco-centric approach to the protection of environmental resources and reliant populations.

Notes

1. Hector Jaime has asked for his name, and the name of his community, not to be anonymized so as to draw further attention to the growing list of real people who are currently being threatened in this way (personal communication, 5 August 2020). I have anonymized the names of individuals in all other instances unless they are public officials or have expressed themselves openly to the media.
2. Cañamomo Lomaprieta Resguardo (indigenous reserve) in western Colombia
3. BACRIM organizations have their roots in demobilized paramilitary organizations.
4. International Work Group on Indigenous Affairs. Seer https://www.iwgia.org/en (Retrieved 2 November 2020).
5. State of the Union Address Part II (1904). Retrieved 2 November 2020 from http://teach ingamericanhistory.org/library/document/state-of-the-union-address-part-ii-9.
6. 'President John F. Kennedy: On the Alliance for Progress, 1961'. *Modern History Sourcebook*. Archived from the original on 3 September 2006. Retrieved 2 November 2020 from https://sourcebooks.fordham.edu/mod/1961kennedy-afp1.asp.
7. Fuerzas Armadas Revolucionarias de Colombia—Ejército del Pueblo (FARC-EP).
8. Ejército de Liberación Nacional (ELN).
9. In writing this, I do not mean to ignore situations in which indigenous peoples have opposed the state or have even attempted to remove themselves from contact with state institutions and wider society. Instances of 'uncontacted tribes' in the Amazon are, for

example, instances of indigenous tribal societies who have sought refuge in isolation from the damaging impacts of both disease and the expansive impacts of state-building.

10. Flammable Societies was a research project financed by the Norwegian Research Council between 2008 and 2011.

11. An emphasis on greed over grievance is also retained in the more recent work of Collier (2011).

12. Contested Powers was a research project financed by the Norwegian Research Council between 2010 and 2013.

13. In 1960, Latin America accounted for 6% of the global economy (Tissot 2012). In 2009, that share had increased to 7.2 % and outperformed global GDP per capita growth by at least 1.5%. While foreign investments have been falling in developing countries, FDI inflows in Latin America rose by 40% between 2009 and 2010.

14. *Bricolage* is a French word: 'to make creative and resourceful use of whatever materials at hand, regardless of their original purpose'.

15. Qualitative research has included extended periods of multi-sited ethnographic research (from two years to two weeks depending on the year) and the use of semi-structured interviews, archival work and focus groups.

References

Acheson, James. 2006. 'Institutional Failure in Resource Management'. *Annual Review of Anthropology* 35. 117–34.

Alpert, Megan. 2016. '15 Years and 10 Billion USD Later, US Efforts to Curb Colombia's Cocaine Trade Have Failed'. *Foreign Policy*, 8 February 2016. Retrieved 2 November 2020 from https://foreignpolicy.com/2016/02/08/15-years-and-10-billion-later-u-s-efforts-to-curb-colombias-cocaine-trade-have-failed.

Alsema, Adriaan. 2019. 'Trump Urges Aerial Fumigation as He Certifies Colombia as Cooperative in War on Drugs'. *Colombia Reports*. 9 August. Retrieved 2 November 2020 from https://colombiareports.com/trump-urges-aerial-fumigation-as-he-certifies-colombia-as-cooperative-in-war-on-drugs.

Altamonte, Hugo; Nelson Correa and Giovanni Stumpo. 2011. *La Dinámica del Consumo Energético Industrial en América Latina y Sus Implicaciones para un Desarrollo Sostenible*. Santiago: CEPAL/ECLAC.

Ambrose, Jillian. 2020. 'Oil Prices Dip Below Zero as Producers Forced to Pay to Dispose of Excess'. *The Guardian*. 20 April. Retrieved 2 November 2020 from https://www.theguardian.com/world/2020/apr/20/oil-prices-sink-to-20-year-low-as-un-sounds-alarm-on-to-covid-19-relief-fund.

Anderson, Jon Lee. 2010. *Che Guevara: A Revolutionary Life*. New York: Grove Press.

Apter, Andrew. 2005. *The Pan-African Nation: Oil and the Spectacle of Culture in Nigeria*. Chicago: University of Chicago Press.

Archer, Margaret. 1982. 'Morphogenesis versus Structuration: On Combining Structure and Action'. *British Journal of Sociology*. 33(4): 455–83.

———. 1995. *Realist Social Theory*. Cambridge: Cambridge University Press.

Auty, Richard. 1993. *Sustaining Development in Mineral Economies: The Resource Curse Thesis*. London: Routledge.

Beaulieu, Devin. 2020. 'The Bolivian Amazon Burns in the Shadow of COVID-19'. *Medium. com*, 15 May. Retrieved 2 November 2020 from https://medium.com/@devin.beaulieu/the-bolivian-amazon-burns-in-the-shadow-of-covid-19-2551ac117a1d.

Berkes, Fikret. 2007. 'Community-Based Conservation in a Globalized World'. *Proceedings of the National Academy of Sciences of the United States of America.* 104(39): 15188–93.

Bernauer, Thomas, and Tobias Siegfried. 2012. 'Climate Change and International Water Conflict in Asia'. *Journal of Peace Research.* 49(1): 113–27.

Bhaskar, Roy.1975. *A Realist Theory of Science.* London: Verso.

Binningsbø, Helge, Indra de Soysa and Niles Petter Gleditch. 2007. 'Green Giant or Straw Man? Environmental Pressure and Civil Conflict 1961–1999'. *Population and Environment.* 28(6): 337–53.

Blackburn, Robin.1997. *The Making of New World Slavery: From the Baroque to the Modern 1492–1800.* London: Verso World History Series.

Blom Hansen, Thomas, and Finn Stepputat (eds). 2001. *States of Imagination: Ethnographic Explorations of the Postcolonial State.* Durham: Duke University Press.

Blom Hansen, Thomas, and Finn Stepputat. 2006. 'Sovereignty Revisited'. *Annual Review of Anthropology.* 35(1): 16.1–16.21.

Bocarejo, Diana, and Diana Ojeda. 2015. 'Violence and Conservation: Beyond Unintended Consequences and Unfortunate Coincidences'. *Geoforum.* 69: 176–83.

Bringa, Tone, and Synnøve Bendiksen. 2018. *Engaged Anthropology: Views from Scandinavia.* New York: Springer.

Buroway, Michael. 2000. *Global Ethnography: Forces, Connections and Imaginations in a Postmodern World.* Berkeley: University of California Press.

Carius, Alexander. 2007. *Environmental Peacemaking: Conditions for Success.* Special Report, Wilson Center. Retrieved 2 November 2020 from https://www.wilsoncenter.org/publication/environmental-peacemaking-conditions-for-success.

Carius, Alexander, and Geoffrey Dabelko. 2004. 'Institutionalizing Responses to Environment, Conflict and Cooperation', in *Understanding Environment, Conflict and Cooperation.* Nairobi: UNEP.

Chesterton, Bridget. 2017. *The Chaco War: Environment, Ethnicity and Nationalism.* London: Bloomsbury Academic.

Chotray, Vasudha. 2007. 'The Anti-politics Machine in India: Depoliticization through Local Institution Building for Participatory Watershed Development'. *Journal of Development Studies* 43(6): 1037–56.

Clark, Patrick. 2010. 'Sowing the Oil? The Chavez Government's Policy Framework for an Alternative Food System in Venezuela'. *Humbolt Journal of Social Relations.* 33(1/2): 135–65.

Cleaver, Francis. 2000. 'Moral Ecological Rationality, Institutions and the Management of Common Property Resources'. *Development and Change.* 31(2): 361–83.

———. 2012. *Development through Bricolage: Rethinking Institutions for Natural Resource Management.* London: Earthscan/Routledge.

Colloredo-Mansfeld, Rudi. 2009. *Fighting Like a Community: Andean Civil Society and an Era of Indian Uprisings.* Chicago: University of Chicago Press.

Collier, Paul. 2011. *Plundered Planet: Why We Must – and How We Can – Manage Nature.* Oxford: Oxford University Press.

Collier, Paul, and Anke Hoeffler. 1998. 'On Economic Causes of Civil War'. *Oxford Economic Papers* 50: 563–73.

———. 2005. 'Resource Rents, Governance, and Conflict'. *Journal of Conflict Resolution.* 49(4): 625–33.

Conca, Ken, Alexander Carius and Geoffrey Dabelko. 2005. 'Building Peace through Environmental Cooperation'. *State of the World: Redefining Global Security.* Washington, DC: W.W. Norton/Watchworld Institute.

Conca, Ken and Geoffrey Dabelko. 2002. *Environmental Peacemaking*. Baltimore and Washington: Johns Hopkins University Press and Woodrow Wilson Center Press.

Coronil, Fernando. 1997. *The Magical State: Nature, Money and Modernity in Venezuela*. Chicago: University of Chicago Press.

Corrigan, Philip, and Derek Sayer. 1985. *The Great Arch: English State Formation as Cultural Revolution*. Oxford: Basil Blackwell.

De Stefano, Lucia, Jacob Petersen-Perlman, Eric Sproles, Jim Eynard and Aaron Wolf. 2017. 'Assessment of Transboundary River Basins for Potential Hydro-political Tensions'. *Global Environmental Change*. 45: 35–46.

Douglas, Mary. 1987. *How Institutions Think*. Milton Park: Routledge and London: Kegan Paul.

Dunning, Ted. 2005. 'Resource Dependence, Economic Performance and Political Stability'. *Journal of Conflict Resolution* 49: 451–82.

Endfield, Georgina, Isabel Tejado and Sarah O'Hara. 2004. 'Conflict and Cooperation: Water, Floods and Social Response in Colonial Guanajuato, Mexico'. *Environmental History* 9(2): 221–47.

'Enemies of the State? How Governments and Businesses Silence Land and Environmental Defenders'. 2019. *Global Witness*. Retrieved 2 November 2020 from https://www.global witness.org/en/campaigns/environmental-activists/enemies-state.

Evans, James. 2012. *Environmental Governance*. Routledge.

Ferguson, James. 2006. *Global Shadows: Africa in the Neoliberal World*. Durham, NC: Duke University Press.

Field, Thomas. 2014. *From Development to Dictatorship: Bolivia and the Alliance for Progress in the Kennedy Era*. Ithaca: Cornell University Press.

Gaillard, Jean-Christophe, Elsa Clave and Ilan Kelman. 2008. 'Wave of Peace? Tsunami Disaster Diplomacy in Aceh, Indonesia'. *Geoforum* 39(1): 511–26.

Galeano, Eduardo. 1997; 1973. *Open Veins of Latin America: Five Centuries of the Pillage of a Continent*. Monthly Review Press.

Gledhill, John. 2008. 'The Peoples' Oil: Nationalism, Globalization and the Possibility of Another Country in Brazil, Mexico and Venezuela'. *Focaal* 52: 57–74.

Gotkowitz, Laura. 2008. *A Revolution for our Rights: Indigenous Struggles for Land and Justice 1880–1952*. Durham, NC: Duke University Press.

Grann, David. 2009. *The Lost City of Z: A Tale of Deadly Obsession in the Amazon*. Vintage Departures. New York: Penguin Random House.

'Grave Aumento de Asesinatos de Quienes Defienden los Derechos Humanos en Colombia'. 2017. *PBI Colombia*. Retrieved 2 November 2020 from https://pbicolombiablog.org/20 17/03/21/grave-aumento-de-asesinatos-de-quienes-defienden-los-derechos-humanos-en-colombia.

Günel, Gökçe, Saiba Varma and Chika Watanabe. 2020. 'A Manifesto for a Patchwork Ethnography'. *Cultural Anthropology*. 9 June. Retrieved 2 November 2020 from https://culanth.org/fieldsights/a-manifesto-for-patchwork-ethnography.

Hardin, Garrett. 1968. 'The Tragedy of the Commons'. *Science* 162(3859): 1243–48.

Hendrix, Cullen and Idean Salehyan. 2012. 'Climate Change, Rainfall and Social Conflict in Africa'. *Journal of Peace Research* 49(1): 35–50.

Hickel, Jason. 2015. 'Enough of Aid – Let's Talk about Reparations'. *The Guardian*, 27 November. Retrieved 2 November 2020 from https://www.theguardian.com/global-de velopment-professionals-network/2015/nov/27/enough-of-aid-lets-talk-reparations.

Homer-Dixon, Thomas. 1994. 'Environmental Scarcities and Environmental Conflict'. *International Security* 19(1): 5–40.

Humphreys, Macarten, Jeffrey Sachs and Joseph Stiglitz. 2007. *Escaping the Resource Curse.* New York: Columbia University Press.

Ide, Tobias. 2019. *Environmental Peacemaking and Environmental Peacebuilding in International Politics.* University of Hamburg. Research Group Climate Change and Security. Working Paper CLISEC-35.

———. 2020. 'The Dark Side of Environmental Peacebuilding'. *World Development* 127: 1–9.

Jones Luong, Pauline, and Erika Weinthal. 2006. 'Rethinking the Resource Curse: Ownership Structure, Institutional Capacity and Domestic Constraints'. *Annual Review of Political Science* 9: 241–63.

Joseph, Gilbert, and Daniel Nugent. 1994. *Everyday Forms of State Formation: Revolution and Negotiation of Rule in Modern Mexico.* Durham, NC: Duke University Press.

Kahl, Colin. 2006. *States, Scarcity and Civil Strife in the Developing World.* Princeton: Princeton University Press.

Kaldor, Mary. 1999. *New Wars: Organized Violence in a Global Era.* Cambridge: Polity Press.

Kaplan, Richard. 1994. 'The Coming Anarchy: How Scarcity, Overpopulation, Tribalism and Disease Are Rapidly Destroying the Fabric of Our Planet'. *Atlantic Monthly*, February. Retrieved 2 November 2020 from https://www.theatlantic.com/magazine/archive/1994/02/the-coming-anarchy/304670.

Karl, Terry Lynn.1997. *The Paradox of Plenty: Oil Booms and Petro-States.* Berkeley: University of California Press.

Knight, Alan. 1994. *Weapons and Arches in the Mexican Revolutionary Landscape.* Durham, NC: Duke University Press.

Kreutz, Joakim. 2012. 'From Tremors to Talks: Do Natural Disasters Produce Ripe Moments for Resolving Seperatist Conflicts?' *International Interactions* 38(4): 482–502.

Larsen, Brooke, and Olivia Harris (eds). 1995. *Ethnicity, Markets and Migration in the Andes: At the Crossroads of History and Anthropology.* Durham, NC: Duke University Press.

Le Billon, Phillipe, Cecilia Roa-Garcia and Angelica López-Granada. 2020. 'Territorial Peace and Gold Mining in Colombia: Local Peacebuilding, Bottom-up Development and the Defence of Territories'. *Conflict, Security & Development* 20(3): 303–33.

Lemieux, Frederic. 2014. 'The Impact of a Natural Disaster on Altruistic Behaviour and Crime'. *Disasters* 38(3): 483–99.

Lund, Christian. 2006. 'Twilight Institutions: Public Authority and Local Politics in Africa'. *Development and Change* 37(4): 685–705.

Mallon, Florencia.1995. *Peasant and Nation: The Making of Postcolonial Mexico and Peru.* Berkeley: University of California Press.

March, James, and Johan Olsen. 1984. 'The New Institutionalism: Organizational Factors in Political Life'. *American Political Science Review* 78(3): 734–49.

Markham, Lauren. 2019. 'How Climate Change Is Pushing Central American Migrants to the US'. *The Guardian*, 6 April 2019. Retrieved 2 November 2020 from https://www.theguardian.com/commentisfree/2019/apr/06/us-mexico-immigration-climate-change-migration.

McGinnis, Michael. 2010. *Building a Programme for Institutional Analysis of Socio-ecological Systems: A Review of Revisions to the SES Framework.* Working Paper. Workshop in Political Theory and Policy Analysis. Indiana University.

McNeish, John-Andrew. 2006. 'Stones on the Road: The Politics of Participation and the Generation of Crisis in Bolivia'. *Bulletin of Latin American Research* 25(2): 220–40.

———. 2017. 'A Vote to Derail Extraction: Popular Consultation and Resource Sovereignty in Tolima, Colombia'. *Third World Quarterly* 38(5): 1128–45.

McNeish, John-Andrew, Axel Borchgrevink and Owen Logan (eds). 2015a. *Contested Powers: The Politics of Energy and Development in Latin America*. London: Zed Books.

———. 2015b. 'Recovering Power from Energy: Reconsidering the Linkages between Energy and Development', in John-Andrew McNeish, Axel Borchgrevink and Owen Logan (eds), *Contested Powers: The Politics of Energy and Development in Latin America*. London: Zed Books.

McNeish, John-Andrew, and Owen Logan (eds). 2012. *Flammable Societies: Studies on the Socioeconomics of Oil and Gas*. London: Pluto Press.

Migdal, Adam, and Joel White. 2013. *The Everyday Life of the State*. Seattle: University of Washington Press.

Nel, Philip, and Marjolein Righarts. 2008. 'Natural Disasters and the Risk of Violent Conflict'. *International Studies Quarterly* 52(1): 159–85.

Nem Singh, Jewellord, and France Bourgain. 2013. *Resource Governance and Developmental States in the Global South*. Camden: Palgrave Macmillan.

Nugent, David. 1993. 'Building the State, Making the Nation: The Bases and Limits of State Centralization in "Modern" Peru'. *American Anthropologist* 96(2): 333–69.

———. 1997. *Spent Cartridges of Revolution: An Anthropological History of Namiquipa Chihuahua*. Chicago: University of Chicago Press.

Omeje, Kenneth (ed). 2008. *Extractive Economies and Conflicts in the Global South: Multiregional Perspectives on Rentier Politics*. Farnham: Ashgate.

Ongh, Aiwa. 2006. *Neoliberalism as Exception: Mutations in Citizenship and Sovereignty*. Durham, NC: Duke University Press.

Ostrom, Elinor. 1990. *Governing the Commons: The Evolution of Institutions for Collective Action*. Cambridge: Cambridge University Press.

———. 2005. *Understanding Institutional Diversity*. Princeton University Press.

Parkin Daniels, Joe. 2020. 'Colombian Death Squads Exploiting Coronavirus Lockdown to Kill Activists'. *The Guardian*, 23 March. Retrieved 2 November 2020 from https://www.theguardian.com/world/2020/mar/23/colombian-groups-exploiting-coronavirus-lockdown-to-kill-activists.

Porpora, Douglas. 2015. *Restructuring Sociology*. New York: Cambridge University Press.

Poteete, Amy. 2009. 'Defining Political Community and Rights to Natural Resources in Botswana'. *Development and Change* 40(2): 281–305.

Postero, Nancy. 2017. *The Indigenous State: Race, Politics and Performance in Plurinational Bolivia*. Berkeley: University of California Press.

Postero, Nancy, and Nicole Fabricant. 2019. 'Indigenous Sovereignty and the New Developmentalism in Plurinational Bolivia'. *Anthropological Theory* 19(1): 95–119.

Piketty, Thomas. 2020. *Capital and Ideology*. Cambridge: Belknap Press/Harvard University Press.

Robbins, Paul. 2004. *Political Ecology: A Critical Introduction*. Oxford: Blackwell.

Rosen, Jonathan. 2014. *The Losing War: Plan Colombia and Beyond*. New York: SUNY Press.

Ross, Michael. 2004. 'What Do We Know about Natural Resources and Civil War?' *Journal of Peace Research* 41(3): 337–56.

———.2012. *The Oil Curse: How Petroleum Wealth Shapes the Development of Nations*. Princeton: Princeton University Press.

Rosser, Andrew. 2006. *The Political Economy of the Resource Curse: A Literature Survey*. Working Paper Series, Number 268. Brighton: IDS.

Rydin, Yvonne. 2010. *Governing for Sustainable Urban Development*. London: Earthscan.

Sambanis, Nicholas. 2004. 'What Is Civil War? Conceptual and Empirical Complexities of the Operational Definition'. *Journal of Conflict Resolution* 48(6): 814–58.

Sànchez-Garzoli, Gimena. 2017. 'July Update: Dangerous Trends Continue to Affect Human Rights Defenders and Social Leaders'. *WOLA*. Retrieved 2 November 2020 from https://www.wola.org/analysis/july-update-dangerous-trends-continue-affect-human-rights-defenders-social-leaders.

Sawyer, Suzana, and Edmund Terrance Gomez. 2012. *The Politics of Resource Extraction: Indigenous Peoples, Multinational Corporations and the State*. Houndsmills/Geneva: Palgrave Macmillan.

Scott, James. 1999. *Seeing Like a State: How Certain Schemes to Improve the Human Condition Have Failed*. New Haven: Yale University Press

———. 1987. *Weapons of the Weak: Everyday Forms of Peasant Resistance*. New Haven: Yale University Press.

Sexton, Jay. 2012. *The Monroe Doctrine: Empire and Nation in 19ᵗʰ Century America*. New York: Hill & Wang.

Sieder, Rachel. 2017. 'Legalizing Indigenous Self-Determination: Autonomy and *Buen Vivir* in Latin America'. *The Journal of Latin American and Caribbean Anthropology* 22(1): 9–26.

Sieder, Rachel, Line Schjolden and Alan Angell. 2011. *The Judicialization of Politics in Latin America*. London. Palgrave Macmillan.

Slettebak, Rune. 2012. 'Don't Blame the Weather! Climate-Related Natural Disasters and Civil Conflict'. *Journal of Peace Research* 49(1): 163–76.

Stavig, Ward, Ella Schmidt and Charles Walker. 2008. *The Tupac Amaru and Catarista Rebellions: An Anthology of Sources*. Indianapolis: Hackett Classics.

Steven, Paul, and Evelyn Dietsche. 2008. 'Resource Curse: An Analysis of Causes, Experiences and Possible Ways Forward'. *Energy Policy* 36(1): 56–65.

Stern, Steve. 1987. *Resistance, Rebellion and Consciousness in the Andean Peasant World, 18ᵗʰ to 20ᵗʰ Centuries*. Madison: University of Wisconsin Press.

Stiglitz, Joseph. 2007. 'What is the Role of the State?', in Macarten Humphreys, Jeffrey Sachs and Joseph Stiglitz (eds), *Escaping the Resource Curse*. New York: Columbia University Press.

Swyngendouw, Erik. 2005. 'Governance Innovation and the Citizen: The Janus Face of Governance beyond the State'. *Urban Studies* 42(11): 1991–2006.

Taussig, Michael. 1997. *The Magic of the State*. London: Routledge.

Theisen, Ole Magnus. 2008. 'Blood and Soil? Resource Scarcity and Internal Armed Conflict Revisited'. *Journal of Peace Research* 45(6): 801–18.

Tissot, Roger. 2012. *Latin America's Energy Future*. IADB Discussion Paper. IDB-DP-252, December. Retrieved 2 November 2020 from https://publications.iadb.org/publications/english/document/Latin-America-Energy-Future.pdf.

Tsing, Anne. 2004. *Friction: An Ethnography of Global Connection*. Princeton: Princeton University Press.

Tucker, Roger. 2002. Environmentally Damaging Consumption: The Impact of American Markets on Tropical Ecosystems in the 20ᵗʰ Century', in Thomas Princen, Michael Maniates and Ken Conca (eds), *Confronting Consumption*. Cambridge: MIT Press.

Van Cott, Donna. 2000. *The Friendly Liquidation of the Past: The Politics of Diversity in Latin America*. Pittsburgh: University of Pittsburgh Press.

———. 2007. *From Movements to Parties in Latin America: The Evolution of Ethnic Politics*. Cambridge: Cambridge University Press.

Vandenberghe, Frederic. 2015. *What's Critical about Critical Realism?* London: Routledge.

Veltmayer, Henry and James Petras. 2014. *The New Extractivism: A Post-neoliberal Development Model or Imperialism of the 21ˢᵗ Century*. London: Zed Books.

Vidal, John. 2017. 'Why is Latin America So Obsessed with Mega Dams?' *The Guardian*, 23 May. Retrieved 2 November 2020 from https://www.theguardian.com/global-development-professionals-network/2017/may/23/why-latin-america-obsessed-mega-dams.

Young, Kevin. 2017. *Blood of the Earth: Resource Nationalism, Revolution and Empire in Bolivia*. Austin: University of Texas Press.

———. (ed.). 2019. *Making the Revolution: Histories of the Latin American Left*. Cambridge: Cambridge University Press.

Young, Oran (ed). 1997. *Global Governance: Drawing Insights from the Environmental Experience*. Cambridge, MA: MIT Press.

Watts, Michael. 2008. 'Blood Oil: The Anatomy of a Petro-insurgency in the Niger Delta'. *Focaal* 52: 18–38.

Wennmann, Achim. 2007. 'The Political Economy of Conflict Financing: A Comprehensive Approach beyond Natural Resources'. *Global Governance* 13(3): 427–44.

Williams, Aled, and Philippe Le Billon. 2017. *Corruption, Natural Resources and Development: From Resource Curse to Political Ecology*. Cheltenam: Edward Elgar.

Wolf, Erik. 1982. *Europe and the People without History*. Berkeley: University of California Press.

Figure 1.1. Protesters opposing the TIPNIS road project carry the Bolivian flag, La Paz, September 2011. © John-Andrew McNeish

Chapter 1

SOVEREIGNTY WITHIN AND BEYOND THE STATE

On 10 November 2019, Evo Morales Ayma formally resigned from his position as President of the Plurinational Republic of Bolivia. Morales had risen to prominence following his election as the first indigenous President of the Republic in 2005. Two days after his resignation, apparently fearing for his life, he jetted off to Mexico in a search of political exile (mirroring the departure of his predecessor Gonzalo Sanchez de Lozada to Miami in 2003). Since then, widespread debate has occurred both within Bolivia and around the world as to what were the circumstances behind his rapid fall from power. Opinions are significantly divided as to why his resignation had been necessitated. Commentators in opposition to Morales highlighted the suspicion and drastic drop in public support caused by the Morales' administrations 'malicious' and 'intentional manipulation' of the national elections in preceding weeks, which had been uncovered in detail in an Organization of American States audit (Graham-Harrison 2019). Supporters of the Morales administration – and Morales himself – claimed in contrast that his resignation was the result of soft coup whereby the Bolivian armed forces and police, supported by elements of the lowland right-wing political opposition, had drawn on the ensuing political crisis to forcibly request that the President stand down (Hetland 2019). An interim government led by Jeanine Áñez Chávez from the centre-right Democratic Social Movement was formed in the days following Morales' resignation ('¿Quién es Jeanine Áñez, la nueva presidenta interina de Bolivia?' 2019).

Both of these interpretations of event have their logics and convincing evidences – some of which have since been refuted (Curiel and Williams 2020), but little attention in most media coverage and analysis was given to the changing pattern of support evident in the years leading up to these events. There is widespread awareness of the fact that Morales enjoyed significant backing from the Bolivian population for a fourth electoral attempt, despite a 2016 referendum voting down the constitutional reform required to legally enable it. However, recent reporting on the resignation largely ignored the facts that Morales' support base was beginning to erode long before 2019. As I aim to emphasize in this chapter, two events in particular should be recognized as sparking a growing disaffection with the Morales government amongst urban poor, rural peasant and indigenous communities, i.e. social sectors that were once essential in his rise to power ('Evo Morales' Popularity Declines' 2016). These are events that featured prominently in my own research in the country and that I argue here are both important in explaining Morales' fall from grace and in initiating a discussion of the significance of resource sovereignty aimed at in this book.

December 2010 to December 2011 was the year of the *gazolinazo* and the TIPNIS protests in Bolivia. In this chapter, I start with these events and suggest that they are not only telling of persisting tensions in Bolivian politics, but also indicative of the complex nature of sovereignty in the country. Indeed, I suggest that both events help to open more general discussion of the close relationship that exists between the politics of natural resources, territory and sovereign claims within and beyond the state in Latin America. The *gazolinazo* and TIPNIS events indicate the negotiable nature of environmental governance and reveal sovereignty to be much more than its traditional static conception as a state's claim, or exercise of a monopoly and control over a defined territory and its resources. In this chapter, it will become evident that sovereignty is a changing and multiscalar concept. Moreover, sovereignty's contestation from beyond and below the state is recognized here as a dynamic that contributes significantly to state institutional and national identity formation over time. Recent events in Bolivia further demonstrate the centrality of territory and resources in this dynamic, and the political volatility it can cause.

A Year of Troubling Sovereignty

On 27 December 2010, the Bolivian government announced that it would remove a subsidy on fuel prices and that the price of a litre of petrol would increase by 72% and diesel by 82%. The Bolivian government justified the removal of the subsidy on the basis of its efforts to prevent the further uncontrolled growth of costs and subsidies' link to a 'bleeding of the economy' due to their encouragement of the contraband sale of fuel with neighbouring countries (Achtenberg 2011). According to data produced by the Ministry of Hydrocarbons and Energy, the value of the actual transfers carried out by the National Treasury to cover its quota share in subsidising liquefied petroleum gas (LPG) and diesel increased significantly after 2007[1] (Wanderley 2015). While Bolivia is an exporter of natural gas, since the late 1990s, the country has imported gasoline and diesel (mostly from Venezuela and Argentina) at the market price to cover domestic demand, reselling it at a discount to domestic consumers. This 'neoliberal' fuel subsidy, Morales argued, had cost the state $380 million in 2010. Indeed, it had primarily benefited Santa Cruz-based agribusiness and smugglers on Bolivia's borders with Peru and Brazil, who resold the fuel at double or triple the price across the border. An estimated $150 million was said by the government to have been siphoned out of the national economy in this manner. In a defence of the government's actions, Morales commented: 'For a small country like Bolivia, that's a lot of change' ('Ending Fuel Subsidies Cuts Bolivia's Losses, President Says' 2010).

Despite the government's explanations, the subsidy removal was broadly considered to be unexpected by the Bolivian population as there had been no previous debate with broad sectors of society regarding the financial justifications for the measure. Economic optimism was also at a high point before the measure was introduced almost simultaneously with government statements on the positive national financial situation and its links to hydrocarbon potential (Wanderley 2015). In 2006, the Morales government had placed the hydrocarbons industry largely under state control. Since then, Bolivia had benefited from a vast increase in royalties and tax revenues from natural gas exports (exceeding $1.5 billion annually in 2017) to fund social and economic programmes. Under these conditions Bolivians expected the subsidies to continue and for fuel prices to drop.

During the first hours following the subsidy removal and price hike, spontaneous protests broke out on the streets of all the cities in Bolivia. Overnight, bus and taxi fares doubled, food prices soared, and panic buying caused long lines for disappearing staples at state-run markets. Some $200 million in bank deposits were withdrawn, sparked by rumours of imminent government restrictions (Achtenberg 2011). In Cochabamba, the unemployed, who gathered daily on the street to wait for work, protested and were driven back by the police; heavy transport drivers also marched, announcing an increase in freight costs (Wanderley 2015). In La Paz and El Alto (its satellite city), spontaneous protests from residents, public transport passengers and market venders expressed their rejection of the measure. In different parts of the country, various sectors called town meetings, marches and protests. The process escalated to become an aggressive mobilization. The government pledged compensatory measures to soften the impact, including a freeze on utility rates, a 20% pay increase for public sector and minimum wage workers, and emergency jobs for the unemployed. Funds were also promised for rural infrastructure projects and agricultural price supports. The army baked and distributed bread at pre-*gasolinazo* prices to counter a bakers' union strike and provided free transportation (Achtenberg 2011). But this was not enough.

Fears spread throughout the government (and were publicly expressed by Alvaro Garcia Linera, the Vice-President who was in charge whilst Morales was out of the country on a diplomatic mission) that this instability could foster a repeat of the political and economic crises of the Water and Gas Wars experienced in the country in the early 2000s. The rise of Morales to the presidency was strongly tied to these two events (McNeish 2006). On the third day of unrest, the government relented and reinstated the pre-existing fuel prices. Debate raged between social movements, political parties and economic interests in the country, and questions were raised as to who was responsible for the measure, and its contradiction of the Morales government's earlier claims of a 'process of change'. Raúl Zibechi, a Uruguayan political analyst, called the episode 'an unprecedented event in recent Latin American history: the first massive popular uprising against a leftist government' (Achtenberg 2011).

Still reeling from the political disquiet produced by the *gasolinazo*, the Bolivian government found itself once again in political controversy in August and September 2011. The Morales government, which had claimed an end to the historical exclusion of the country's indigenous majority under the leadership of an Aymaran president, was observed by the national and international media to be callously suppressing the protests of indigenous communities that were in disagreement with its announced road development plans for the Isobore Sécure National Park and Indigenous Territory (TIPNIS). The TIPNIS is a triangular piece of land covering 1.2 million hectares, straddling the southern part of the department of Beni and the northern part of Cochabamba. On 15 August 2011, 2,000 marchers left the city of Trinidad, the lowland regional capital of the department of Beni, to follow a route that would take them 66 days and 600 km before their arrival in La Paz (Laing 2015).

The march was not the first of its kind and Bolivia is well known for its rich history of politically militancy. It was, however, of great surprise to observers and protesters alike that government security forces would attempt to impede the progress of the protest with direct repression. On Sunday 25 September 2011, Bolivian police raided the encampment (La Chaparina) of resting protesters near the town of Yucumo on the border between the Bolivian departments of Beni and La Paz. Within minutes of arriving, the police fired tear-gas canisters into the campsite. Having arrived to carry out interviews with people in the camp myself, I witnessed men, women and children being beaten to the ground, having their mouths taped and their hands tied behind their backs before being hauled away into a fleet of waiting hired buses (McNeish 2013). Dozens of television crews and newspaper reporters broadcast images of bloodied protesters being arrested and dragged by their limbs or their hair out of the field. In the aftermath of analysis in the press, observers made the association between this event and the attack on indigenous protesters by the military government of Banzer in 1976. Many citizens and experts also argued that by sanctioning this action, the administration had attacked its own support base (McNeish 2013).

Clearly surprised by the public outcry and embarrassed by the scenes of blood and aggression that the national media had captured during the raid, but also reluctant to assume personal responsibility, Morales held a press conference during which he apologized for the violence and promised that an investigation would be carried out into who was responsible for its instigation. Marcos Farfán, the Deputy Interior Minister, immediately denied any involvement in giving the order, as did the Minister, Sacha Llorenti. Cecilie Chacón, the newly appointed Minister of Defence, also resigned, stating her desire to separate herself from the irresponsible actions of the government and the police in connection with the raid. Following a series of meetings between the protesters and the President in the Presidential Palace, the government agreed to pass a legal decree (*ley corta*) on 24 October 2011 guaranteeing that the Villa Tunari–San Ignacio de Moxos road would not pass through the TIPNIS. Furthermore, the law stated that from now on, the TIPNIS would be protected by the state as an 'intangible' territory, effectively making it out of bounds for all forms of future state or development projects.

This was not what any of the TIPNIS communities wanted, despite divisions between those opposed and those in support of the road project. By deeming the TIPNIS intangible, the Morales government were seen to remove the right to autonomy and decision-making over territory and resources by any of the key stakeholders in the region. New protests and marches followed in the months after the first TIPNIS protest. The government also attempted to regain popular support in the TIPNIS through the sponsorship of a large-scale consultation exercise in 2012. However, breaching international standards on the 'prior' nature of consultation and by clearly manipulating the conditions of the vote, the government was broadly seen to contradict its own claims of taking the higher moral and democratic ground. The lasting impression given to local people and to the national organizations and international community now actively involved in the observation of the TIPNIS crisis was one of contradiction. Indeed, the crisis generated the largest fall in public confidence in the government since its election in 2006.[2] As if resigned to a gradual fall in confidence, the government reinitiated plans to build the road through the TIPNIS in 2017 with the expected results – a new round of significant (several indigenous leaders have been jailed) albeit smaller-scale confrontations between local communities and the government.

The Morales administration weathered both the *gasolinazo* and the TIPNIS crises, but their impact on the popularity of the administration and wider government–community relations were much longer-lasting. According to local analysts (Wanderley 2015), the *gasolinazo* and the resulting crisis confirmed the sectoral and fiscal problems of the new hydrocarbon management model. It revealed the non-transparent management of the country's financial situation, the inefficiencies of government management and the absence of alternative proposals to resolve structural problems that the *gasolinazo* sought to correct. For critics of the government, these problems were also linked to wider problems in the economy – the difficulties in providing food and construction materials, the rise in inflation, the increase in internal debt and the unsustainability of government spending. Many saw these problems as having their root in the absence of a social, territorial and financial pact that would give the hydrocarbon policy legitimacy and rationality. Other analysts (Salman 2012) recognized what the *gasolinazo* said about the government's lack of control over both the country's borders and influential social movements within the country. In the aftermath of the crisis, the government's efforts were judged to be an error that cost it not only in statistical terms of spot polls, but also the long-lasting goodwill of important social and civil society movements, including the historically important Bolivian Central Workers Union (COB).

The clear disagreement and growing split between the Morales government and important elements of Bolivian civil society was made even more obvious by the TIPNIS protest. Again, whilst not entirely defining in terms of political destiny, the crisis further eroded the image and relations propping up the Morales government. As a result of the TIPNIS protest, splits within the uneasy pact between social sectors and organizations that had delivered Morales to the presidency would be increasingly highlighted. In the lowlands, one of the lasting impacts of the crisis would be the division of the region's main indigenous organization, the Confederation of Indigenous Peoples of Bolivia (CIDOB), into two ('CIDOB dividida por el Gobierno de Morales' 2013). Members of the organization who were won over by the government's pressure and enticements split to form an organization loyal to the ruling governmental party, the Movement for Socialism (MAS). The other half of CIDOB remained loyal in its opposition to the road project and the government. Some individuals prominently associated with CIDOB, including Pablo Nuni (one of the protest leaders), announced in frustration their support for elements of the right-wing political opposition, including Ruben Costas, the governor of Santa Cruz.[3]

In the Bolivian highlands, the TIPNIS protest would also result in a difficult re-alignment of political interests. During the course of the TIPNIS crisis, the National Council of Ayllus and Markas of Qullasuyu (CONAMAQ), a significant indigenous organization in the Andes and part of the movement for change responsible for the election of Morales, would also divide into two opposing factions – one in favour of the protesters, the other in support of the government ('CIDOB dividida por el Gobierno de Morales' 2013). In December 2012, representatives from CONAMAQ denounced the President and the MAS government before the UN Human Rights Council and the International Labour Organization (ILO) in Geneva (von Hirsch 2019). In December 2013, the disputed election between rival factions led to a police siege of CONAMAQ's La Paz headquarters and a series of violent confrontations, followed by hunger strikes, vigils and road blockades. Other splits and re-alignments have continued to take place. In August 2017, representatives of the Highland community of Achacachi, known for their political militancy, announced their alliance with the indigenous populations of the TIPNIS in opposition to the government and their continued development plans ('Indígenas del TIPNIS y pobladores de Achacachi se unen contra el Gobierno' 2017).

As such, the *gasolinazo* and TIPNIS crises are political events with lasting impacts. Indeed, their details suggest the complicated dynamics of Bolivian politics and of efforts to further govern and develop the country's extractive economy. Certainly, the study of these two events illustrates the difficulties of constructing legitimacy for collective agreements on how 'to govern oil and gas' and related infrastructural development (Wanderley 2015). Interestingly, parallels can also be drawn between these events and similar moments of protest elsewhere in the world (see e.g. Houland 2018). From this perspective, institutions and political platforms are understood as collective constructions, the stability of which requires continuous affirmation. Importantly for this book and this chapter in particular, they also exemplify the challenge of a nation-state to ensure sovereignty over the control of territory and natural resources.

The sovereign authority of the state visibly requires negotiation and adjustment in response to competing perspectives of the nation, the access and use of resources and territory, and the direction of its economic development. Taken together, the *gasolinazo* and TIPNIS crises further reveal that these competing perspectives are not only a matter of opposition to the ideology and dynamics of global markets as a source of rules for the hydrocarbon sector or a driving force for development. Rather, they highlight the complexities of sovereignty as competing claims (at once driven by formal political platforms, the difficult relationship between the formal and informal economic sectors stretching into smuggling and cross-border movements and contrasting – often contingent – ethnic alliances and cultural perspectives on territory and resources). Sovereignty is revealed to be singular and plural at the same time, and as an inroad into understanding conflict. Recognizing this, I propose in the next few pages to move on to a deeper consideration of ideas about sovereignty. In the chapter's conclusion, I will return to the context of Bolivia and Latin America and a reading of events through the lens of this expanded discussion of sovereignty.

The Birth of the Sovereign

As a category of scholarship, activism, governance and cultural work, sovereignty matters in consequential ways in terms of understanding the political agendas, strategies and cultural perspectives of peoples across the world. Many take for granted what sovereignty means and why it is important. As a result, sovereignty can be confused and confusing, especially as its normalization masks its own ideological origins in colonial legal-religious discourses as well as the heterogeneity of its contemporary histories, meanings and identities. Sovereignty is therefore a concept that should be treated and studied more carefully. By taking the time to study sovereignty more closely, it becomes clear that it does not have a singular history of creation and application, but rather a story that can only be reconstructed out of the confluence of different historical events and processes. It becomes clear that this is a story that is intimately related not only to claims to territory and resources; it is also an account dealing with the constitution of knowledge and the expression of political power. It also becomes clear that sovereignty is a political idea that has gone through and continues to go through significant changes. For the people this book takes as its central focus – indigenous and peasant peoples – these changes are important to recognize because they may determine the possibility that persisting colonial conditions of settlement can change and their struggles for rights and autonomy may be more fully realized.

In one narrative of history and political science, sovereignty is the product of changes in religious and political thinking within Europe in the period from the Reformation to the Enlightenment (Jackson 2007). Although originally a theological term, sovereignty was appropriated by European political thinkers in the centuries following the Reformation to characterize the person of the king as the head of state. The king or the sovereign was thought to have inherited the authority to rule from God. This 'divine right' was understood to be absolute, a power that was accountable only to God, from whom it originated. The Protestant and Catholic Churches were important governing powers during the early uses of sovereignty and consequently Church doctrine impacted its meaning in its initial application. The Church maintained that only God was the true sovereign and that the Church was the medium of God's will on earth, while the king claimed to be a sovereign who inherited from God the right to rule. However, the powers of the Church and the king slowly gave way through various political shifts and revolutions to the ideologies and structure of the nation (Bourke 2016).

The transition from the 'vertical' structure, headed by the Pope and the Holy Roman Empire, to the 'horizontal' structure of independent states (equal in authority and legal legitimacy) was consolidated in 1648 with the end of the 30 Years' War in Europe and the Peace of Westphalia (Jackson 2007). With the introduction of Westphalian sovereignty, a number of states acquired uncontested independence. As such, kings and princes were no longer subject to interference from the Holy Roman Empire with regard to the territories subjected to its sovereignty. The principle of non-interference by any sovereign power in the territorial affairs of other states became an uncontested rule that governed the system of international relations, and the authority of kings and princes over their respective territories became 'supreme'.

Key political thinkers of this period such as Niccolo Machiavelli, Jean Bodin and Thomas Hobbes shared a conception of sovereign power as a supreme entity, governing the law and the life and death of the subjects (Jackson 2007). Suggesting a break with the past, such an idea was also proposed as the result of considerations of realpolitik rather than of supernaturalism-based thoughts. On this basis, the objective of sovereignty that emerged in early modern Europe was a power concentrated in the hands of an authority bundled into a single entity, which governed a collectively unified set of interests that were confined within territorial borders. The sovereign authority held supremacy in the collective interest. Rights to 'exclusive jurisdiction, territorial integrity and non-intervention in domestic affairs' would now characterize the nation, and these rights would be correlated to concepts of sovereignty (Jackson 2007). The nation reorganized concepts of social status and responsibility from the obligations of subjects either of the Church or of the kingdom to notions of citizenship, civil society and democracy.

In contrast to the historical narrative of sovereignty born out of war and scientific discovery within Europe, other writers suggest that it is equally an idea formed through the history of European exploration and conquest (Bertelsen 2016). Here the concept of 'chunk theory' in which sovereignty is possessed 'in full or not at all' is tested by the realities of encounters in which the extent of territory, resources and the people within it are uncertain, unknown and changing. In this historical narrative, sovereignty is directly tied to a European need to codify and regulate the practices of conquest and settlement and to come to terms with lands with peoples deemed as different and uncivilized, and hence *unsovereign* (Anghie 2012; see also Silva 2007). During this period, notions of civilization, citizenship, personhood and humanism became established and developed – not as mere descriptors, but as discursive categories within an interested debate over the reach of European power. The colonial project spurred the need to define the terms of territorial ownership and political belonging, to draw distinctions between savages and barbarians, citizens and subjects, incorporation and inclusion, occupation and settlement.

The concept of sovereignty provided a legal technology with which to lay claim to putatively unowned lands (i.e. *terra nullius*), to dispossess native communities or, alternatively, to establish treaties with native peoples in ways that incorporated them into an ontological order of civilizational difference (Anghie 2012). Such legitimacy was sanctioned by Pope Alexander VI in the Bull Inter Caetara of 3 May 1493, which recognized Spain's sovereignty over all territories discovered after Christmas 1492 located west of an imaginary line drawn through the Atlantic Ocean from the Arctic Pole to the Antarctic Pole. The papal bull also granted Portugal sovereignty over whatever it discovered in Africa. This was not a process that involved only military and economic mastery, but also a significant philosophical and institutional reworking, as the protracted theological and legal debate between Bartolome de las Casas and Juan Gines de Sepulveda in 1550 reveals (Hancke 1994). Sovereignty as a legal concept is thus grounded in concrete material practices of dispossession, the practical work of disenfranchisement and the creation of legal regimes of difference. The European global encounter added meaning and force to the concept of sovereignty (Cooper 2014; Kelly and Kaplan 2001, 2009).

The People as Sovereign

A slow dismantling of European colonial rule would start to take place in the late eighteenth and early nineteenth centuries, and with it the meaning of sovereignty would shift again. Popular movements inspired by European and North American political liberalism would arise that aimed at freeing peoples from the domination of despotic colonial governments. The argumentative structure of the American Declaration emphasized independence – rather than simply natural rights or the statement of grievances – as its primary message would influence many other actions towards postcolonialism. The consequence of that separation was that Americans would, as 'Free and Independent States . . . have full Power to levy War, conclude Peace, contract Alliances, establish Commerce, and to do all other Acts and Things which

Independent States may of right do' (Armitage 2005). By means of their Declaration, they announced that the United States had left the transnational community of the British Empire to join instead an international community of free and independent states. The American Declaration provided the primary model for the first great wave of declarations of independence that swept the transatlantic world in the first half of the nineteenth century. In Spanish American territories, the authorities tried to prevent the spread of independence by banning the circulation of the US Declaration. Despite their efforts, it was nonetheless widely transmitted and translated, for example by the Venezuelan Manuel García de Sena, by the Colombian Miguel de Pombo, by the Ecuadorian Vicente Rocafuerte and by the New Englanders Richard Cleveland and William Shaler, who distributed translations of the Declaration and the US Constitution among creoles in Chile and Indians in Mexico in 1821. The Declaration also reached Portuguese America, initially by way of the Brazilian medical student 'Vendek' (José Joaquim Maia e Barbalho), who had met secretly with Thomas Jefferson in Nîmes in 1786 (Armitage 2005: 12). As liberal ideas took hold, various Latin American republics would issue a series of imitative declarations between 1811 and 1849.

The formal understanding of sovereignty representing a peoples' democratic determination of independence became an accepted legal and diplomatic norm following 1776, but its assertions of the 'self-evident' truths that 'all men are created equal' with unalienable rights to life, liberty and the pursuit of happiness would remain largely unused in law and politics until the end of the nineteenth century. John Adams, the second President of the United States writing in 1781, called the Declaration in simple terms 'that memorable Act, by which [the United States] assumed an equal Station among the Nations'. Even Abraham Lincoln, speaking in 1857, suggested that the assertion that 'all men are created equal' was of no practical use in effecting the separation from Great Britain. Whilst Thomas Jefferson is best known for his role as the principal author of the US Declaration of Independence, he was also the first to propose broad policies calling for the removal of North American Indians from their homelands. Many men in the new republic were denied the full measure of citizenship. These included the indigenous men of the land, who were seen as savage forces to be controlled rather than fellow Americans. Wars between the European settlers and indigenous peoples were regular elements of the colonial period and throughout Jefferson's life (Zimring 2015: 15). Jefferson was also the author of a more ominous strategy to acquire Indian land: the use of trading posts to drive Indians into debt, forcing them to relinquish acreage to pay their bills. The result was treaties with a dozen tribal groups that ceded to the United States nearly 200,000 square miles of land in nine states (Landry 2016).

The US Constitution functioned as a document of national formation and was used by colonists, rebellions and commonwealths to assert territorial boundaries and the authority and terms of the nation-so-formed to govern within them. Yet the declarative status of the Constitution disguised the fact that the nation so defined was contingent upon it being recognized as legitimate by other already recognized nations. Custom within international law emerged around the treaty as a mechanism for both the exercise of nationhood and the recognition of national sovereignty. However, law also covered over the reality of postcolonial sovereignty whereby indigenous and slave populations were pushed or fooled into states of no sovereignty (Bonilla 2013, 2015). Other counties would adopt this practice. England, France, Canada and New Zealand notably negotiated, signed and ratified treaties with indigenous peoples. However, many observe that such efforts were less about the recognition and provision for the sovereignty of indigenous peoples than they were about the assertion of the respective nation's status as the more powerful sovereign within a given territory against other European powers and over indigenous peoples.

In Latin America, similar contradictions in the application of ideas of liberty would become evident through continued genocide and the continued marginalization of indigenous populations from political and economic decision-making. After independence, political elites in Latin America attempted to dismantle the colonial regimes that had institutionalized racialized difference; they adhered to a liberal emphasis on universalism and the creation of equal citizens (Viotti da Costa 2000; Larson 2004; Lasso 2007). However, as usual in liberal regimes, there were major limits to equality. Simón Bolívar, the central architect of the rebellion against Spain and the father of the Latin American republics, himself denied that South America was suited to full liberal democracy, as the participation of the (non-white) popular classes would, he said, 'lead to Colombia's ruin' (Lasso 2007). Indigenous and free black people were not usually explicitly excluded, although indigenous people were more likely to be named in this respect (Wade 2016). More usually, however, literacy requirements – which persisted in Colombia until 1932 and in Brazil until 1988 – were used to exclude them from suffrage, along with many other poor people (Sanders 2004; Agudelo 2005; Engerman and Sokoloff 2005; Yashar 2005). The idea of *Mestizaje* as a political idea also started to be commonly used in the region to refer to purposeful racial mixing and the forcible eradication of difference. This sometimes excused or enabled the conditions for extreme violence that operated outside the boundaries of the law. Examples of this violence include the massacres of Afro-Cubans in the 1912 Guerrita del 12, the Conquest of the Desert in late nineteenth-century Argentina, the massacres of Matagalpa people by the Nicaraguan state repressing an 1881, and the extreme abuses practised by rubber companies in the Colombian Amazon in the early twentieth century that created *a space of terror* (Wade 2016: 328).

Indigenous Sovereignty

It was not until after the Second World War that the idea of sovereignty inclusive of the idea of both a right to self-determination (independence) and equality between all peoples would be considered anew in international and national law. Following the Second World War, the opportunity to continue the process of decolonization that had started in the nineteenth century occurred as European powers retracted their financial holdings abroad and as new social movements and political agendas expressing social justice were articulated. Often contradicting their own geopolitical interests, these articulations were of course assisted by the reconfiguration of the great powers after the war and the new ideological confrontation between allied clusters of states that would go on to become the Cold War.

In this period, the idea of sovereignty was re-articulated to mark the complexities of global efforts to reverse ongoing experiences of colonialism as well as to signify both local and international efforts at the reclamation of specific territories, resources, governments and cultural knowledge and practices. Indeed, the idea of permanent sovereignty over natural resources emerged as a principle in international law (Schrijver 2013: 95).

In the aftermath of the Second World War, the newly formed UN sought to assist independent states to secure the possible benefits of exploiting natural resources. The UN also hoped to create a legal shield against infringements of their economic sovereignty as a result of property rights or contractual rights claimed by other states (often former colonial powers) or private corporations. Signed in 1945, the UN Charter expressed the conception of sovereignty as a prerogative of states as independent entities enjoying political domination over a territorial area. It banned the threat or use of force against the territorial integrity or political independence of any state. Over the years the political and legal debate on resource sovereignty has both broadened and deepened. It broadened by extending its scope to include natural wealth and marine resources. It also deepened by increasing the number of resource-related rights, including those relating to foreign investment (Schrijver 2013: 96).

The evolution of international law that has taken place since 1945 led not only to the restriction of the scope of state sovereignty, but also to the conditioning of its constitutive elements, and particularly its legitimacy. Indeed, the international community has progressively recognized the legal relevance of a number of values (including the right of people to participate in the

government) that erode the traditional idea of sovereignty as the uncondi-
tioned prerogative of the state. In order to be legitimate, sovereignty must
be representative of the people living in the territory over which it extends
its scope and control. Starting in the 1950s, the practice of the UN led to
the evolution of the principle of self-determination of peoples, already proclaimed by Article 1, paragraph 2 and Article 55 of the UN Charter, towards
a principle of customary international law granting the right of independence
to any people subjected to foreign colonial domination. These developments
would also lead to the Warsaw Declaration of 27 June 2000, which states
that the will of the people shall be the basis of authority of government,
as expressed by exercise of the right and civic duties of citizens to choose
their representatives through regular, free and fair elections with universal
and equal suffrage. These transformations in the international understanding
of sovereignty did not go unnoticed or encouraged by peoples who under
colonial rule lacked an 'impartial' governmental body to whom they could
refer in their claims of autonomy and territorial rights. In the mid-twentieth
century, subaltern populations took up the notion of sovereignty (tied to the
idea of self-determination) in the hopes of transforming their status through
entry into a system of states and nations as equal sovereigns. Reflecting this,
1955 postcolonial governments across the developing world announced at
the Bandung Conference their *non-alignment* with earlier colonial powers
and insistence on independence, sovereignty and territorial integrity.

The starting point of claims for *indigenous sovereignty* lies in the fact that
indigenous peoples were illegitimately deprived of the lands ancestrally occupied and governed by them as entities owning the attributes of sovereignty
pursuant to international law (Lenzerini 2007). An objective assessment of
the inherent characters of most indigenous nations demonstrates that in
numerous cases, they possess the qualities necessary for qualifying as a state
according to international law i.e. (a) they have a permanent population; (b)
a defined territory; (c) a government; and (d) a capacity to enter into relations with other states (i.e. independence) (Lenzerini 2007).

The shared idiom of sovereignty became a specific discursive response
to living under conditions of settler colonialism (external and internal), a
concept that had gained immense traction among indigenous intellectuals
during the course of the 1990s, and particularly in North America and Australia (Barker 2007). Sovereignty has emerged as a key discursive framework
for indigenous self-determination in these territories in part because of the
shared experiences of British colonialism and its successor states, and what
was now a largely anglophone context that facilitated intellectual exchanges
among indigenous actors across the region. Whilst geographical and linguistic differences complicated communication, the shared history of conquest
and the new institutional context of the UN system enabled a parallel – and

not entirely separate – discourse of indigenous rights to develop in Latin America.

Although a debated term (Catellanos 2017), settler colonialism is recognized in general to involve common and ongoing attempts at political erasure and a refusal of the idea that nation-states are in any sense *post*colonial societies. A distinction is made here between settler and franchise colonialism (as established in other colonial territories such as India, some parts of Africa and the Far East). The primary natural resource extracted under this history of colonialism is indigenous land, a practice that leads to a second key distinction, i.e. 'the logic of elimination' (Wolfe 1999: 27). This replacement serves the goals of the new settler society, because the logical assumption is that the ongoing existence of indigenous peoples threatens the new social order; thus, to avoid them making an alternative claim to the land and their own political authority over it, they must be made to disappear.

Following Wolfe's (1999) influential tour-de-force publication on the subject, most scholars have viewed the term 'settler society' as not being relevant to the Latin American context. However, several scholars have significantly revised this position in recent years. Castellanos (2017) and Speed (2017) convincingly argue that the logic of elimination was equally as prevalent in conquest of Latin America as it had been in the history of the establishment of the colonies in North America and Australia. One reason why Latin America was thought to be characterized by colonialism of the non-settler variety is the perception that, while colonial processes in the anglophone north focused on land dispossession and the correlated elimination of the native, in the south the focus was on resource extraction and the corresponding marshalling and control of indigenous labour. Speed (2017) suggests that by looking at the contrasting experiences across the region, Wolfe's land-labour binary becomes evidently too rigid a description of how colonialism played out in Latin America. Colonialism in Latin America can be characterized by both land dispossession and labour extraction, to which indigenous peoples were simultaneously subjected. Indigenous land dispossession was a fundamental aspect of colonialism, combined with various regimes of labour extraction.

Unlike metropole and administrative colonialism imposed on other parts of the world, in Latin America white Europeans came to stay. And stay they did. According to Gott (2007), the birth of settler Latin America coincides with independence when settlers gained full control of the native population and its land. Importantly, in contrast to many other authors (Castellanos 2017), he also contests the notion that colonialism ended with the formation of the republics after independence, stressing instead the ongoing nature of colonial nature of power relations. According to Speed (2017: 786), 'by failing to address settler colonialism *as settler*, they accept the basic premise that the settler has settled, rather than acknowledging that there is a state of ongoing occupation, in Latin America as elsewhere in the hemisphere'. European settler colonialism was the catalyst for capitalism's expansion and continues to structure life under capitalism as it moves through different phases. Capitalism's current iteration – neoliberalism – continues to be shaped by the settler imperative of dispossession/extraction/elimination justified by racialized and gendered logics (Speed 2017: 788). It is a practical experience of the terms of continued settler colonialism by indigenous peoples themselves that motivated common calls for indigenous sovereignty at the international level.

A reconsideration of the possibility of indigenous sovereignty was seriously set in motion by the parallel efforts of the UN General Assembly and the ILO. Once sceptical of international human rights, indigenous rights advocates in the 1980s and 1990s began to articulate their claims in terms of human rights, particularly the human right to culture (Engle 2011). In the 1970s, a UN subcommittee and a global study on the problem of discrimination faced by indigenous peoples led by the Ecuadorian diplomat Jose Martinez Cobo was established.[4] The study's definition of indigenous peoples was widely cited and had a clear influence on later formal legal formulations and claims of indigenous identity:

According to the subcomittee's report, indigenous communities, peoples and nations have a historical continuity with pre-invasion and precolonial societies that developed in their territories and consider themselves distinct from prevailing societies in those territories (or parts of them). They form at present nondominant sectors of society and are determined to preserve, develop and transmit to future generations their ancestral territories and their ethnic identity as the basis of their continued existence as peoples, in accordance with their own cultural patterns, social institutions and legal systems.

In 1982, the Economic and Social Council (ECOSOC) established a Working Group on Indigenous Populations as a subsidiary organ to the Sub-Commission on the Promotion and Protection of Human Rights. The Working Group was granted the mandate of developing a set of minimum standards that would protect indigenous peoples. In parallel to the Working Group, the ILO forged ahead with its own definition of the rights and legal protection of indigenous populations. This included the revision of the assimilationist goals of previous conventions.

The ILO is a specialized UN agency that aims to improve the living and working conditions of people around the world. It was founded by the League of Nations in 1919 as part of the Treaty of Versailles. Being the oldest of the specialized agencies of the UN system, it was also the first international body to address indigenous issues (starting in the 1920s) in a comprehensive manner through establishing the Indigenous and Tribal Populations Convention,

1957 (No. 107) and the Indigenous and Tribal Peoples Convention, 1989 (No. 169). A new convention (ILO 169) proposed that existing cultures and institutions of indigenous peoples should be respected by ratifying governments. It also presumes the right of indigenous peoples to continued existence within their national societies, to establish their own institutions and to determine the path of their own development. Controversially the ILO's formulation of indigenous sovereignty emphasized that it was 'self-determined' and that states should seek approval of development activities on indigenous land through mechanisms of consent and consultation:

> Article 6 of ILO 169: requires, among other things, that ratifying States consult indigenous and tribal peoples through appropriate procedures, particularly through their representative institutions when legislative or administrative measures that may directly affect them are being considered and provides that States should establish means for the peoples concerned to develop their own institutions.

> Article 7: establishes, among other things, the right of indigenous and tribal peoples to decide their own priorities for the process of development and to exercise control over their own economic, social and cultural development, and establishes the obligation of ratifying States to take measures to protect and preserve the environment of the territories inhabited by these peoples.

ILO 169 was ratified by over twenty countries and led to significant shifts in the constitutional law throughout Latin America and other countries where it was adopted.[5] It would also encourage the UN General Assembly to further expand its work towards a Universal Declaration. This resulted in the formulation and tabling for debate within the UN of a Draft Declaration on the Rights of Indigenous Peoples in 1993 in which acknowledgement was further made of indigenous sovereignty. Article 26 states that: 'Indigenous peoples have the right to own, develop, control and use the lands and territories, including the total environment of the lands, air, waters, coastal seas, sea-ice, flora and fauna and other resources which they have traditionally owned or otherwise occupied or used. This includes the right to the full recognition of their laws, traditions and customs, land-tenure systems and institutions for the development and management of resources, and the right to effective measures by States to prevent any interference with, alienation of or encroachment upon these rights (Draft Declaration on the Rights of Indigenous Peoples 1994).

The idea of self-determination provided the foundation for the principle of free, prior and informed consent (FPIC) that will be discussed further in Chapter 5. However, it is notable at this early stage that the results of the work of the Working Group were delayed for several years due to concerns within the UN regarding the core provisions of the Draft Declaration, specifically the right to self-determination of indigenous peoples and the control over natural resources existing on indigenous peoples' traditional lands (Barker 2007). Ultimately states that had opposed earlier drafts – African states in particular – were swayed to support the formation of a convention by the inclusion of a compromise: Article 46(11) makes clear that that self-determination only applies to nations trying to free themselves from the yoke of colonialism (Draft Declaration on the Rights of Indigenous Peoples 1994).

In September 2007, a vote in the Assembly of 143 in favour and 4 against (Australia, Canada, New Zealand and the United States), with 11 abstentions, enabled the formal adoption of the United Nations Declaration on the Rights of Indigenous Peoples. The Declaration sets out the individual and collective rights of the world's 370 million native peoples, calls for the maintenance and strengthening of their cultural identities, and emphasizes their right to pursue development in keeping with their own needs and aspirations ('General Assembly Adopts Declaration on Rights of Indigenous Peoples' 2007). Part 1 recognizes their right to be consulted with regard to 'legislative or administrative measures which may affect them directly' and to participate at all levels of decision-making concerning programmes or policies affecting them directly. They also have the right to decide their own priorities 'for the process of development as it affects their lives, beliefs, institutions and spiritual well-being and the land they occupy or otherwise use'. It also recognizes their right to have their customs with respect to penal matters 'taken into consideration' by the judicial authorities dealing with such matters. Although it is a nonbinding text, the Declaration states that indigenous peoples have the right 'to the recognition, observance and enforcement of treaties' concluded with states or their successors. It also prohibits discrimination against indigenous peoples and promotes their full and effective participation in all matters that concern them. Article 14 proclaims the obligation of recognizing 'the rights of ownership and possession of the peoples concerned over the lands which they traditionally occupy', adding that 'measures shall be taken in appropriate cases to safeguard the right of the peoples concerned to use land not exclusively occupied by them, but to which they have traditionally has access for their subsistence and traditional activities'.

The United Nations Declaration on the Rights of Indigenous Peoples (UNDRIP) 2007 has been described by rights campaigners and academics as a victory and a 'milestone' in international indigenous struggles (Wiessner 2008). It appeared that indigenous peoples finally had formal legal defence of their collective rights, the right to culture, and self-determination (Engle 2011). The UN Permanent Forum on Indigenous Issues states on its webpage that the UNDRIP gives prominence to collective rights to a degree unprecedented in international human rights law. The adoption of this instrument is the clearest indication yet that the international community is committing itself to the protection of the individual and collective rights of indigenous peoples. However, while many international legal scholars maintain that the UNDRIP is a vital source of protection for indigenous peoples, many indigenous organizations and analysts have qualified their support for the convention. Indeed, many indigenous organizations and analysts now argue that UNDRIP is at best a devastating compromise for indigenous people and at worst an insidious attempt by state actors to maintain structures of international injustice.

Within the framework of the UNDRIP, self-determination was reconstituted to mean 'the right of autonomy or self-government in matters relating to their internal and local affairs'. This means that indigenous peoples are granted only certain administrative powers, and only within state recognized communities and territories (Engle 2011: 147). The international ratification of the UNDRIP was secured only by ensuring that the power to secede from existing states was denied. As a result, the final text of the Declaration is 'more concerned with the broad human rights' of indigenous peoples than with their survival as 'distinct peoples' (Watson 2011: 507). This was less threatening to the international state system, represented by the UN, and one that complied with the further stabilization of the international order. The legacy of the civilizing mission of colonial states remained deeply encoded into the very strictures of international law (Anghie 2005). Whilst appearing engender a legal revolution, the fine print of the UNDRIP repeated the logics and practice of state legal practice evident in colonial settings such as the Americas and other European settled territories since the eighteenth century, in which sovereign rights are recognized, but do not amount to internationally relevant sovereign powers.

Given the conflicting evaluations of the UNDRIP, it is evident that the idea of *indigenous sovereignty* remains a contested idea. Indeed, as will become evident in the exploration of socio-environmental conflicts in subsequent chapters in this volume, the ambiguity surrounding indigenous rights to land and territory – sustained since the arrival of European settlers – is generative of significant and frequently violent disagreement. Although states in Latin America have largely ratified the UNDRIP and have made provisions in respect to it within constitutional law and public policy, they maintain an interpretation of indigenous autonomy and self-determination as granted within the limits and strictures of the state. Whilst indigenous communities increasingly recognize the presence and power of national legal governing institutions, conflicts with authorities regarding the practice of development consultation and indigenous involvement in regional and national decision-making regarding the use of local territory and resources abound.

Bolivia has perhaps surpassed other Latin American states in its constitutional recognition of ethnic plurality (it is now officially known as the Plurinational Republic of Bolivia). Nonethelesss, in common with its neighbours with significant populations of indigenous peoples, multiple conflicts have developed throughout the country regarding the correct implementation of the UNDRIP and its strictures regarding consultation and self-determination (Schilling-Vacaflor and Eichler 2017). This was clearly reflected in the legal and political disagreements of the TIPNIS struggle described above.

Renewed Scholarly Debates on Sovereignty

There has been a renewed interest in the meaning and use of the concept of sovereignty across the legal and social sciences in recent years. This has in part been generated by the internal reworking of theory within different disciplines, but also as a result of the need to sufficiently respond to the persisting controversies and contradictions observed in politics and law. The legal and political interpretation of sovereignty and sovereign rights remains a central factor in ongoing conflicts and social contestation at different scales, e.g. from international discussions on terrorism and migration, state reactions to regional calls for national independence, and state, corporate and community confrontations on local property and resource rights. Recognizing that the concept of sovereignty has shifted over time and has never reached a universally agreed meaning, recent scholarship has focused on the changing and multiple meanings of this concept across a variety of historical and political contexts.

Across the constellation of the social sciences and political theory, diverse writers (including Max Weber, Carl Schmitt and Franz Neumann) have touched on the historically complex and unsettled configurations of sovereignty in European countries. In political and legal studies, renewed debate has recently surfaced regarding the significance of the sovereign state in a globalized market economy. On the one hand, it is suggested that the sovereign state is no longer the main locus of political authority and community in the future. It is now challenged by new constellations of authority and community that transcend the divide between the domestic and the international spheres and will soon be replaced by new forms of political life that know nothing of this distinction (Bertelsen 2006: 464). According to the second view, the sovereign state is likely to remain a potent source of authority and community in the future. According to this view, emergent constellations of authority and community that allegedly challenge the predominance of the sovereign state are ultimately only the manifestation of its successful claims to sovereignty.

According to Bertelsen (2006), the persistence of this debate results from the ontological status of concepts, a question that has been conveniently neglected by many of those who have taken the linguistic turn within political science and law. Indeed, many constructivists assume that this question has been settled once and for all, and are thus blind to the ontological implications of their own arguments. Bertelsen (2006: 466) suggests that some of the problems resulting from a nominalist interpretation of the concept of sovereignty are highly visible in Ilgen's book *Reconfigured Sovereignty* (2003). Ilgen argues that sovereignty is a much more fluid and malleable concept than its standard characterization as fixed and immutable in international affairs. The introductory chapter posits that sovereignty nowadays is seldom monopolized by the state, but is regularly divided and shared among state and nonstate actors at all levels of governance, depending on the issue or problem at hand. Furthermore, while most existing scholarship has argued that the principal challenge to state sovereignty comes from outside the state, there is a need to also recognize internal challenges to state sovereignty. While the history of sovereignty culminates in its concentration in the nation-state, it has been increasingly challenged by the market economy and its natural tendency to expand beyond the politically defined boundaries of states. Consequently, crucial features of state sovereignty have been weakened, such as its ability to make and enforce laws, the power to define and defend territorial borders, as well as the capacity to shape and direct economic performance. According to Ilgen (2003), this has led to the creation of supranational institutions of global governance and to a downward diffusion of power to subnational actors such as cities and regions.

Reflecting on the constitution of popular sovereignty in the present, Ochoa Espejo (2011) mirrors Ilgen's observations on the downward diffusion of power. However, this is further developed to consider the way in which power is now made legitimate. In doing so, she suggests, 'we should conceive of the people as a process rather than as an aggregation of individuals' (2011: 3). The traditional conception of the people is problematic because it holds that only a unified popular will legitimizes the foundation of the state. Hence, in order to govern, a ruling administration has to demonstrate that a given people is or was unified in order to prove that a state is legitimate. Yet the conception cannot point to any instance of this unification because the populace changes constantly. Every time you try to frame an actual populace according to the traditional conception of a unified people, the populace has already changed. Ochoa Espejo suggests that:

> When you consider time and change, you realize that a people do not originate when individuals merge into a bigger thing. Instead, a people arise when many

actions and movements combine into novel patterns of change. For a people is always in the making or unmaking. (2011: 2)

Ochoa Espejo's emphasis on sovereignty as something in the making and unmaking is further echoed by a recent reworking of the idea of sovereignty within social anthropology. Whilst anthropology appears to be passing through parallel and sometimes overlapping theoretical discussions or 'turns' (ontological, political ontological, geontological, etc.), an important one of these has been a new consideration of the idea and sociocultural manifestations of sovereignty. This is to a large degree influenced by earlier developments in both the anthropology of the state and of globalization, in which institutions, law and bureaucracy are recognized not as neutral, but as deeply cultured constructs (e.g. Corrigan and Sayer 1985; Blom Hansen and Stepputat 2001; Kapferer 2004). Here ideas of political philosophy become merged with ethnographic observation of ideas and transformations in a series of postcolonial contexts. As part of this process, traditional categories and divisions between nature and society, humans, animals and inanimate objects are also questioned. As revealed by two special editions of the journal *Current Anthropology* (Kauanui 2017), sovereignty has been considered in new ways in social anthropology since the rise of a focus on globalization (see e.g. Humphrey 2004; Wachspress 2009).

The rise of globalization studies, whatever its limits, demonstrated that political borders were porous and fickle, and that the persistent and long-standing flows of peoples, goods, and ideas across national boundaries made nation-states unsuitable units for many forms of analysis (Bonilla 2017: 331). The anthropological turn to sovereignty emerged out of that intellectual conversation, but was also rooted in a particular geopolitical context in which, despite blurred borders and brokered interactions, states themselves remain powerful entities in both the political system and the political imagination. Works on the 'anthropology of the state' emerged in the 1990s and quickly became central to the discipline, unseating more conventional studies of 'political anthropology' that had focused mainly on putatively traditional modes of power, kingship and authority (Bonilla 2017: 331). More recent political anthropology has focused on the historical formation of modern forms of governance, state authority, and the modern management of bodies, populations and peoples through discourses of science, health and security. Even as they broker duties among nongovernmental institutions and entities, states continue to wield power – fiscal, military, economic, discursive and imaginative. They continue to act as agents: they legislate, they deport, they invade, they build and they borrow. Even as governments are toppled, states themselves persist. However, this does not mean that they hold sovereign power (Bonilla 2017: 331).

New anthropological interest in sovereignty draws significantly on Agamben's (1998) reworking of the historicity of Foucault's (Burchell, Gordon and Miller 1991; Foucault 1995) earlier work on power and governmentality. Foucault's interventions in the interdisciplinary social sciences enabled new understandings of political authority, sovereignty, the state and power (Clarke 2017: 362). Foucault (Clarke 2017: 363) expanded and decentralized a view of sovereignty and legitimate power that had led to many decades of writing about how power is produced and how it produces certain effects. In Agamben's work, sovereignty is understood as an externality, an outside constitutive force that is independent of orders and of moralities. It is a wild power that defines itself in its unconstrained capacity to act independently of the rules it institutes. This sovereign power is also conventionally exercised against persons defined outside the sovereign order. This externality, like the sovereign, is defined as an asocial, amoral being – or as 'bare life' – and therefore beyond the protection of the sovereign order, open to being killed with legal and moral impunity. Arguing that this form of power is most apparent in its contestation or dispute, or in moments of the transformation or transmutations in the order of power, Agamben argues that there has been a resurgence of wild sovereignty in the context of the recent 'war on terror' and that it is visible in contexts of legal and political contestation, such as Iraq and Afghanistan. Drawing on Agamben, Kapferer argues that wild sovereignties are also evident in the operation of corporate capitalism when corporations subvert state orders and institute their own regimes of war and violence.

Expanding further on Foucault and Agamben's characterization of sovereignty as an expression of violence and struggle, Blom Hansen and Stepputat (2001, 2006) demonstrate how the ambiguity and contested nature of sovereignty is particularly marked in postcolonial contexts. Blom Hansen and Stepputat highlight how classical works on kingship failed to provide an adequate framework for understanding the political imaginations of a world after colonialism. Moving away from the conceptual straitjacket of state control, they emphasize sovereignty as an uncertain form of authority, grounded primarily in violence that needs to be repeatedly performed and redesigned to generate loyalty, fear and legitimacy that operates at different levels from the neighbourhood to the summit of the state and beyond. Blom Hansen and Stepputat (2006) argue that the sovereignty of the state is always idealized and that it is particularly tenuous in postcolonial societies in which sovereign power has been historically distributed among many forms of local authority. They also emphasize studies of informal sovereignties such as vigilante groups, insurgents and illegal networks – while tracing the relationship between market forces that also serve to reconfigure sovereign power. They thus chart and advocate an ethnographic approach to sovereignty 'in practice' (Blom Hansen and Stepputat 2006: 297).

Recent writing in the 'anthropology of sovereignty' focuses on how states vying for a monopoly on violence contend with social forces challenging that authority – and especially in urban areas across the Global South. In a recent opus revisiting the anthropology of 'Kings', Sahlins and Graeber (2017:2) write that one 'unanticipated side-effect of the collapse of European colonial empires has been that this notion of sovereignty has become the basis of constitutional orders everywhere – the only partial exceptions being a few places, like Nepal or Saudi Arabia, which had monarchies of their own already'. It follows from this that 'any theory of political life that does not take account of this, or that treats kingship as some sort of marginal, exceptional, or secondary phenomenon, is not a very good theory' (Sahlins and Graeber 2017: 2). Anthropologists pay particular attention to how colonial forms of government leave enduring marks on the performance and legitimation of political power beyond Europe and the United States. Whilst recognizing that the modern nation-state remains a central form of political authority and imagination in the contemporary period, recent studies acknowledge that it has taken new forms throughout the world, without completely removing or superseding older languages of power and public authority (see Jennings 2011). Anthropological studies on such topics as the operation of bureaucrats, the dynamics of political factions, actors, movements and stateless subjects draw attention to practices of power and provide crucial insights into how power and social life manifest, intersect and become mobile (Kauanui 2017: 325). Reinforcing this, Gupta (2012: 42) argues that states are not just functional bureaucratic apparatuses, but powerful sites of symbolic and cultural production. These analyses have grown into a corpus of research focused on a broad range of questions, including ones about citizenship, crime and policing, contemporary legal systems, governance, language and the law, ritual violence and state organization, sovereignty, state formation, socialism and post-socialism (Kauanui 2017: 326).

Returning to think critically on the topic of indigenous sovereignty a number of anthropologists have placed colonial theory in productive conversation with Agamben's ideas of 'states of exception'. Agamben argues that modern state societies enact a particularly insidious form of sovereign violence by creating a state of exception, one that gives them the power to kill and to strip certain human beings of their political significance, reducing them to bare life and making them subject to state-sanctioned biological death. Sturm (2017) and Morgensen (2011) suggest that the idea of violent exceptionalism dovetails productively with the logic of elimination in settler society theory.

Ziarek (2008: 89–90) notes that Agamben's concept of bare life – at least as described in its original formulation – remains insufficient as a complete expression of sovereign violence. She suggests that the concept takes us only so far, because it reduces the social and political distinctions that once characterized human subjects (race, gender, class and sexuality), even though these differences are often the very grounds by which modern populations are targeted for bare life in the modern exercise of biopower (Kauanui 2017: 343). It is proposed that indigeneity should be added to this list, which is understood here not merely as a distinct racial, social or cultural identity, but rather as an explicitly political subjectivity tied to the experience of living in the shadow of settler colonialism and with an everyday sense of ongoing territorial invasion and dispossession (Rifkin 2009). With indigeneity and settler colonialism as added lenses, we see that policies intent on social and political death, such as assimilation, missionization, relocation, allotment, termination and even political incorporation via citizenship, were all designed to eliminate indigenous assertions of sovereignty over the land.

Postero's (2017) recent work on the 'indigenous state' in Bolivia further highlights the way in which state formation and indigeneity interact as cultural expressions that control. However, it also reveals in great detail that the states' efforts to eliminate counter-assertions of sovereignty might not only take the form of interethnic struggle, but also of 'decolonizing' intra-ethnic struggles between competing indigenous interests. Describing the recent formation of the Bolivian plurinational state under the 'indigenous' leadership of Morales, Postero writes that the 'Bolivian state is not coherent by any means, but its actors engage in a wide range of decolonizing activities, ranging from legislation and policy to public speeches and spectacular performances'. These dynamics are described as constituting a cultural revolution in the context of the Morales government that seeks to form certain acceptable subjects of the pluri-national state. As such, some cultural practices are used to silence others. Postero draws heavily in her recent book on Ranciere (1999), who defines politics as a process of emancipation brought about by disagreement. Drawing on Ranciere's (1999) idea of *policing*, Postero suggests that a social partitioning has taken place in which some people have a recognizable 'part' of society, whilst others are silenced as 'the part with no part'.

Drawing on the background of these writings on the ethnography of state formation, it is suggested that the study of colonialism in the Americas provides further correctives to standard understandings of sovereignty. In the context of this book's focus on Latin America, I suggest that there is something important to be learned in this regard. Settler colonialism insists on the need to acknowledge different forms of colonialism (Kauanui 2017: 343). Moreover, it reveals that different colonialisms have led to multiple and competing forms of sovereignty that are messy and incomplete (Bruyneel 2007; Moreton-Robinson 2007; Rosen 2007). This fact becomes obvious in the context of US federalism, where the federal government, states and tribes all assert different forms of sovereignty and vie for political authority over the same land base. Cattelino (2008) in the empirical context of Seminole Gaming in Florida moves us beyond classical debates about sovereignty that view it as either *autonomous* and *inherent* (a by-product of peoplehood or kingly authority, for instance) or *derivative* and *dependent* (as something that stems from external political recognition by other sovereigns). Instead, she explores *interdependent* forms of sovereignty that are negotiated, partial, insecure and demand diplomacy on all sides. She explores how the circulation of capital is a sovereign force in and of itself, one that provides a key to how sovereignty functions in these more interdependent forms. The upshot of this body of work in Native North America is that the state power generated by colonialism, in any of its forms, remains highly insecure and is not a privileged site of sovereign authority.

In fact, state sovereignty as a repressive force generates various forms of resistance to that sovereignty, including a whole slew of counter-sovereignties that exceed its more legal, formal, authorized, recognized and official versions (see Povinelli 2002; Miller 2003; Cramer 2005; Klopotek 2011). Simpson (2014) in the context of the anthropological exploration of Mohawk sovereignty takes on the concept of *resistance* and offers instead the idea of *refusal*. Theories of resistance tend to focus attention on how aspects of domination get reproduced by those doing the resisting, meaning that in countering oppression, the terms of debate and terrain of conflict are already predetermined, and thus the idea that counterhegemony retains a kernel of hegemony, heterodoxy that of orthodoxy, violence begets more violence and so on. Simpson's theory of refusal offers something else entirely: refusal is neither derivative nor reproductive, but rather is an outright rejection of the externally imposed logics of settler-state sovereignty (Sturm 2017: 344–45).

Territory, Land, Food and Energy

Further important academic contributions to the rethinking of the meaning and significance of sovereignty focus on the connections between the social and material. By now, it should be evident that any discussion of sovereignty requires reflection on a history of land use and territorial claims. Indeed, Elden (2009) reminds us that political elites and popular movements exercise sovereign claims in relation to concrete territories. By making this deceptively simple point, Elden seeks to demonstrate that power aims to exercise itself over something that is tangible, not an abstraction of itself (McNeish and Logan 2012: 26). In writing about the connections between the war on terror and its links to ideas and claims to territory, Elden (2009) emphasizes the importance of social geography and that space is the ultimate locus and medium of struggle. Drawing on the work and thought of Lefebvre (1992) and paralleling earlier works on territory and territoriality (e.g. Delaney 2005; Storey 2012), he reminds us that 'there is a politics of space, because space is political' (Elden 2009: 16). Sovereign claims to space were made possible because of the coincident developments in the age of exploration of technologies that made them possible. Advances in geometry, such as coordinate or analytic geometry by Descartes, which uses algebra and equations, were partnered with development in cartography and land surveying as well as the accurate measure of time, enabling longitude to be determined more accurately (Elden 2009: 16).

Elden recognizes that as a result of technologically driven market globalization and the changed context of international security generated by 9/11, international and national understandings of sovereignty have been disturbed. In much contemporary literature, initially inspired by Deleuze and Guattari (1972), the term 'deterritorialization' is used. Some have seen this as demonstrating the lack of weight that territory has in a globalized world. Elden emphasizes that deterritorialization is significant, but 'this does not mean that there is no territorial aspect to state practice, or that territory does not continue to be an object of non-state actors (2009: 11). Today's territorial logic is not the same as earlier imperial practices, but war (even in its unending form) has thus far been 'fought with a very conventional sense of territoriality in mind – territory has been targeted, bombed, invaded'. Yet deterritorialization, in spite of its name, should not be interpreted as an argument for the end of the importance of territory. Indeed, the reverse is true, because territory is both its condition of possibility and, in some newly configured form, its necessary outcome (Elden 2009: 17).

The persistence of the territorial logics of sovereignty and the formation of political claims are evident not only in current geopolitics but also at the national and subnational levels. As indicated in the Introduction to this volume, the operation of subnational claims have been under-emphasized in earlier research on resource and energy politics (McNeish and Logan 2012; McNeish 2017). Following Mitchell (2011), there has been a growing acceptance that 'forms of political, economic, and social relations are in fact engineered out of the flows of energy, that energy helps organize politics and that the oil and gas world manufactures a vast archive of knowledge produced and fought over by multiple and complex actors and agents' (Appel, Mason and Watts 2015). As a result, the academic conversation regarding resource and energy politics has shifted beyond earlier concerns with developmental pathologies (Ross 2012), corporate oil and geopolitics (Klare 2011) to a wider exploration of the manner in which oil and other energy resource extraction impact on consumption and ways of life (Strauss, Rupp and Loue

2013) and the social imagination (Apter 1993; Coronil 1997). Together with my colleagues (Strønen 2017; McNeish, Borchgrevink and Logan 2016), I recognize the importance of this broadening field of study, but also recognize that the subnational dynamics of resource and energy politics is still little explored. Moreover, we have suggested that the histories of subnational sovereign claims for territory and resources within the context of resource and energy politics have not been given sufficient attention as a means to understand the frequent appearance of conflict and contestation. Put simply, the relationship between sovereignty and resources helps in simple terms to explain why subnational claims such as 'this land is ours; these resources are ours' frequently elicit competition and violence (McNeish 2017: 1136).

An emphasis on the territorial orientations of sovereign claims at the subnational level requires acknowledgement of the complexity of territoriality. As earlier anthropologists and social geographers have realized, claims to territory or claims to sovereignty in which they are included involve particular ways of thinking about geographical space, about land and about human interactions with the environment. Indeed, territories are not only a matter of thought, but also a matter of contrasting territorial and community practices (Escobar 2008; Storey 2012). There has been considerable discussion of the extent to which territorialization and territorial behaviour should be seen as 'natural' or 'social' phenomena. These debates echo wider longstanding arguments over the relative influence of nature and nurture, a division that many see as somewhat artificial and itself a discursive construction. This is a debate that will be revisited in Chapter 4. For now, it is important to signal that territorial thinking, the production of territories and the employment of territorial strategies are bound up with constituting sovereignty. Indeed, they are both ways of maintaining power or with resisting the imposition of power by a dominant group. Moreover, forms of exclusion can be consolidated and reinforced through territorial practices, yet they can also be resisted through similar means.

Evidence of the relationship between different understandings of territory and resources, and competing expressions of state, corporate and popular sovereignty is visible not only in recent academic research, but also in the slogans, statements and actions of social movements. These movements represent not only indigenous communities, but also a coalition of marginalized interests (caused by different settler histories) in which alliances have been formed between indigenous, smallholder, landless and peasant communities. It is perhaps important to stress here that as a result of political histories in which indigenous peoples were rebranded with the class identity of peasant communities, it is often not possible or even correct to distinguish clearly between these social sectors. Class and ethnicity have become bound together throughout Latin America. This is particularly the case in Bolivia, as a result of its conjoined histories of resource extraction and revolution.[6]

The international food sovereignty project emerged in the 1990s in response to the rapid expansion at the time of the corporate food regime and related moves by wealthy countries to acquire great tracts in the Global South to feed their current and prospective growth. It emerged as the antithesis of the calls from the World Trade Organization (WTO) and other international institutions for 'food security', which had been based on the assumption that people were dispossessed because they did not have formal property rights over their land (McMichael 2014). Peasant organizations – La Via Campesina being key amongst them in Latin America and beyond – and agrarian analysts recognized that instead of promoting or protecting the exclusive property rights of owners and users, efforts to create 'security' were more often than not used by states and corporate actors to alienate and separate people from their land. Use of the term 'sovereignty' is made here as a form of strategic essentialism' that overrides international WTO trade rules and forms the basis of a substantive alternative claim on states to guarantee domestic food provision and protect those who work, care and live on the land (McMichael 2014). It also foreshadowed application of a more complex notion of 'territory of self-determination' according to which societies are seen as self-governing via their rural producers, agricultural capacities and domestic food needs

In the 2000s, further dramatic changes in relation to food, climate, energy and finance pushed common questions of land use and land control back to the centre stage of development debate. Inspired by food sovereignty debates, proposals are made to extend mobilization to 'land sovereignty' (Borras and Franco 2012). The notion of land sovereignty repoliticizes and historically grounds the popular mainstream conception of land governance by bringing in social relations as the key unit of analysis, and the object of policy and political advocacy, rather than 'things' like papers and titles (Borras et al. 2014). States have historically demonstrated a compulsion to always simplify – 'make legible' – complex and dynamic land-based social relations as part of the logic of modern state-building. Land and food sovereignty are explained by major social movements that support them (such as La Vía Campesina) as the right of working peoples to have access to, use of and control over land and the benefits of its use and occupation, where land is understood as resource, territory and landscape. Land and food sovereignty connote a sense of 'belonging': the land belongs to the people who work it, care for it and live on it, and the people belong to a particular land as a people.

Land and food are therefore an active focus of sovereign claims in agrarian movements such as la Via Campesina. In its preparatory statements made in the build-up to the United Nations Climate Change Conference (COP23) in Bonn (2017), la Via Campesina issued a statement in which land and food sovereignty were also connected to energy sovereignty. Recognizing the links between the burning of fossil fuels and climate change, and between extractive practices and the environmental degradation of their own lands, the peoples supporting la Via Campesina 'reaffirm the importance of struggling for public policies that promote and support agro-ecology, local community-controlled energy systems and collective action for a just energy transition' ('Food Sovereignty to Answer World Food and Energy Crisis' 2008). Furthermore, they bolster the claim in the climate talks that food sovereignty is an important route to a solution to the global food and energy crisis.

Conclusions: Contested Sovereignty in Bolivia and Beyond

The history of ideas summarized above demonstrates the central role played by the concept of sovereignty in global political shifts. With its common history of liberal revolution and legalism, Latin America has not been immune to these dynamics. Indeed, the outcome of regional history has been a significant contributor to the shifting understanding of sovereignty. It should also be evident on the basis of this discussion that the centrality of sovereignty in political dynamics is not dependent on a fixed and universal understanding, but rather on its role as a malleable and changing concept. Sovereignty is a conceptual vehicle by which states, peoples and corporations differently construct their claims for and understandings of territory and resources. These claims and understandings sometimes coincide and sometimes clash completely – and often violently.

Returning to the context of Bolivia with which the discussion in the chapter started, there should now be some sense of the clashes and controversies described as not only being momentary disagreements over economic policy or national development, but the reflections of a much longer and complex history of contested sovereignty. The *gasolinazo* and TIPNIS controversies were not only disagreements over fuel prices and the effects of road-building, but the constitution of national territory and sovereignty vis-à-vis popular and cultural understandings of territory and sovereignty. Indeed, these events in Bolivia parallel the multi-scalar, overlapping temporality and plurality of sovereign claims expressed throughout the region and even worldwide.

Aside from its indications of the problems of balancing the books of state-sponsored fuel subsidies (ref), the *gasolinazo* highlights the incomplete and contested physical and economic frontiers of Bolivia. Bolivia is a postcolonial state that has had difficulty in consolidating its national sovereignty. This is in part due to its complex geography, history of armed conflict with neighbouring countries (e.g. the War of the Pacific and the Chaco War) and territorial size. However, as earlier authors have recognized, Bolivia's incomplete territorial sovereignty is also explained by significant political and social factors. As in other settler societies, the hunger for land and resource wealth of political and economic elites resulted in a series of significant but complex social (ethnic assignations of identity, i.e. indigenous, *chola, mestizo, criollo, colla/ camba* overlap with class divisions) and spatial divisions (*occidente/ oriente*, highlands/lowlands).

Whilst significant legal and political developments have recently been made to address the racial divides and historical legacy of external and internal colonialism, no singular understanding of sovereignty exists (other than perhaps support for the national football team). Indeed, for many communities, the state only made its permanent presence known to them in the 1990s as a result of moves to re-establish the map of municipal boundaries and the introduction of policies for decentralization. Until the 1990s, the state had operated according to a racial and urban bias that had left many indigenous and rural communities outside of steady contact with the system of state political and economic governance (McNeish 2001). State forces would periodically arrive before the 1990s, but only to exploit available people and resources, not to directly foment economic development or a stable system based on the rule of law. Because these efforts remain incomplete, even insincere, state efforts to control and patrol its borders and markets are constantly challenged by populations that have learned to bend the rules and profit from engagement in a large-scale industry of illegal exports. The price shifts of the *gasolinazo* not only threatened potential profits from contraband, but also highlighted anew that local communities do not share the state's view of territorial borders or the state's legitimacy to monopolize the governance in these zones (see Chapter 2 for more on this).

The TIPNIS further mirrors the developments in the legal, theoretical and popular political understanding of sovereignty. Sovereignty, and with it claims to land and territory and to a particular extractivist development trajectory, is visibly in dispute. Indeed, given the fragmentation that occurred both within the indigenous movements and within national politics, it is clear that multiple notions of sovereignty were being expressed at the same time. These expressions picked up on contrasting interpretations of the value of the state as well as differing interpretations of much longer histories of social and cultural relations, settlement and colonization, and of territory, resources and territorialization.

Whilst many of the communities in the TIPNIS did not disagree with the idea of the road (McNeish and Arteaga Böhrt 2012), they vehemently disagreed with the presumption of the Bolivian state to decide without consultation the placement and conditions under which the road was to be built. The TIPNIS was declared a national park in 1965, and in 2009 the Mojeño-Ignaciano, Yuracaré and Chimán indigenous groups living in the area received legal title to territory (i.e. *territorio indígena originario campesino*

(TIOC)), amounting to over a million hectares, by the Morales government. The Morales government had proclaimed itself to be in support of the country's indigenous majority population and to have set in motion under the leadership of President Morales, whose Aymara background was widely publicized, a process to reform the state and the Constitution in order to establish a new postcolonial order. For many of the communities of the TIPNIS, this meant that they would at the very least be given the right to 'free, prior and informed consent' regarding the future of their land and territory, in line with the Bolivian state's earlier ratification of ILO 169 and the UNDRIP.

That the government had granted a contract for the road to the Brazilian corporation Odebrecht and had failed to carry out any prior consultation was considered intolerable by the local community and regional indigenous leadership. Indeed, despite the government's claims that respected local indigenous territorial claims, it was seen not only to be favouring national economic interests in opening up the road (opening improved communication access to the eastern Beni and giving access to oil and gas blocks within the territory), but also to be siding with peasant coca farmers (*cocaleros*) hungry for access to occupy more land (see McNeish 2013). In this way, the state was, despite its claims employing an enlightened postcolonial economic strategy supporting communitarian forms of production (Garcia-Linera 2011), replicating the attitude and actions of earlier governments. Events would show that it was also willing to do this with the same direct repression (the Chaparina) and political manipulation (the staging of consultation, the buying-off of local leaders and the splitting of local political organizations) as earlier governments had done.

The TIPNIS protesters rejection of the government's – now clearly temporary – decision on the 'intangibility' of the TIPNIS territory is also indicative of significantly different notions of sovereignty from that of the state. Indeed, this made it clear that protesters were not necessarily against the identification of new economic opportunities or development interventions in their communities (McNeish 2013). A deep respect for nature and its sustainable use was shared and commonly expressed by the protesters, but this was also more pragmatic than environmentalists' posters portrayed at the time – which depicted the inhabitants of the TIPNIS as singularly interested in the protection of the forest. New projects for sustainably hunting caiman for their skins and for the production of cacao had recently started in the region, and local communities hoped to continue with these trading activities. They were instead mostly opposed to the idea that the Bolivian state had the right to act as the gatekeeper in this respect. As my own research in the territory would reveal, the isolated communities of the TIPNIS had governed and policed themselves successfully for generations (McNeish and Arteaga Böhrt

2012) and had been formally recognized for this. It did not make sense to cede this again to the state. The arrival of the military to enforce the rulings of the Bolivian state on the fate of the territory and to control access has also sown further confusion regarding the identity and claims of the Bolivian 'indigenous state' (Postero 2017).

As I have also indicated above, the TIPNIS protest also sowed confusion regarding the identity of the state at other levels of national politics. Government officials left their posts and politicians, and civil society leaders and academics shifted their political allegiances because of the contradictions and abuse of power and identity it revealed. Following on from the *gasolinazo*, it became increasingly evident that whilst Morales retained popularity in many rural and urban areas, the government's ambitions were also persistently at odds with the flexible requirements of sovereignty required at the country's borders or in remote areas where the presence of state institutions was still ill-defined (see also Chapter 4 for further features of this in relation to the politics of lithium). Despite Morales' claim that he respected the Andean ethical goal of 'governing whilst listening to the people' (*mandar mientras obedeciendo*), the great game of the Bolivian state was clearly still at odds with the sovereign claims and practice of many of its people. It is this context of contested sovereignty that forms the background to the increasing fragmentation of support for Morales and his rapid fall in the context of electoral failures.

Notes

1. In the case of LPG, the increase was 1,000%, going from US$22 million in 2007 to US$250 million in 2008. In the case of diesel, this rose from US$123 million to US$180 million in the same years (Wanderley 2015).
2. Morales' public support was registered as dropping to 37% (down 7%) in the month following the police raid (Young 2011).
3. Costas had led the 'Media Luna' autonomist white nativist movement against Morales and orchestrated attacks against the CIDOB offices in 2008.
4. UN Doc. E/CN.4/Sub.2/1986/7 and Add. 1-4. The conclusions and recommendations of the study, in Addendum 4, are also available as a UN sales publication (UN Sales No. E.86.XIV.3). The study was launched in 1972 and was completed in 1986, thus making it the most voluminous study of its kind, based on thirty-seven monographs.
5. The countries that ratified ILO 169 were: Argentina, Bolivia, Brazil, the Central African Republic, Chile, Colombia, Costa Rica, Denmark, Dominica, Ecuador, Fiji, Guatemala, Honduras, Mexico, Nepal, the Netherlands, Nicaragua, Norway, Paraguay, Peru, Spain and Venezuela
6. In the case of Bolivia, the 1952 Nationalist Revolution was and remains a key factor in determining this.

References

Achtenberg, Emily. 2011. 'Gasolinazo Challenges Bolivia's "Process of Change"'. North American Congress on Latin America. *NACLA Report on the Americas*, 28 February. Retrieved 5 November 2020 from https://nacla.org/news/gasolinazo-challenges-bolivia's-process-change.

Agamben, Giorgio. 1998. *Homo Sacer: Sovereign Power and Bare Life*. Translated by Daniel Heller-Roazen. Redwood City: Stanford University Press.

Agudelo, Carlos. 2005. *Retos del multiculturalismo en Colombia: política y poblaciones negras*. Medellín: La Carreta Editores, Institut de recherche pour le développment, Universidad Nacional de Colombia, Instituto Colombiano de Antropología e Historia.

Anghie, Antony. 2012. 'Western Discourses of Sovereignty', in Julie Evans, Ann Genovese, Alexander Reilly and Patrick Wolfe (eds), *Sovereignty: Frontiers of Possibility*. Honolulu: University of Hawaii Press.

Appel, Hannah, Andrew Mason and Michael Watts. 2015. *Subterranean Estates: Life Worlds of Oil and Gas*. Ithaca: Cornell University Press.

Apter, Andrew. 1993. *The Pan-African Nation: Oil and the Spectacle of Culture in Nigeria*. Chicago: University of Chicago Press.

Armitage, David. 2005. 'The Contagion of Sovereignty: Declarations of Independence since 1776'. *South African Historical Journal* 52: 1–18.

Barker, Joanne. 2007. *Sovereignty Matters: Locations of Contestation and Possibility in Indigenous Struggles for Self-Determination*. Lincoln: University of Nebraska Press.

Bertelsen, Jens. 2006. 'The Concept of Sovereignty Revisited'. *European Journal of International Law* 17(2): 463–74.

Bonilla, Yarimar. 2013. 'Ordinary Sovereignty'. *Small Axe* 17(3): 152–65.

———. 2015. *Non-sovereign Futures: French Caribbean Politics in the Wake of Disenchantment*. Chicago: University of Chicago Press.

———. 2017. 'Unsettling Sovereignty'. *Cultural Anthropology* 32(3): 330–39.

Borras, Saturnino, and Jennifer Franco. 2012. *A Land Sovereignty Alternative? Towards a Peoples' Counter-enclosure*. TNI Agrarian Justice Programme Discussion Paper. Amsterdam: Transnational Institute.

Borras, Saturnino, Jennifer Franco and Wang Chunyu. 2014. 'The Challenge of Global Governance of Land Grabbing: Changing International Agricultural Context and Competing Political Views and Strategies'. *Globalizations*. Retrieved 5 November 2020 from https://www.researchgate.net/publication/263569276_The_Challenge_of_Global_Governance_of_Land_Grabbing_Changing_International_Agricultural_Context_and_Competing_Political_Views_and_Strategies.

Bourke, Richard. 2016. *Popular Sovereignty in Historical Perspective*. Cambridge: Cambridge University Press.

Blom Hansen, Thomas, and Finn Stepputat. 2001. *States of Imagination: Ethnographic Explorations of the Postcolonial State*. Durham, NC: Duke University Press.

———. 2006. 'Sovereignty Revisited'. *Annual Review of Anthropology* 35: 295–315.

Bruyneel, Kevin. 2007. *The Third Space of Sovereignty: The Postcolonial Politics of U.S.–Indigenous Relations*. Minneapolis: University of Minnesota Press.

Burchell, Graham, Colin Gordon and Peter Miller. 1991. *The Foucault Effect: Studies in Governmentality*. Chicago: University of Chicago Press.

Castellanos, Bianet. 2017. 'Introduction: Settler Colonialism in Latin America'. *American Quarterly* 69(4): 777–81.

Catellino, Jessica. 2008. *High Stakes: Florida Seminole Gaming and Sovereignty*. Durham, NC: Duke University Press.

'CIDOB dividida por el Gobierno de Morales'. 2013. *Página Siete*, 25 September. Retrieved 5 November 2020 from https://www.paginasiete.bo/nacional/2013/9/25/cidob-dividida-gobierno-morales-1311.html.

Clarke, Kamari. 2017. 'Rethinking Sovereignty through Hashtag Publics: The New Body Politics'. *Cultural Anthropology* 32(3): 359–66.

Cooper, Frederick. 2014. *Citizenship between Empire and Nation: Remaking France and French Africa, 1945–1960*. Princeton: Princeton University Press.

Coronil, Fernando. 1997. *The Magical State: Nature, Money, and Modernity in Venezuela*. Chicago: University of Chicago Press.

Corrigan, Philip, and Derek Sayer. 1985. *The Great Arch: English State Formation as Cultural Revolution*. Oxford: Blackwell Publishing.

Cramer, Renée. 2005. *Cash, Colour, and Colonialism: The Politics of Tribal Acknowledgment*. Norman: University of Oklahoma Press.

Curiel, John, and Jack Williams. 2020. 'Bolivia Dismissed Its October Elections as Fraudulent. Our Research Found No Reason to Suspect Fraud'. *Washington Post*, 27 February. Retrieved 5 November 2020 from https://www.washingtonpost.com/politics/2020/02/26/bolivia-dismissed-its-october-elections-fraudulent-our-research-found-no-reason-suspect-fraud.

Delaney, David. 2005. *Territory: A Short Introduction*. Oxford: Blackwell.

Deleuze, Gilles, and Felix Guattari. 1972. *Anti-Oedipus: Capitalism and Schizophrenia*. London: Penguin Classics.

'Draft Declaration on the Rights of Indigenous Peoples'. UN Doc. E/CN.4/Sub.2/1994/2/Add.1. 1994. Retrieved 5 November 2020 from http://hrlibrary.umn.edu/instree/declra.htm.

Elden, Stuart. 2009. *Terror and Territory: The Spatial Extent of Sovereignty*. University of Minneapolis: Minnesota Press.

———. 2010. 'Land, Terrain, Territory'. *Progress in Human Geography* 34(6): 799–817.

'Ending Fuel Subsidies Cuts Bolivia's Losses, President Says'. 2010. *CNN*, 31 December. Retrieved 5 November 2020 from http://edition.cnn.com/2010/WORLD/americas/12/30/bolivia.morales.gas/index.html.

Engerman, Stanely, and Kenneth Sokoloff. 2005. 'The Evolution of Suffrage Institutions in the New World'. *Journal of Economic History* 65(4): 891–921.

Engle, Karen. 2011. *The Elusive Promise of Indigenous Development: Rights, Culture and Strategy*. Durham, NC: Duke University Press.

Escobar, Arturo. 2008. *Territories of Difference: Place, Movements, Life, Redes (New Ecologies for the Twenty-First Century)*. Durham, NC: Duke University Press.

Espejo, Paulina. 2011. *The Time of Popular Sovereignty: Process and the Democratic State*. University Park: Pennsylvania State University Press.

'Evo Morales' Popularity Declines'. 2016. *Economist Intelligence Unit*, 24 October. Retrieved 5 November 2020 from http://country.eiu.com/article.aspx?articleid=1004738884&Country=Bolivia&topic=Politics&subtopic=Forecast&subsubtopic=Political+stability&u=1&pid=365857020&oid=365857020&uid=1.

'Food Sovereignty to Answer World Food and Energy Crisis'. 2008. *Via Campesina*. Retrieved 5 November 2020 from https://viacampesina.org/en/food-sovereignty-to-answer-world-food-and-energy-crisis.

Foucault, Michel. 1995. *Discipline and Punish: The Birth of the Prison*. New York: Vintage Books.

Garcia-Linera, Alvaro. 2012. *Las Tensiones Creativos de la Revolución. La quinta fase del proceso de cambio*. La Paz: Vicepresidencia del Estado. Estado Plurinacional de Bolivia.

'General Assembly Adopts Declaration on Rights of Indigenous Peoples: Major Step Forward Towards Human Rights for All, Says President'. 2007. United Nations, 13 September. Retrieved 5 November 2020 from https://www.un.org/press/en/2007/ga10612.doc.htm.

Gott, Richard. 2007. 'Latin America as White Settler Society'. *Bulletin on Latin American Research* 26(2): 269–89.

Graham-Harrison, Emma. 2019. 'Is It as Coup or a Return to Democracy? Battle for Bolivia's Soul Rages'. *The Guardian*, 17 November. Retrieved 5 November 2020 from https://www.theguardian.com/world/2019/nov/17/bolivia-more-volatile-than-ever-as-president-flees-and-leaders-denounce-a-coup.

Gupta, Aradhana, and Akhil Sharma. 2012. 'Introduction: Rethinking Theories of the State in an Age of Globalization', in Aradhana Sharma and Akhil Gupta (eds), *The Anthropology of the State: A Reader*. Malden, MA: Blackwell.

Hancke, Lewis. 1994. *All Mankind Is One: A Study of the Disputation between Bartolome De Las Casas and Juan Gines De Sepulveda in 1550 on the Religious and Intellectual Capacity of the American Indians*. DeKalb: Northern Illinois Press.

Hetland, Gabriel. 2019. 'Many Wanted Morales out. But What Happened in Bolivia Was a Military Coup'. *The Guardian*, 13 November. Retrieved 5 November 2020 from https://www.theguardian.com/commentisfree/2019/nov/13/morales-bolivia-military-coup.

Houland, Camilla. 2018. 'Between the Street and Aso Rock: The Role of Nigerian Trade Unions in Popular Protests'. *Journal of Contemporary African Studies* 36(1): 103–20.

Humphrey, Caroline. 2004. 'Sovereignty', in David Nugent and Joan Vincent (eds), *A Companion to the Anthropology of Politics*. Oxford: Blackwell Publishing.

Ilgen, Thomas. 2003. *Reconfigured Sovereignty: Multi-layered Governance in the Global Age*. Farnham: Ashgate.

'Indígenas del TIPNIS y pobladores de Achacachi se unen contra el Gobierno'. 2017. *Página Siete*, 24 August. Retrieved 5 November 2020 from https://www.paginasiete.bo/nacional/2017/8/24/indigenas-tipnis-pobladores-achacachi-unen-contra-gobierno-149511.html.

Jackson, Robert. 2007. *Sovereignty: The Evolution of an Idea*. Cambridge: Polity Press.

Jennings, Robert. 2011. 'Sovereignty and Political Modernity: A Genealogy of Agamben's Critique of Sovereignty'. *Anthropological Theory* 11(1): 23–61.

Kapferer, Bruce. 2004. 'Democracy, Wild Sovereignties and the New Leviathan'. *Bulletin of the Royal Institute for Inter-Faith Studies* 6(2): 23–38.

Kauanui, Kêhaulari. 2017. 'Sovereignty: An Introduction'. *Cultural Anthropology* 32(3): 323–29.

Kelly, John, and Martha Kaplan. 2001. 'Nation and Decolonization: Toward a New Anthropology of Nationalism'. *Anthropological Theory* 1(4): 419–37.

———. 2009. 'Legal Fictions after Empire', in Douglas Howland and Louise White (eds), *The State of Sovereignty: Territories, Laws, Populations*. Bloomington: Indiana University Press.

Klare, Michael. 2011. 'The Changing Geo-politics of Oil', in Richard Looney (ed.), *Handbook of Oil Politics*. London: Routledge.

Klopotek, Brian. 2011. *Recognition Odysseys: Indigeneity, Race and Federal Tribal Recognition Policy in Three Louisiana Communities*. Durham, NC: Duke University Press.

Laing, Anna. 2015. 'Resource Sovereignties in Bolivia: Re-conceptualizing the Relationship between Indigenous Identities and the Environment during the TIPNIS Conflict'. *Bulletin of Latin American Research* 34(2): 149–66.

Landry, Alysa. 2016. 'Thomas Jefferson: Architect of Indian Removal Policy'. Retrieved 5 November 2020 from https://indiancountrytoday.com/archive/thomas-jefferson-architect-of-indian-removal-policy-kV7p2W8yLUeb47XLS5kJmg.

Larson, Brooke. 2004. *Trials of Nation Making: Liberalism, Race, and Ethnicity in the Andes, 1810–1910*. Cambridge: Cambridge University Press.

Lasso, Marixa. 2007. *Myths of Harmony: Race and Republicanism during the Age of Revolution, Colombia 1795–1831*. Pittsburgh: University of Pittsburgh Press.

Lenzerini, Federico. 2007. 'Sovereignty Revisited: International Law and Parallel Sovereignty of Indigenous Peoples'. *Texas International Law Journal* 42: 155–89.

Lefebvre, Henri. 1992. *The Production of Space*. Hoboken: Wiley-Blackwell.

McNeish, John-Andrew. 2001. 'Globalization and the Reinvention of Andean Tradition: The Politics of Community and Ethnicity in Highland Bolivia', in Tom Brass (ed.), *Latin American Peasants*. London: Routledge.

———. 2006. 'Stones on the Road: The Politics of Participation and the Generation of Crisis in Bolivia'. *Bulletin of Latin American Research* 25(2): 220–40.

———. 2013. 'The TIPNIS Effect: Extraction, Protest and Indigeneity in Bolivia'. *Latin American and Caribbean Ethnic Studies* 8: 221–42.

McNeish, John-Andrew and Anna Cecilie Arteaga Böhrt. 2012. 'An Accumulated Rage: Legal Pluralism and Gender Justice in Bolivia', in Rachel Sieder and John-Andrew McNeish (eds), *Gender Justice and Legal Pluralities: Latin American and African Perspectives*. London: Routledge.

McNeish, John-Andrew, Axel Borchgrevink and Owen Logan. 2016. *Contested Powers: The Politics of Energy and Development in Latin America*. London: Zed Books.

McNeish, John-Andrew and Owen Logan. 2012. *Flammable Societies: Studies on the Socioeconomics of Oil and Gas*. London: Pluto Press.

McMichael, Philip. 2014. 'Historicizing Food Sovereignty'. *Journal of Peasant Studies* 41: 933–57.

Miller, Bruce. 2003. *Invisible Indigenes: The Politics of Nonrecognition*. Lincoln: University of Nebraska Press.

Mitchell, Timothy. 2011. *Carbon Democracy: Political Power in an Age of Oil*. London: Verso.

Moreton-Robinson, Aileen. 2007. *Sovereign Subjects: Indigenous Sovereignty Matters*. Crow's Nest, Australia: Allen & Unwin.

Morgensen, Scott. 2011. 'The Biopolitics of Settler Colonialism: Right Here, Right Now'. *Settler Colonial Studies* 1(1): 52–76.

Postero, Nancy. 2017. *The Indigenous State: Race, Politics and Performance in Plurinational Bolivia*. Stanford: Stanford University Press.

Povinelli, Elizabeth. 2002. *The Cunning of Recognition: Indigenous Alterities and the Making of Australian Multiculturalism*. Durham, NC: Duke University Press.

'¿Quién es Jeanine Áñez, la nueva presidenta interina de Bolivia?'. *El Tiempo*, 13 November. Retrieved 5 November 2020 from https://www.eltiempo.com/mundo/perfil-de-jeanine-anez-nueva-presidenta-interina-de-bolivia-432904.

Ranciere, Jaques. 1999. *Disagreement: Politics and Philosophy*. Minneapolis: University of Minneapolis Press.

Rifkin, Mark. 2009. 'Indigenizing Agamben: Rethinking Sovereignty in Light of the 'Peculiar' Status of Native Peoples'. *Cultural Critique* 73: 88–124.

Rosen, Deborah. 2007. *American Indians and State Law: Sovereignty, Race, and Citizenship, 1790–1880*. Lincoln: University of Nebraska Press.

Ross, Michael. 2012. *The Oil Curse: How Petroleum Wealth Shapes the Development of Nations*. Princeton: Princeton University Press.

Sanders, James. 2004. *Contentious Republicans: Popular Politics, Race, and Class in Nineteenth-Century Colombia*. Durham, NC: Duke University Press.

Sahlins, Marshall, and David Graeber. 2017. *On Kings*. Chicago: HAU Books.

Salman, Thomas. 2012. 'The MAS Six Years in Power in Bolivia: Review Essay'. *European Review of Latin American and Caribbean Studies* 92(April): 89–98.

Schilling-Vacaflor, Almut, and Jessika Eichler. 2017. 'The Shady Side of Consultation and Compensation: Divide and Rule Tactics in Bolivia's Extraction Sector'. *Development and Change* 48(6): 1439–63.

Schrijver, Nico. 2013. 'Fifty Years Permanent Sovereignty over Natural Resources: The 1962 Declaration as the Opinio Iuris Communis', in Marc Bungenberg and Stephan Hobe (eds), *Permanent Sovereignty over Natural Resources*. New York: Springer.

Silva, Denise. 2007. *Toward a Global Idea of Race*. Minneapolis: University of Minnesota Press.

Simpson, Audrey. 2014. *Mohawk Interruptus: Life across the Borders of Settler States*. Durham: Duke University Press.

Speed, Sharon. 2017. 'Structures of Settler Capitalism in Abya Yala'. *American Quarterly* 69(4): 783–90.

Storey, David. 2012. *Territories: The Claiming of Space*, 2nd edn. London: Routledge.

Strauss, Sarah, Stephaine Rupp and Thomas Love. 2013. *Cultures of Energy: Power, Practices, Technologies*. London: Routledge.

Strønen, Iselin. 2017. *Grassroots Politics and Oil Culture in Venezuela: The Revolutionary Petro-state*. Camden: Palgrave Macmillan.

Sturm, Circe. 2017. 'Reflections on the Anthropology of Sovereignty and Settler Colonialism: Lessons from Native North America'. *Cultural Anthropology* 32(3): 340–48.

Von Hirsch, Cecilie. 2019. 'Contentious Forests: From Global Climate Change Policies to Bolivian Forest Communities'. Unpublished Ph.D. thesis. Norway: NMBU.

Viotti da Costa, Emilia. 2000. *The Brazilian Empire: Myths and Histories*, 2nd edn. Chapel Hill: University of North Carolina Press.

Wanderley, Fernanda. 2015. 'The Continuous Negotiation of the Authority of Oil and Gas Dependent States: The Case of Bolivia', in John-Andrew McNeish, Axel Borchgrevink and Owen Logan (eds), *Contested Powers: The Politics of Energy and Development in Latin America*. London: Zed Books.

Wachspress, Megan. 2009. 'Rethinking Sovereignty with Reference to History and Anthropology'. *International Journal of Law in Context* 5(3): 315–30.

Wade, Peter. 2016. 'Mestizaje, Multiculturalism, Liberalism, and Violence'. *Latin American and Caribbean Ethnic Studies* 11(3): 323–43.

Watson, Irene. 2011. 'The 2007 Declaration on the Rights of Indigenous Peoples: Indigenous Survival – Where to From Here?'. *Griffith Law Review* 20(3): 507–14.

Wiessner, Siegfried. 2008. 'Indigenous Sovereignty: A Reassessment in Light of the UN Declaration on the Rights of Indigenous Peoples'. *Vanderbilt Journal of Transitional Law* 41(4): 1141–76.

Wolfe, Erik. 1999. *Settler Colonialism and the Transformation of Anthropology: The Politics and Poetics of an Ethnographic Event*. London: Cassell.

Wolfe, Patrick. 1999. *Settler Colonialism and the Transformation of Anthropology*. London: Cassell.

Yashar, Deborah. 2005. *Contesting Citizenship in Latin America: The Rise of Indigenous Movements and the Post-liberal Challenge*. Cambridge: Cambridge University Press.

Young, Kevin. 2011. Bolivia Dilemmas: Turmoil, Transformation and Solidarity. *Zblogs*, 1 October. Retrieved 5 November 2020 from https://zcomm.org/zblogs/bolivia-dilem mas-turmoil-transformation-and-solidarity-by-kevin-young.

Ziarek, Ewa. 2008. 'Bare Life on Strike: Notes on the Biopolitics of Race and Gender'. *South Atlantic Quarterly* 107(1): 89–105.

Zimring, Carl. 2015. *Clean and White: A History of Environmental Racism in the United States*. Washington and New York: New York University Press.

Figure 2.1 Contraband fuel being shipped across the Bolivian–Chilean border.
© Jorge Montesinos

Chapter 2

RESOURCE POLITICS AT THE MARGINS

At the start of this volume, I highlighted the role that natural and energy resources have played in the history of state-building and contemporary politics of Latin America. I suggested in the Introduction to this volume – on the basis of my own past research and a growing alternative academic consensus – that resources do not automatically play a role in constituting environmental conflicts or insecurity. Instead, they are an important catalyst for social, economic and political change. Historic and contemporary conflicts do not originate in resource discoveries themselves. The material constraints of resource discoveries play a role in helping to determine the way in which they can be exploited, but resource governance and resource conflicts are generated by political ambitions, divisions and the friction between the contrasting norms and values that are placed upon them in different times and contexts. As the previous chapter has explored in detail, these political ambitions, divisions and cultural values are commonly expressed through, or informed by, contrasting visions and political definitions of sovereignty.

In this chapter, I aim to further explore the links between resource governance and contrasting visions and political definitions of sovereignty introduced in the last chapter. I emphasize that resource politics and conflicts are a dynamic in which local actors effectively influence state and regional positions. The chapter aims to deepen an understanding of the multi-scalar and contested nature of sovereignty and of the actively contrasting perspectives of resources and territory. It does this through an empirical focus on local practices of smuggling (of fuel resources in particular) and an expanding panorama of militancy focused on the terms and impacts of environmental resource exploitation (also further explored in the following chapter). These practices persist despite the State's frequently violent efforts to stop and police them. They also have a significant influence on the conditions and character of states and markets that follow from a need to respond to their economic and security knock-on effects.

Repeated reference has been made in recent writing on resource and energy politics (e.g. Appel, Mason and Watts 2015; Szeman and Boyer 2017) of Mitchell's (2011) observation that energy extraction and the development of governance structures are mutually constitutive in the course of history. In *Carbon Democracy: Political Power in the Age of Oil*, Mitchell convincingly argues that energy helps to organize politics. He suggests that it does so in such a way that the political, economic and social relations needed to guarantee the flows of energy are engineered to make their use more palatable to Western consumers. The extraction of natural resources, and energy resources in particular, links together local social and political transformations with capitalism and the global economy – the setting of the interventionist interests of the great powers. Such insight is invaluable in terms of providing a comprehensive understanding of the political economy of energy extraction and the intertwined dynamics of resource-rich and resource-reliant economies. However, whereas these insights are important, they are not comprehensive. Indeed, they provide an impression that local contexts and communities are entirely powerless in the face of imperialist and corporate interests.

Mitchell importantly recognizes the political significance of material dependencies and the development of energy systems. However, whilst rich details of local histories and political dynamics are included in his analysis, the force of geopolitics and dominant expressions of governmentality appear utterly hegemonic. Indeed, whilst far more nuanced in a consideration of historic dynamics (including the meeting of international and national ambitions), Mitchell's work does not question the reductionist lens of earlier arguments of a resource curse. Academics (Auty 1993; Collier 2000; Humphreys et al. 2007) and policy-makers alike have commonly observed that the discovery of natural resource wealth does not lead to increased wealth for all, but instead to the inevitable stimulation of violent competition between political elites who are intent on the capture of extractive rents.

This chapter aims to highlight that these characterizations of resource politics are not wrong but are insufficient in their avoidance of competing claims of territorial and resource sovereignty that come from below the level of the nation-state. They are also insufficient in terms of acknowledging the political ambitions of elites, political parties and governments in Latin America with regard to national development and the exploitation of natural resources. Despite obvious imbalances of power, they have to respond to, negotiate and curry popularity amongst non-elites. Indeed, Latin American politics today, as in the past, is marked by democratic, militant and violent confrontations with powerful alternative visions of development and sovereignty. These are expressed by what are often assumed to be marginal social sectors of civil society (indigenous peoples, peasant communities, the urban poor, etc.).

In line with other social scientists and historians (Scott 1987; Nugent 1993; Mallon 1995; Nugent 1997; Migdal and White 2013), I highlight with empirical examples that subjects traditionally regarded as being weak, passive and obedient manage not only to resist the authority of state actors but also actively subvert and appropriate it in an everyday process of making and remaking the boundaries of the state, nation and their society. The capture and harnessing of energetic and natural resources are a focus and force that enable large-scale political ambitions, including the polar-opposite outcomes of conservatism and revolution. However, as I intend to demonstrate here, these do not go unquestioned or unaltered in response to expressions of sovereignty from below. I also highlight that these efforts of determining sovereignty from below are not necessarily heroic acts, but necessarily pragmatic practices that are frequently made in response to conditions of economic inequality and insecurity.

Out of the Corner of My Eye

Between 1997 and 1998, I lived and worked in the Aymaran highland community of Santuario de Quillacas in the department of Oruro, Bolivia. I arrived in Santuario de Quillacas as a result of an invitation from the indigenous leadership in the community and with the openly announced intention of completing my Ph.D. research. The research focused on the status of community–state relations following the introduction of government-sponsored reforms aimed at establishing popular participation and decentralization in the country. These were a set of reforms that the international community, including the World Bank, heralded as game-changing in terms of stimulating democracy and development. Indeed, for close to a decade, Bolivia would be a point of reference for the World Bank and other governments in their encouragement of a similar blueprint for change across the world.

As described in detail in my completed Ph.D. thesis (McNeish 2001), Santuario de Quillacas was a community that could be characterized in different ways. It was a religious sanctuary, as the name suggests, where every September people from all over the Southern Andes (Bolivia, Chile and Argentina) would gather in order to demonstrate their devotion and ask assistance from the local saint – a figure preserved in a colonial church that in a syncretic manner combined both Catholic and Andean beliefs in its murals and construction. The landscape surrounding the town of Santuario de Quillacas, situated in the bowl of an extinct volcano, is marked by deep paths that radiate like a wheel across the landscape, suggesting the many points on the compass from where pilgrims have arrived over many generations.

Santuario de Quillacas is now a rather sleepy Andean town, dedicated mostly to pastoralism and agriculture on the harsh and dry Altiplano and some seasonal labour in nearby mines and towns. However, it gained its regional fame as a religious sanctuary to a large degree because it had also once been the site of significant political power. As the local leaders in the town instructed me, Santuario de Quillacas had once been Jatun Quillacas (where Jatun refers in Aymara to 'great'), the centre of an indigenous 'kingdom' or 'estate' (señorío) that had significant power over the local landscape in the years both leading up to and immediately following the Spanish Conquest. Indeed, the Spanish recognized the importance of the town in a period of time in which load-bearing llamas and alpacas, and labour for the silver mines were of importance. Religion and cultural tradition in Santuario de Quillacas run deep. In one corner of the municipal offices, colonial-age documents recognizing the significance of Santuario de Quillacas as a political centre and its territorial limits were stacked in dusty and decaying piles in one corner of the municipal office building.

With these characteristics as background, Santuario de Quillacas was also an interesting place to study social and political change. Indeed, as described in detail in my Ph.D. thesis, the introduction of popular participation and decentralization created a scenario in which tradition and modern development aspirations were pitched in significant tension together. With the problematic political space created by the reforms, local community leaders also became actively engaged not only in discussing local concerns and possibilities, but increasingly within regional and national indigenous politics. Through their collective efforts, the Federación de Ayllus de Sur Oruro (FASOR) was established and the Katarista movement (a movement that takes its names from a eighteenth-century Aymaran rebellion leader) that was aimed at re-establishing indigenous culture and political transformation in the Bolivian Highlands would continue to grow to the point that the Consejo Nacional de Ayllus y Markas del Qullasuyu (CONAMAQ) could be established. Here the Aymaran words 'Ayllus' and 'Markas' denominate local understanding of the conformation of indigenous territories – sixteen in total in this case. The establishment of CONAMAQ would play an important role in the establishment of the political support base that would push for the removal of traditional political parties from power and the election of Evo Morales Ayma as President in 2005 (McNeish 2006).

These political transformations filled the pages of my Ph.D. thesis and several subsequent articles, but there was another particular role that Santuario de Quillacas played at the time that I lived there. This was highly evident in my life there, but no more than a footnote in the study conducted at that time. Out of the corner of my eye, I noted whilst living there that Santuario de Quillacas was an important refuelling point on the route used by smugglers to avoid customs authorities, police and the military in their efforts to bring cars and other goods into the country. Every week, a convoy of dusty (but apparently new) cars would arrive at dusk in the town on paths that avoided the main highways. The convoy of cars would be divided up and ushered as quickly and quietly as possible into the backyard and hidden patios of the houses in the community. Drivers would be given food and lodging for the night, and a little information regarding the observation of police and military movements in the area. In the early morning, the convoy would move on, continuing their off-road journey towards the markets for *autos chutos* (smuggled and often modified vehicles) in Santa Cruz and El Alto and other parts of the country.

This was obviously a means of supplementing income for many Quillacans, for whom traditional activities such as pastoralism, agricultural and seasonal work in the mines covered little more than their basic subsistence. Communities on the Bolivian Altiplano persist due to their continued use of a surprising array of context-specific productive technologies (terracing raised fields, storage silos, underground irrigation channels, etc.) and the careful husbandry of hardy food plants (quinoa, rice, corn, etc.) and animals (llamas, alpacas, cattle, etc.), but climate change (evident in increased frosts and a reduction in rainfall) and the actions of local mining companies to over-exploit and contaminate local waters sources has made this life increasingly difficult for local farmers and pastoralists. In a recent article, *The Guardian* newspaper reported that Lake Poopó had dried up as a result of these factors ('Bolivia's Second-Largest Lake Dries up and May Be Gone Forever, Lost to Climate Change' 2016). Lake Poopó – Santuario de Quillacas is located a short distance inland from its southern end – was Bolivia's second-largest lake and was an important hunting and gathering resource for the local communities in the Oruro area. The number of abandoned villages and settlements were already increasing in the 1990s when climate migration and increasing anthropogenic environmental degradation also started to become evident.

When asked about the legality of their activity, Quillacans acknowledged that state authorities would see their actions as criminal. However, they also stressed that whilst the Bolivian state considered them illegal, this was part of a celebrated tradition for trading and self-sufficiency in Quillacas. Whilst the state had arrived with recent political reform, it historically had little presence other than periodic visits by state officials and law enforcement, and gave little assistance to the economic and social development of the community, which had received periodic handouts of money and equipment, but local institutions and infrastructure were sustained by their own labour and were not sufficiently supported by the state. Despite the package of reforms and opportunities granted by popular participation and decentralization, the ambitions of the Bolivian government and the international community to establish modernity, development and change contrasted sharply with a lived history in which other conceptions and requirements for subsistence applied. This included the local community's concerns with balancing economic development with their further spiritual development. When the municipal council decided to place the expenses of renovating the central square and walls of the church into its 5 year operative plan for the municipality – recognizing the role of annual pilgrimage to the community as one of both of economic and spiritual importance – it was quickly denounced by the consultants sent by the state to oversee the decentralization process. Indeed, it was used by the consultants as an excuse to stress not only differing economic priorities, but also the flawed moral character of local residents who, they suggested, 'would prefer to buy beer for their festivals than pay taxes' (McNeish 2001).

Deeply contrasting perspectives between state and community perspectives of development were also visible in the coverage in my thesis of local territorial conflicts. A detailed account is given in my Ph.D. thesis of the local history of the efforts of one of the local sections of the community to split-off from the municipality of Santuario de Quillacas in order to join a wealthier neighbouring municipality (McNeish 2002). A clear complication in this political conflict was the contrasting understanding of the territorial extension of municipal geographical boundaries and of its relationships to new and existing maps. Typical of other Andean communities, Quillacans did not see the local territorial boundaries of the *ayllu* (territory) as being sharply divided by clear fence lines or lines on a map. Territory was held in common and land divisions tended in local community perspectives to overlap with one another. Although land was carefully divided and rotated between different community members, at times it was also not continuous, but rather broken into different areas of productive activity, including sites for ritual and offering to ancestral spirits. The contrast between these understandings of territory became a problem when new political and productive boundaries were to be produced by the new decisions of the Bolivian state (McNeish 2002). The state's efforts to both map and form agreement on municipal divisions became evidently incompatible with local perspectives.

This mismatch between local and state perspectives of territory in the Andes has been a subject of much broader anthropological interest for some time. In 1967, Murra proposed the idea of the *vertical archipelago* as a way to capture the broken and multilevel nature (ecological layers) of the Andean landscape. More recently, Orlove (1991) also importantly described the lack of commensurability of territorial and resource understandings between the Peruvian and Andean communities in the vicinity of Lake Titicaca. Studying the highly contrasting maps produced by the state and local communities, Orlove (1991: 29) concluded that 'each side holds distinct, complex notions of use, control and ownership of resources'. Recognizing these differences, he further suggested (1991: 31) that Benedict Anderson's influential idea of 'imagined communities' should be supplemented by a more spatially oriented idea of *imagined countrysides*. Interestingly, this idea of competing imagined countrysides also maps on to historical trade routes and persisting cross-border smuggling routes. Originating from rural Andean communities such as Santuario de Quillacas, the car smugglers described above used mental maps and landscape knowledge that contrasted with the state's political boundaries and military-geographic oriented maps of roads and borders.

Contrasting logics were also evident in local perceptions of the state's provision of law and order. The community relied on national legal institutions to intervene when serious crimes occurred, and the police and military periodically visited the community – often on the lookout for smugglers. Many of the Quillacans I got to know closely nonetheless felt that they were by and large left alone to look after themselves. Municipal authorities relied heavily on the traditional leaders and the application of customary law in the community to guarantee everyday law and order, and to ensure that inhabitants abided by agreements on local land and resource use. This mirrors the experience of other rural, indigenous and peri-urban communities in Bolivia (Goldstein 2004, 2012; McNeish and Arteaga Böhrt 2012). Indeed, it is relevant to acknowledge that the conditions of contested sovereignty and economic marginalization that provide the rationale and context for smuggling in Bolivia – and of the *gasolinazo* described in the previous chapter – are also evident in the contraband economy elsewhere in Latin America. A significant element of that trade is fuel. Indeed, recognizing that trucks, boats and planes represent the main vehicles of this trade – other than animal and human muscle – it is fossil fuel that makes this informal economy possible at all.

Everything Moves with Fuel

It is tempting when considering the enormity of the Bolivian informal economy to single out the country as an exceptionally unruly space, as a smuggler's paradise. In Bolivia, everything is on the move in the smuggling economy. Whilst Bolivia is famed as one of the locations for the production and smuggling of cocaine, this is in reality only a small (albeit highly lucrative) part of a vast contraband economy that includes a multitude of other goods, e.g. fuel, clothing, electronics, vehicles, people, animals, falsified medicines and foodstuffs. The problem with such a claim would be that there is evidence of a similar political economy at multiple sites and border crossings throughout the region. Fuel and everything moved by fuel is smuggled over borders from Bolivia to Peru (Ødegaard 2015), from Mexico to Guatemala (Galemba 2017), from Venezuela to Colombia (Kaplan 2016) and over multiple borders to Brazil (Gurney 2015). This is also not a new or recent phenomenon.

For centuries, inter-regional barter and trade have played an important role among people in the Andes (Murra 1980). Indeed, contemporary cross-border trade in southern Peru follows the same routes as trade during the colonial period – that is, along the routes of mule drivers who brought goods between highland towns such as La Paz, Puno and Arequipa, and towns along the Pacific coast, to Chile (Ødegaard 2016). For residents on the Mexico–Guatemala border, transporting goods across the border has also long been a legitimate form of making a living and accessing goods in a relatively neglected region (Galemba 2017: 6). Chiapas is Mexico's poorest state and Huehuetenango is one of Guatemala's poorest departments. Border populations have often historically shared stronger ties across the border than with their fellow nationals.

Whilst they were nothing new, these activities increased significantly in the 1980s and 1990s, the period in which neoliberal economics expanded in the region. The 1980s and early 1990s are often referred to as the 'lost decade' in Latin America, characterized by increasing unemployment, inequality and poverty. As economies became increasingly liberalized, unemployment and self-employment levels increased, and at the same time, an expansion of the informal economy, both legal and illegal, occurred (Ødegaard 2016; Galemba 2017). In Andean countries, the need for alternatives to waged labour was further reinforced by the continued migration of people from rural areas to the cities. These changes combined to make self-employment (e.g. through trade) the only alternative for many, often taking place at the margins of the formal economy.

In Mexico, structural adjustment also meant abandoning its model of state-directed development, which resulted in decreased public spending and investment, a decline in the minimum wage and rising unemployment. In particular, agricultural liberalization dealt a drastic blow to small peasants, especially in Mexico's southern states (Galemba 2017: 9). On the Mexico–Guatemala border, smuggling also intensified in the 1990s due to economic crises on both sides of the border, the collapse of traditional livelihood options, and improvements in infrastructure and technology. Although intended to serve mega-development or extractive projects and facilitate regional trade integration, highway expansion in Chiapas in the 1990s also expedited extra-legal commerce and communication in the region (Galemba 2017: 7). Residents began to acquire both the trucks and the capital to invest in smuggling businesses as a result of rising migration to the United States in the 1990s.

Other economic and political factors also encouraged the expansion of cross-border trade and smuggling. At the beginning of the 1990s, also in response to the pervading logic of neoliberalism, many NGOs shifted their interest away from direct development assistance and towards the establishment of microcredit programmes focused on small producers and women in particular. In these programmes, the value of entrepreneurship is promoted alongside the expectation of reliance on family and kin networks rather than traditional community foundations. A series of free trade and duty-free zones were also established throughout Latin America, perhaps the most significant of these being Panama, Manaus and the tri-border area of Ciudad del Este between Brazil, Argentina and Paraguay. According to Ødegaard, free trade zones have also been established close to the borders of both Chile (in Tacna) and Bolivia (in Puno), the latter being established in 2007/2008. These free trade zones are located along the historical roots of cross-border trade and can be considered a way to incorporate, or make legible (Scott 1998), already-existing practices of trade. There is and has been a majority of women in these forms of cross-border trade in the Andes. This can be understood in light of the historical traditions for women to be involved in barter and trade in this part of the Andes, and a gender complementarity whereby women manage money and economic matters, while men manage politics (Harris 2000).

Authors working with what now appears to the ubiquity of smuggling in border areas acknowledge that whilst these practices may be connected to larger networks of crime, those working with small-scale trade and smuggling over borders should not simply be defined as criminals. While cartels and criminal syndicates tax and directly rely on the labour of petty traders and smugglers to move their wares, the majority of people involved in these activities are not the part of any defined organization. They look at these activities as possibilities to cope with 'stressful periods of biographic transition such as unemployment and poverty' (Bruns and Migglebrink 2012: 12). Writing about the smuggling of fuel on the Bolivian–Peruvian border Ødegaard (2015: 141) adds that:

> The smuggling of combustible fuel reflects long-standing inequalities and a deep sense of local autonomy in border areas characterized by an ambiguous presence of state. A focus on smuggling thus serves to illustrate how controversy and contestation over energy may be responsible for uncovering and renewing long-standing social cleavages. Indeed, the smuggling reveals not only controversy over energy resources, but also how state legitimacy is negotiated and questioned.

Especially in the villages close to the border, many people are engaged in the contraband businesses and think about the delineated border not primarily as a delimitation of the nation-state, but as representing a possibility to earn money. The smuggling of fuel and other goods takes place in border areas characterized by a strong sense of local autonomy, infused by a history of marginalization and the ambiguous presence of state actors. It is also not uncommon for smugglers to question the right of state officials to intervene in their efforts at making a living, and often with reference to what they either see as corruption of the state and large-scale enterprises, including energy and extractive industries. Latin American newspapers regularly carry stories about corrupt government officials and their connections to oil and mining contracts and projects. Galemba (2017) is also explicit in detailing local frustrations and contradictions along the Mexican border with regard to the inequalities of national development and energy production.

As of 2015, there were ninety-nine mining concessions in Chiapas, which were awarded by the Mexican government primarily to Canadian and Chinese companies and constituted over 14% of the territory of Chiapas. Licences will last until 2050 or 2060; activists argue that more concessions are also under way to plans for five hydroelectric dams along Chiapas' Usumacinta River. According to Mexico's National Institute of Statistics and Geography (INEGI), Chiapas provides 44.5% of Mexico's hydroelectric power, 7.5% of its electrical production, 1.8% of its crude oil and 3.1% of its natural gas. Although coverage has improved, Chiapas also ranks toward the bottom of Mexican states with regard to the percentage of households possessing electricity. In the context of securitized neoliberalism, a heightened security and military presence in Chiapas has created a climate for securing investment, resource extraction and road construction that serves mega-development projects, but also acts to silence and criminalize opposition and attempts to control mobility (Galemba 2017: 13).

A focus on the smuggling of combustible fuel demands a pluralized and multi-layered understanding of sovereignty. We recognize, as was indicated in the last chapter, that as a result of subsidies in some (but not in all) countries, energy prices in Latin America can vary quite significantly from one country to another. The nationalization of the energy sector in Bolivia by Evo Morales in 2005 involved a subsidization of energy prices for the national market, causing a significant price difference between Bolivia and neighbouring countries. This differentiation in fuel prices has encouraged the illegal trade in fuel to flourish. In another context, similar dynamics are visible. Galemba (2017) highlights that petrol and diesel were significantly cheaper in Mexico than in Guatemala in the years leading up to a 2006–7 rise in petrol smuggling at the border. Guatemalan prices also began to soar in the summer of 2007 to some of the highest in Central America, reaching almost twice those of

Mexican prices, paralleling global concerns in 2007 over rising oil prices. The price for a gallon of petrol in Guatemala rose by 11.4% between July and August 2007, which made it increasingly profitable for Guatemalans to smuggle petrol from Mexico. Gabenda also notes the effect of recent energy privatization moves in Mexico. In early 2017, protests against the effects of privatization, called 'el gasolinazo', erupted throughout Mexico as a falling peso and subsidy cuts led food and fuel prices to surge by 20% (Galemba 2017: 202).

A recent article focused on the Venezuelan–Colombian border link describes similar price imbalances and its relationship to a rise in petrol smuggling. The article notes that:

> While both Colombia and Venezuela produce and export oil, Venezuela has the world's largest crude reserves and is among the top producers in the world, miles ahead of Colombia's supply. This bounty and a history of state subsidies long kept gas prices in Venezuela low. But over the last two decades, local officials essentially froze domestic gas prices at already low rates, drastically widening its price gap with its neighbours year by year. This subsidy system, which now costs the state about $15 billion a year, meant that (until a few months ago) locals could buy a litre of gas for $0.01. Going by the artificial official exchange rate (about a tenth of a cent to the dollar's black-market value), that figure represents cheapest gas prices in the world – cheaper than water – while Colombians paid about $0.50. (Hay 2016)

The experience of a serious loss of revenue generates reactions whereby new and intensified attempts to control the borders are introduced by state structures in order to reduce the extent of these practices. As Chalfin (2006) has suggested, these state reactions should be recognized as an effort to defend state sovereignty. Ødegaard (2015) suggests that seen in this light, the illegal exportation of fuel represents not only economic loss for countries like Bolivia, where energy prices are subsidized, but also a questioning of the legitimacy and territoriality of the state. The smuggling may in this regard be considered a double challenge to state sovereignty in the countries involved, involving denials both of the state's legitimacy in controlling the flow of commodities and of the territorial boundaries themselves.

However, noting the vagaries of state security arrangements in her study of contraband on the Mexican–Guatemala border, Galemba (2017: 5) proposes that we should not simply assume that this challenge to sovereignty is geared towards undermining the state or the formal economy; rather, these illegal activities depend on the uneasy relationship with the state and formal economy. This position is further supported by the work of Jorge Montesinos, who has been working on small-scale trade and smuggling across the Bolivian–Chilean border (the picture above of the petrol tanker is his). Asked directly in a seminar I intended – during my sabbatical at the University of California at San Diego (UCSD) – if he saw smuggling across the border as a form of resistance to the state, he was clear in answering no, it was not. These expressions of 'parallel citizenship', as he termed smuggler socio-economies, existed in tension with the state. However, they also required the state to set the boundaries that they would then negate. As a result, there is an uneasy symbiosis between these contrasting expressions of sovereignty.

Galemba (2017: 5) also suggests that: 'At the border, informality, illegality, the formal economy, and security logics intertwine and blur in the context of . . . securitized neoliberalism, or the wedding of security policies to neoliberal economic policies and logics.' Securitized neoliberalism works to value certain economic activities and actors, and exclude and criminalize others in a context where the informal and illicit economy in increasingly one of the poor's remaining options and informality also permeates the formal sector. Instead of accepting illegality as static and from a state-centred standpoint, it is necessary to interrogate how and under what conditions certain activities or people are deemed informal, illegal or illicit. Rather than distinct realms, informal, formal, legal and illegal commerce merge together, and are mutually constituted, in the flow of global commerce across borders (Galemba 2017: 16). The borders between legality and illegality are therefore often blurred and fluid when engaging in smuggling (Bruns and Miggelbrink 2012: 13). Indeed, the status of (il)legality qualifies a relationship between a trading activity and a state's law. Smuggling and small-scale trade are hence the effects, and perhaps vagaries, of a state's regulations.

Small-scale border trade and smuggling are commonly family businesses involving entire households and kin groups (Ødegaard 2015). Central to these forms of trade is also an overlap between social and spatial embeddedness, being based on networks of cooperation through households and extended kinship relations. Success in these businesses depends on relationships of trust and cooperation, and there is an intense cultivation of social relations among vendors and *contrabandistas*, through sharing and giving, and the establishment of godparenthood and relationships to customers and suppliers. Many smugglers also offer ritual payments to saints and *earth beings* (the *achachillas*, or ancestors in the landscape)[1] as a way of maintaining good relations with the sources of wellbeing, health and prosperity (Ødegaard 2015). Such payments are meant to reproduce the sources of prosperity and improve success in business, and major-league vendors have a particular responsibility to serve as sponsors for festivals or parties. Among successful smugglers, it is also common to use a percentage of profits to make pilgrimages to luck- or wealth-bringing places (such as Santuario de Quillacas).

Olivia Harris (2000) has previously suggested that people involved in legal and illegal cross-border trade understand prosperity and progress then being maintained through reciprocity, exchange and circulation. Such understandings not only diverge from the public discourse of development as facilitated by development models dependent on natural extraction, but also serve to legitimize the contraband businesses. Indeed, *smugglers* are generally respected for their ability to make and manage money, and for their independence, whether their work is illegal or not. They are seen as important suppliers of merchandise, performing a valuable social service by travelling to bring in goods that other vendors can sell. There is thus a general appreciation of the often hardworking *contrabandistas* in a way that reflects the appreciation of circulation and exchange as a cultural value in this context (Ødegaard 2015).

Contraband therefore demonstrates that the borders of the state are not only marked by a spatial and material divide, but are borderlands crisscrossed by contrasting personal conceptions and ideas of political legitimacy and social and economic development. At the frontier, contrasting and frequently shifting understandings of boundaries and limits – physical, spiritual, legal and ethical – and of a desired present and future development are generative of contrasting understandings of sovereignty. In this context, everything moves with fuel. Even notions of state security, economic policy, regulation and law are determined by the movement of fuel given its importance to wider trade both legal and illegal. Although only one of many products and resources on the move across borders, and clearly not a cause in its own right of social differences, its centrality to movement, political and productive activities results in fuel becoming a catalyst for both confrontation and creative thinking. Through their involvement in the smuggling and supply of fuel, peasant and indigenous communities living in isolated areas close to state frontiers actively deny and engage with the state. The state in return has to reluctantly respond.

To some extent, this ambiguous relationship with the state is akin to the 'anarchist' history of a search for self-determination and community–state relations described by Scott in Southeast Asia (2010). Through their involvement in smuggling, indigenous and peasant peoples are not passive, but actively carry out acts of resistance and engagement with the state, which have lasting impacts on the character and operation of the state itself. The state is at once questioned and reimagined in a zone of 'awkward' engagement (Tsing 2004). However, the ethnographic details of this engagement at least in Andean countries do not entirely fit the 'nobility' of the *weapons of the weak* threading through Scott's work. The history of economic development in the region (extensively based on mining and other forms of natural resource extraction), and of cultural domination and of state formation, has not produced an outright rejection of capital or state authority.

As many analysts have recognized before me (Albó 1977; Nash 1993; Harris 2000; Taussig 1991, 2010), this history has instead instilled a critical engagement with the state and marketplace in local communities and with the significance of capital to their lives. This is a history of active cultural engagement that includes *commodity fetishism* (Taussig 2010) i.e. where states and state institutions have magical powers, and the value and use of money is given cultural revision (Taussig 1991; Harris 2000). In this context exploitation and dependency also coexist, albeit in uneasy fashion in work, land and resource use (Albó 1977). It is a history of hybridity whereby individuals and communities defy cultural stereotypes of the indigenous through the coalescence of class and ethnicity.

It might be assumed that the Andean area stands out within the region of Latin America in terms of the level of interaction between the local and the global, given the intensive presence of extractive projects in the area. However, it is important to acknowledge that whilst the Highland region might be exceptional in terms of intensive resource extraction, the economic history of the Lowlands is not delinked or without similar characteristics. Indeed, given that other countries in Latin America (e.g. Colombia and Guatemala) have similar histories of extractive or plantation economies and have experienced similar dynamics of internal economic migration and seasonal labour, it is possible to suggest, as Fabricant and Gustafson (2011: 8) have done in the case of Bolivia, that economic articulations across space leave these spaces (*lo andino* and *el oriente*) politically and culturally embedded in each other. They are also commonly intertwined with the global. It is also through these processes that contestation of sovereignty at the margins become connected to similar processes in other areas of the nation.

A New Ecological Context for Protest

Smuggling, in which fuel plays a key role, can be seen here to be a significant context in which indigenous and peasant communities reformulate their relationship with the state – and in response, the state reformulates itself. Physical and mental boundaries are also encountered and questioned in an effort not to remove sovereign claims, but to redefine sovereignty and its contextual significance. Sovereignty is significant here as a vehicle for claims to economic rights, territory, resources and identity. However, smuggling, whilst an important and little-recognized feature of sovereign forces, is only one of the dynamics through which local indigenous and peasant peoples frame unruly engagements with the state and influence the direction of politics.

Protest is perhaps a more obvious dynamic of engagement and pressure for change. From the time of European conquest to the present day, the exploitation of natural resource wealth has determined Latin America's links to both international markets and destiny as the site of periodic social and political contestation (Nash 1993). Protest and periodic rebellion by peasant and indigenous communities have perhaps been the more common source of political pressure from below, and of social and legal transformation in Latin America from the colonial period to the present.

Although not a common feature of the elite histories of the nation (such as those taught in schools), of struggles against colonialism and independence or of ideologically driven revolutions against tyranny and foreign intervention, the protests and rebellions of indigenous and peasant peoples are nonetheless recognized as critical agents of change by many historians of the region (Stern 1987; Thompson 2003; Gotkowitz 2008). Significant shifts in regional history (e.g. the Wars of Independence, the Mexican Revolution, the Chaco War, the Bolivian Nationalist Revolution, the armed conflict in Colombia, the Shining Path struggle in Peru, the Sandinista Revolution and the Contras War) would not have taken place – or at least would not have taken place the way they did – had it not been either for preceding protests and rebellions by these populations, or the manpower they granted to the warring sides.

Another common element in these histories is also the failure of victors and political elites to honour the promises made to indigenous and peasant communities (of protection, territory and political inclusion) in exchange for their alliances following the cessation of the conflicts. Despite this, it seems that the gravity of persistent struggle does change. Indeed, everyday protest and political engagements by indigenous and peasant communities with their states should also be recognized as an important source of pressure, which when combined with other political dynamics contributes over time to the expansion of political, economic and social rights. Debates in the republican period regarding the integration of the indigenous population, the *indigenista* shift in several countries, and the adjustments made to national constitutions throughout the 1990s and 2000s all speak of the way in which national attitudes regarding indigenous and peasant peoples have shifted and, with it, the proclaimed identities of the *patria* (nationhood).

As mentioned in the Introduction to this book, there has been a common relationship between processes of political conflict and change in Latin America and claims made for territory and resources. Since colonial times, Latin America's relationship with natural resources has been a source of conflicting political, social and economic dynamics (Raftopolous 2017). Indeed, as Haarstad (2012: 1) argues, natural resources have traditionally been considered a curse on Latin American societies, from the plundering of the colonial era to the ills of commodity dependency in later years. Moreover, the socioeconomic conditions produced by extractivist economies have contributed to ecological destruction, widespread poverty and social injustice throughout the region. Schmink and Jouve-Martín (2011: 3) highlight that

'Latin America's historical dependency on natural resources, both for local livelihoods and to supply an evolving global market, has made environmental issues central in policy debates and in widespread contests over the meaning and use of natural species and habitats, carried out against the region's persistent legacy of inequality'.

Indigenous and peasant claims and political struggles fall within and have significance within these dynamics. Struggles over land and resources, including periodic land invasions by both lesser-known and well-known agrarian organizations such as the Movimento dos Trabalhadores Rurais Sem Terra (MST), remain a feature of social movement politics in the region. However, in recent years, these land claims have been joined by new political expressions in which claims to territory and resources are seated within wider concerns and claims regarding economic benefits, political participation and the quality of the local environment in face of the impacts of extractive activities. There are two important time periods that can be roughly defined as marking stages of these developments: the 1990s to the early 2000s, and the early 2000s to the present (this expands on the summarized political economic history in the Introduction).

The 1990s to the Early 2000s

During the 1990s, a number of global and regional political and economic transformations contributed to significant shifts in land, labour and capital determinants, and ushered in a new period of widespread growth of extractive industries across Latin America (Bury and Bebbington 2013). The end of the Cold War led to a reconfiguration of geopolitical relationships (Hobsbawm 1995) that affected trade, the investment climate, and political and development relations between Latin America and the rest of the world (Sikkink 1997). In this new geopolitical climate, the formal support for democratic as opposed to military (which had been accepted to some extent in the 1970s) governance increased, and the importance of earlier nationalism and economic protectionism were pushed aside in favour of the ideology of a global free market. Among the various effects of the spatial reordering of geopolitics under neoliberalism was the creation of new international trade and investment opportunities for many countries, even where dictatorships persisted, as in the case of Chile and Guatemala. In the decades since 1990, a new contingent of rapidly developing and highly populous countries emerged, among them the so-called BRICS countries (Brazil, Russia, India, China and South Africa). In their quest for rapid development, these countries have enthusiastically sought the necessary mineral and hydrocarbon supplies needed to support their plans for extensive urbanization and industrialization. As a result, Africa and Latin America would become the key sources of these raw materials.

The extractive sector has remained a critically important driver of economic growth by both global and national policy-makers seeking to overcome the economic and political crises spurred by successive oil price shocks and massive national debt burdens in the 1990s. Import substitution industrialization policies and the nationalization of extractive industries during the decades prior to 1990 were viewed to have culminated in several periods of hyperinflation and little economic growth. At the behest of the World Bank and the international community, Latin American governments adopted structural adjustment programmes aimed at controlling government spending and currency markets, and attracting new flows of foreign capital, generating foreign exchange for debt service and fostering economic growth. Many structural adjustment programmes were initiated during hyperinflation crises, under pressure from international lending institutions such as the World Bank and the International Monetary Fund, and in accordance with the emerging 'Washington Consensus' that sought to reintegrate Latin America into the global system of neoliberal trade and exchange (Bury and Bebbington 2013: 44).

Structural adjustment resulted in the significant liberalization of the extractive sector throughout Latin American. Regionally, state-led industrialization and public ownership of extractive industries decreased considerably. All of these features would disturb previous assumptions regarding the national ownership of natural resources, and with it create new questions regarding sovereignty or resource sovereignty (at different geographical and social scales) more specifically. In this period, many operations and proven mineral and hydrocarbons deposits were privatized or sold to foreign and domestic investors. New regulations to assist the inflow of foreign direct investment (FDI) were put in place that mandated the non-discrimination of foreign capital, freedom to remit profits abroad, the reorganization and clarification of mining and hydrocarbons concessions, the removal of local hiring and sourcing requirements, limitations on state expropriation rights, ratification of international arbitration accords, and the creation of investment protection (Bury and Bebbington 2013: 45). Previous natural resource extraction legislation was either abolished or amended to limit legal public interests and claims of eminent domain, reform environmental protections, establish minimal taxation regimes, formalize mineral and hydrocarbons concessions taxation and leasing, and create investment incentives. In this period, many countries also developed the infrastructure to provide access to remote areas where new hydrocarbons and mineral deposits were being discovered. Provision was also made where necessary for military and police support to ensure the safety of new extractive operations and their frequently foreign personnel (Bury and Bebbington 2013: 45).

The changes to the regulation of the natural resource extractive sector co-incided with the introduction of new techniques in open-pit mining, operations engineering, mineral processing, drilling, geotechnical modelling and petroleum-intensive transportation (Bury and Bebbington 2013). Drilling operations on land have accounted for much of the growth in operations, which is in large part due to the introduction of new technologies such as directional drilling, super-deep ocean drilling platforms, and new 'fracking' technologies that allow surface operations to hydraulically fracture subterranean rock layers to release natural gas. The development of new biomining extraction technologies is also reworking mining in Latin America, again modifying the assemblage of activities that constitute the extractive complex of the region (Bury and Bebbington 2013: 65). For most of the twentieth century, gas was not commercially viable, given that it was too difficult to store and transport. However, technological change has since made gas more attractive, and new gas discoveries led to dramatic increases in reserves in Bolivia, Guatemala and Peru. Significantly in terms of labour relations, all of these technological changes have meant a reduction in the workforce at mining, drilling and processing sites.

The confluence of these broad currents of change in the extractive sector initiated what has often been referred to as a 'super-cycle' of growth in mineral and gas production across the region (Humphreys Bebbington 2012). Between the early 1990s and late 2008, the rapid growth of this cycle, though uneven in terms of its geographical extent, was historically unprecedented in terms of its magnitude and velocity. Overall, between 1990 and 2007, Latin America received US$969 billion in FDI (Bury and Bebbington 2013: 41). New flows of FDI to Latin America financed extensive mining and hydrocarbons exploration. While reliable exploration investment data are largely non-existent and do not include the state held operations that dominate petroleum production as well as many of the largest mining operations, global investments in exploration by transnational private-sector corporations accounted for approximately US$2 trillion in the hydrocarbons sector and US$91 billion in the mining sector between 1996 and 2007 (Bury and Bebbington 2013: 42). Comparatively, hydrocarbons exploration in Latin America accounted for roughly 10% of global investment between 2005 and 2007, while mineral exploration accounted for 26% between 1996 and 2007. Exports of minerals and mineral products grew significantly in this period, increasing by US$123 billion between 1990 and 2006. (Bury and Bebbington 2013: 47). Natural gas exports more than tripled between 1990 and 2007.

Whilst the expansion of non-renewable natural resource extraction is highly significant; it should be noted that its social and environmental impacts were reinforced by related developments in both infrastructural and renewable energy developments. Many of the projects for hydrocarbons that started in the 1990s required the supporting construction of related infrastructure (roads, bridges, ports, processing facilities) and sometimes renewable energy projects such as hydroelectric dams. In 2000, twelve Latin American countries signed an agreement creating the Initiative for Integration of the Regional Infrastructure of South America (IIRSA). As a result of this initiative, funds were to be channelled towards the massive expansion of roads, riverways, hydroelectric dams and telecommunications throughout the region. The IIRSA initiative was further supported by regional financial institutions, including the Andean Development Corporation (CAF),[2] the Inter-American Development Bank (IDB) and the River Plate Basin Financial Development Fund (FONPLATA). Whilst clearly with a larger remit than just the extractive industries, many of the activities related to IIRSA concerned the provision of support to a variety of extractive activities, including oil and gas production.

Renewable energy projects without any links to hydrocarbons have also grown significantly throughout Latin America in line with the rise in prices for hydrocarbon fuels. In addition to hydroelectric schemes (reflecting its ample water resources, Latin America produces 65% of its domestic energy from hydropower), solar energy projects, biofuels production and thermal energy projects have significantly expanded throughout the region over the last two decades. Whilst not with the same severity as non-renewable energy production, it is important to place an emphasis on these infrastructure and renewable developments, recognizing that they also entail serious social and environmental costs.

With the expansion of new extractive frontiers, the environmental and social impacts have also been extended. Despite attempts at regulation, oil and petrochemical production has led to the dumping of millions of barrels of a cocktail of chemicals, drilling fluids and formation water into the rivers, coastal seas and forests. Mining practices, including those for rare earths, have caused river courses to change, and heavy metals and chemicals used in processing to leach into drinking water. Beyond the diversion and contamination of water, the persistent toxic leaks and periodic catastrophic spills, large-scale mining and oil exploitation projects play an important role in opening new areas of sensitive biodiversity and human population to industrial development. The construction of supporting infrastructures (roads, pipelines, hydroelectric dams, pylons and cable networks, ports and storage facilities) have also had their own direct cost on the environment and have frequently forced the further displacement and problematic resettlement of local communities. Whilst renewable energy projects are often considered to have a lower social and environmental impact, similar issues regarding contamination (to water supplies and soil, but also of noise and light pollution), land and property rights (given the requirement of private titling and the construction of perimeter fences) and the unequal distribution of labour and profits (these are still capital-intensive projects governed by market principles) have surfaced in their development.

On their own, these factors could be considered enough to generate responses of rejection and protest amongst local communities. However, other significant contextual factors have also been noted as adding to this potent recipe for reaction. In addition to a shift in economic ideology and policy, in the 1990s most Latin American countries underwent a process of democratization and political decentralization. The trend towards civil government and electoral democracy that restarted in the 1980s increased in the 1990s and former exclusionary forms of governance gave way to electoral forms of political representation. At the same time, the role of the state was limited by far-reaching structural adjustment policies imposed by international institutions, in particular the International Monetary Fund, the World Bank and the Inter-American Development Bank (Leverman and Villas 2006). The self-governance mode, as conceptualized by the World Bank, called for the shrinking of state regulation and an emphasis on market-based mechanisms such as privatization, self-designed corporate conduct guides (e.g. corporate social responsibility (CSR)) and voluntary mechanisms (certification and compensation schemes) (Raftopolous 2017: 6). While promising environmentally and socially sound initiatives, the market-based approach to self-governance primarily also sought to improve the image of transnationally operating companies vis-à-vis their shareholders and to consequently ease their insertion into host countries (Lyon 2009).

The 1990s was also the period in which the idea of rights-based development also became firmly established within both non-governmental development efforts and state-led experiments with territorial co-management. Both NGOs and states encouraged the formation of a large number of community-based management studies (see McKay and Acheson 1990; Berkus and Folk 1998). While self-governance through collective action became important in more remote areas during this period (Schmink and Jouve-Martín 2011), in areas of large-scale economic production, a type of self-governance based on market-based mechanisms thrived, leading to a wave of natural resource privatization in the region. These experiments would be further expanded in the early 2000s. These experiments in participatory governance range from co-management models, in which state and local communities develop a sustainable plan for traditional territories (de Castro 2012) to more complex arrangements that include multistakeholders and multiscale institutions, such as that of climate governance. Here, governments, transnational social movements and transnational corporations are engaged in the shaping of an international institutional arrangement that combines semi-legal agreements to tackle climate change and related environmental issues, such as emission targets, Agenda 21 and the Convention on Biological Diversity (Biermann and Pattberg 2008).

With encouragement from the World Bank and other international institutions, many Latin American countries, in line with global trends, also implemented in this period widespread policies for fiscal decentralization and popular participation that were thought to be means to assist democratization through the streamlining of state institutions and spending, as well as the transfer of fiscal and governance responsibilities to local municipalities and community-level institutions. My Ph.D. research, which was mentioned in connection to smuggling activities above, was directed specifically towards studying the impacts of the Bolivian decentralization and popular participation reforms on state–community relations in the 1990s (McNeish 2001). Described as a programme for 'municipalization plus popular vigilance', the popular participation legislation had the combined effect of decentralizing a significant percentage of government expenditure to local government budgets, the creation of new opportunities for rural communities to partake in the planning and regulation of local government, and formal recognition of indigenous and popular organizations as political entities with rights (McNeish 2002: 229). Under the administrative decentralization law, nonpayroll responsibilities of central government ministries – including health and education – were devolved to the departmental level, and for the first-time prefectural governments at those levels were advised by and made accountable to elected councils representing the municipalities of their area (McNeish 2002: 229).

These experiments in participatory governance also notably occurred in direct relationship with the ratification of ILO 169 and revisions of indigenous sovereignty discussed in the previous chapter. Importantly, in 1992, Latin American states, following pressure from the international community, celebrated the quincentennial of the conquest of the Americas with statements and policy actions emphasizing their commitment to the protection of indigenous rights under ILO 169. It is also notable that Rigoberta Menchu, an indigenous activist from Guatemala, was granted the internationally recognized Nobel Peace Prize that same year. Indeed, in the early 1990s, many national constitutions in Latin America were revised in recognition of indigenous peoples and of the need to create legal and political provision in defence of the heterogeneity of their populations. In the 1990s and early 2000s, increasing support was given by Latin American states and international organizations to the idea of multiculturalism, intercultural dialogue and development with identity. In 2004, the United Nations Development Programme (UNDP) released a Human Development Report focused on 'Cultural Liberty in Today's Diverse World'. The report made the case for

respecting cultural diversity and making efforts to build more inclusive societies through the adoption of policies that explicitly recognize cultural
differences (Human Development Report 2004: 2). In a parallel move, the
World Bank officially adopted the notion of rights-based development by
establishing links between cultural diversity and public action to reduce
poverty (Rao and Walton 2004). This was a marked revision of earlier constitutional statements and elite-driven expressions of nationalism that even
whilst recognizing *mestizaje* (racial mixing) and *indigenismo* (recognition of
indigenous identities within the state) emphasized the need for integration
(forced if need be) and social homogeneity.

Earlier in Latin American history, there had been a strong tendency to
deny the political and economic significance of ethnicity (Thorp, Caumartin
and Grey Molina 2006). During the colonial period, Indians were relegated
to the bottom of the social, economic and political hierarchy by a system of
tribute and labour responsibilities that went together with 'protections' such
as special legal status (often as minors), exemption from military service, and
inalienable land rights often enforced by moving indigenous communities
from their traditional territories to crown-controlled, town-based settlements
(*reducciones*). After independence, the new Latin American creole elites set
about creating political and economic institutions to serve their interests.
Although some countries accorded indigenous peoples protected status, the
laws and institutions of the independent states excluded them from the benefits of citizenship while also expecting them to fulfil citizen obligations and
demonstrate devotion to the new nation-states. Although different lines of
policy were used to address the lingering 'Indian question' (van Cott 1994),
indigenous groups were generally viewed as 'backward', as an obstacle to development and as people who had to be modernized and assimilated into the
wider society and market. In the 1950s and 1960s, earlier nationalist policies
for *mestizaje* were updated and included in the political agendas of some
governments that were influenced by ideological trends of the day. While
they offered different explanations to account for the Indian problem, liberals
and Marxists shared a disdain for ethnic and cultural politics and an interest
in nurturing a homogeneous vision of the nation (Stavenhagen 2002).

For many indigenous and peasant communities, the moves in thinking and
policy during the 1990s were extremely important in encouraging renewed
reflection in relation to the possibilities of enabling an interest in expressing self-determination and renewed control over their ancestral territories.
Various marginalized sectors of Latin American society now found room to
advocate and push for a pluralist, ethnically heterogeneous state 'based on
tolerance, respect for difference and intercultural dialogue' (Sieder 2002: 5).

With the end of the Cold War, political expressions and movements for
indigenous identity found new roots in the ideological vacuum left behind

by the perceived fall of communist and socialist alternatives. In the 1990s, these movements would grow in line with expanded formal support and financing for rights-based development and participatory governance strategies. New indigenous political organizations, such as the Katarista movement mentioned above, grew and gained increasing influence in national political discourse and direction. In Guatemala, the signing of the Peace Accords in 1996 formally provided Mayan activists – who had been the targets of both the state and left-wing guerrilla forces during the 35-year long conflict – with a new dawn in terms of political formation and interaction with the state. Provisions within the Peace Accords made explicit the basis of the legal entitlements of the Guatemalan indigenous majority and its right not only to make claims upon the state, but also to participate in decision-making regarding both local and national development. This was further backed up by financial support from countries such as Norway in the form of financing for the training of indigenous leadership and participatory development projects. In Colombia, the reform of the national constitution in 1991 not only recognized indigenous rights through the ratification of ILO 169 but also stipulated that indigenous peoples in the country would secure clear mechanisms of political participation in the operation of the state and the governance of their territories. It did so by creating a series of senatorial posts for indigenous representatives (up to five) and by emphasizing that municipal councils were opened for indigenous participation and leadership, or that governing bodies within indigenous territories could be legally established according to their own organizational principles.

With these changes, there was a growing expectation amongst indigenous communities and political movements that they could regain control of land, resources and identity through the political spaces generated by new participatory mechanisms of states and international actors. However, this was not really the case. Instead, research (including my own) revealed that indigenous and peasant communities in Bolivia and other Latin American countries encountered a series of contradictions in which, on the one hand, they were encouraged to assume governance responsibilities and participate in financial and development planning, and, on the other hand, they were told that many of their aspirations simply did not fit within the prescribed format and directions of participatory and decentralized governance mechanisms (McNeish 2001, 2002). Indeed, despite their invitation into the performance of decentralized governance, this did not extend to decision-making and questions of ownership surrounding a now booming industry of natural resource extraction.

As Engle in *The Elusive Promise of Indigenous Development: Rights, Culture and Strategy* (2010) makes clear, the emergence of the conceptualization of indigenous rights as cultural rights in the 1990s displaced or deferred many of the economic and political issues that initially motivated much indigenous advocacy. By asserting static, essentialized notions of indigenous culture that matched prevailing ideas of rights-based development and cultural liberty, indigenous rights advocates have often made concessions that excluded many claimants, forced others into norms of cultural cohesion and further curtailed efforts to claim indigenous economic, political and territorial autonomy. Indigenous communities were granted new possibilities for rights and territory, but these had to fit the prescribed logics of state and international institutions. In this way, it has been argued (Hale 2004) governments and international institutions used cultural rights to divide and domesticate indigenous movements. As expressed by Hale (2004: 17), the idea of *indio permitido* used by indigenous political actors in both Bolivia and Guatemala at this time emphasized the ways in which neoliberalism, as a cultural project, contributes to the rising prominence of indigenous voices at the same time as it creates limits to their transformative aspirations. Indigenous communities are recognized as citizens with acceptable political agency as long as they do not question or threaten the integrity of the existing regime of productive relations, especially in the sectors most closely connected to the global markets (McNeish 2008: 34).

Multicultural reforms then produced novel spaces for conquering rights, stimulating the development of new skills that often give indigenous struggles a sophisticated allure. However, as Hale (2002) argues, we must become aware that a menace resides in the accompanying, unspoken parameters of these spaces: the reforms have predetermined limits; benefits to a few indigenous actors are predicated on the exclusion of the rest; and certain rights are to be enjoyed on the implicit condition that others will not be raised. Neoliberal multiculturalism structures the spaces to be occupied by the cultural rights activists. It also defines the language of contention (Joseph and Nugent 1994), deciding which rights are legitimate, what forms of political action are appropriate and even arbitrating basic questions about the meaning of being indigenous. We see here then the formation of a setting in the 1990s in which at first glance, the conditions are set to enable Latin American and indigenous and peasant communities in Bolivia, Guatemala and Colombia to make concrete gains in asserting new expressions of sovereignty. However, upon closer inspection, it is visible as a setting in which innovations in governmentality mislead and contradict indigenous sovereign claims.

The Early 2000s to the Present

The contradiction between a new discourse and set of policy experiments, and the realities of an expanding extractive economy and sustained social and economic boundaries did not go unnoticed by local populations in Latin

America. Indeed, as the gap between political rhetoric and political and economic realities became painfully clear, the frustration generated would provide the impetus for new expressions of protest and confrontation focused on environmental resources (the social and environmental impacts of extraction, consultation and the terms of their management and the distribution of their financial benefits). This was made dramatically clear in the case of the 'water and gas wars' in Bolivia in 2002–5. These were years in which I visited the country sporadically, but also published several articles considering the background to these conflicts (McNeish 2005, 2006). Countrywide protests opposing government decisions on the management and sale of water services and gas resources generated sufficient instability to topple the Sanchez de Lozada administration.

In 1999, the Bolivian government granted a multinational consortium (Aguas de Tunari) headed by the US-owned Bechtel Corporation a forty-year concession lease to manage the water supply of the city of Cochabamba, the country's third-largest city, in return for its commitment to modernize and expand the existing system (Assies 2003). Although the local population was already paying for water services, the local government and consortium failed to recognize both the history of impoverishment in many neighbourhoods and prevailing ideas of water as a public good. The introduction of a three-fold increase in local water prices resulted in a massive public outcry that became formalized in a social movement, the Cochabamba Coordinadora. The Coordinadora organized an open rebellion against what it stated was an effort to 'lease the rain'.

Barricades were erected throughout the city and roadblocks were established along the route of Bolivia's main east–west highway that cuts the city in two. In response to the growing militancy of the protests in Cochabamba, the government declared a state of emergency and sent in the police and the army to remove the barricades and roadblocks. A lack of sufficient control of these forces led to the use of live fire against protesters and several deaths. An army sniper was filmed shooting a student dead. Fearing for their safety, the leaders of the Coordinadora left the city, but also inspired the protest to spread to other parts of the country. With the country effectively closed down as a result of protests, the Bolivian government rescinded its contract with Bechtel in April 2000 and offered some of the protest leaders a place on the board of a new publicly owned water company in Cochabamba (SEMAPA). However, the anger with the Bolivian government and its decisions on resource governance did not end there.

Aguas de Tunari pursued international arbitration regarding its contract with the Bolivian government, resulting in a settlement in 2006. The water war also became the inspiration for a further wave of protests focused on the Bolivian production of natural gas. On 19 September 2003, the National

Coordinadora (Coordination) for the Defence of Gas mobilized 30,000 people in Cochabamba and 50,000 in La Paz to demonstrate against the project to export gas through a pipeline connected to a Chilean port (McNeish 2008). The following day, six Aymara villagers, including an eight-year-old girl, were killed in a confrontation in the town of Warisata after government forces used planes and helicopters to circumvent the road blockades and evacuate several hundred tourists who had been stranded for five days in Sorata. In response to the killings, Bolivia's Trade Union Confederation (COB) called for a general strike that paralysed the country, insisting that the strike would continue until the government backed down on its decision. Poorly armed Aymara community militias drove the army and the police out of Warisata and the towns of Sorata and Achacachi. Eugenio Rojas, coordinator of the regional strike committee, and Felipe Quispe, leader of the highland Aymara Indigenous Movement Pachakuti party, announced that if the government refused to negotiate in Warisata, the insurgent Aymara communities would surround La Paz and cut it off from the rest of the country (McNeish 2008).

As the protests continued, residents of El Alto, a sprawling indigenous city of 750,000 people on the periphery of La Paz, joined the mobilization, blocking key access routes to the capital and causing severe fuel and food shortages (McNeish 2008). The El Alto protesters linked their local grievances over the higher prices of water introduced by Aguas de Illimani to the demands of the National Coordinadora for the Defense of Gas. In Cochabamba, Santa Cruz and Oruro, further demonstrations were staged raising issues relating to regional investment and autonomy. Teachers, university students, public service workers, market traders and transport workers also joined the protests, adding their complaints about wages and the cost of services to the general demands of the National Coordinadora. Shouting 'Lozada assassin, the people do not want you, carajo!', the protesters demanded the resignation of the President and his ministers. On 13 October 2004, the government suspended the gas project. However, as a result of the universal repudiation of the 'excessive force' used against the protesters and the withdrawal of Vice-President Carlos Mesa's support, the ruling coalition was fatally weakened. As a result, President Sanchez de Lozada was forced to resign.

Carlos Mesa assumed the presidency, declaring his commitment to the proposal of convening a new Constituent Assembly. Over the next few months, however, his indecision encouraged renewed protests (McNeish 2008). Finally, on 2 June 2005, the President announced that he was willing to hold elections for the Assembly and address the issue of regional autonomy in a referendum. But the announcement came too late. Because of the government's previous reluctance to address these issues, the leaders of the different opposition movements refused to end their protests and Carlos

Mesa was forced to resign. This was the background of Evo Morales's success-ful bid for the presidency on an electoral platform that emphasized social and political inclusiveness.

The scale and impact of the Bolivian water and gas wars are without doubt unusual if not exceptional in the history of socioenvironmental conflicts in Latin America. However, it is worth considering whether despite exceptional features, there are otherwise common foundations and dynamics that match other occurrences of socioenvironmental protest and militancy in the region. Leading on from the international economic and political changes described above, instances of socioenvironmental conflict have become a growing fea-ture of rural areas in many Latin American countries since the late 1990s. Indeed, these conflicts have so evidently become a part of the political pro-cess and a theme of national and subnational debates (at the departmental or municipal level) that they have become a growing focus of media coverage, international donors and NGOs, academic writing and large-scale research projects. One of the most significant efforts to try and chart the occurrence of socioenvironmental conflicts (conflicts focused on the politics and manage-ment of nature and environmental resources) is that represented by the work of the Environmental Justice Atlas (EJA) and its multiple partners in Latin America.[3]

In 1996, Martinez-Alier and Martin O'Conner coined the term 'Ecologi-cal Distribution Conflicts' (EDCs) to refer to social conflicts they observed that had emerged as a result of the unfair access to natural resources and the unjust burden of pollution. They observed that environmental benefits and costs were generated in a way that caused conflict ('Ecological Distribution Conflicts' 2016). The globalizing scale of the contemporary capitalist global economy means we are seeing more instances of resource extraction conflicts in poor or indigenous communities being brought into the frontline of con-tests about the values of environmental resources and services. Drawing on wider efforts to establish the field of environmental justice, Martinez-Alier (2013) acknowledged that given the unequal distribution of social and envi-ronmental impacts on lower-income and marginalized-income communities, the resulting conflicts could be seen to form part of the wider expression of an 'environmentalism of the poor'. Such movements have a double face: they can be interpreted as classical land conflicts, but they also have an ecological content (Martinez-Alier 2013: 239).

With funding from the EU, Martinez-Alier established a large-scale re-search initiative to study the spatial spread of socioenvironmental through the formation of an electronic atlas of 'environmental justice'. The EJA has since its formal establishment in 2011 generated a series of living thematic and regional maps that pinpoint the distribution and type of ecological conflicts around the world. In the work of the EJA, socioenvironmental conflicts are identified as mobilizations by social movements against particular economic activities, in which concerns about current or future negative environmental impacts are an important part of the grievances (Muradian, Walter and Martinez-Alier 2012: 564). At other times, the agents of violent conflicts are not those directly damaged in their livelihood by resource extraction, but armed groups aiming to gain access to natural resources, such as a rebel group fighting to control a diamond mine. These conflicts by social groups become visible through legal cases, campaigning, demonstrations or direct (even violent) confrontations. Although the map, given the need for constant updating, misses some conflicts and central qualitative details in some cases, it nonetheless represents an extraordinary and unparalleled large-scale effort to evidence and observe socioenvironmental conflicts around the world. In these maps, Latin America is not only a region where ecological conflicts are observed to have spread; the maps emphasize that Latin American countries, and the Andean region in particular, represent territories where these conflicts are deeply concentrated.

According to Martinez-Alier et al. (2010), the rising number of socioenvironmental conflict at the global level can be attributed to a changing global *social metabolism*. By social metabolism, Martinez-Alier and colleagues refer to the manner in which human societies organize their growing exchanges of energy and materials with the environment (Fischer-Kowalski 1997; Martinez-Alier 2009). The concept of social metabolism (Fischer-Kowalski and Haberl 2007) refers to the physical throughput of the economic system in terms of the energy and materials associated with economic activities, either as direct or indirect inputs or wastes. The social metabolism perspective then refers not only to extractive industries (mining for metals and building materials or extraction of fossil fuels, but also to biomass extraction conflicts (resulting from tree plantations, agrofuels and other export crops, deforestation and mangrove destruction and fisheries). In these processes, biomass is being extracted in nonsustainable ways (Martinez-Alier et al. 2010: 153).

Muradian, Walter and Martinez-Alier (2012: 559) suggest that combining the social metabolism perspective with that of political ecology makes it possible to establish links between the use of material and energy by some social actors and the environmental impacts experienced by others. Indeed, these links can be seen to exist between geographically distant locations. It can also provide an explanation of the resistance to these effects, which may take the form of socioenvironmental conflicts. These conflicts might take place all along the different nodes of commodity chains, from extraction to final disposal, and by a single social group or a coalition of them, through social alliances and networks at different scales. They observe that: 'When we consider, for instance, communities in Peru affected by new mines, or mangroves (and human livelihoods) sacrificed in tropical coastal areas for the rising production of shrimps for exports, global interdependencies between resource use patterns in some world regions and socio-economic dynamics in the places of extraction become apparent' (Muradian, Walter and Martinez-Alier 2012: 599). They suggest a series of dynamics with global impact as part of the pattern of recent socioenvironmental conflicts, i.e. emerging economies and their material and energy requirements, the rise of Brazil, India and China as economic poles and new centres of the global economy, the impact of rising energy prices on food prices and conditions of scarcity, and the new conditions of bundling aid, financial flows, labour mobilization, investments and infrastructure projects together in bilateral agreements.

The links that are highlighted by Martinez-Alier between an expanding social metabolism, political ecological impacts and the growth in the occurrence of socioenvironmental conflicts are extremely important. Indeed, by focusing on threatened livelihoods, a basis for conflict analysis is established that contrasts with the literature tackling the relationship between natural resources and the incidence of civil wars and other armed conflicts, particularly in Africa (Collier and Hoeffler 2005; Collier 2011). Contrary to rebels aiming to reap the rents from the extraction of natural resources, in a considerable proportion of socioenvironmental conflicts, social movements actually resist the expansion of the extraction frontiers, often as a strategy to defend a particular rural livelihood (Muradian, Walter and Martinez-Alier 2012: 564). As indicated at the Introduction to this volume, this basis for conflict analysis is more in line with my own view and an expanding alternative consensus that emphasizes a proactive interrelationship between localized social responses and sovereign claims with global economic pressures and changing international policy trends. In these processes, social movements and protest communities use a language of contestation either with explicit reference to environmental claims, appealing to the dependency of local livelihoods on the threatened resources, or making use of religious/worldview concerns for defending natural ecosystems or the right to a clean environment (Muradian, Walter and Martinez-Alier 2012: 564). Regularly, social groups also protest against decision-making procedures that exclude or minimize their claims and concerns. Furthermore, social movements involved in these kinds of conflicts are typically organized in networks and coalitions across several scales (Muradian, Walter and Martinez-Alier 2012: 564).

Whilst accepting and incorporating the importance of the global observations of Martinez-Alier and his colleagues at the EJA, the generalized level of analysis passes over some features at a regional and a local level that are also causes of the growing incidence of socioenvironmental conflict in the context of Latin America. The extractives boom that started in Latin America in the late 1990s would continue on until at least 2013/14. Fed by the activity and possibilities of a new source of public funding, significant political changes would also occur in parallel with the expanding extractive frontier. In the early 2000s, a number of countries in Latin America experienced a political shift to the left. The so-called 'pink wave' (i.e. not entirely red as they did not carry out state expropriation of private assets) peaked in 2010, when Peru was added to a list of countries including Argentina, Bolivia, Brazil, Chile, Ecuador, Honduras, Nicaragua, Paraguay, Uruguay and Venezuela. In many of these contexts, political agendas claimed that public money generated by the nationalization of import industries and heightened taxation of extractive industries would be redirected through heightened levels of economic redistribution and social and economic development.

In some contexts, such as Bolivia, new left administrations were the outcome of protracted struggles against neoliberalism and the perceived injustices of governmental policies that favoured international corporate interests over those of the needs and interests of the local population. These policies, such as those that sparked the Bolivian Water and Gas Wars, were seen as particularly unfair, given the high prices of primary commodities[4] in the international markets and the previous promises of participation and inclusion made by neoliberal governments. New left governments promised to redress these imbalances through the introduction of welfare policies that would instead 'sow the oil' in a manner favourable to endogenous democratic development. For example, in Venezuela, the Chavez government made a great show of using nationalized oil revenues to expand and invest in new health, social, economic and cultural programmes in poor urban and rural areas (Strønen 2017). In Brazil, the Lula government expanded welfare spending through the establishment of a conditional cash transfer programme (Bolsa Familiar) aimed at reducing poverty and inequality (Hall 2008). In Bolivia, the Morales government used funds generated by a new hydrocarbons tax to form the basis of programmes aimed at the provision of basic pensions, improved national literacy and conditional cash transfers to mothers and schoolchildren (Kaup 2010).

The alternative platforms of these governments – termed by some as neo-extractivism (Gudynas 2009, 2010; Acosta 2013; Veltamayer and Petras 2014) – purported to transcend traditional growth-centric economic models and break imperialist dependency by offering radical alternatives to the way in which socioeconomic development discourses are constructed. In contrast to conventional extractivism, characterized by the limited role of the state and subordinated to the interests of transnational corporations, under the framework of neo-extractivism, the state is able here to take on a more interventionist and regulatory role, introducing a new socio-political dimension into the practice of extractivism (Raftopolous 2017: 392). In the case of Ecuador and Bolivia, this new positioning of their extractive economies was further supported by constitutional and legal changes that recognize indigenous cosmological ideas expressing the need to live in harmony with mother earth, or *pachamama*, as the basis for the formal protection of the rights of nature.[5]

On the face of it, these new policy experiments represented an effort to revise the region's history of extraction and capitalist accumulation, and provide an alternative to the concurrent doubling down on neoliberalism in neighbouring countries (Chile, Colombia, Guatemala and Mexico). However, beyond the official discourse and launch of formal plans, there was little practical evidence of a genuine shift. Acosta (2013: 72), drawing on Gudynas (2009, 2010), argues that although South America's progressive governments are 'creating a new type of extractivism, both in terms of some of its components and in the combination of old and new attributes', there are no substantive changes in the current structure of accumulation. Neo-extractivism keeps involvement in the international market in a subordinate position that serves the globalization of transnational capitalism. It not only maintains but also increases the fragmentation of territories, with relegated areas and extractive enclaves linked to global markets. The social and environmental impacts of the extractive industries remain unaltered and in some cases have even got worse. Indeed, beyond the ownership of the resources, the rules and operations of productive processes that focus on competitiveness, efficiency, maximizing profits and externalizing impacts are the same as before (Acosta 2013: 72).

Humphreys Bebbington (2012) also comments that 'the troubling face of this policy convergence has been the predisposition toward authoritarian imposition of the model combining occasional use of force with efforts to delegitimize those who question extraction'. It has been argued (Bebbington 2009, 2011) that the progressive governments of Bolivia and Ecuador are just as likely as that of Peru to tell activists and indigenous groups to get out of the way of national priorities, just as likely to allow extractive industry into fragile and protected ecologies, and just as determined to convince indigenous peoples that the extractive industry is good for them but without fulfilling their rights. This policy disposition has led to a plethora of social conflicts that are not just manifestations of struggles over human rights, forced displacement, citizenship and control over political economic processes and natural resources.

In this light, the Bolivian TIPNIS conflict, which was mentioned in the previous chapter, and a series of other socioenvironmental conflicts are in reality all of a similar ilk and explanation, despite the claimed ideologies of different governments. Here a long list of *cause célèbre* cases can be linked together, e.g. the Bagua confrontation, the Chevron legal case in Ecuador, the Belo Monte protests in Brazil, protests against mining in Tambo Grande, Las Bambas and Cajamarca in Peru, and protests in opposition to mining and hydroelectric dams in Guatemala, and mining and oil extraction in Colombia. Veltmeyer and Petras (2014: 28) argue that the social and political struggles surrounding extractivism throughout Latin American have given rise to a new class struggle predominately in rural areas. This has created a new proletariat composed of waged workers and miners, indigenous communities, peasant farmer communities and semi-proletarianized rural landless workers who form the backbone of the forces of resistance against the 'workings of capitalism and imperialism in the economic interests of the dominant class'.

The responses of governments on the right and left of the political spectrum to local efforts at protest and contestation have also, despite political claims of contrasting ideologies and practices, been strikingly similar. Governments on both the left and right of the political spectrum have denounced protesters involved in anti-extractivist campaigns as standing in the way of development, modernity and the common good (Humphreys Bebbington 2012). For example:

> Extractivism is not a destiny but may be the point of departure to conquer it. Certainly, it can be found condensed in all of the world's territorial divisions – much of it colonial. And to break with this colonial subordination is not enough to fill the mouth with insults against extractivism, to stop producing and sink the population into further misery, to return to rights without modification and partial satisfaction of the basic needs of the population. This is precisely the trap of inflexible critique in favour of opposing extractivism. (Alvaro Garcia Linera, Vice-President of the Plurinational State of Bolivia 2012: 106–7)

> We are committed to maintaining, if not increasing levels of production. We are aware of a series of problems that you are facing, and we are considering how we can resolve these together . . . Yes there are social protests, there is a form of fundamentalist environmentalism. We see this not only in Colombia, but also throughout the world. NGOs are moving from climate change and a defence of human rights to attack all entities that supposedly place the environment in risk. Unfortunately, as a result of lies the oil industry is the first on the list . . . So, we have to consider how do we confront these new problems . . . we have to be creative and innovative . . . For example, I spoke with President Correa of Ecuador regarding the consultations and he told me 'I have a difficult population in the sense that 50% of the population are indigenous and very opposed to oil production . . . but I say the following that has been very effective, very practical, go to the communities before drilling and ask what your needs are, what do you want, and make an agreement with them . . . here is your road, here is your hospital. Say that this is possible if we can drill here'. This changes the mentality away from being aggressive, to make them complicit. This is what President Correa told me and I think

it very important . . . This is one example of how we can respond to these kinds of problems . . . You said that peace is essential for the oil industry, and the oil industry is essential for peace. This is correct. (Juan Manuel Santos, Colombian President, 26 September 2016, Second International Conference of the Colombian Association of Oil Producers)

Responses to rising levels of socio-environmental protest have also sadly not only been rhetorical in form. In this process, commitments to the recognition of rights and the use of available mechanisms of consultation and dialogue have been put to one side. Throughout the region of Latin America, governments on the left and right of the political spectrum have attempted to suppress protest through the use of increasingly militarized policing. On multiple occasions, police heavily equipped with riot gear, and occasionally military units, have attempted not only to control peaceful demonstrations but also to disperse them by force. This has resulted in heightening levels of violence, such as those seen in the TIPNIS conflict, and even more serious results in terms of the loss of life in multiple other confrontations across the region between protesters and security forces.

Although there remains some debate on the seriousness of a recent economic downturn in the commodity markets, it now appears that the supercycle of high commodity prices, which kickstarted many of the political and economic shifts discussed above, has significantly slowed down. Although Latin American economies weathered the 2008 global economic crisis pretty well, between 2010 and 2013, there was a steady decrease in foreign investment and global demand for its primary commodities, including those resulting from extraction.[6] Some analysts observe that a slowdown in the formation of international value chains and reduced liberalization due to an increase in protectionism in the region has had an impact on levels of trade. A number of analysts also suggest that a slowdown in global demand for primary commodities is a direct result of an economic slowdown in China (Porter 2014; Werner 2015). Commodity prices are seen by analysts to have fallen in two phases. Producers of metals (such as copper and iron ore, for which China had become a dominant source of demand) and agricultural goods have seen their export prices decline since 2011 (Werner 2015). Oil prices, in contrast, held firm, sustaining historically high levels until June 2014. Since then, the price of oil has suffered a sharp decline, which intensified in the last quarter of 2014 and early 2015.

It is important to recognize that whilst a downturn has occurred in Latin American commodity markets in recent years, this does not mean that governments in the region are exploring avenues to reduce their economic reliance on extractive industries. Indeed, throughout the region, there has been clear political hope that the economic downturn would end and, with it, profits from extraction would increase. Although the financial institutions ('Outlook for Latin America and the Caribbean: New Challenges to Growth' 2020) would continue to depict a slowdown, this political optimism meant that expansion continued in the extractive sector. In line with this, socioenvironmental conflicts have continued to spread to new areas as new projects and extractive blocks are granted licences. Indeed, politicians in the region are making new commitments to this effect. In the 2018 Colombian presidential campaign, all of the candidates on the political right (Vargas, Duque and Pinzón) guaranteed that should they be elected, they would take steps to significantly expand the mining sector and allow for the new establishment of unconventional oil exploration in the form of fracking. In 2018, the Colombian High Court suspended the previous rule introduced in 2008 to regulate fracking, citing concerns over its effect on the environment and human health. Since then, its legal status has been in limbo, with President Duque and government ministries continuing to push for an opening of this sector ('Colombia: To Frack or Not to Frack?' 2019).

Conclusions

Although they are distinct arenas of interaction with the state, smuggling and protest can be seen above as being both means to test the terms and legitimacy of the state and as spaces where alternative sovereignties are proposed and defended. The importance of territory and resources, or rather radically different perspectives on the value of land and energetic resources, is visibly important in both of these dynamics. Crucially, they are also suggestive of the contrasting strategies and ideas of different local indigenous and peasant communities. Communities' relationships to territory and resources visibly become the basis of contrasting interactions with the state and relationships to the capitalist market.

At first glance, smuggling can appear to be an effort to escape the supervision and control of the state, to directly circumvent national law and state attempts at economic control and taxation. It is also a response to the result of extended histories of economic marginalization and state neglect of peripheral areas or particular ethnic and social groups. As such, contexts of smuggling might be seen to mirror Scott's (2010) description of the peripheral 'shatter zones' of Southeast Asia, where large numbers of people were driven to seek refuge in out-of-the-way places and adopt unruly practices in an effort to avoid the violent expansion of nation-states. Smuggling could in this way be one more expression of the 'art of not being governed' by local peoples in marginal areas. However, such an interpretation would not be correct.

As revealed above, upon closer analysis, it becomes evident that whilst smugglers are antagonistic towards the state and are fully aware of the illegality of their actions, petty border trading and smuggling are not conscious acts that deny the existence of the state; rather, they are ways in which communities in border areas, and communities linked through trading with border areas, come to terms with the state and the inconsistencies of national economies. Indeed, the practice of smuggling is in large part formed in response to, not denial of, changing national security policy and action, albeit through the use of inconsistencies and weaknesses in these cases. These actions reveal the contrasting values that are applied to territory and resources, contrasting ideas and knowledge of landscape, and that contrasting claims are made regarding the significance and right to benefit from the key elements therein. Although fuel may not be a product of that immediate territory, there is a common perspective amongst traders and smugglers that it should belong as much to the people as it does to the state. The resource-nationalist rhetoric of sowing the 'people's oil, or people's mines' expressed by some governments (e.g. Bolivia and Venezuela) may have heightened an embedding of such logics at the local level. It was observed in the last chapter that local-level reactions to the removal of fuel subsidies were driven both by the perceived threat to local contraband incomes and the mismatch with a wider politics in which claims had been made by the government of spreading resource wealth.

Socio-environmental protests of course differ from smuggling, in that they are efforts to not only quietly live and express parallel citizenship, but also to directly confront the state regarding the terms and fairness set by its own terms of sovereignty. Through protest, local communities and social movements at the same time question the right of the state to decide over their lives and land, and attempt to stop or limit the worst consequences as they see it of state and corporate extractive development. As we have seen, these contexts of protest are fraught not only with legal actions and the policing of protests by state law-enforcement institutions, but direct and indirect forms of violence

Importantly, it is also clear from the text above that protesters' expressions of opposition to state sovereignty – the right to access territory and the right to the subsoil – together with their efforts to vocalize local understanding sovereignty have an accumulative impact on the formation of the state itself. State institutions shift to address both the direct 'threat' of militancy and, given the legacy and presence of both democratic institutions and liberal political ideology, to address the rights and territorial claims of local peoples. As I suggested in the introduction to this chapter, there is an important parallel here with the observations of other writers regarding 'everyday state-formation' (Scott 1987; Nugent 1993; Mallon 1995; Nugent 1997; Migdal and White 2013).

This perspective in no way denies the imbalance of power that exists between states, corporations and local communities. Nor does it ignore the contrasting levels of power between state sovereignty, corporate sovereignty and expressions of popular sovereignty. Mindful of romanticizing a 'history from below', there is recognition of the need to demonstrate an awareness of power relations that tie local society, and local expressions of sovereignty over land and resources, into larger contexts of region, country, international economy and geopolitics (Joseph and Nugent 1994: 11). This should be evident from the discussion of both smuggling and protest given above. These dynamics of popular sovereignty are also clearly replete with a series of internal contradictions, i.e. smuggling and the informal sector seek to constitute a more local and culturally appropriate understanding of the market, but still exploit formal capitalist logics and market mechanisms; protesters denounce the violence of the state's rule of law. They also employ violence and coercion in their own efforts to confront state authorities, and coerce support for mobilization and frequently rely on cultural mechanisms of discipline and sanction.

Sovereignty can then be seen at all levels to be as much a problem as it is a means to express identity and belonging. Accepting all of this, something can be gained analytically by a revisionist history in which the participation of people in state-formation 'is brought back in'. Standard histories of the region of Latin America and of key events that emphasize institutional histories and elite dynamics have ignored the state's contested relationship with popular culture. These histories have also ignored the broader socio-political dynamics in which states, elites and marginalized rural communities have been pushed into a relationship with each another. I suggest here that they have also ignored the way in which sovereignty, strongly fixed to claims to and understandings of territory and land, is also dynamically constituted through this interaction.

In conclusion, smuggling and protest are then two important dynamics through which state sovereignty is both tested and contested in contemporary Latin America. Territory and natural resources are evidently central elements of these political and cultural dynamics. I do not mean to suggest here that they are the only dynamics through which competing ideas of 're-source sovereignties' are generated. On their own, the last two chapters could be interpreted as suggestive of an argument that the agency of rural peasant and indigenous peoples not only takes expression through acts of avoidance and practices of resistance. This is only part of the story. Acts of avoidance and resistance are in reality only part of a repertoire of agency. In the next chapter, we move on to a consideration of the manner in which local peasant and indigenous communities act to directly engage with the state using its own logics and understanding of law and governance. In Colombia and

Guatemala, attempts are being made to 'counterwork' existing law and political institutions as a means to recover control over territory and resources, and to attempt to constitute other ways of understanding sovereignty.

Notes

1. For more on this, see Chapter 4.
2. Corporación Andina de Fomento.
3. See http://www.ejolt.org.
4. For example, the price of copper, below US$1 per pound in 2000–3, rose above $3 in 2006 and peaked at $4 in 2011 (Monaldi 2014).
5. The importance of the ideas of living-well (*buen vivir*) and their formal political adoption will be explored in detail chapter 5.
6. During the commodities boom of the late 1990s and early 2000s, the volume of exports grew at 6.3% per annum, but shortly after the world economic crisis in 2008 growth fell to a more meagre 2.2% (Monaldi 2014).

References

Acosta, Alberto. 2013. 'Extractivism and Neoextractivism: Two Sides of the Same Curse'. Amsterdam: Transnational Institute. Retrieved 6 November 2020 from https://www.tni.org/files/download/beyonddevelopment_extractivism.pdf.

Albó, Xavier. 1977. *La paradoja aymara: solidaridad y faccionalismo*. La Paz: CIPCA.

Appel, Hannah, Andrew Mason and Michael Watts. 2015. *Subterranean Estates: Life Worlds of Oil and Gas*. Ithaca: Cornell University Press.

Assies, Willem. 2003. 'David versus Goliath in Cochabamba: Water Rights, Neoliberalism and the Revival of Social Protest in Bolivia'. *Latin American Perspectives* 30(130): 14–36.

Auty, Richard. 1993. *Sustaining Development in Mineral Economies: The Resource Curse Thesis*. Milton Park: Routledge.

Bebbington, Anthony. 2009. 'Latin America: Contesting Extraction, Producing Geographies'. *Singapore Journal of Tropical Geography* 30(1): 7–12.

———. 2011. 'An Andean Avatar: Post-neoliberal and Neoliberal Strategies for Securing the Unobtainable'. *New Political Economy* 16: 131–45.

Berkus, Fikret, and Carl Folk. 1998. *Linking Social and Ecological Systems: Management Practices and Social Mechanisms for Building Resilience*. Cambridge: Cambridge University Press.

Biermann, Frank, and Philipp Pattberg. 2008. 'Global Environmental Governance: Taking Stock, Moving Forward'. *Annual Review of Environment and Resources* 33(1): 277–94.

'Bolivia's Second-Largest Lake Dries up and May Be Gone Forever, Lost to Climate Change'. 2016. *The Guardian/Associated Press*, 22 January. Retrieved 6 November 2020 from https://www.theguardian.com/world/2016/jan/22/bolivias-second-largest-lake-dries-up-and-may-be-gone-forever-lost-to-climate-change.

Bruns, Bettina, and Judith Miggelbrink (eds). 2012. *Subverting Borders: Doing Research on Smuggling and Small-Scale Trade*. VS Research.

Bury, Jeffrey, and Anthony Bebbington. 2013. *Subterranean Struggles: New Dynamics of Mining, Oil and Gas in Latin America*. Austin: University of Texas Press.

Chalfin, Brenda. 2006. 'Global Customs Regimes and the Traffic in Sovereignty: Enlarging the Anthropology of the State'. *Current Anthropology* 47(2): 243–76.

Collier, Paul. 2000. 'Doing Well Out of War: An Economic Perspective', in Mats Berdal and David Malone (eds), *Greed and Grievance: Economic Agendas in Civil Wars*. Boulder: Lynne Reiner.

———. 2011. *The Plundered Planet: Why We Must – and How We Can Manage – Nature for Global Prosperity*. Oxford: Oxford University Press.

Collier, Paul, and Anke Hoeffler. 2005. 'Resource Rents, Governance and Conflict'. *Journal of Conflict Resolution* 49(4): 625–33.

'Colombia: To Frack or Not to Frack?' 2019. *The Dialogue*, 27 September. Retrieved 6 November 2020 from https://www.thedialogue.org/blogs/2019/09/colombia-to-frack-or-not-to-frack.

De Castro, Fabio. 2012. 'Multi-scale Environmental Citizenship: Traditional Population and Protected Areas in Brazil', in Alex Latta and Hannah Wittman (eds), *Environmental Governance and Citizenship in Latin America: Natures, Subjects and Struggles*. New York: Berghahn Books.

'Ecological Distribution Conflicts'. 2016. *Ejolt*. Retrieved 6 November 2020 from http://www.ejolt.org/2016/04/ecological-distribution-conflicts.

Engle, Karen. 2010. *The Elusive Promise of Indigenous Development*. Durham, NC: Duke University Press.

Fabricant, Nicole, and Brett Gustafson. 2011. *Remapping Bolivia: Resources, Territory and Indigeneity in a Plurinational State*. Santa Fe: School for Advanced Research Press.

Fischer-Kowalski, Marina. 1997. 'Society's Metabolism: On the Childhood and Adolescence of a Rising Conceptual Star', in Michael Redclift (ed.), *The International Handbook of Environmental Sociology*. Cheltenham: Edward Elgar.

Fischer-Kowalski, Marina, and Helmut Haberl. 2007. *Socioecological Transitions and Global Change: Trajectories of Social Metabolism and Land Use*. Cheltenham: Edward Edgar.

Galemba, Rebecca. 2017. *Contraband Corridor: Making a Living at the Mexico-Guatemala Border*. Stanford: Stanford University Press.

Garcia Linera, Alvaro. 2012. *Poder hacendal-patrimonial y acumulación capitalista*. La Paz, Bolivia: Vicepresidencia del Estado.

Goldstein, Daniel. 2004. *The Spectacular City: Violence and Performance in Urban Bolivia*. Durham, NC: Duke University Press.

———. 2012. *Outlawed: Between Security and Rights in a Bolivian City*. Durham, NC: Duke University Press.

Gotkowitz, Laura. 2008. *A Revolution for Our Rights: Indigenous Struggles for Land and Justice in Bolivia 1880–1952*. Durham, NC: Duke University Press.

Gudynas, Eduardo. 2009. 'Diez tesis urgentes sobre el nuevo extractivismo', in Centro Andino de Acción Popular (CAAP) and Centro Latino Americano de Ecología Social (CLAES) (eds), *Extractivismo, política y sociedad*. Quito: CAAP/CLAES.

———. 2010. 'The New Extractivism of the 21st Century: Ten Urgent Theses about Extractivism in Relation to Current South American Progressivism'. Americas Program Report, 21 January. Retrieved 6 November 2020 from http://postdevelopment.net/wp-content/uploads/2016/10/NewExtractivism10ThesesGudynas10.pdf.

Gurney, Kyra. 2015. 'Crime without Punishment: Brazil's Massive Contraband Trade'. *Insight Crime*, 19 March. Retrieved 6 November 2020 from https://www.insightcrime.org/news/analysis/brazil-contraband-smuggling-trade-networks.

Haarstad, Haavard. 2012. *New Political Spaces in Latin American Natural Resource Governance*. New York and Shanghai: Palgrave Macmillan.

Hale, Charles. 2002. 'Does Multi-culturalism Menace? Governance, Cultural Rights and the Politics of Identity in Guatemala'. *Journal of Latin American Studies* 34: 484–524.

———. 2004. 'Rethinking Indigenous Politics in the Era of the "Indio Permitido"'. *NACLA Report on the Americas*, September/October.

Hall, Anthony. 2008. 'Brazil's Bolsa Familiar: A Double-Edged Sword'. *Development and Change* 39(5): 799–822.

Harris, Olivia. 2000. *To Make the Earth Bear Fruit: Ethnographic Essays on Fertility, Work and Gender in Highland Bolivia*. London: ILAS.

Hay, Mark. 2016. 'Inside the Illicit Venezuela-Colombia Gas Smuggling Trade'. *Vice.com*, 24 August. Retrieved 6 November 2020 from https://www.vice.com/en_us/article/vdqvb4/inside-the-illicit-venezuela-colombia-gas-smuggling-trade.

Hobsbawm, Eric. 1995. *The Age of Extremes: A History of the World 1914–1991*. New York: Pantheon.

'Human Development Report 2004: Cultural Liberty in Today's Diverse World'. 2004. New York: UNDP.

Humphreys, Macartan, Jeffrey Sachs and Joseph Stiglitz (eds). 2007. *Escaping the Resource Curse*. New York: Columbia University Press.

Humphreys Bebbington, Denise. 2012. 'Post What? Extractive Industries, Narratives of Development and Socio-environmental Disputes across the (Ostensibly Changing) Andean Region', in Haavard Haarstad (ed.), *New Political Spaces in Latin American Natural Resource Governance*. Camden: Palgrave Macmillan.

Joseph, Gilbert, and Daniel Nugent. 1994. *Everyday Forms of State Formation: Revolution and the Negotiation of Rule in Mexico*. Durham, NC: Duke University Press.

Kaplan, Ezra. 2016. 'Inside the Booming Smuggling Trade between Venezuela and Colombia'. *Time Magazine*, 31 March. Retrieved 6 November 2020 from https://time.com/4254619/inside-the-booming-smuggling-trade-between-venezuela-and-colombia.

Kaup, Brent. 2010. 'A Neoliberal Nationalization? The Constraints on Natural Gas Led Development in Bolivia'. *Latin American Perspectives* 37(3): 123–38.

Leverman, Diana, and Silvina Villas. 2006. 'Neoliberalism and the Environment in Latin America'. *Annual Review of Environment and Resources* 31: 317–63.

Lyon, Thomas. 2009. 'Environmental Governance: An Economic Perspective', in Magali Delmas and Oran Young (eds), *Governance for the Environment: New Perspectives*. Cambridge: Cambridge University Press.

Mallon, Florencia. 1995. *Peasant and Nation: The Making of Postcolonial Mexico and Peru*. Berkeley: University of California Press.

Martinez-Alier, Joan. 2009. 'Languages of Valuation'. *Economic & Political Weekly* 43(48): 28–32.

———. 2013. 'The Environmentalism of the Poor'. *Geoforum* 54: 239–41.

Martinez-Alier, Joan, Giorgio Kallis, Sandra Veuthey, Mariana Walter and Leah Temper. 2010. 'Social Metabolism, Ecological Distribution Conflicts, and Valuation Languages'. *Ecological Economics* 70(2): 153–58.

McKay, Bonnie, and James Acheson. 1990. *The Question of the Commons: The Culture and Ecology of Communal Resources*. Tucson: University of Arizona Press.

McNeish, John-Andrew, and Anna-Cecilie Arteaga Böhrt. 2012. 'An Accumulated Rage: Legal Pluralism and Gender Justice in Bolivia', in Rachel Sieder and John-Andrew McNeish (eds), *Gender Justice and Legal Pluralities: Latin American and African Perspectives*. Milton Park: Routledge.

McNeish, John-Andrew. 2001. 'Pueblo chico, infierno grande: Globalization and the Politics of Participation in Highland Bolivia'. Unpublished Ph.D. dissertation. London: University of London.

—. 2002. 'Globalization and the Reinvention of Andean Tradition' in *Latin American Peasants*. London: Frank Cass.

—. 2005. 'Luchando para la Prosperidad: Reflexiones sobre él crisis y la política de pobreza en Bolivia', in Sonia Alvarez (ed.), *Trabajo y la Producción de Pobreza*. Buenos Aires: Consejo Latinoamericano de Ciencias Sociales.

—. 2006. 'Stones on the Road: The Politics of Participation and the Generation of Crisis in Bolivia', in Sian Lazar and John-Andrew McNeish (eds), *Bulletin of Latin American Research* 25(2). Wiley Blackwell: Cambridge.

—. 2008. 'Beyond the Permitted Indian? Bolivia and Guatemala in the Age of Neoliberal Developmentalism'. *Latin American and Caribbean Ethnic Studies* 3(1): 33–59.

Migdal, Joel, and Adam White. 2013. *The Everyday Life of the State: A State-in-Society Approach*. Seattle: University of Washington Press.

Mitchell, Timothy. 2011. *Carbon Democracy: Political Power in the Age of Oil*. London: Verso.

Monaldi, Francisco. 2014. The Mining Boom in Latin America. *ReVista*. Baker Institute, Winter. Retrieved 6 November 2020 from https://www.bakerinstitute.org/media/files/Research/98baf386/The_Mining_Boom_in_Latin_America.pdf.

Muradian, Roldan, Mariana Walter and Joan Martinez-Alier. 2012. 'Hegemonic Transitions and Global Shifts in Social Metabolism: Implications for Resource-Rich Countries'. *Global Environmental Change* 22(2): 559–67.

Murra, John. 1967. 'La Visita de los Chapacu como fuente Etnológica', in John Murra (ed.), *Visita de la Provincia de León de Huánuco en 1562, Vol 2*. Huanuco: Universidad Nacional Hermilio Valdizán.

—. 1980. *The Economic Organization of the Inca State*. Greenwich, CT: JAI Press.

Nash, June. 1993. *We Eat the Mines and the Mines Eat Us*. New York: Columbia University Press.

Nugent, Daniel. 1993. *Spent Cartridges of Revolution: An Anthropological History of Namiquipa, Chihuahua*. Chicago: University of Chicago Press.

—. 1997. *Modernity at the Edge of Empire: State, Individual, and Nation in the Northern Peruvian Andes 1885–1935*. Stanford: Stanford University Press.

Ødegaard, Cecilie. 2015. 'Everything Moves with Fuel: Energy Politics and the Smuggling of Energy Resources', in John-Andrew McNeish, Axel Borchgrevink and Owen Logan (eds), *Contested Powers: The Politics of Energy and Development in Latin America*. London: Zed Books.

—. 2016. 'Border Multiplicities. at the Crossroads between Regulation and Improvisation in the Andes'. *Journal of Borderlands Studies* 31(1): 23–38.

Orlove, Benjamin. 1991. 'Mapping Reeds and Reading Maps: The Politics of Representation in Lake Titicaca, Peru'. *American Ethnologist* 18(1): 3–38.

'Outlook for Latin America and the Caribbean: New Challenges to Growth'. 2020. *International Monetary Fund*, 29 January. Retrieved 6 November 2020 from https://blogs.imf.org/2020/01/29/outlook-for-latin-america-and-the-caribbean-new-challenges-to-growth.

Porter, Eduardo. 2014. 'Slow Down in China Bruises Economy in Latin America'. *New York Times*, 16 December. Retrieved 6 November 2020 from https://www.nytimes.com/2014/12/17/business/international/slowdown-in-china-bruises-economy-in-latin-america.html.

Raftopolous, Malayna. 2017. 'Contemporary Debates on Social Environmental Conflicts, Extractivism and Human Rights in Latin America'. *International Journal of Human Rights* 21(4): 387–404.

Rao, Vijayendra, and Michael Walton. 2004. *Culture and Public Action*. Stanford. Stanford University Press.

Schmink, Marianne, and José Jouve-Martín. 2011. 'Contemporary Debates on Ecology, Society and Culture in Latin America'. *Latin American Research Review* 46: 3–10.

Scott, James. 1987. *Weapons of the Weak: Everyday Forms of Peasant Resistance*. London: Yale University Press.

———. 1998. *Seeing Like a State: How Certain Schemes to Improve the Human Condition Have Failed*. London: Yale University Press.

———. 2010. *The Art of Not Being Governed: An Anarchist History of Upland Southeast Asia*. London: Yale University Press.

Sieder, Rachel (ed.). 2002. *Multiculturalism in Latin America*. London: Palgrave Macmillan.

Sikkink, Karen. 1997. 'Reconceptualizing Sovereignty in the Americas: Historical Precursors and Current Practices'. *Houston Journal of International Law* 19(3): 705–29.

Stavenhagen, Rodolfo. 2002. 'Indigenous Peoples and the State in Latin America: An Ongoing Debate', in Rachel Sieder (ed.), *Multiculturalism in Latin America*. London: Palgrave Macmillan.

Stern, Steven. 1987. *Resistance, Rebellion and Consciousness in the Andean Peasant World, 18th to 20th Centuries*. Madison: University of Wisconsin Press.

Strønen, Iselin. 2017. *Grassroots Politics and Oil Culture in Venezuela: The Revolutionary Petro-State*. London: Palgrave Macmillan.

Szeman, Imre, and Dominic Boyer. 2017. *Energy Humanities: An Anthology*. Baltimore: Johns Hopkins University Press.

Taussig, Michael. 1991. 'Tactility and Distraction'. *Cultural Anthropology* 6(2): 147–53.

———. 2010. *The Devil and Commodity Fetishism in South America*. Chapel Hill: University of North Carolina Press.

Thompson, Sinclair. 2003. *We Alone Will Rule: Native Andean Politics in the Age of Insurgency*. Madison: University of Wisconsin Press.

Thorp, Rosemary, Corinne Caumartin and George Grey Molina. 2006. 'Inequality, Ethnicity, Political Mobilization and Political Violence in Latin America: The Cases of Bolivia, Guatemala and Peru'. *Bulletin of Latin American Research* 25(5): 453–80.

Tsing, Anne. 2004. *Friction: An Ethnography of Global Connection*. Princeton: Princeton University Press.

Van Cott, Donna (ed.). 1994. *Indigenous Peoples and Democracy in Latin America*. New York: St Martin's Press.

Veltamayer, Henry, and James Petras. 2014. *The New Extractivism: A Post-neoliberal Development Model or Imperialism of the 21st Century*. London: Zed Books.

Werner, Alejandro. 2015. 'The Latin American Growth Slowdown'. *Americas Quarterly*, 7 May. Retrieved 6 November 2020 from https://www.americasquarterly.org/fulltextarticle/the-latin-american-growth-slowdown.

Figure 3.1 Section of a mural in Bogota depicting the relationship between mining and conflict in Colombia. Mural by Grupo Animal. © John-Andrew McNeish

Chapter 3

CONTESTING EXTRACTION AND SOVEREIGNTY IN COLOMBIA AND GUATEMALA

'Yes, we could do it', 'For the defence of our sovereignty', 'Anglo-Gold Ashanti out!', chanted a jubilant crowd. On 26 March 2017, the citizens of the rural community of Cajamarca in the Colombian Department of Tolima organized a popular referendum (*consulta popular*). The referendum was held to help democratically decide on whether proposals for gold mining should proceed. In response to the question[1] posed in the referendum, there was a clear response: 98% of voters (36.6% of the municipal population) rejected proposals for mining, with only seventy-six people voting in favour. With the look of both joy and disbelief, campaigners connected to the local Socio-environmental Youth Collective of Cajamarca (Cosajuca) and the regional Committee for the Defence of the Environment in Tolima relayed these figures to a waiting crowd gathered in the streets outside the municipal government building. In response to this news, tears ran, old and young clapped and danced in unison. Joyful chants reverberated in the narrow-cobbled street of a normally sleepy and quiet small town of approximately 20,000 people. Until now, Cajamarca had only one other major claim to fame – the main producer of the *arracacha* (an Andean root vegetable). In this moment they had won – and seemingly had won big.

The campaign against mining in Cajamarca had succeeded despite all of the odds stacked against them during the course of a decade of campaigning. The campaign had been through a lot. In rapid summary, this included the initial rejection by the town council of the proposal for a referendum, the claim by the regional Attorney General of the illegality of such a vote, the death of a supportive mayor, death threats and the possible assassination of a community leader by a paramilitary organization, police arrests, the efforts of the mining company AngloGold Ashanti to launch legal injunctions against the referendum and buy local favour through a series of local investments and payments, and the persisting formal support for the mining project by central government (see also McNeish 2017a, 2017b). In the weeks and months that would follow the referendum, local activists' surprise at victory would be echoed in a series of news articles in the national ('Cajamarca, el pueblo que prendío la mecha de las consultas populares' 2017) and international media ('Cajamarca, el pueblo de Colombia que le dijo no a la explotación minera' 2017).

Somewhat dumbfounded by the results of the election and the support granted to it by the National Constitutional Court (most importantly as a result of sentence T-445/16 that recognized the rights of local territorial institutions to decide on the prohibition of mining), a series of national media channels carried out special reports discussing the significance and legality of the vote. In a debate organized by national current affairs magazine *Semana*, Senator Navarro commented: 'Nobody can debate that this vote is going to change the life of the region'. The referendum was not made by the mayor, it was made by society' ('¿Cual es la aplicabilidad de la Consulta en Cajamarca?' 2018).

In April 2017, AngloGold Ashanti announced that it was suspending its activities in Cajamarca and the Department of Tolima, citing the negativity produced by the referendum as a principal reason for its decision ('Cajamarca definió su posición en la consulta minera: Anglogold' 2017). A multimillion-dollar investment and the prospectively largest gold mine in the Americas was not to be. Although the legality of the referendum continued to be debated, the referendum was recognized to not only have consequences for the proposed La Colosa mine project in Cajamarca, but to have set legal precedent and changed the political debate on mining and extractive politics throughout the country. By the end of the year, local anti-mining, oil and hydroelectric campaigns had registered formal applications to hold popular referenda in forty other municipalities across Colombia. Cajamarca and Tolima were also made reference points in campaigns against mining and extraction throughout Latin America.

The idea that sovereignty resides with the people is nothing new in Colombia, despite its difficult political history. The mechanism of popular referenda (*consultas populares*) has been part of Colombian law since the Constitutional Reforms of 1991. However, the Cajamarca vote was hailed as a sign by environmental activists, civil society leaders, indigenous organizations, lawyers, academics and politicians that a new era of popular sovereignty has finally arrived in Colombia. Indeed, so strong was the sense of this idea that as the national elections of 2017–18 began, representatives on the political left such as Gustavo Petro would make clear references to popular referenda (as exemplified in Tolima) as a positive example of community action he would encourage if elected. In clear contrast, but also in acknowledgement of the political and legal upset produced by the Cajamarca referendum, representatives of the right – including Ivan Duque, who would win the presidency in 2018 – suggested that constitutional reform was necessary to avoid the threat to business produced by these referenda and to 'limit the excessive abuse of citizens' participation' (¿Qué proponen los candidatos presidenciales sobre sector minero y participación popular?' 2018).

The Romance of Sovereignty

The Cajamarca vote changed the debate regarding popular sovereignty in Colombia and made significant practical advances in terms of the legal right of local communities to decide on their own development futures in the face of mining and other extractive or energy-related developments. These topics remain central to the domestic political debate even after the recent change in government ('Colombia: activistas denuncian impactos ambientales de multinacionales' 2018). The referendum was also recognized at the time as a rare win ('Cajamarca, el pueblo que prendío la mecha de las consultas populares' 2017) in a national and regional context that can otherwise be characterized by the largely unchecked expansion of projects for natural resource extraction, and a model for national development based on the sale of primary commodities and large-scale energy developments.

Importantly for this book, it is also an instance highlighting yet again the manner in which claims to resources mobilize contrasting expressions of sovereignty. Its positioning at the beginning of this chapter aims to further advance an exploration of the dynamics of resource sovereignty. Despite occurring in one particular location and at one moment in time, and its apparent flavour of resistance to the state and capitalism, the detailed history of this win suggests that questions need to be asked as to whether was so 'momentous'. By characterizing in more detail the backstory in the pages below, I do not mean to reduce the significance of this win, but to make it evident that complex forces and relationships spanning decades, and crisscrossing Latin America, have been at work to enable it to take place. In this chapter, a connection will be made between the events in Tolima and the earlier history of indigenous communities' use of referenda to confront the Marlin project in northern Guatemala. In approaching these forces and relationships and by digging deeper into these histories of contestation, it also becomes evident that whilst expressions of resource sovereignty – or resistance (Abu-Lughod

1990) – carry a romance, they are never quite so pure or clear-cut as they appeared at first glance. Nevertheless, this does not reduce their significance in helping to catalyse legal and political change.

In earlier chapters, I have demonstrated the manner in which popular sovereignty can be constituted in different ways. As we have seen, it can be constituted at different scales of protest and confrontation with the state, or through efforts to circumvent state authority over territory and resources. In this chapter, I mean to emphasize that whilst these are important dynamics that impact on ideas and practices of environmental governance, other expressions of popular sovereignty exist. In contrast to other global contexts in which indigenous and peasant peoples have learned the 'art of not being governed', popular sovereignty in Latin America and, in particular, focused expressions of resource sovereignty are not only expressed through confrontation or avoidance; instead, there are multiple examples, including the Tolima anti-mining campaign, in which claims to sovereignty over land and territory have necessitated a proactive engagement with state and private sector institutions. In Latin America, new political and legal spaces are not only granted to local communities, but are also actively shaped by community engagement with state entities.

Indigenous and peasant communities, together with representative social movements and civil society organizations, draw on existing legal and political institutions and mechanisms in their efforts to gain a formal response to sovereign claims. These engagements with government departments and legal institutions demand an effort by local communities to come to terms with the logics of the nation-state and national market economy. However, as I will show here, proactive engagement is not the same as full acquiescence with the terms and logics of state sovereignty and expectations of a capitalist market. Strategies of engagement with state legal and political institutions often take place concurrently with efforts to reaffirm distinct cultural and social identities, other meanings and values, and strategies of circumvention. Indeed, as should become evident as I detail the deep backstory to the Cajamarca vote, the articulations with state institutions often take the form of what might be called 'creative articulation' (Hale 2011).

Hale recognizes the curious paradox whereby the rise of neoliberalism in Latin America coincided with an opening for multiculturalism, cultural plurality and indigenous rights. He also importantly highlights the structural break that neoliberal governmentality makes with regard to regional political economy. The neoliberal state has divested itself of a mandate for territorial encompassment, opting instead for differentiated zones of governance fashioned according to entrepreneurial criteria (Hale 2011: 202). These developments, he suggests, are largely compatible with the partial recognition of indigenous and cultural rights and with a limited acceptance of territorial autonomy. In this context, claims for indigenous autonomy and land rights (epitomized in reference to an interview with a local informant as the 'para que', or rationale for indigenous politics) have become captured by broader efforts to regularize land tenure and to establish clear rules by which individuals and communities can turn their resources into commodities. He also recognizes that by devolving limited authority to far-flung places, political claims and participation are constrained, especially with regard to broader structures of political-economic inequity (Hale 2011: 195).

However, whilst recognizing the debilitating nature of neoliberal politics on struggles for autonomy and sovereignty, Hale warns of only seeing one side of this story. 'It is commonplace', he suggests, 'to portray neoliberal hegemony as suppressing anti-systemic critique and censuring radical alternatives' (Hale 2011: 189). The debilitating effect of this is to discourage awareness of the 'creative articulation' that persists between utopian sensibilities and the always compromised, always urgent struggles for relief from oppression and for modest wellbeing in the here and now (Hale 2011: 189). There needs, he further argues, to be a 'reminder of the material gains they [land rights movements] can achieve, of the substantive rights they can push the state to grant of the utopian promise that they keep alive' (2011: 197). Without such reminders, analyses of governmentality can all too easily slip into a scholarly conceit, the flip side of what Abu-Lughod (1990) rightly criticized as the 'romance of resistance' (2011: 197).

It is within this nuanced perspective on governmentality that recent popular claims for sovereignty, such as the case of Tolima, need to be placed. Indeed, in focusing in this chapter on one particular means to voice sovereignty and participate in governance (i.e. popular referenda), this need for nuance is of particular importance. Critical social theory recognizes that formal instruments of participation are often constitutive elements in regimes of domination (Cooke and Kothari 2001; McNeish 2001). The implicit intention and force behind state-led participation mechanisms are observed to craft 'rituals of verification', i.e. formalized acts involving the population in the confirmation of policy practice of the state and the state's powerful allies (Power 1999). Yet, whilst recognizing the importance of these insights, it is also important to observe the 'backflows' (Bruun Jensen and Winthereik 2012) that occur despite efforts to constitute governmentality (Burchell, Gordon and Miller 1991). People relate to 'technologies of invited participation' in pragmatic and strategic ways as means to access the recognition and material resources they otherwise cannot obtain. Participating in public hearings of an environmental impact assessment (EIA), claiming prior consultation, petitioning participatory environmental inspection and engaging in independent environmental monitoring cannot be understood on the basis of the norms of deliberation formulated in formal and legalistic discourse. Participation can also be part of the rationale of resistance, and frequently one that aims to repoliticize state–community interactions that bureaucratic procedure otherwise seeks to neutralize or simply 'render technical'. Although efforts at subaltern pushback may be frequently fragile and temporary (Sousa Santos and Rodriguez Gavarito 2005), studies of indigenous and peasant efforts to repoliticize the objectives and actions of governance nonetheless emphasize results in the generation of 'openings' (Murray Li 2007), i.e. ways in which expert knowledge and practice are challenged and contested by populations that are subject to development interventions. In this regard, a 'switch' (Murray Li 2007: 11) can occur. There are conditions under which expert or bureaucratic discourse become punctured by a challenge or rationale it cannot contain.

Indeed, this lack of containment has increased as the years have passed and the contradictions of neoliberal governance have become increasingly evident. The state remains an object of local politics – for financial resources, political legitimation and recognition – and sometimes physical security and protection. However, the ambiguities and violence of state practices have led indigenous, peasant and other marginalized populations in many specific sites in Latin America to organize and demand higher degrees of autonomy. Centralized forms of sovereignty appear increasingly fragmented as attempts are made by local communities to strengthen their own forms of law and security, and communal and supracommunal forms of governance (Sieder 2013).

In this chapter, I describe the dogged determination of indigenous and peasant communities in Guatemala and Colombia to respond to the threat of large-scale mining to both the land and community through legal and political means. Of central importance is an acknowledgement that whilst they do not start out as clearly stated campaigns for popular sovereignty, in the course of defining their social and cultural foundation and territorial extension, explicit use of the term sovereignty is activated – or re-activated – as contestation moves from the streets to political and legal process. Indeed, it is perhaps surprising to note that it is not the communities themselves that at first term their struggle in sovereign terms (see the discussion in Chapter 2, in which earlier political claims for self-determination were replaced by a language of rights and territory within the state).

New sovereign claims and histories are gradually born or formulated anew as communities and movements are forced by changing circumstances to negotiate and collide with the reductionist expectations of legal and political institutions. As such, these sovereign claims are reflections of identity and indigeneity that are not static, but are the result of local communities and individuals encounters with ever-new iterations of capitalism, state-building and dispossession. They are also generated as communities become frustrated with the gap between the rhetoric and reality of mechanisms such as prior consultation exercises (the focus of Chapter 5), and the discovery of other means to democratically express their needs and interests. Interestingly, they are also formed not only (as might be expected) by retrospection on distinct social and culture practices, customary law and settlement patterns, but through surprising alliances between historically distinct yet neighbouring communities and at times as pragmatic coalitions between otherwise clearly contrasting social groupings. Studies of environmental protest and campaigns have long acknowledged the manner in which these situations temporarily draw together people with different class backgrounds into a singular social movement (McNeish 2017a).

In the context of resource extraction in Latin America, the related contestation of impacts, benefits, rights and territorial control have led to more lasting claims to popular sovereignty. However, the formation of coalitions does not mean that new sovereign platforms are solid or without controversy. In line with new social movement theory, they are constantly at risk of internal fragmentation, infighting and the requirement of periodic crisis and reconstruction. Sovereignty does not avoid conflict or difference. There is a hybridity or a *ch'ixi* aesthetic and sensibility (Rivera Cusicanqui 2012) to claims of popular sovereignty in which difference is both productive and unresolved. Indeed, violence is an inevitable part of both their expression and external reaction.

It should already be evident that the violence surrounding sites of extractive development also forms an important element in catalysing the conditions for popular claims for sovereignty. As was emphasized at the start of this book, the violence surrounding extractive projects does not only come in the forms of clashes between environmental protesters and state forces, or the destruction caused by these projects on the natural environment. Other forms of direct violence are observed in connection to these projects, including the threats made against, attacks on and assassinations of community leaders and environmental defenders. As is made clear from the start in the accounts that follow, there has been a rising level of insecurity surrounding extractive projects and related infrastructure in what are otherwise considered post-conflict countries. In expressing their rights and sovereignty, communities and their members and leaders take enormous risks.

These direct forms of violence are also intimately connected to other more structured or institutional forms of violence and racism represented by legal and political institutions and practices. These are contexts not only defined by democratic fragility and a weak rule of law, but also where the practice and constitution of law and regulation can be complicit and supportive of illegal activities. As I aim to emphasize in this chapter, recognition of the gaps between state discourse on law and regulation and the reality in which there are clear signs of cooperation between economic elites, state institutions and illegal actors has added further to local claims that other claims to law and justice, and therefore of political sovereignty, may be justified. There is a gaping chasm between what exists on paper and what takes place in practice.

An Awkward Journey

'The mayor does not want to come out, he is scared to come out and talk to you.' This was the response we received when we knocked on the door of the mayor's house in Sipacapa, Guatemala in the autumn of 2006. Although my colleague and I could see the shadow and tousled black hair of a man behind the net curtains of a front window, we were being waved back down the small garden path and stairs by the voice and hand of a woman standing partly hidden in the crack of the front door of the house. This was a disappointing result given the difficult journey of two days (and requiring a 4x4) that we had taken from the capital city. The Municipality of Sipacapa lies in the Northern San Marcos Department of Guatemala close to the frontier with Mexico. On our drive to the Municipality, we not only crossed mountains and forded rivers, but also – to my uncomfortable surprise – we had driven through areas of poppy production controlled by the drug cartels.

We had travelled to the Municipality of Sipacapa to follow up on reports in the national media that the local community were in open confrontation with Glamis Gold – a North American mining company later bought by Goldcorp – that had opened operations of the first open-cast mine in the country in 2005 (the mine had been purchased in the late 1990s). I had decided to make the journey to Sipacapa as part of a postdoctoral research project in which I was studying the politics of poverty reduction in the country. This project was part of a larger project financed by the Norwegian Research Council under the title of 'Poverty Politics: Current approaches to its production and reduction' based at the Department of Social Anthropology of the University of Bergen (2004–7).[2] At that time, it occurred to me that something could be revealed regarding the politics of marginalization in the country by studying the flashpoints that had started to take place in connection with the development of large-scale mining. At the time, political discussion on the unequal impacts of mining on marginalized communities was starting to heat up as new political spaces opened up following the peace accords in 1996. However, it was not clear at that time just how extensive these debates and conflicts would become as the years passed and extraction projects spread in line with high commodity prices.

National media reports highlighted that protests connected to what would become known as the Marlin project had not only taken place in the immediate vicinity of the mine, but had dogged the mining companies' efforts to move equipment at several locations along a route from a port on the Southern Pacific coast to the mine in San Marcos. This had included protests in March 2006 that had turned into a violent confrontation between the local Mayan population and the national police at a major road junction near Sololá on the main road leading from the south to the north. The municipality of Sololá was the main site of my research at that time (see McNeish 2008). However, whilst the media was quick to reveal that the Marlin mine project had become part of a nationwide protest against mining, it had reported little on why reported efforts at prior consultation in the neighbouring communities of Sipacapa and San Miguel Ixtahuacán had ended acrimoniously.

My colleague (a researcher at the Faculty of Latin American Social Sciences – FLACSO, Guatemala) and I had then set out to find out more about the details of the prior consultation and the disagreements surrounding the mine project. We had contacted the mining company by mail, then Glamis Gold, and following some emailing back and forth had received a letter of invitation to come and visit the mine in person. The letter of invitation specified the time and date at which we were to report to the security guards at the main gate to the mine area, and that in the interests of personal security, we would be expected to wear work helmets and reflective jackets during the tour. Given that the granting of this kind of invitation to researchers was rare according to other colleagues, we anticipated that the hardest part of our research trip was over.

With the mine invitation in hand, we set about contacting people in the local municipality and local neighbourhood association with the hope of scheduling a series of interviews aimed at revealing local perspectives on the mine and prior consultation. This part of our preparations did not go as well as hoped. We managed to get hold of names and telephone numbers. We managed to call and explain our intentions, but whereas the people we talked to did not dismiss the possibility of an interview, they would not commit to a time and date when this could take place. We were told to travel to the Sipacapa, come to the municipal government and take it from there. This was not really what we wanted to do. People in rural areas were reported at the time to act aggressively against strangers arriving in their community. Indeed, the media carried stories in those months of lynching that had occurred in local communities when strangers arrived unannounced. However, we did not see a way around this. If we wanted to get closer, we would have to take this risk. So, a little awkwardly, this is what we agreed to do. We would travel and knock on doors when we got there.

The door of the mayor's house was not the first door we had knocked on when we arrived in Sipacapa. We had initially hoped to meet and interview the mayor within the buildings of the municipal government. We had stopped at these offices and had asked the secretary in attendance there if it was possible to talk with the mayor. She had asked us to wait. We waited for two hours before the secretary informed us that the mayor was no longer there. He had gone home. I still do not know why she then followed this by giving us his home address, but this is what she did and this is why we ended up on his doorstep. His refusal to meet with us seemed exaggerated at the time. We thought it odd, but we continued on back to the municipal government to see if someone else was willing to talk to us. We were told to wait, and again after a time were told politely that there was nobody present who was able to respond to our request for an interview on the topic of the mine and the recent consultation. Left without direction, my colleague and I sat outside for a while; we took several rounds walking the streets of the small town. In the middle of the day, we met very few people out in the street. We knocked on the doors of the local agricultural cooperative, the local school and local shops, but to no avail. Nobody we met was at all interested in even stopping and saying hello, let alone answering our questions. Nevertheless, we did manage to find a simple guesthouse and spend the night there.

Our appointment to visit the mine was the following morning. So, we arrived at the gate of the mine site at the specified time and checked in with the security officers. They read through the invitation letter we had been sent and checked our IDs. They asked about our purpose visiting the mine and joked that it was about time someone wrote something positive about the place. They then ushered us into a small room lined with mining helmets, reflex vests and rubber boots. We were asked to grab a set of these and to change. A short time afterwards, we were asked to get in a large SUV so that the tour of the mine site could start. I did not really know what to expect. I had visited several mines over the course of my earlier research in Bolivia, but this was the first time visiting an open cast mine. At that time, the activity of the mine was still relatively recent, but already it was clear that a massive area of the top of a hillside and its green vegetative cover had been scraped away. As we drove higher up the hillside, there were massive banks of gravel and stone that lined the edges of the road. I remember we stopped a couple of times so that we could get a vantage point over the massive area of the mine. However, the security guard guides did not want to stay too long at these locations. They were keen to show us the processing site where crushed ore was brought in by massive conveyor belts to be ground, mixed with water, lime and steel ball bearings. The resulting slurry of ground ore, water and a weak cyanide solution was then fed into large steel leaching tanks where the gold and silver are dissolved. Following this leaching process, the slurry passed through absorption tanks containing carbon granules that adsorbed the gold. The loaded carbon was then fed into an elution (or absorption) column where the bullion was washed off. In demonstrating this process, our guides were keen to stress that at every step of the process, care was taken to endure that no dangerous chemicals were allowed to escape into the local surroundings and that every effort was made to recycle the vast amount of water used. 'This is a closed system', we were told. 'Unlike other open cast mines, the Marlin Mine will cause no contamination to the local environment.' Significant effort was also made to show us their water treatment plant and the solidity of the embankments of the tailing ponds. In these ponds solids are allowed to settle before water is fed back to the processing plant or 'excess' water discharged into the local environment.

Ending our tour, we were asked to sign a guest book and were encouraged to write a few lines about our impression of the mine. My colleague and I signed our names; we had been impressed by the tour and corporate salesmanship, but felt unsure whether what we had seen was not just a piece of corporate theatre. Overwhelmed by the size and technicality of the mine, we did not know what to say. We headed back to the municipal government hoping to discuss our recent impressions with someone there. We were again asked to wait and again after some time were told that none of the municipal council was available that afternoon. Leaving the municipal buildings, we also discovered that the doors of the town were as equally shut to us as they had been the day before. Something was clearly not quite right in Sipacapa. It was clear that some kind of conflict had taken place, but the details had avoided us. Frustrated and a bit confused, there was only one course of action. We left Sipacapa and returned after yet another long and stressful drive to the capital Guatemala City. At that time, it felt that this had been an awkward and wasted journey.

Persistent Claims

On our return to Guatemala City, my colleague scheduled an interview with Magali Rey Rosa, a representative of the Guatemalan environmental NGO Madre Selva. Thankfully, this led to a breakthrough. The interview finally helped to clarify why we had encountered refusals and silence from local people in Sipacapa. Moreover, it made us realize that we had stumbled into a context of contestation that was much larger, more intense and more long-lasting that either of us had first suspected. Rey Rosa nodded and grimaced when we told her of the mayor's apparent fear and refusal to talk with us. She was surprised that we had attempted to carry our research in the area of the mine, but was not surprised that this had met with a wall of silence at the level of the community. Madre Selva had been actively involved in writing critical op-eds in the national media regarding the mine since the Berger administration had awarded Glamis Gold the concession in 2003. They reported on the evidence of the environmental and social damage that had been caused by Glamis Gold's San Martin mine in Honduras and warned that similar consequences would unfold in Guatemala (van de Sandt 2009). Madre Selva had also closely observed the establishment of the mine in Sipacapa and the neighbouring municipality of San Miguel Ixtahuacán. She recounted to us the fear and confusion in these two communities that had resulted from the process surrounding the establishment of the mine. This account is embellished here with the inclusion of details captured in academic and activist organization and media reports.

When the Marlin mine began operations, Montana – incorporated as a Guatemalan company – was a wholly owned subsidiary of Glamis Gold (the project would be later inherited by the Vancouver-based gold giant Goldcorp Inc. when the company merged with Glamis in 2006). At the time that it was awarded the concession, Glamis Gold looked to the Marlin project as a means to increase the 'low cost' production of gold. Study of the local geology promised a high yield of gold (2.3 million ounces) as well as silver (36 million ounces). The company estimated that it would be able to extract 217,000 ounces of gold and 3.5 million ounces of silver annually. The total sale value of exported minerals was estimated to be US$893 million (Witte 2005). The expectations of the profitability of the mine were significantly increased when Glamis Gold was granted a US$45 million-dollar loan from the International Finance Corporation (IFC). The IFC, which is part of the World Bank, provides loans to companies owned by the private sector for projects in developing countries as a means to encourage competitive markets whilst also improving the social wellbeing of people in these countries. Glamis had received the loan on the basis of the apparent effort it had made since 2002 to prepare the ground for the mine project. Glamis first began to meet with municipal officials in the San Miguel Ixtahuacán and Sipacapa areas in 2002. During its exploration activities, Glamis conducted thirty meetings in San Miguel Ixtahuacán and seventeen in Sipacapa between June and September 2003. According to Glamis, these meetings attempted to address environmental and other community concerns. To acquire the land for the Marlin project, Glamis has also made land purchases from individual landowners. Apparently, land was bought from 254 landowners and all transactions were witnessed by municipal staff members. At the time, Glamis said that no complaints had been raised regarding the sale of these lands and that all individual land transactions were conducted successfully. It reported that it paid Q4,000 per *cuerda* (US $4,567 per acre) to landowners for land that usually sells for Q350 to Q1,500 per 52 *cuerda*. It also emphasize that the average income in Guatemala is US$1,670 per year, making its land purchase offers a 'fortune' to landowners (Imai, Mehranvar and Sander 2007).

Yet, the claims made by the corporation that it had carefully responded to local environmental and other community concerns were, according to Madre Selva and the proximate communities, an empty bluff made to simply enable its loan application to the IFC. Countering the company's claims of a transparent approach, local people interviewed by Madre Selva and independent researchers suggested that Glamis Gold had not been honest when it arrived. Promises had been made regarding its intention to assist in the foundation of a wider set of productive activities, including orchid production (Bunch and Loarca 2013). The local subsidiary to Glamis (i.e. Montana) had organized a series of public events, but these took more of a form of information meetings than of consultations. One researcher reports, for example, a local inhabitant commented on these meetings: 'In none of these meetings did the company ask us if we agreed [to the mine]' – Mariana, a Maya-Mam Catholic sister in her late thirties, interview, July 2012 (MacLeod 2016). They also report on the failure of the company to recognize the particular conditions of consultation needed in a community that was largely indigenous.

A total of 98% of San Miguel's nearly 40,000 inhabitants are Maya-Mam and the majority live in rural areas. Most also speak Spanish, but some only speak Mam. A high percentage of the 14,000 inhabitants of the Municipality of Sipacapa are considered Sipakapense-Maya (a language group largely unique to the municipality). It is perhaps important to note here that Guatemala is one of two countries in Latin America where indigenous peoples constitute the majority of the overall population. While it is difficult to quantify the proportion of the indigenous population of any country, it is estimated that the indigenous population of Guatemala comprises roughly 55% of the total population (Holden and Jacobson 2008). Collectively, the indigenous are referred to as 'Mayans' and there are approximately 21 different ethnolinguistic groups, with Mam being the most prominent (Holden and Jacobson 2008). Historically (and still today), people of indigenous and mixed ancestry have been confronted with institutionalized racism, mostly due to Guatemala's demographic situation and highly unequal distribution of wealth. Government figures indicate that 80% of people with indigenous descent live in poverty, compared with 40% of the Ladino (*mestizo* or ethnically mixed) population.

No formal process of prior consultation had occurred in line with the requirements of free, prior and informed consent as stated by Article 6(2) of ILO 169, which was ratified by the Guatemalan government in 1996. The company claims to have widely distributed the EIA report in the area, including a version in the regional language of Mam. However, following a visit to the town in April 2005, researchers from the Food First International Action Network (FIAN) and the German Catholic Bishop's Organization for Development Cooperation (Misereor) reported that 'none of the regional groups in San Marcos or the NGOs working on the issue had a copy of this document, and residents stated that they never received this information in their native language (Castignino 2006). In an interview with the Peace Brigades, Mario Tema of the Association of Indigenous Nations of Sipacapa commented that whilst the mining company was not evicting peasants, but was buying their land instead, these purchases were far from transparent: 'Until the work began in January 2004, we were never informed about the intentions of the company to mine metals in the area' (Castignino 2006: 22). Mario Tema claimed that land was purchased without the company informing local people of the mineral resources beneath it.

Opposition in both San Miguel and Sipacapa grew as people became increasingly aware of both the true intentions of the company, as well as of the scale and impact of what was planned. The mine was to be located in an area covering approximately 5km^2, but this was located in a 1,000 km^2 parcel of land that was being actively prospected (a total of seventy-three exploratory holes were drilled in 2008). The mine consists of two open pits and one underground facility. Once made available, the EIA also made it clear to those who could access it that the Marlin project would require 250,000 litres of water per hour. According to Madre Selva, a typical family in the area consumes around 30 litres a day. It would therefore take a family twenty-two years to use the same amount of water as that used by the mining company in one day. In addition to its impact on the local water supply, which was essential for local agricultural production, concerns also started to be voiced regarding the possibilities of wider local environmental damage being caused by the mine. A poll released on 4 November 2004 in San Marcos showed that 95.5% of those surveyed were against the implementation of the mine project due to fears that the mining would damage the environment. Debates regarding national development elsewhere in the country contributed directly to these concerns.

Imai, Mehranvar and Sander (2007) write that residents in San Miguel and Sipacapa were concerned about the environmental impact of the mine, but they were also concerned about the possibility that mining would impact on the wider direction of development. In line with a growing anti-mining movement throughout the country, expressions were made in favour of alternative development proposals controlled by the community. On 6 November 2004, a meeting held in Sipacapa resulted in a declaration against the mine, at which it was stated, amongst other things: 'We publicly declare at the national and international level, that the granting of the license for open pit metal mining violates the collective rights of the indigenous peoples' (Imai, Mehranvar and Sander 2007). This differed entirely from the position of many politicians, civil society representatives and journalists who emphasized the benefits over the risks of strip mining.

Mining for the Nation

The Berger government argued that mining was an opportunity that Guatemala should take advantage of. It said that mining would ensure the wellbeing of the population in the area of the mining activities. 'Mines not only bring investment', said Carolina Roca, Vice-Minister of Energy and Mines, 'but also rural development and jobs.' The Berger government's promulgation of the mining industry coincided with an emphasis on neoliberal reform. New legislation and economic reforms guarantee access to territories and natural resources, but also grant tax exemptions and generous benefits that guarantee profits for transnational companies. The state has been won over by market forces, constraining itself in developing public services to better economic conditions (Yagenova, Donis and Castillo 2012). Neoliberal restructuring and the proliferation of free trade agreements have played a central role in creating new spaces of accumulation. Free trade agreements are strategies for gaining access to the economics of the Global South by codifying neoliberalism and investment rights of capital from developing nations (Gordon and Webber 2007). In Guatemala, the signing of the Dominican Republic–Central America Free Trade Agreement (CAFTA-DR) in 2004 represented such a strategy, signalling a new phase of capitalist accumulation by protecting investor rights. Mining companies could now sue the government for noncompliance with the Agreement. CAFTA-DR continued the neoliberal recipe of reducing the functions of the state and promoting increasing dependence on technology and imported food products (Gordon and Webber 2007).

Large-scale FDI has also played an important role in the neoliberal restructuring (Gordon and Webber 2007). National policies attempt to reposition their country as a more attractive target for mining investment activity by improving their risk/reward radio relative to other countries (Bridge 2004). With the signing of the peace accords in 1996 bringing an end to the civil war, the Guatemalan government wanted to attract FDI in all the sectors of the economy to rebuild a shattered economy.

Guatemala experienced civil war between 1960 and 1996. Democratic elections during the Guatemalan Revolution in 1944 and 1951 had brought popular leftist governments to power, but a US-backed coup d'état in 1954 installed the military regime of Carlos Castillo Armas, who was followed by a series of conservative military dictators (Grandin 2000). In the 1970s, continuing social discontent gave rise to insurgency among the large populations of indigenous people and peasants, who traditionally bore the brunt of unequal land tenure. During the 1980s, the Guatemalan military assumed almost absolute government power for five years; it had successfully infiltrated and eliminated enemies in every socio-political institution of the nation, including the political, social and intellectual classes (Grandin 2000). As well as fighting between government forces and rebel groups, the conflict included, much more significantly, a large-scale, coordinated campaign of one-sided violence by the Guatemalan state against the civilian population from the mid-1960s onwards. The Guatemalan state was the first in Latin America to engage in widespread use of forced disappearances against its opposition, with the number of disappearances estimated at between 40,000 and 50,000 from 1966 until the end of the war (Grandin 2000). In rural areas where the insurgency maintained its strongholds, the repression amounted to the wholesale slaughter of the peasantry and massacres of entire indigenous villages, first in the Departments of Izabal and Zacapa (1966–8) and later in the predominantly Mayan western highlands from 1978. Peace talks started between the government and the guerrilla forces in the late 1980s, but it was only as a result of considerable pressure from the international community, including the United States (the military regime's earlier ally), that talks would proceed to the signing of an accord in 1996 (Grandin 2000).

Mining was to serve as an engine of economic growth and development in the name of 'Public Need and Utility' in the post-conflict period, as stated in the Mining Law of 1997. To attract the interest of foreign capital, the new law sharply reduced state income from mining activity. The income tax rate was reduced from 53% to 31% and the royalty reduced from 6% to 1%, the lowest in the country's history. Moreover, only 0.5% of the royalties collected were earmarked to the communities hosting the mine, depriving impoverished communities of much-needed resources. There were also no guarantees that the revenue from the royalties would be spent in environmental protection and mitigation and/or for community development (Yagenova, Donis, and Castillo 2012). The law also simplified mine site access by the project proponent, abolishing all limits to foreign ownership of mines and granting all mining operations duty-free imports (cited in Holden and Jacobson 2008). This type of regulatory dispersion and disorder provided significant advantages to transnational mining companies in terms of accumulating capital in Guatemala (Yagenova, Donis and Castillo 2012).

Rejecting the Blessing

However, the government position that mining represented an opportunity to generate the necessary income after war was increasingly criticized by civil society organizations. Critical voices included prominent members of the Catholic Church in Guatemala such as Cardinal Rodolfo Quezada Toruño and Bishop Álvaro Ramazzini Imeri. In response to the growing critique from the Church, President Berger offered to explain the advantages of mining to church officials personally. He told the bishops that, after he explained the project to them, they would come away 'blessing anyone who carries out such projects' (Castignino 2006). He added that he considered the cardinal's view on mining to be old-fashioned and populist. The cardinal was quick to respond that making 'the best choice for the poor is not populism'. Echoing what was fast becoming a nationwide anti-mining lobby, the residents of San Marcos mobilized with support from the Bishop of San Marcos in February 2004 to demand that the permit for operating the Marline mine be revoked. Throughout 2004, environmentalist organizations including Madre Selva warned about how the communities would react if local concerns were not heard. They 'will not stand by watching passively as their water, quality of life and dignity are carried off'. In March 2004, the Ministry of Energy and Mines (MEM) carried out an information campaign on how 'to avoid problems with residents', targeting municipal governments in areas being explored for gold and silver.

In December 2004, machinery belonging to the Montana company arrived in the village of Los Encuentros in Sololá located at kilometre 127 on the Inter-American Highway on its way to the Marlin mine. Although initially sparked off by rumours that the machinery was intended for use in a new mine project in the local municipality, the protest quickly became termed in much larger national terms. The anger and numbers of protesters grew to the extent that a blockade was sustained for forty-two days. The blockade only ended on 11 January 2005, when more than 1,200 soldiers and 400 police agents began firing to disperse unarmed protesters. The security forces in this confrontation killed Rafil Castro Bocel, an indigenous farmer. Twenty other protesters were injured. Paralleling what had occurred at Los Encuentros, Bishop Ramazzini led a new 3,000-person protest against the Marlin mine in the departmental capital of San Marcos. This led to the establishment of the Western Front Against Mining, an organization aimed at representing the concerns of indigenous populations regarding metal mining. Afterwards, indigenous representatives, such as the Indigenous Mayor of Sololá, organized regional meetings, conferences and workshops with the goal, according to Carlos Guarquez, of 'reaffirming their rejection of mining' (Castignino 2006). Large events were organized, such as the First Regional Conference of Indigenous Authorities of the Western Highlands (30 March and 1 April 2005) and the Regional Mayan Legislative Meeting (9 August 2005). At these events, people overwhelmingly rejected metal mining and demanded respect for indigenous peoples via compliance with their land rights, as well as respect for their right to define their own path to development, as established in ILO 169.

The Marlin Referendum

Angered and politically fuelled by events occurring elsewhere in the country, the communities in the Municipality of Sipacapa decided to take their own action. The municipal council passed the first of three resolutions in January 2005 establishing a Consulta de Buena Fe (a popular referendum). The referendum would take place in Sipacapa and ten other communities within the municipality. Although the Berger government had supported popular referendums on other development issues, this was the first time that a popular referendum was to be used to test the popular will regarding territory and subsoil resources in Guatemala. It is worth noting that it was an Italian pastoral worker who suggested the use of a referendum for this purpose to local community leaders in Sipacapa (Øveraas 2013: 63). This was in light of the successful community consultation on a local gold mine in Tambo Grande in Peru in 2002 (van de Sandt 2009). Drawing on the reputation of this earlier example, the local referendum was intended to give 'the Indigenous authorities, the Indigenous Maya Sipakapanese population and the residents over 18 years old in the Municipality of Sipacapa to pronounce in favour or against the mining activity, exploration and exploitation of minerals in open pit mines' (Imai, Mehranvar and Sander 2007). It was also envisaged as a means of exercising their rights to prior consultation as indigenous communities, given that Guatemala was a signatory of ILO 169. Using existing municipal ordinances, a commission was formed by the local government to organize and publicize the event. With support from the Catholic Church and other civil society organizations, the community also arranged for seventy national and international observers to be present during and after the referendum. The presence of the observers was meant to both secure the objectivity of the vote and to provide some moral constraint on both state and corporate responses to the referendum.

On 8 June, ten days before the referendum, Glamis Gold issued a press release that characterized the event as sinister, secretive and intimidating. It claimed that it had received threats from the referendum organizers suggesting that they would shut off the water supply or burn crops if it attempted to oppose the referendum. Glamis Gold 'communicated its concerns' about the 'undemocratic and abusive process' suggesting that the referendum was 'patently corrupt'. Five days before the referendum, the company also requested a court injunction to stop the referendum from taking place. This was granted, despite the efforts by the municipality to appeal the decision. The Mayor of Sipacapa followed this by withdrawing his support for the referendum.

My colleague and I arrived in the community long after this decision (in the autumn of 2016), but the cause of the mayor's unwillingness to open his door to an interview had a lot to do with the unpopularity that this withdrawal generated at the local level. In addition, reports from the time suggested that the corporations had used illegal means to bully the supporters of the referendum. Bishop Alvaro Ramazzini, who led the march against the mine, had received death threats and had to be provided government protection. There were death threats against other anti-mine activists and a car belonging to one of the local leaders was set on fire. After members of Madre Selva received threats and attacks, the Inter-American Human Rights Commission ordered the government to provide them with police protection. Although there is no evidence of a direct connection, this situation of threats and violence should of course also be seen in the light of the persisting conditions of insecurity resulting from the armed conflict and the expanding operation at that time of illegal cartel operations in the region of San Marcos.

Despite the different forms of opposition encountered by the community leaders of Sipacapa, they were determined to continue with plans for the vote, and announcements were made on the radio. In response to the court decision, the municipal government of Sipacapa determined that the referendum was a 'sovereign decision of the will of the indigenous and non-indigenous population' (Imai, Mehranvar and Sander 2007). The attempt to issue an injunction was also not considered to be valid within local indigenous law. The referendum was finally scheduled for 18 June 2005. The referendum was held simultaneously at three sites within the town of Sipacapa and in ten rural communities in the region. Each community met at its local community hall, where benches or individual chairs were placed in rows facing the front stage. Each community hall was also connected to the local radio station, which covered the process live, ensuring a simultaneous vote. The question put out to the communities was: 'Are you in favour of mining on the territory of the Sipacapense people?' The people of Sipacapa overwhelmingly voted 'no' to the mine (Sieder 2007). In total, 2,426 people voted against mining, 35 people voted for mining, 8 ballots were illegible, 1 was blank and 32 abstained. Of the thirteen community assemblies, eleven rejected mining (the great majority unanimously), one supported it and another community abstained from voting. In total, 98.5% of the participating population rejected mining. A total of 2,502 people participated in the referendum (44.3% of the total voting population in the municipality). At a press conference, the Ombudsman's Office for Human Rights ratified the results as valid and said they should be respected (Imai, Mehranvar and Sander 2007: 159–61).

Following the June 2005 referendum, the population of Sipacapa carried our further political and legal actions that simultaneously attacked the company's actions in the municipality and strengthened local organizational cohesion. In the view of many in Sipacapa, the popular referendum had closed the discussion about mining and made their position clear. A new local organization, the Sipakapense Civic Committee (Comite Civico Sipak-apense (CCS)), was founded with the strategic goal of building alternative popular political power and defending collective rights and the resounding 'No to mining' gained in the referendum. The Committee would eventually participate in and win the municipal elections in 2007.

The Committee would also have to respond to Glamis Gold and the government's refusal to accept the results of the referendum as having any legal value. After the company and its workers were expelled from the centre of the municipality in mid-2007, the company opened information offices in five different communities, using these to intensify its offensive against the municipality. Although the local government has implemented some projects to benefit residents, the company offered cash to those who requested it for household or community microprojects. Through its NGO Fundación Sierra Madre and in collaboration with the US NGO Citizens Development Corps, the company funded school repairs and the hiring of teachers in local community schools. It also built a 24-hour medical clinic, purchased and equipped an ambulance and helicopter rescue service, and installed chlorina-tors in the water systems in both municipalities. According to their reports, they also trained midwives, provided vocational training in carpentry, sewing and cooking, renovated health care centres and established eighteen com-munal banks. The company has also amassed a group of local lobbyists, who received USD 1,000 monthly payments, travel costs (including fuel expenses) and vehicles for the purpose of going door to door to extol the benefits of mining and to persuade residents to sell their land. According to Glamis Gold, it only conducted exploration activities in communities where it received expressed support and consent. From the point of view of local indigenous law, this was seen as a clear violation of rights. According to local indigenous leaders, the referendum had not only made local opposition to the mine clear, but also that land should not be sold to the mine.

Contamination and Insecurity

While Sipacapa had decided to organize and reject the Marlin project, in the neighbouring municipality of San Miguel Ixtahuacán (where approximately 85% of the mine is located), people were confused and divided about the mine. Some saw it as an opportunity that would provide much-needed jobs, while others held the mining project in deep distrust (Macleod 2016: 90). Indeed, the actions taken by Sipacapa encouraged an increasing divide to develop in San Miguel. Reports from San Miguel at this time detailed seri-ous internal community conflicts and problems involving the presence of government security forces, assassinations, intimidation, threats, structural damage to homes and the legal persecution of those who have fought the company.

In 2005, the true environmental damage caused by the open cast mine had also started to become increasingly evident to residents in both Sipacapa and San Miguel. The first formal analysis of the environmental impact of the mine was contained in a report commissioned by the World Bank itself following a complaint made to the Bank in March 2005, i.e. before the referendum was held. The World Bank sent a representative of the Office of the Compliance Advisor to investigate the complaints. The Compliance Advisor produced two different reports (one in September 2005 and the other in May 2006). In the first of these reports, the Compliance Advisor noted that the initial EIA was incorrect in stating that there was no habitation downstream from the mine's Tailings Storage Facility. It also concluded that it was unclear how the IFC had determined the adequacy of the initial EIA (Imai, Mehranvar and Sander 2007). However, the Compliance Advisor concluded that there was no significant risk of water contamination to local communities near the mine. Furthermore, due to updated project design, there would be no experience of water shortage in the local district due to mine activities.

The conclusions of the first formal report (Moran 2004) contrasted significantly with an independent analysis of the company's EIA. In 2004, Madre Selva funded Robert Moran, a US based hydrologist, to carry out a review of the EIA and to travel to the local area in order to carry out further measurements. According to his technical analysis, the hydro geologist consulted by the Compliance Advisor for its assessment had never visited the mine site and had based his opinion on documents provided by Glamis Gold. Moran also concluded that the impact assessments in the Compliance Advisor's report were too simplistic and had failed to take into account many factors and long-term scenarios. He noted that the Marlin project is an area of frequent seismic activity. He criticized the company for studying only the short-term earthquake risk, having based his own conclusions on an analysis of the last nineteen years, a period of 'extremely destructive earthquakes in Guatemala'. The Chixoy-Polochic Fault on which the mine is located was the cause of the last major earthquake that occurred in Guatemala in 1976.

Moran, in line with the position of Madre Selva, was also concerned about the toxic rock that will remain at the site. The rock will be full of cyanate, for which potential environmental problems cannot be discarded, since cyanate is not 100% safe. It also has a capacity to convert into cyanide if it comes into contact with diesel or chlorine, contaminants that are regularly found at a mine site. According to Moran, the Marlin project had also not considered the natural toxicity of the piles of rock produced by the open cast mine. The rubble from the processed rock contains a high level of naturally occurring sulphur. Whilst not dangerous if it remains trapped in the rock, the sulphur remains suspended in the air when the rock is pulverized to extract gold. Rainwater coming into contact with the sulphur affects the surface and ground water as 'acid drainage'. In Moran's opinion, the probability of acid drainage in the Marlin mine was very high, given the seismic activity in the region and the natural toxicity of the rock extracted. Whilst the company had tested for Acid Rock Drainage ('ARD') over 20 weeks, Moran indicates in his report that industry commonly uses a longer measurement period (i.e. 40 weeks to a year) in order to properly predict the possible development of ARD.

Moran's report also considered the impact of the mine on the local water supply. Robert Moran expressed doubts about the viability of sharing water resources between the Marlin project and small farmers and residents of the area. Moran predicted competition between the company and the local population, which will become worse during the dry season.

In the second of the two formal reports, the Compliance Advisor concluded that '[t]he mine should declare a temporary, voluntary suspension of exploration activities in Sipacapa' because of the 'the risks of continuing with exploration activities in Sipacapa, particularly in the current climate of a tense calm'. By now, the Compliance Advisor (CAO 2015) was forced by circumstances to be critical about the lack of attention paid by Glamis Gold to security issues:

> The lack of a clear policy on human rights and the management of security forces is a significant oversight on the part of both the company and IFC to adequately safeguard against the potential for violence . . . Local people remain gravely concerned about security force issues, and the company to date does not have policies in place for management of security forces.

In response to these conclusions, Glamis Gold publicly took some steps to address the issue of security, including adopting the US–UK Voluntary Principles on Security and Human Rights in its operations. However, the intimidation and targeting of leaders continued.

Most of the land was purchased in San Miguel in September 2005. The government's Compliance Advisor reported that there were no complaints from people selling the land. Despite this formal conclusion, dozens of protesters blocked entrances into the mines for a week in January 2007, complaining about the land transactions (Imai, Mehranvar and Sander 2007). In March 2007, a group called the Communal Front of Resistance to Mining Exploitation located in San Miguel Ixtahuacán released a declaration stating that they had been pressured and intimidated into selling their land. They also complained of water wells drying up and the deaths of animals due to the contamination produced by tailings deposits. Residents of San Miguel who attempted to carry out protests and peaceful demonstrations against the mine experienced their actions being turned against them as the justification of criminal charges. On 2 May 2007, the Association for Integrated Development in San Miguel sent a letter to shareholders of Goldcorp revealing that the Guatemalan army had 'disappeared' two members of their community in the middle of the night and that there were arrest warrants out for fourteen others (Imai, Mehranvar and Sander 2007).

Concerns regarding both contamination and security would persist until the final closure of the mine in 2017. In 2008, a report produced by the Human Rights Office of the Archbishop of Guatemala highlighted allegations by local residents in both Sipacapa and San Miguel (Mayan Mam indigenous peoples) that the Marlin mine had caused negative effects on human health, broad environmental degradation and social unrest. Part of the evidence included in the report comprised photographs claiming that indigenous residents, especially young children and the elderly, residing near the Marlin mine suffered from skin rashes, hair loss, respiratory difficulties and other disorders, and that these were due to the mine's pollution (Spring and Guindon 2009). Following this report, a request was made by the Archbishop's office for an independent investigation of these claims by a multidisciplinary team of researchers from the NGO Physicians for Human Rights. Having conducted their research, this team of investigators published their results in the journal *Science of the Total Environment*. Their peer-reviewed paper corroborated claims that higher levels of mercury, copper, arsenic and zinc could be found in mine-adjacent rivers and that elevated levels of aluminium, manganese and cobalt were found in the blood of individuals residing near the mine (Basu et al. 2010).

A series of other studies conducted in the late 2000s also reported on a series of socioeconomic impacts, including worsening levels of security and violence. Although the Marlin mine increased the quality of life and income of a small number of families, the quality of jobs was recognized to be poor. Community members mostly received lower-paid jobs, whilst outside workers were hired to fill higher positions. Zarsky and Stanley (2011) reported that the number of jobs peaked with 870 local people during the construction phase, but this figure dropped dramatically once the mine became operational. Montana's employment of community members had also created social division and tensions within the community, given that mine wages were significantly higher than those gained from local subsistence farming. Tensions related to the income gap were also exacerbated by the introduction by foreign workers of new consumption patterns and problematic social behaviour (gun-carrying, prostitution, drinking and drug use; see van de Sandt 2009)

Competition for water access also became one of Marlin's social problems. Montana purchased a number of private water sources, such as streams and springs, to supply water to workers and mine-adjacent communities. This resulted in Montana maintaining the control of water and a rise in local water prices. Unrest and conflict grew between water clients and providers within and between neighbourhood communities (van der Sandt 2009: Øveraas 2013: 6).

Montana's response to accusations regarding contamination and economic insecurities was also observed to further intensify local tensions. Montana was seen to actively promote the division of communities as a tactic to undermine organized opposition (van der Sandt 2009). It exclusively focused on the positive aspects of the mine's presence and the work carried out by its own local development organization, Foundation Sierra Madres. It refused to discuss the results of independent water quality studies, calling into question the standards and technical expertise of the laboratories and experts involved. Montana was seen to purchase the support of the municipality of Sipacapa by offering a €100,000 gift, as well as the promise of jobs, development and small development projects. Montana's response to growing opposition was also observed to have a subversive side to it. The acquisition process was beset with allegations of illegality and intimidation. Local civil society organizations accused Montana of leading an aggressive, individual-oriented negotiation campaign that avoided traditional authorities and social structures. It was also accused of the intimidation of community leaders as well as smear campaigns and threats to anti-mining activists. The presence of a private contingent of armed security guards was also seen as a method of intimidating communities into ceasing their opposition (Holden and Jacobson 2008). Indeed, reports of the company's involvement in a series of killings, beatings, corruption and bribery was reported internationally. In *The Guardian* newspaper in the UK, an article revealed the grotesque nature of some of this violence by citing the following commentary of an informant who had lost her husband: 'They took him and poured gasoline all over him. Then they struck a match and lit him' ('Welcome to Guatemala: Gold Mine Protester Beaten and Burnt Alive' 2014).

A Lasting Legacy

In 2010, the sum of these horror stories and the heightening levels of both domestic and international activism surrounding them led the Inter-American Commission on Human Rights to pressure the Guatemalan government to suspend all activities relating to the concessions granted to Goldcorp and Montana, including the Marlin project. Initially the government ignored the Commission's request and the Commission itself backtracked on its suggested action. However, further pressure (resulting from a visit by

James Anaya, the UN Special Rapporteur on Indigenous Rights, to Guatemala the same year, the further organization of a series of twenty-three other popular referenda in communities in the region close to the mine and a class action lawsuit launched by eighteen Mayan communities that highlighted the failure of the company to sufficiently address legal requirements regarding prior consultation) built sufficient critical mass and legal trouble to sway the opinion of the state. Responding to this, the Alvaro Colón government of Guatemala announced its decision to start a process towards the closure of the mine.

It is evident from the account given up to this point that the campaign by the communities of Sipacapa and San Miguel against the Marlin mine was a process demanding year of persistence and risk-taking. It is also evident that it was a process demanding both militancy and pragmatic dialogue between local communities, civil society organizations and the state. Although not 'momentous', the campaign against the Marlin mine did leave a significant lasting legacy in terms of how local communities in the country and beyond confront proposals for large-scale mining. In particular, it inspired the formation of an anti-mining movement in the country and helped instruct other communities throughout the country on the relevance of popular referenda as a legal mechanism to demonstrate local opposition to other extractive and energy projects. The consultation in Sipacapa in 2005 marked the beginning of a new type of resistance, a new repertoire of 'constrained collective action' (Øveraas 2013), based on community consultation as a primary tactic (Bunch and Loarca 2013). By 2013, over sixty-five separate popular consultations had taken place in Guatemala. By 2015, this number had risen to seventy-two (Costanza 2015: 238). In all of the consultas the overwhelming majority voted 'No' when asked whether they wished to allow extractive projects on indigenous land. In these referenda, over one million people, both indigenous and non-indigenous, expressed their opposition to mining and hydroelectric dams in their territories.

The Guatemalan Constitutional Court has repeatedly deemed these consultations to be legally nonbinding. Although taking place in indigenous communities, they does not recognize the consultations as having any relevance as the expression of a right to veto in connection with the right to free, prior and informed consent as stipulated in ILO 169. Many lawyers view constitutional articles and international conventions as abstract statements of principle rather than judiciable rights, arguing that secondary legislation is required to make the principles binding law (Sieder 2007: 223). The nebulous wording of human rights accords also often hinders compliance; indeed, it allows for the legality of consultations to be interpreted according to politics. Laws dealing with mining projects are similarly controversial. Although legally municipal governments have 'autonomy' to govern, the nation state controls all subsoil natural resources. Overlapping legal regimes (local, national, international) such as those governing mining activities in Guatemala leave consultations open to ad hoc interpretations (Fulmer et al. 2008). The result is a legal vacuum and a political opportunity that indigenous activists attempt to exploit (Costanza 2015).

Although the *consulta* of 2005 in Sipakapa was denied legal legitimacy by the state and the mining company, it nonetheless set a rights-based example of resistance for indigenous communities in the Western Highlands of Guatemala (Costanza 2015). Whilst realistic about the bar to legality put in place by the government and the Constitutional Court, communities nonetheless recognize that popular consultations represent 'a way for indigenous peoples to have a voice in national economic development and a back door strategy for claiming the right to collectively control territory at a community, municipal and occasionally regional scale' (Costanza 2015: 271).

Most of these consultations are pre-emptive, reflecting a fear that the government is selling off the entire country including their livelihood, but also an awareness of 'a politics of time' (Kirsch 2014) as well as scale. Indigenous activists have learned a lesson from the extended time period in which the Marlin case and others like it played themselves out. To build coalitions on the ground, attract and enrol international allies, and experiment with different strategies in order to find out what works and what does not take time. In common with environmental movements elsewhere (Kirsch 2014), indigenous and environmental activists in Guatemala attempt to accelerate this process by moving resistance to an earlier moment in time, i.e. to address the problems caused by mining before they take place. In some places, indigenous peoples from bordering municipalities and similar ethnolinguistic groups (there are twenty-one Mayan language groups) have jointly asserted the pre-emptive claims for territorial control.

Learning from the Marlin case, many activists also see the consultations as part of a larger process of rescuing, revalorizing and even creating communities' organizational culture and ethnic identity. Consultation procedures are made to respect local decision-making customs and make them accessible and understandable by all. However, common to all these consultations is the self-directed nature of the consultations, i.e. they are led by indigenous peoples and communities themselves, not by the state. Supporting this interpretation of consultations, Juárez (2007: 86) reports the comments of a local leader: 'for the first time in the history of 500 years, our people met together, discussed, proposed, without any kind of intervention from outside; it was their own effort'. A common sentiment is that consultations disrupt a long history of socio-political exclusion and forced assimilation that has prevented these peoples from living lives they have reason to value. Of particular importance to this volume, communities also make their decisions regarding popular referenda as communities, in many cases rejecting the principle of individual sovereignty and the basis of the country's liberal democratic system. In many cases, the entire community is welcome to participate in the consultation, regardless of whether a person is registered to vote or has a national identification card (which many women and elders lack). Juárez reports these consultations as means by which the community and its leadership defy standard state understandings of citizenship. It is 'not as the Constitution tells us, that a certain age we are citizens, in our Mayan worldview we are citizens from the moment we are conceived by father and mother' (Juárez 2007: 86). In the course of participating in the referenda and their preceding campaigns, participants' conceptions of indigenous identity, rights and the state are transformed (Constanza 2015: 275). In other words, as new forms of citizenship are expressed (Rasch 2012), state sovereignty is contested and forced into tension with popular sovereignty.

Major opposition from the state and corporations of course place this expression of sovereignty under significant duress and risk. In early 2011, in order to prevent 'a situation of violence and confrontation for the future of this country', the Colom administration began a campaign to regulate the right to consultation via Presidential Decree (Costanza 2015: 276). Since the Guatemalan government has rarely supported indigenous rights and given that few countries have domestic legislation elaborating the right to consultation, this move suggests that the Colom administration viewed the consultations as an implicit demand for territorial autonomy and the consultation movement as a threat to the balance of political power in the country. Legally regulating the right to consultation could address both threats. This move prompted intense resistance from indigenous activists. Though many of them had previously pressed for regulation, they now felt excluded and manipulated (Constanza 2015). The absence of indigenous participation in writing the Regulation violated Article 6 of ILO C169, which requires that the government consult indigenous peoples on any legal initiative that may affect them. Consultation activists accused the government of 'institutionalizing indigenous protest' in a similar manner to the way in which the law limits how and when labour can strike. They worried that the Regulation would transfer the consultations from the realm of social protest to the realm of judicial procedure, awarding more power to the state and large corporations, and possibly making it easier to divide and manipulate indigenous communities.

Although a moratorium on hard rock mining was suggested in 2013 by the Pérez Molina government as a response to rising levels of instability and critique, this was not supported by the Guatemalan Congress. Not having been held in check, under the last two Guatemalan governments (the Pérez Molina and Jimmy Morales administrations), the number of extractive and large-scale energy projects in the country has expanded. With this expansion, there have been increasing levels of local socioenvironmental protest and legal action, and also violent reactions by the state and private actors to protests.

Multiple scholarly works deal with these cases of conflict in the mining and hydropower sectors (Hurtado and Lungo 2007; Fulmer et al. 2008; Holden and Jacobson 2008; Nolin and Stephens 2010; Urkidi and Walter 2011; Rasch 2012; Pedersen 2014; Aguilar-Støen and Hirsch 2015; Sieder 2017). The United Nations High Commissioner for Human Rights in Guatemala has expressed concern over conflicts associated with natural resources in the country, particularly those related to mining, hydropower, logging, palm-oil production and sugar-cane developments. In May 2018, a spokesman for the Commissioner issued a statement expressing concern for the 'deteriorating climate for the defence of human rights in Guatemala' (Vidal 2018). Acknowledging the existence of over fifty land conflicts in the country, the statement condemned the rising number of murders of land defenders in the country, including the leaders of indigenous communities, and asked for the government to promptly ensure that those responsible are held accountable.

Both domestic and international media coverage of the country have provided multiple further accounts of the violence and insecurity surrounding sites of resource extraction and hydropower development in the country ('Guatemala: Seven Human Rights Defenders Killed in Four Weeks' 2018; 'Indigenous Xinca March in Guatemala to Banish Canadian Mine' 2018; Vidal 2018). In these reports, there are indications of connections between the perpetrators of these acts of violence, economic elites and the companies behind each project (Aguilar-Støen 2015). *The Guardian* newspaper in the UK reported in August 2018 that since the start of the year, eighteen human and indigenous rights defenders had been targeted in this violence (Vidal 2018). Of these, thirteen were involved in land conflicts and nine were Codeca leaders, a growing organization of indigenous farmers. Amongst this litany of cases, a number of conflicts such as the case of the Cementos Progresos project and San Juan Sacatepéquez, the El Tambor Mine and La Puya, the Escobal Mine in the Department of Santa Rosa stand out because of their record of violent confrontations and killings. In each of these cases, local popular referenda did not in themselves bring an end to violence or the projects.

Despite the successes of official efforts in terms of controlling or suppressing consultations, and other more violent actions aimed at suppressing activism and protest, the legacy of indigenous and peasant activism has nonetheless been sustained. Indeed, at the national level, the consultation, protests and campaigning have helped indigenous activism to grow. Through the consultations, an increasing number of indigenous municipalities, communities and human rights organizations have united in an identity-framed movement to demand local control over land and natural resources. This is a significant development in Guatemala, given the ingrained ideological and spatial divisions among the indigenous population (Costanza 2015: 275). Moreover, despite the risks and setbacks, these actions have provoked a state and institutional response moving towards forms of desired action and governance, even if these are imperfect.[3] In 2011, the Constitutional Court of Guatemala partly supported the position of consultation activists, ruling that the actions of the Colón administration were unconstitutional because insufficient effort was made to consult with indigenous people while drafting regulations. Whilst the Court also ruled that the Municipal Code and Development Council Law, which indigenous activists use to justify their consultation procedures, was not a sufficient legal framework for carrying out consultations, it also ruled that Congress should draft legislation and make an honest effort to include indigenous voices in the process. More recently, in the cases of both the Tambor and Escobal mines, community organization and expressions of popular sovereignty, rather than just rising levels of unrest and violence, pushed the Guatemalan government to suspend the projects.

Colombian Activists Learn from Guatemala

The history of the Marlin referendum continues to influence ongoing efforts to confront extraction and large-scale developments in Guatemala. In this process, expressions of popular sovereignty and an effective anti-mining movement have both been crystalized through a history of significant adversity. It is also important to note that according to interview respondents in the Colombian anti-mining movement, the Marlin case directly formed part of a history – i.e. the use of popular referenda across Latin America – that guided their actions and outlook.

In her Ph.D. thesis, Marian Walter (2014) places Guatemala together with Colombia as part of a common *travel path* or *context of emergence* for a wave of anti-mining activism across Latin America that uses popular referenda. The first popular referendum in Colombia occurred in 2009 in response to the perceived threat of the arrival of Muriel Mining (owned by Rio Tinto and other companies) into the Antioquia and Chocó regions. Local indigenous and Afro-descendant communities started a search for information and contacted church organizations in the area. A support group was created, bringing information, documentaries and activists from other countries and communities to Carmen de Darién ('Colombia: No a la Minería en territorio indígena' 2009). Communities, inspired by the Sipacapa experience, promoted the organization an inter-ethnic consultation for the indigenous and Afro-descendant communities affected by the mining project, following their own procedures (i.e. the use of their own language, those that were registered as being older than fourteen years old). Human rights, indigenous, church and anti-mining organization representatives from Colombia, Paraguay, Honduras, Guatemala, Germany and Canada observed the process. The consultation was grounded in international and national indigenous consultation rights, including the Colombian Constitution's special consideration for indigenous consultation rights. The legality and legitimacy of the process was confirmed by an important verdict (T-769, 2009) of the Colombian Constitutional Court that led to the suspension of the project.

Other communities in Colombia would quickly pick up on this experience and its background history (McNeish 2017b). I conducted research focused on the popular consultations held in Tolima for the *Extracting Justice* project[4] between 2014 and 2017 (McNeish 2017a, 2017b). Responding to my question regarding the inspiration for their use of popular referenda in the La Colosa campaign, one of the leaders of the local anti-mining social movement in Tolima commented in an interview:

> We had to see what experiences function in other places and consider if they could be implemented in Colombia. It was on this basis that we started to look at the case of the consultation in Tambo Grande (Peru) that was successful in opposing another mine project. All the question of the Argentine resistance in the case of Esquel, where there was not only another consultation, but also the theme of 'social license' we thought of great importance . . . Also, the example of Sipacapa in Central America. All of these examples helped us to consider what would work, and what would not. (Interview with leader of the Comite Defensa del Medio Ambiente, Tolima, 22 September 2014)

From 2002 to 2012, sixty-eight community consultations/referenda on large-scale mining activities took place in Latin America (Peru, Guatemala, Argentina, Colombia and Ecuador) that aimed at challenging centralized decision-making procedures. Between 2012 and 2018, many others, including the popular consultations in Tolima, were added to this number. For the growing number of scholars studying these processes, consultations not only challenge hegemonic scales of governing mining activities but also reconstruct and put in practice an emerging scale of regulation and governance, i.e. one based on community participation and ownership or, in simple terms, sovereignty. Popular consultations are now occurring throughout the hemisphere and gaining attention as an alternative way for communities to register their concerns about extractive projects.

In common with Guatemala, the adoption of popular referenda (*consultas populares*) also reflects a growing call for and expression of popular sovereignty resulting from a history of parallel developments in neoliberal governance, expanding resource extraction, violence and judicialization. Indeed, whilst many of the contextual details differ between the two countries, there are a series of qualitative similarities. They both demonstrate the local impact of larger political economic dynamics and the interactions between vernacular responses to these wider pressures and influences by states and populations. As well as finding a new voice throughout Latin America and beyond, the expression of popular sovereignty reflects both the common challenge of 'transnational states' and contrasting histories of land ownership and state formation.

Land, War and Neoliberalism in Colombia

In contrast to Guatemala (and many other Latin American states), Colombia has no formal history of military dictatorship. Colombia's armed forces have never supplanted or even forced a power-sharing arrangement with the country' s traditional elite. With the exception of one short period (1953–58),[5] the Colombian economic elites have always wielded more political power than the generals. However, rather than being an expression of the strength of democracy in the country, the details of continued civilian government are instead a reflection of the historic capture and continued control of government and the state apparatus by the country's economic elites. The government and the military have faithfully co-implemented and enforced conservative economic elite interests. A military coup or power-sharing agreement has never been required because elites have managed to retain control over both the government and the military throughout its postcolonial history. Of course, this does not mean that there has been no challenge to elite control over the state or that political factionalism and ideological differences have not had an impact on history and governance. Nor does it mean that economic elites have remained entirely unchanged by the changing conditions of geopolitics and the international economy, or pressures from the wider population in the country. Indeed, whilst Colombian rural and urban elites are culturally conservative, they have periodically pressured state institutions to adjust to changing circumstances (Sankey 2018). This has in particular occurred with the reform and removal of laws seen to stand in the way of FDI or the establishment of private companies in Colombia, such as in the extractive and energy sectors.

Colombia is well known internationally for its history of armed conflict. This was a conflict sparked to a large degree by the extreme imbalance of land ownership in the country. Between 1823 and 1931, the Colombian state had offloaded vast chunks of land into private hands in order to pay off debts that it accrued in the course of the independence war ('Understanding the Causes of Colombia's Conflict: Land Ownership' 2018). As a result, the top 0.2%

of the population owned nearly 30% of all farmland in Colombia. Landless peasants in the country became locked into sharecropping contracts with wealthy landowners and the Catholic Church. In the 1930s, an effort was made to partially redistribute unused land by the Liberal Party. However, the pushback from the political and economic elites had reversed these efforts by 1948. The Conservatives' assassination of the Liberal presidential candidate in 1949 further provoked rioting in the capital city resulting in the death of 5,000 people. This was also the start of a period known in Colombian history as 'The Violence' (*la Violencia*), in which Liberals and Conservatives used paramilitary forces (that included the participation of the national police and military) to violently assume control over each other's property and rural landholdings. An amnesty was signed between the opposing forces in 1953, but by then between 200,000 and 300,000 people had been killed and millions of rural peasants and indigenous communities had been forced from their homes. Peace and democracy would return to Colombia in the late 1950s and early 1960s. However, without significant changes to the distribution of land and social structure, the threat of a return to violence would never remain far away.

In 1961, the short-lived military government of Gustavo Rojas introduced a law that was intended to become the 'true agrarian' reform in a bid to completely restructure land tenure. The government pledged to redistribute large, mainly unused plots of land to the country's poor farmers. But this attempt also failed. The 1972 Chicoral Pact squashed any chance of a 'true agrarian' change to land concentration. Counter-reform stemmed from the collective effort of cattle ranchers, the industrial bourgeoisie and even drug traffickers to neutralize land redistribution attempts and concentrate land ownership even further. In this context of extreme and growing land concentration. communist groups in the country – already the target of a US-backed counter-insurgency initiative – became enraged. In 1964, a new armed conflict emerged as some of the earlier community self-defence units of 'The Violence' morphed politically into left-wing oriented rural (the Revolutionary Armed Forces of Colombia-Peoples' Army (FARC-EP) and the National Liberation Army (ELN)) and urban (M19) guerrilla movements focused on delivering greater land equality through communism. This conflict would continue to rage in the country for over fifty years right up to the present day. In these years, approximately 220,000 people would be killed, 11,000 of them from land mines, and five to seven million people would be forcibly displaced from their homes and communities. Multiple large-scale human rights abuses would also be carried out by all armed actors in the conflict, but most notably by paramilitary organizations backed in successive waves of action by large-scale landowners in the 1980s and 1990s. The increasing fragility of the country due to the armed conflict and the significant growth of the drug trade from the 1970s onwards, and the increasing connections between the two as the guerrilla also became involved with the cartels, would also result in the US government's support for a significant increase in both direct military intervention and spending by the late 1990s ('Plan Colombia: A Retrospective' 2012).

In 2000 Plan Colombia (also mentioned in the Introduction), billed as a 'pro-democracy' aid package but resulting in a massive expansion and re-equipping of the Colombian armed forces, was introduced with the stated aim of ending drug trafficking in Colombia. In the wake of the experience of 9/11 in the US, the Colombian government of Alvaro Uribe was given greater latitude in its use of Plan Colombia funds. This enabled the rebranding of both cartels and guerrillas alike as terrorists. Although the Uribe administration made important gains in terms of improving national security and reducing the number of kidnappings (a strategy used by the guerrilla forces to add to their dwindling funds), the general human rights situation in the country worsened. By increasing the pressure to pursue violent actors – and particularly the FARC-EP – the Uribe administration created a security environment that was prone to new and disturbing abuses. A notorious example of this was the 'false positive' scandal between 2004 and 2008, which arose from a programme that rewarded military officers who captured or killed insurgents. According to the UN High Commissioner for Human Rights, security forces (mostly from the army) killed an estimated 3,000 innocent civilians whilst this programme was running (*Americas* Quarterly 2012). In these years, the forced conscription of Colombian adolescents by both the guerrilla and state forces also increased significantly.

Between 2012 and 2016, hopes for peace returned to Colombia in the form of talks between the Santos government and the FARC guerrilla. Whilst earlier efforts to establish a peace accord had floundered as a result of persisting insecurities and the assassinations of demobilized guerrilla members, supporters of the new peace talks hoped that political and economic conditions had changed sufficiently to allow an agreement to be reached. Whilst leaving in its wake a controversial history of human rights abuses, much of which resulted from the joint actions of security forces and paramilitary organizations, the expansion of military action under Plan Colombia succeeded in reducing the ranks of the FARC from 17,000 to an estimated 8,000 fighters by its conclusion in 2015 (Cosoy 2016). The peace talks conducted by the Colombian government with the FARC also appeared to be distinct from earlier efforts at brokering peace, in that they succeeded in drawing up a plan aimed at peace and reconciliation for all citizens affected by the armed conflict. Through a series of agreed ceasefires, the levels of violence in the country were reduced in the period of the talks to levels not seen in forty years (Dennis 2015). In the peace talks, agreement was reached on creating an amnesty for combatants, but a commitment was also made to prosecute the perpetrators of war crimes. An agreement was reached on rural reform aimed at returning stolen land to individuals and communities displaced by war. The FARC-EP made a clear commitment to not only disband but also to refrain from further involvement in the drugs trade (from which it had funded its armed struggle). Of vital importance to the sustainability of the peace accord, the Colombian state not only agreed to support the re-settlement of FARC-EP fighters back into civilian life, but also to provide security measures for their protection. In the early 1990s, efforts to demobilize the urban guerrilla organization M19 and to establish the Patriotic Union political party saw thousands of its members massacred by paramilitary groups, leading the FARC-EP to again intensify its military campaigns. These achievements in the talks were also formed in a different context from earlier peace initiatives. Taking place in Havana, the 2012–16 peace talks were hosted by the Cuban government, but also with the considerable support of the UN, Norway and Canada as international guarantors.

These conditions and agreements enabled a process that would lead to the signing of an eventual peace agreement between the Colombian government and the FARC-EP in November 2016. Recognized for his efforts in actively supporting the peace process and accord, President Juan Manuel Santos was awarded the Nobel Peace Prize in December of the same year. Encouraged by the success of the talks with the FARC, the ELN, the second-largest guerrilla movement in the country, would also enter into a round of peace talks with the Colombian government. With the FARC-EP peace deal in hand, it appeared to most observers that Colombia was reaching the conclusion of a long history of political and economic violence. However, such judgements proved to be premature.

Complications in terms of the ability of the peace accords to establish a new political atmosphere of peace were already evident in the run-up to its signing. When the contents of the draft peace accord were submitted to the public vote in a national referendum in October 2016, the results were not what the government, the FARC or the international community expected. Expecting overwhelming support, they had already organized a lavish launch for the accord at a ceremony attended by multiple international dignitaries in Cartagena in September 2016. According to the results of the referendum, 50.02% of the population opposed the draft accord. The Colombian government was then forced to reconsider and redraft the accords in response to this opposition. Media coverage attempting to explain the referendum's results highlighted the influence of the far-right Democratic Centre party and its efforts to tarnish the peace agreement in the run-up to the referendum (Idler 2016). It was broadly claimed that the Democratic Centre party had successfully convinced the majority Colombian public that the peace agreement would 'let the rebels get away with murder' ('Colombia Referendum: Voters Reject FARC Peace Deal' 2016). Under the agreement, special courts would have been created to try crimes during the conflict. Those who confessed to their crimes would be given more lenient sentences and would avoid serving time in conventional prisons. They would have also paid FARC rebels a monthly stipend and offered financial help to those interested in starting a business as part of a demobilization strategy. In its attempt to mollify opponents' claims that the peace deal would reward criminal behaviour, fifty major modifications were made to the redrafted peace accord, including a prohibition on foreign magistrates judging alleged crimes and a commitment from the rebels to forfeit assets in order to help compensate victims ('Colombia's Government Formally Ratifies Revised FARC Peace Deal' 2016). To further avoid public rancour, the newly drafted peace deal would be signed without a second referendum. This directly set in motion a process in which the FARC's 8,000 guerrillas were expected to concentrate in approximately twenty rural areas and turn over their weapons to the UN monitors.

The referendum heightened national and international awareness of the political and social divisions in Colombia regarding peace and its terms. Indeed, it clearly revealed that there were significant spatial and class differences in terms of voting patterns. In the referendum, Colombia was divided regionally, with most of the outlying rural provinces voting in favour of the agreement and those closer to the capital and in other urban centres voting against it. This spatial and social division would become evident again in the results of the national presidential elections in Colombia in 2018. In the final round of the national elections, it became clear that there was a significant match between the rural areas supporting the left-wing red-green coalition led by Gustavo Petro and Progress Movement Party, and the urban or central areas of the country represented by the right-wing candidate for the Democratic Centre party, Iván Duque. Indeed, it was also revealed how these patterns in the referendum and election also corresponded with maps produced by NGOs identifying areas that were particularly vulnerable in the post-conflict period ('Colombia Presidential Elections 2018: What Next for Peace?' 2018). Areas of high vulnerability had voted both for the peace accord in the referendum and for the left-wing coalition in the national elections.

Although it would be Iván Duque who would win the presidential election with 39.1% of the vote, the 25.1% (over 8 million votes) garnered by Petro, the left-green coalition candidate, would nonetheless be highly significant. Petro is the first left-wing candidate in Colombian history to receive such a large level of support and on that basis to enter the second round of the presidential elections. Support for Petro is also significant because of its indication of the growing democratic opposition in parts of Colombia to the government's commitments to a neoliberal and largely extractive economy. In his election commitments, Petro had made a clear alignment with the position of the Green Alliance promoting a politics founded on environmental democratization. Clear statements and signals to this effect were made throughout the campaign, including a set of Ten Commandments he had etched in marble. The commandments made it clear that the party opposed 'the politics of expropriation' represented by the right. It would also support different mechanisms to establish democratic decision-making regarding resources and the environment, and would set the country on a course of transition towards the use of renewable energy resources. Many voting for Petro had voiced concern that Duque's support for established development policy, which aimed at making Colombia more attractive to multinational corporations through a reduction in business taxes, would further exacerbate high levels of inequality and tension in rural mineral-rich regions of the country.

This politics of transition contrasted entirely with the position represented by the political right. Commenting on the country's neoliberal extractive development model, Ivan Duque highlighted during the election campaign that oil production had fallen from one million barrels a day to 800,000 barrels. In response to these changing circumstances, he suggested that Colombia did not need to transition away from fossil fuels, but rather should exhaust all possible options regarding conventional oil and mining production and then look to focus on fracking as an alternative.

The Energy-Mining Locomotive Steams On

Paralleling the trajectory of economic development in Guatemala described above, Colombia's conversion to a neoliberal mining country had important ramifications in terms of the further reconfiguration of class relations, governance and conditions of security.

Although Colombia's formal history of mining and resource extraction dates back to the colonial period, its centrality to the national economy was vastly increased following the boom in commodity prices in the early 2000s. Under President Uribe (2002–10), FDI in the mining sector was promoted through the further privatization of public resources, labour flexibilization, new labour laws (including the extension of the working day and flexible dismissal) and direct incentives for the extractive industry (Sankey 2018). The government's strengthening of its commitments to free trade also further encouraged the expansion of the extractive frontiers to cover over 40% of national territory by the end of the decade. As the peace talks progressed, the Santos government also reiterated its clear support for the mining and hydrocarbons sector, now as an essential future source of funding for peace and development. The goal laid out in Santos' *National Plan for Mining and*

Energy Policy was to turn Colombia into the most important mining country in Latin America by attracting FDI, particularly in oil, coal, gold and other minerals (UPME 2006). The Colombian government stated it was naïve to suggest, as the Green Alliance (which entered an alliance with Santos in the 2014 presidential elections), that the country's dedication to a model of development premised on the export of primary commodities should also be on the negotiating table. Promises were made in the peace process regarding the redistribution of land previously controlled by the guerrilla forces and the reskilling of the rural population. However, suggestions regarding a wider – sustainable – transformation of land titling and the market economy were blocked on the pretext that they were being unreasonable.

The influx of investment in the mining, energy and related infrastructure sectors in these years precipitated a land and resource grab driven by multinational corporations (Sankey 2018). Dispossession, political violence and corruption played a central role in facilitating this land grab. A UN investigation reported that 'a pattern of displacement has also appeared in relation to the exploration and exploitation of natural resources and the implementation of large-scale development projects, in some cases involving multinational corporations' ('Returning Land to Colombia's Victims' entry in the References' 2011). Taking place in a context otherwise characterized by armed conflict between the state and left-wing guerrilla forces, and the drug violence caused by ascendant drug cartels, the expansion of the extractive frontier in the country attracted a series of armed actors interested in its taxation or direct control.

The context of rising instability would also encourage new processes of elite class formation at odds with democratic development. Alliances between far-right sectors of rural landlords, rural politicians, drug traffickers and multinational mining companies were strengthened. The rural caudillos and private regional armies with origins in the violence of the 1940s and 1950s were reconstituted as a reactionary force of land speculators, agribusiness, multinational corporations and narco bourgeoisie. Fearful of the incremental growth of the guerrilla forces in the countryside, sectors of the urban industrial and financial elite also allied themselves with this bloc. Together they would sponsor the rise of a series of paramilitary organizations focused on the eradication of the left wing and the 'forced displacement of populations from areas of strategic economic and/or military importance including those rich in non-renewable natural resources' (Hristov 2014: 97). The land grab that ensued displaced an estimated 6 million predominantly rural inhabitants from 10 million hectares of land and initiated anti-union violence that saw the assassination of over 2,800 union representatives. Paramilitary terror devastated workers and rural communities, but was key to securing and maintaining the conditions for capital accumulation through extraction (Sankey 2018: 62).

Under Santos, mining remained the most important export sector of the Colombian economy, representing 20% of total exports between 2010 and 2015 ('Colombia: Policy Priorities for Inclusive Development' 2015). In 2010, 5.8 million hectares of land were licensed for mining exploitation. Colombia is now the world's fourth-largest exporter of coal and Latin America's fourth-largest oil producer. Wider hydrocarbon production has also increased. Gas production rose from 200 billion cubic feet in 1999 to 400 billion cubic feet in 2010. New investment in the energy sectors has also stimulated infrastructure construction, including the building of new roads, bridges and ports at key points throughout the country in order to assist the export of raw materials. In January 2015, a new decree (2041) was passed by the central government to speed up the licensing process. Commonly referred to by critics as the decree of 'express licences' (*licencias express*), the government claimed that this would reduce the time and cost of new exploration. However, since 2013, a slump in global commodity prices has increasingly revealed the weaknesses and contradictions of this economic growth strategy.

In 2015, FDI fell to US$500million, a quarter of the level seen in 2010–14, resulting in declining rates of economic growth and increasing fiscal debt (Sankey 2018: 65). Rather than consider options to diversify the national economy, the Santos administration responded to the devastation of the country's economic base by deepening the country's dependency on raw-material extraction. Recently elected President Ivan Duque has continued this commitment with even more enthusiasm. In the 2018 election campaign, he emphasized that oil production had fallen from one million barrels a day to 800,000 barrels. A total of 43 fracking concessions have been handed out to multinational companies, including Exxon Mobil, Conoco Philipps and Drummond.

The violence associated with extraction in the previous decade has persisted as the energy-mining locomotive has steamed on. Indeed, somewhat counter-intuitively given the conditions outlined in the Peace Agreement of 2016, serious expressions of unrest and violence have continued to take place in close proximity to sites of resource extraction. According to journalists and researchers, the apparent end of the armed conflict has simply shifted violence to new venues, under new pseudonyms. Although paramilitary organizations were formally disbanded following a series of amnesty agreements between 2006 and 2008, the territory and the power vacuum left behind as the FARC have demobilized has encouraged a resurgence of paramilitarism in the country. New paramilitary groups and related criminal organizations (BACRIM – *bandas criminales*) with a series of new names (Aguilas Negras, Los Rostrojos, Los Urubeños, Los Paisas, Los Machos, Renacer, Los Giatanistas, Nueva Generación, etc.) have appeared in areas previously controlled by the FARC and especially in areas where there are extractive projects. According to at least one recent report, following the election of President Duque, the attacks have reached new heights with 'once social leader every week' (Alsema 2018). As in the past, there are rumoured connections between these organizations and business and political interests in the country. Over the last ten years the Colombian drug cartels have also increasingly invested in and moved to control gold mining concessions in the country as a way to whitewash and move its 'cash'.[6]

Directly linked to this renewed rise in paramilitarism, a wave of targeted assassinations of 'land defenders' (indigenous and peasant leaders, human rights activists, environmentalists, etc.) has been taking place in rural areas (see also the Introduction). Again, there is a clear correspondence between areas of extraction and areas of assassination. The current and the previous governments have done little to address this violent picture. Promises have been made that the presidency would take direct responsibility for the investigation of these killings, but no acknowledgement has been made of the fact that they are the result of paramilitary action or that there is a clear correspondence with areas of non-renewable extraction. Nor have any arrests been made of the perpetrators of these crimes to date.

Contesting Sovereignty in Colombia

The expression of civil society opposition and resistance to the expansion of extractive, energy and infrastructure projects in Colombia has also resulted in further instances of violence and unrest. Responding to the insecurity and negative impacts on their communities, territories and local natural environment, multiple communities in rural areas have organized campaigns in open and militant opposition to extractive projects. Visualization of the extent and spread of these socioenvironmental contestations is evident in the current efforts by the Environmental Justice Atlas[7] based at the University of Barcelona and the Observatory of Social Conflicts (OCA)[8] at the National University in Colombia. The interactive maps produced by these two research-based projects demonstrate the high concentration of socioenvironmental conflicts in the Colombian Andes and Amazonian areas, and their close relationship with extractive, energy and infrastructure projects. Whilst the reactions to extractive projects are most often local in focus and scope, it is also important to acknowledge the efforts by civil society organizations to put pressure on the government through joint mobilizations and protest in the nation's capital. In many cases, indigenous (approximately 4% of the national population)[9] and Afro-descendant (approximately 10–14% of the national population) organizations have formed coalitions with other social actors (students, labour unions, environmental organizations, church organizations, etc.) who share their common concerns regarding environmental destruction and displacement, and that are similarly proactive in their opposition to the state's reliance on and promotion of an extractive model of development.

Social movements in Colombia have periodically employed the concept of *minga* – which translates from its Quechuan origins (*mink'a*) as a form of joint labour – as means to call for common action and popular sovereignty. In 2008, Colombia's popular movements, headed by the country's indigenous organizations, carried out an unprecedented six-week mobilization to protest the Uribe government's economic and security policies, as well as ongoing violations of human and indigenous rights (Poole 2009). The *minga popular* was described by its leadership as the beginning of a nationwide 'conversation with the people' designed to transform Colombian society and politics through coordinated and nonviolent mobilization. The mobilization received considerable popular support from the Colombian population, as well as expressions of international solidarity. It was also the event that would inspire other mass mobilizations. In August 2012, Colombia experienced another mass mobilization of civil society against the terms of the national economic model that analysts referred to as a *social earthquake* ('Fogonazo y memoria de paro' 2013). Thousands of indigenous peoples, small farmers and small-scale miners from municipalities across the country paralysed Colombia for a week through a series of coordinated strikes, protests and blockades. The protesters used these actions to highlight the public rejection of the government's neoliberal economic model and, in particular, the terms of recent free trade agreements and the extremely liberal concessions granted the extractive and agribusiness corporations. Student organizations and industrial workers gave further support to this movement as the protests and strikes reached the nation's cities and capital. On each of these occasions of protest, the government sent in heavily equipped riot police (ESMAD) to physically manage the protests and arrest ringleaders. The heavy-handed actions of the police have escalated violent confrontations and resulted in the injury and deaths of protesters.

Other than through open protests, indigenous, Afro-descendent, peasant and environmental social movements in the country have also looked to other democratic legal and political mechanisms to raise public awareness and to block extractive projects. Indigenous, peasant and Afro-descendant communities have been strong proponents of formalizing alternative development plans and renewing legal recognition of their territories. In other cases, they have joined broad cross-class social movements and campaigns to confront, stop or tame extractive activities. Importantly in terms of national legal and political debates, several attempts have been made by local municipalities in connection with these movements to organize in the defence of their territories through the use of popular referenda. As well as further revealing contrast visions of development between the state and rural communities throughout the country, the use of popular referenda in Colombia has also made public a series of significant legal and political divisions at different levels and between different parts of the state regarding the meaning and position of sovereignty (Chapter 6 deals specifically with the politics of prior consultation)

Even before the introduction of Decree 2041, Colombian indigenous organizations had highlighted the gap between de jure rights and their flawed de facto respect and practice by the government. In the face of the insecurities of the current legal and political system for prior consultation, a search has been made for other relevant political and legal mechanisms that can be used to confront extractive development. In this effort, indigenous and Afro-descendant communities have joined broad social movements to organize popular referenda. Following on from the 1991 Constitution's support for popular sovereignty, Law 99 (1993) establishes that environmental policy should follow the principles of democratic and participatory environmental management. According to Chapter 4 of Law 134 (1994), which regulates the mechanisms for citizens' participation, popular consultation is a mechanism that grants the people the right to decide on questions of vital importance. According to Law 134, there is no need to go to Congress to gain formal backing, but regional governors or local mayors must meet certain requirements defined in the general regulations for territorial organization. However, these regulations have remained disputed, resulting in the persistent controversial nature of local municipalities' and social movements' use of popular consultation.

Extracting Justice in Tolima

We have been strengthening our community sovereignty by appropriating mechanisms of citizen participation clearly recognized in the political constitution of Colombia. This includes popular referenda. Popular sovereignty represents the possibility to surmount the selfishness that we sometimes have as human beings, an opportunity to overcome the extremes of individualism that stop us from being a collective, above all when we know that we share the same difficulties, the same problems and same inconveniencies. (Renso Garcia Parra, Committee for the Defence of the Environment, Tolima, private communication, August 2017)

The case of Tolima and the vote in Cajamarca with which this chapter started is an important case in which the use of popular referenda has successfully resulted in the suspension of extractive activity. As the quote above further underlines, it is also a case that importantly demonstrates the link between organized opposition to extraction and the expression of popular sovereignty.

However, again in line with the earlier described history of extraction and resistance in Guatemala, this has only been possible because of a protracted history of struggle over the meaning of sovereignty and its legal and political recognition as popular expression of rights to resource rights and territory (or as a popular expression of resource sovereignty). What follows is a further summary of that history in which it will become evident that the referendum in Cajamarca was the continuation of wider strategies that had been explored and tested by community activists in previous years. This further updates my analysis of this case in two earlier published articles (Hristov 2014:123; McNeish 2017a and b).

In the years following AngloGold Ashanti's (AGA's) 2007 announcement of the discovery of the La Colosa gold deposit, local communities within 100 km of the mine noted the increasing presence of AGA company technicians and their efforts to both survey and purchase land needed for the mega-project. When AGA first entered the municipality of Piedras in mid-2012, it was guarded about the company's plans. The Mayor of Piedras received a letter stating that the company was interested in carrying out an assessment of the flora and fauna in the municipality. Functionaries of the company also went to the local school to meet with the teachers, with the expressed intention of giving classes on recycling. At the time, no clear indication of the company's plans for infrastructure development connected to the mine was given, but suspicions grew when the company started to install exploration platforms on private land in the neighbouring municipality of Doima. Through contacts in Ibagué, local landowners and teachers accessed more detailed information about AGA's real plans.

With this new information, concerns flourished in Doima and Piedras over the possible impact of AGA's revealed plans to build a metallurgical plant and a series of leaching pools in the area. In particular, the communities wanted to avoid any impact on the quality of water in the River Opia, on which their rice crops and local fishing depended. Tolima is one of Colombia's most productive agricultural regions. These concerns grew to the degree that they sparked local protests and the blocking of company traffic on roads in the area for six months starting in January 2013. Responding to a changing security context, the government sent in the military to protect AGA company employees entering the area. Following the circulation of independent research carried out by the Colombia Solidarity Campaign and the London Mining Network in 2013, it became clear to local communities and the district authorities that the company envisaged not just a single massive mine, but a complex of storage areas and roads for tailings, toxic waste and refinement (i.e. the Anaima Tocha complex). While the mine would be located in Cajamarca, because of the area's steep, mountainous geography, the company aimed to situate the tailings dam that collects waste close to the town of Doima, where land is flatter, rich in water and covered with rice fields. A giant conveyor belt would be constructed to move the rock from the mine to the tailings dam. The report also made clear the legacy of human rights and environmental abuses previously connected to the company. Emphasis was also placed on the impact that the mine would have on the southern end of the protected Paramo Los Nevados nature reserve.

Assisted by environmental organizations based in Tolima as well as diverse sectors of civil society, there was now growing interest and ability within the region to mount a campaign to stop the mining project. AGA had started its operations in the area without the proper licences from the local environmental authority (Cortolima) and without having undertaken a genuine consultation of the local community. Local civil society organizations (thirty in total) banded together in late 2010 to form the Committee in Defence of the Environment (CDE), which was tasked with organizing a campaign to stop the mining project. Student and academic associations from the local universities circulated information widely regarding the company's record of environmental and social damage elsewhere in the world. Weekly public lectures and discussions (resulting in the granting of popular diplomas) co-organized by the CDE and Ecotierra, a national environmental NGO, gained high levels of popularity and attendance. A number of social media channels and blogs also circulated information and contrasting perspectives regarding the mine project. Public protests and events, frequently mixed with festivities such as the Gran Marcha Carnival, were organized to draw attention to the dangers of an open cast mine project and to celebrate local agrarian traditions. By organizing protest as carnival, the CDE successfully attracted a broad cross-section of social support and avoided the violent confrontations with the security forces seen at environmental rallies and protests elsewhere in the country. Rural and urban participants in these protests coined the movement's slogan: 'If we can stop the Giant [Calosa is the Spanish for giant], we can stop anything.'

Parallel to activism in the street, a series of public hearings and consultations took place at the district level. This built on an earlier history of consultations between civil society and the local indigenous community (the Pijao) in particular. Both the regional government and the local indigenous population in the district had recognized conventions on free, prior and informed consent (Decision C-366/2011 of the Constitutional Court and Decree 1320/2008) as important legal mechanisms. However, awareness of the limited results from previous efforts to use these legal mechanisms and of their relevance being limited to the indigenous population pushed campaigners to search for other democratic tools. A public hearing in 2009 made cross-sectoral concerns clear along with widespread public demand that government agencies and environmental authorities fulfil their responsibility with regard to the public management and protection of environmental resources in the Department of Tolima. The participants at the hearing drew up a petition seeking an immediate halt to the La Colosa project. Usocoello, a users' organization responsible for managing the largest irrigation area in the Department of Tolima, also filed a class action lawsuit against the environmental and mining authorities of the Colombian state in the same year.

The regional environmental authority (Cortolima) and regional Personería (human rights ombudsman) joined this legal action as co-sponsors, denouncing the risks to human life and ecosystems that the continuance of the project would bring. The Cortolima convened a Citizen's Environmental Meeting in Ibague in February 2013 to discuss the mining project publicly. In this space, various organizations were able to hear the warning in the report of the Contraloria (the national statistics bureau) about the environmental impacts of the project. National indigenous organizations, agricultural producers' associations, NGOs and regional environmental committees were present at this meeting. The President of Fedearroz, the rice growers' association, stated at this meeting that AGA 'has not told the truth to the people of Tolima about its mega-mining incursion' and that this was 'a threat to the country's food security'.

These meetings added considerably to public knowledge and debate, but frustrations grew with the lack of clear official response to these actions. The suspicious and ostensibly linked circumstances of the assassination of Pedro César García Moreno – a member of Consciencia Campesina, a peasant organization – in 2013 also added to this growing public anger. Moreno was an activist connected to an NGO representing small-scale peasant farmers in Cajamarca that opposed the mine project. It now became apparent that a clearer public statement regarding the local community's rejection of the mine needed to be stimulated. On 12 June 2013, a popular referendum was held by the Municipality of Piedras to measure and demonstrate local public opinion on the question of the mine project.

The national media and civil society organizations reported news of the referendum and its result throughout the country. Although not the first referendum of its kind in the country, the media attention given to the Piedras referendum quickly made it a point of reference for other local communities similarly confronting processes of extraction. For example, civil society organizations in the municipality of Casanare immediately launched a proposal to carry out a referendum in the style of Piedras against oil extraction. Within the region of Tolima, the publicly perceived success of the referendum in Piedras led directly to calls for further referenda.

Legal Backlash

The actions of the community of Piedras and Tolima set a precedent for democratic participation in Colombia. As a colleague of mine at the Faculty of Law at the Universidad de los Andes commented at the time: 'It renewed the claim that the local community represented by the municipality is a qualified and legitimate voice that can question the leadership of the national government.' However, whilst it was clear that civil society received an initial boost from the Piedras referendum, AGA and the national presidency raised questions about its legality (Dietz and Engels 2017). In an interview in July 2014, AGA's representative Felipe Marquez Robledo condemned the *consulta popular* as a 'referendum of the deaf' because of the failure of campaigners to discuss and include the company in its organization or to guarantee truly democratic participation. AGA emphasized that whilst it may have made mistakes in its earlier consultations with the local community in Tolima, it had made considerable investments to demonstrate its corporate social responsibility. A process of EIA had been launched. AGA also highlighted the forms of assistance it was now granting the local community in my interview with its social affairs office in Ibagué in September 2014.

Within the government, further questions were posed about the legality of the referendum and plans for others. This resulted in an unparalleled legal confrontation between the Attorney General (Procurador General) and the Presidency on one side, and the Constitutional Court and the National Office of the Controller General (Contraloria General de la Republica) on the other. Both sides have claimed to be the holders of the legal and political truth in the country. The participation of a series of legal scholars, linked to Dejusticia (a NGO legal collective based in the Colombian capital), and a series of university law faculties in these debates is notable and explains the personal links between some state institutions and civil society organizations.

Using contrasting legal sources, the office of the Attorney General and the executive power represented by the President – together with the National Mining Agency – claim that every decision regarding the use of the subsoil and non-renewable natural resources lies within the jurisdiction of the national government. Seen from the government's position, no local authority is competent to establish the management and use of such resources, and therefore any popular consultation on the matter is illegal. The Attorney General's office holds that the Mining Code (Law 685) of 2001 is of central importance in this interpretation of the law. Article 37 of the Mining Code declares that no regional authority, sectional or local, can exclude areas of the territory from mining, either temporarily or permanently. Concordantly, Regulating Decree 0935/2013 states that according to the provisions of the

Constitution, the state owns the subsoil and all non-renewable natural resources (Articles 5, 7 and 10 of Law 685/2001).

Given their interpretation of events in Tolima, the Attorney General's
office proceeded with an official investigation in which it accused the Mayor
and Municipal Council of Piedras of having abused their powers as public
officials by holding a popular consultation that violated Colombian law.
This procedure in effect froze the accounts of the local municipality and
placed all further administrative decision-making by the office into question.
It also released a formal warning to all the municipal officials in the region
contemplating a referendum on the mine that, following investigation, a
series of disciplinary measures may be taken against them. This has had some
impact. The Municipal Council of Cajamarca decided in February 2015 (by
10 votes to 1) that it could not support a decision calling for referenda on
the mine project, as this was not within its competence. This decision made
direct reference to the recommendations of the Attorney General's office. The
Council also made clear reference to the pressure placed on it by AGA. As
leaks to the press revealed, AGA had sent a letter to the Council stating that
all social and economic programmes started in the community during the
exploration stage would stop if the local municipality carried out a popular
consultation.

The legal wrangling between the Attorney General's office and the Constitutional Court had a dampening effect on local councillors' willingness to
support further referenda. However, the regional campaign against the mine
did not stop because of this. Regional and national politicians, such as Freddy
Perez from the Green Party and Iván Cepeda Castro of the social-democratic
left Polo Democratico Alternativa political party, gave higher-level political
support to the campaign. A further ruling of the Constitutional Court in
October 2016 (T 445-2015) also declared popular consultations over mining
issues to be legal and municipalities to have the right to ban mining activities
in their territory, given their constitutional mandate to regulate the use of the
land and guarantee environmental protection. Further rulings by the court at
the national level have removed concessionary rights to extractive zones on
the basis of the failure of prior consultation and to protect national conservation areas. Coincident with these changes, Ernesto Cardoso Camacho, the
regional Attorney General, resigned.

At the local level, the T445 ruling added significantly to a climate in
favour of a popular referendum on mining in Cajamarca, the proposed site of
the La Colosa mine. In December 2016, the town council revised its earlier
decision on the condition that the question in the referendum was posed in
such a way that it enabled a free and not a directed vote. In March 2017, the
Mayor of the city of Tolima also declared that a reformulated question could
be used. Whereas no popular referendum has occurred to date in Tolima

because of political compromises and changing political dynamics within the city, this did not stop the town of Cajamarca from going ahead with its own referendum plans.

Although delayed by several 'tutela' (legal injunctions based on individual claims of effects on ownership), supporters of a referendum made both reference to T445 and Law 1757, in which a popular referendum can be held on any subject of popular interest if 10% of the local population approve of it. For the local Environmental Committee of Cajamarca and Anaima, this meant that they had to collect a total of 1,604 signatures in a six-month period. The Committee succeeded in collecting 4,800 signatures, 3,364 of which were recognized by the National Registry (Dietz and Engels 2017: 109). The collection of sufficient signatures meant that the Mayor of Cajamarca was legally required to present the initiative for the referenda to the town council. It was approved in August 2016 and, shortly afterwards, the Regional Administrative Tribunal of Tolima declared that the proposed question for the referendum fulfilled constitutional requirements. The question finally proposed in the referendum asked the local public: are you, or are you not, in agreement with the Municipality of Cajamarca's administration of mining projects and activities? Although the local mayor was opposed to the referendum and the local opposition created a movement to abstain from the vote, 38.6% of the population still participated in the vote. As was described at the start of this chapter, the results of the vote were also sufficient to demonstrate the local population's lack of favour in relation to the proposed mine project.

In the aftermath of the Cajamarca, its apparent victory spurred a wave of similar votes throughout Colombia. In the next five months, at least five referendums designed to register public opinion and sovereignty on extractive projects followed and an additional forty were left pending (Noriega 2018).

The *Consulta* Story Continues

It would be misleading to end the story of the campaign for local referenda (*consultas populares*) in Tolima with the successful outcome of the vote in Cajamarca and its spurring of others elsewhere in the country. In reality, whereas this represented a significant win for anti-mining campaigners, the controversy surrounding its legality and further attempts to use local referenda as a means to express local democratic will and sovereignty would persist until the present time of writing. A new Constitutional Court ruling in October 2018 left the future of municipal-level popular referenda in ambiguous territory. The ruling was given in response to a lawsuit filed by the multinational Mansarovar Energy Colombia after the Municipality of Cumaral voted in 2018 (following inspiration from the Cajamarca vote) to prohibit oil exploration (Noriega 2018). While the Constitutional Court's decision only affects the Cumaral referendum, it sets a binding legal precedent that contradicts previous law and court judgements. The apparent reversal could be partially explained by a change in all five judges in the High Court in the last five years. The political effect of the election of President Duque will also not have improved matters. The national government had continued to argue that municipalities do not have the authority to ban energy and extractive projects through votes because the subsoil contended in these referendums is owned by the state.

For oil, mining and infrastructure companies, associations and investors, the new ruling has provided some relief after a rising number of referendums halted and threatened their operations. Still, it is equally important to note that the wave of referendums in Colombia has not shown any sign of stopping. Less than a week after the court ruling, the municipality of Fusagasugá, two hours south of the capital, held the first referendum in Latin America to ban fracking. The 'no' campaign won overwhelmingly with 99% of the vote. The vote, which affects 100,000 inhabitants, was also the largest to be held in the country to date. Local communities still clearly dispute the sovereign claim of the state to decide over the use of their territory and resources.

Conclusions

In this chapter, I have characterized the use of popular referenda as a significant mechanism used by indigenous, Afro-descendant and peasant peoples and others to question the rights of the state and corporations to access their territories and subsoil resources. Although the communities and social movements in Guatemala and Colombia did not start out viewing them in that way, as we have seen above, the significance of local popular referenda as a means to express popular sovereignty has become ever more evident as their histories of campaigning have unfolded. Of significance here is the manner in which the referenda campaigns not only become a means to express the sovereignty of discreet ethnic groups or peasant communities. They become visible here also as a means to form expressions of sovereignty that stretch to accommodate coalitions of diverse social interests. This is seen to take place across historic ethnic, class and spatial social divisions. Indigenous peoples, peasant communities, small-scale farmers, large-scale landowners (in the case of rice farmers in Tolima), students, urban neighbourhood organizations, national and international environmental and human rights organizations, academics from national and foreign universities, lawyers and government monitoring agencies, and representatives from national political parties have become participants and supporters in the anti-mining campaign in Guatemala and Colombia. Although with different initial motivations, all of these actors have also moved in line with the local community in terms of a claim for the importance of local autonomy and democracy. They have accepted the way in which local referenda disturb understandings of national sovereignty and the state's unquestioned right to access subsoil resources.

In the histories summarized in the last two chapters, there is an evident romance attached to the heroic efforts of local communities and their municipal government to use local referenda as a means to confront the state and corporations. There is undoubtedly a whiff of a David and Goliath tale here, and perhaps especially so when one of the mines is named 'La Colosa' (the Giant). However, I have also made it clear that these histories are intertwined with much darker and disturbing events. Guatemala and Colombia share histories of armed conflict, dictatorship, human rights atrocities, failed attempts at peace-building, neoliberalism, corrupt political elites, organized crime, paramilitarism, corporate collusion with armed actors, legal impunity, and rampant and largely unchecked expansion of extractive frontiers, resulting in both widespread environmental contamination and human displacement. These campaigns for local referenda and the expression of popular sovereignty are made at a terrible cost, or in the face of experiences of violence, conflict and contamination. Indeed, it could be argued that the experience of struggle is an inherent part of the fight for popular sovereignty, whether it expressed in the form of referenda or other means. In order to be effective, anti-mining campaigns require a series of supporting actions including protest and militancy in addition to efforts to negotiate with the state through existing legal and political institutions. As such, they must balance a search for order and governance with actions that necessarily destabilize and court conflict.

As I have suggested above, the campaigns surrounding local referenda on extractive, energy and infrastructure-related projects are also important examples of the way in which popular sovereignty is not only expressed in the form of confrontation and circumvention, but also proactive engagement with the state. This is a very different expression of sovereignty from that seen in the previous chapters of the book. Here it is evident that indigenous and peasant communities – and their supporters – are not only the victims of state and corporate initiatives for development, but also the agents who significantly place in question and to some extent tame and change the course of projects and policies. Here it is also evident that in doing so, notions and claims to sovereignty both change and lead to new political and legal expressions. While power relations and political and economic outcomes have negative outcomes, we see here communities that to some extent learn to 'see like a state' and to use new knowledge of law and politics as levers towards their best advantage. In this way, the campaigns against extraction in Guatemala and Colombia match wider patterns of social action, or ExtraActivism (Willow 2019), observed elsewhere in the world. In these ExtraActivist dynamics, direct action protest is complemented by legal challenges, appeals to international, multiscalar alliances, strategic media drives and targeted corporate campaigns (Willow 2019: 3).

Large and small gains, as well as massive losses, are made along the way in these efforts at social action. Extractive, energy and infrastructure projects are in some cases suspended and discontinued, with tremendous financial losses for corporations and loss of face for national administrations. There is still a long way to go in order for these efforts towards popular referenda to substantively change the nature of the state so as to recognize popular sovereignty or to deliver environmental peace. Nevertheless, it is possible to argue that incremental changes are made – albeit often three steps forward and one step back – and gradually the nature of the governance of the environment is changing in response to these claims for popular sovereignty. Even in the face of governments that double down on the economics of extraction, the actual atmosphere and action of law governing territory and resources continue to change, and arguably for the better. A question we will face in the following chapters of this book is whether the power of these sovereign claims to territory and resources can be further enhanced through structured recognition.

Notes

1. Are you in agreement Yes or No that the Municipality of Cajamarca administers mining projects and activities?
2. Poverty Politics project. Retrieved 15 November 2020 from http://www.uib.no/fg/poverty/38794/poverty-politics-research-project.
3. As Costanza (2015: 274–75) notes, there is always a percentage of these communities that support the apparent opportunities provided by extractive projects and that do not agree with the results of the popular referenda. As such, referenda are imperfect expressions of democracy in that they still result in a level of exclusion, even if only of a minority position.
4. Extracting Justice Project. Retrieved 15 November 2020 from https://www.nmbu.no/en/faculty/landsam/department/noragric/research/clusters/rapid/projects-and-assignments/extracting-justice.
5. The military has governed modern Colombia only once at the height of the civil war between the Liberal and Conservative political parties. Following *La Violencia*, a period in which political violence caused the deaths of over 20,000 Colombians, military officers under the leadership of General Rojas Pinilla took power bloodlessly and at the invitation of political and business leaders (Sotomayer 2008).
6. There has been a tripling of coca production in the country over the last three years, most of it destined for the cocaine trade. See: https://www.theguardian.com/world/2017/mar/14/colombia-coca-cocaine-us-drugs (retrieved 15 November 2020).
7. Environmental Justice Atlas. Retrieved 15 November 2020 from https://ejatlas.org.

8. Observatorio de Conflictos Ambientales. Retrieved 15 November 2020 from http://oca .unal.edu.co.
9. National census data reveals that over 80% of the Colombian population to be *mestizo* (i.e. of mixed racial background). However, it is important to stress that, as in other Andean countries, the attribution of ethnic categories in Colombia has resulted from a history of both internal and external colonization. Individuals that have shifted their personal ethnicity may no longer claim indigenous identity, preferring instead a class identifier such as peasant (campesino). There may nonetheless be little distinction in practice between their lived practices and beliefs and those of indigenous peoples.

References

Abu-Lughod, Lila. 1990. 'The Romance of Resistance: Tracing Transformations of Power through Bedouin Women'. *American Ethnologist* 17(1): 41–55.

Aguilar-Støen, Mariel, and Cecilie Hirsch. 2015. 'Environmental Impact Assessments, Local Power and Self-Determination: The Case of Mining and Hydropower Development in Guatemala'. *The Extractive Industries and Society* 2(3): 472–79.

Alsema, Adrianna. 2018. 'The Duque Effect: One Social Leader is Assassinated in Colombia Almost Every Day Now'. *Colombia Reports*, 29 October. Retrieved 15 November 2020 from https://colombiareports.com/the-duque-effect-one-social-leader-assassinated-in-col ombia-almost-every-day-now/?fbclid=IwAR26d9fLaj0i_ZGaQi9VyNDeaeDn83ASt25 54soeibBIefjgJ2s8CP-k7hk.

Anthias, Penelope. 2018. *Limits to Decolonization: Indigeneity, Territory and Hydrocarbon Politics in the Bolivian Chaco*. Ithaca: Cornell University Press.

Basu, Niladri, Marce Abare, Susan Buchanan, Diana Cryderman, Dong-Ka Nam, Susannah Sirkin, Stefan Schmidt and Howard Hu. 2010. 'A Combined Ecological and Epidemiologic Investigation of Metals Exposure amongst Indigenous Peoples Near the Marlin Mine in Western Guatemala'. *Science of the Total Environment* 409(1): 70–77.

Bridge, Gavin. 2004. 'Contested Terrain: Mining and the Environment'. *Annual Review of Environment and Resources* 29: 205–59.

Bruun Jensen, Casper, and Brit Ross Winthereik. 2012. 'Recursive Partnerships in Global Development Aid', in Soumhya Venkatesen and Thomas Yarrow (eds), *Differentiating Development: Beyond an Anthropology of Critique*. New York: Berghahn Books.

Bunch, Angela, and Carlos Loarca. 2013. 'Mining Conflict and Indigenous Consultation in Guatemala'. *Americas Quarterly*, 25 March. Retrieved 15 November 2020 from https://www .americasquarterly.org/article/mining-conflict-and-indigenous-consultation-in-guatemala.

Burchell, Graham, Colin Gordon and Peter Miller. 1991. *The Foucault Effect: Studies in Governmentality: With Lectures by and an Interview with Michel Foucault*. London: Harvester Wheatsheaf.

CAO. 2015. Assessment of a Complaint Submitted to CAO in Relation to the Marlin Mining Project in Guatemala. Office of the Compliance Advisor/Ombudsman International Finance Institution/ Multilateral Investment Guarantee Agency. Retrieved 5 January 2020 from http://www.cao-ombudsman.org/cases/document-links/documents/CAO-Marlin-assessment-English-7Sep05.pdf.

'Cajamarca definió su posición en la consulta minera: Anglogold'. 2017. *El Tiempo*, 27 April. Retrieved 15 November 2020 from https://www.eltiempo.com/colombia/otras-ciudades/ anglogold-se-retira-de-cajamarca-tras-negativa-en-consulta-popular-minera-82440.

'Cajamarca, el pueblo de Colombia que le dijo no a la explotación minera'. 2017. *BBC World*, 27 March. Retrieved 15 November 2020 from https://www.bbc.com/mundo/noticias-america-latina-39407877.

'Cajamarca, el pueblo que prendío la mecha de las consultas populares'. 2017. *El Espectador*. De-cember 3rd 2017. Retrieved 15 November 2020 from https://www.elespectador.com/noticias/medio-ambiente/cajamarca-el-pueblo-que-prendio-la-mecha-de-las-consultas-populares.

Castignino, Vincent. 2006. 'Mineria de metales y derechos humanos en Guatemala: La Mina Marlin en San Marcos'. Report by the *Brigadas de Paz Internacional*: Guatemala.

'Colombia: activistas denuncian impactos ambientales de multinacionales'. 2018. *Telesur*, 3 October. Retrieved 15 November 2020 from https://videos.telesurtv.net/video/743793/colombia-activistas-denuncian-impactos-ambientales-de-multinacionales.

'Colombia's Government Formally Ratifies Revised FARC Peace Deal'. 2016. *The Guardian*, 1 December. Retrieved 15 November 2020 from https://www.theguardian.com/world/2016/dec/01/colombias-government-formally-ratifies-revised-farc-peace-deal.

'Colombia: No a la Minería en territorio indígena'. 2009. *OCMAL – Observatorio de Conflictos Mineros de América Latina*, 20 March 2009. Retrieved 15 November 2020 from https://www.ocmal.org/4680.

'Colombia: Policy Priorities for Inclusive Development'. 2015. *OECD Better Policies Series*. Retrieved 15 November 2020 from https://www.oecd.org/about/publishing/colombia-policy-priorities-for-inclusive-development.pdf.

'Colombia Presidential Elections 2018: What Next for Peace?' 2018. *ABColombia*. Re-trieved 15 November 2020 from https://www.abcolombia.org.uk/colombia-presidential-elections-2018-what-next-for-peace.

'Colombia Referendum: Voters Reject FARC Peace Deal'. 2016. *BBC News*, 3 October. Re-trieved 15 November 2020 from https://www.bbc.com/news/world-latin-america-37537252.

Cooke, Bill, and Uma Kothari. 2001. *Participation, the New Tyranny?* London: Zed Books.

Cosoy, Natalio. 2016. 'Has Plan Colombia Really Worked?' *BBC*, 4 February. Retrieved 15 November 2020 from https://www.bbc.com/news/world-latin-america-35491504.

Costanza, Jennifer. 2015. 'Indigenous Peoples' Right to Prior Consultation: Transform-ing Human Rights from the Grassroots in Guatemala'. *Journal of Human Rights* 14(2): 260–85.

'¿Cual es la aplicabilidad de la Consulta en Cajamarca?' 2018. *Semana*, 15 November. Re-trieved 15 November 2020 from https://www.semana.com/nacion/multimedia/cual-es-la-aplicabilidad-de-la-consulta-en-cajamarca/521301#.

Dennis, Claire. 2015. 'The 5 Most Important Achievements in 3 Years of Peace Talks in Co-lombia'. *Colombia Reports*, 16 November. Retrieved 15 November 2020 from https://colombiareports.com/5-important-achievements-colombias-peace-talks.

Dietz, Kristina, and Bettina Engels. 2017. 'Contested Extractivism: Actors and Strategies in Conflicts over Mining'. *South American Resource Geographies* 148(2–3): 111–20.

'Fogonazo y memoria de paro'. 2013. *Desde Abajo*, 24 September. Retrieved 15 November 2020 from https://www.desdeabajo.info/ediciones/item/22777-fogonazo-y-memoria-del-paro.html.

Fulmer, Amanda, Angelina Godoy and Philip Neff. 2008. 'Indigenous Rights, Resistance and the Law: Lessons from a Guatemalan Mine'. *Latin American Politics and Society* 50(4): 91–121.

Gordon, Todd, and Jeffrey Webber. 2007. 'Imperialism and Resistance: Canadian Mining Companies in Latin America'. *Third World Quarterly* 29(1): 91–121.

Grandin, Greg. 2000. *The Blood of Guatemala: A History of Race and Nation*. Durham, NC: Duke University Press.

'Guatemala: Seven Human Rights Defenders Killed in Four Weeks'. 2018. *Amnesty International*, 11 June. Retrieved 15 November 2020 from https://www.amnesty.org/en/latest/news/2018/06/guatemala-seven-human-rights-defenders-killed-in-four-weeks.

Hale, Charles. 2011. 'Resistencia para que? Territory, Autonomy and Neoliberal Entanglements in the "Empty Spaces" of Central America'. *Economy and Society* 40(2): 184–210.

Holden, William, and Daniel Jacobson. 2008. 'Civil Society Opposition to Nonferrous Metals Mining in Guatemala'. *VOLUNTAS: International Journal of Voluntary and Non-profit Organizations* 19(4): 325–50.

Hristov, Jasmin. 2014. *Paramilitarism and Neoliberalism: Violent Systems of Capital Accumulation in Colombia and beyond*. London: Pluto Press.

Hurtado, Margarita, and Irene Lungo. 2007. *Aproximaciones al movimiento ambiental en Centroamerica*. Guatemala: FLACSO.

Idler, Annette. 2016. 'Colombia Just Voted No in Its Plebiscite for Peace. Here's Why and What It Means'. *Washington Post*, 3 October. Retrieved 15 November 2020 from https://www.washingtonpost.com/news/monkey-cage/wp/2016/10/03/colombia-just-voted-no-on-its-referendum-for-peace-heres-why-and-what-it-means.

Imai, Shin, Ladan Mehranvar and Jennifer Sander. 2007. 'Breaching Indigenous Law: Canadian Mining in Guatemala'. *VOLUNTAS: International Journal of Voluntary and Non-profit Organizations* 19(4): 325–50.

'Indigenous Xinca March in Guatemala to Banish Canadian Mine'. 2018. *Canada's National Observer* 17 April. Retrieved 15 November 2020 from https://www.nationalobserver.com/2018/04/17/news/indigenous-xinca-march-guatemala-banish-canadian-mine.

Juárez, Rigoberto. 2007. 'La experiencia del Parlamento Qánjobál, Chuj y Akateko', in *Memoria: Primera Jornada de Estudios y Experiencias sobre Territorio, Poder y Política Huehuetenango*. Guatemala City: Centro de Estudios y Documentación de la Frontera Noroccidental de Guatemala, CEDFOG.

Kirsch, Stuart. 2014. *Mining Capitalism: The Relationship between Corporations and Their Critics*. Berkeley: University of California Press.

MacLeod, Morna. 2016. 'Development or Devastation? Epistemologies of Mayan Women's Resistance to an Open-Pit Goldmine in Guatemala'. *AlterNative: An International Journal of Indigenous Peoples* 12(1): 86–100.

McNeish, John-Andrew. 2001. 'Pueblo Chico, Infierno Grande: Globalization and the Politics of Participation in Highland Bolivia'. Unpublished PhD thesis. Senate House. University of London.

———. 2008. 'Beyond the Permitted Indian? Bolivia and Guatemala in an Era of Neoliberal Developmentalism'. *Latin American and Caribbean Ethnic Studies* 3(1): 33–39.

———. 2017a. 'A Vote to Derail Extraction: Popular Consultation and Resource Sovereignty in Tolima, Colombia'. *Third World Quarterly* 38(5): 1128–45.

———. 2017b. 'Extracting Justice? Colombia's Commitment to Mining and Energy as a Foundation for Peace'. *International Journal of Human Rights* 21(4): 500–16.

Moran, Robert. 2004. *New Country, Same Story: Review of the Glamis Gold Marlin Project EIA*. Guatemala: Madre Selva.

Murray Li, Tania. 2007. *The Will to Improve: Governmentality, Development and the Practice of Politics*. Durham, NC: Duke University Press.

Nolin, Catherine, and Jaqui Stephens. 2010. 'We Have to Protect the Investors: Development and Canadian Mining Companies in Guatemala'. *Journal of Rural Community Development* 5(3): 37–70.

Noriega, Christina. 2018. 'In Colombia, New Court Ruling Threatens Future of Community-Decision Making Referendums'. *Latino USA*, 13 November. Retrieved 15 November 2020 from https://www.latinousa.org/2018/11/13/colombiareferendums/?fbclid=IwAR10VQBwrHEkg5zN5zH7GoU7MzCwPVBSYG2yYPmaiWelpPLeWAIsrLbssi4.

Øveraas, Per Ernesto, 2013. 'The Community Consultation as a Strategy Against Mining: A Study of the Repertoire Change in Anti-mining Resistance in Guatemala'. Unpublished Master's thesis. Oslo: University of Oslo.

Pedersen, Alexandra. 2014. Landscapes of Resistance. Community Opposition to Canadian Mining Operations in Guatemala. *Journal of Latin American Geography* 13(1): 187–214.

'Plan Colombia: A Retrospective'. 2012. *Americas Quarterly*, 18 July. Retrieved 15 November 2020 from https://www.americasquarterly.org/fulltextarticle/plan-colombia-a-retrospective.

Poole, Deborah. 2009. 'The Minga of Resistance: Policy Making from Below'. *NACLA Report on the Americas*, 16 February. Retrieved 15 November 2020 from https://nacla.org/news/minga-resistance-policy-making-below.

Power, Michael. 1999. *The Audit Society: Rituals of Verification*. Oxford: Oxford University Press.

'¿Qué proponen los candidatos presidenciales sobre sector minero y participación popular?' 2018. *Semana Sostenible*, 24 May. Retrieved 15 November 2020 from https://sostenibilidad.semana.com/opinion/articulo/propuestas-candidatos-presidenciales-sobre-sector-minero-y-participacion-popular/41007.

Rasch, Elisabet. 2012. 'Transformations in Citizenship: Local Resistance against Mining Projects in Huehuetenango (Guatemala)'. *Journal of Developing Societies* 28(2): 159–84.

'Returning Land to Colombia's Victims'. 2011. *ABColombia*, May. Retrieved 15 November 2020 from https://www.globalprotectioncluster.org/_assets/files/field_protection_clusters/Colombia/files/HLP%20AoR/Returning_Land_to_Colombias_Victims_2011_EN.pdf.

Rivera Cusicanqui, Silvia. 2012. 'Ch'ixinakax Utxiwa: A Reflection on the Practices and Discourses of Decolonization'. *South Atlantic Quarterly* 111(1): 95–121.

Sankey, Kyla. 2018. 'Extractive Capital, Imperialism and the Colombian State'. *Latin American Perspectives* 45(5): 52–70.

Sieder, Rachel. 2007. 'Contested Sovereignties: Indigenous Law, Violence and State Effects in Post-war Guatemala'. *Critique of Anthropology* 31(1): 161–84.

———. 2013. 'Sexual Violence and Gendered Subjectivities: Indigenous Women's' Search for Justice in Guatemala', in John-Andrew McNeish and Rachel Sieder (eds), *Gender Justice and Legal Pluralism: Latin American and African Perspectives*. London: Routledge.

Sotomayer, Arturo. 2008. 'Los civiles y militares en América Latina: Avances y retrocesos en mataría de control civil'. *Revista Mexicana de Política Exterior*. 8341–43.

Sousa Santos, Boaventura and Cesar Rodriguez Gavarito. 2005. *Law and Globalization from Below: Towards a Cosmopolitan Legality*. Cambridge: Cambridge University Press.

Spring, Karen, and Francois Guindon. 2009. San Miguel Health Harms. Technical Report. Rights Action and COPAE.

'UN Warns of Deteriorating Climate for Human Rights Defenders in Guatemala'. 2018. *UN News*, 18 May. Retrieved 15 November 2020 from https://news.un.org/en/story/2018/05/1010102.

'Understanding the Causes of Colombia's Conflict: Land Ownership'. 2018. *Colombia Reports*, 3 April. Retrieved 15 November 2020 from https://colombiareports.com/understanding-the-causes-of-colombias-conflict-land-ownership.

UPME. 2006. *Colombia país minero*. Bogota: UPME.

Urkidi, Leire, and Marianne Walter. 2011. 'Dimensions of Environmental Justice in Anti-gold Mining Movements in Latin America'. *Geoforum* 42(6): 683–95.

Van de Sandt, Joris. 2009. *Mining Conflicts and Indigenous Peoples in Guatemala*. Amsterdam: CORDAID.

Vidal, John. 2018. 'How Guatemala Is Sliding into Chaos in the Fight for Land and Water'. *BBC News*, 19 August. Retrieved 15 November 2020 from https://www.theguardian.com/world/2018/aug/19/guatemala-fight-for-land-water-defenders-lmining-loging-eviction.

Walter, Marianne. 2014. 'Political Ecology of Mining Conflicts in Latin America: An Analysis of Environmental Justice Movements and Struggles over Scales'. Unpublished PhD thesis. Autonomous University of Barcelona.

Weitzner, Viviane. 2017. 'Nosotros Somos El Estado: Contested Legalities in Decision-Making about Extractives Affecting Ancestral Territories in Colombia'. *Third World Quarterly* 38(5): 1198–214.

'Welcome to Guatemala: Gold Mine Protester Beaten and Burnt Alive'. 2014. *The Guardian*, 12 August. Retrieved 15 November 2020 from https://www.theguardian.com/environment/andes-to-the-amazon/2014/aug/12/guatemala-gold-mine-protester-beaten-burnt-alive.

Willow, Anna. 2019. *Understanding ExtrActivism: Culture and Power in Natural Resource Disputes*. London and New York: Routledge.

Witte, Benjamin. 2005. 'Multinational Gold-Rush in Guatemala'. *NACLA Report on the Americas* 39: 8–11.

Yagenova, Simona; Claudia Donis and Patricia Castillo. 2012. *La industria extractiva en Guatemala: Politicas Publicas, Derechos Humanos y Procesos de Resistencia Popular en el Período 2003–2011*. Guatemala: CIRMA.

Zarsky, Lyuba, and Leanardo Stanley. 2011. *Searching for Gold in the Highlands of Guatemala: Economic Benefits and Environmental Risks of the Marlin Mine*. Global Development and Environment Institute, Tufts University.

Figure 4.1 Lithium evaporation ponds, Llipi, Bolivia. © John-Andrew McNeish

Chapter 4

CITIZENS OF LITHIUM AND SALT

A low and eerie howl produced by a constant cold wind is now all that blows through the rusting smokestacks of the hulks collected in a locomotive grave-yard on the outskirts of the Altiplano town of Uyuni. For close to a century, salt and dust have sandblasted and corroded the remains of these trains, leaving a ghostly but picturesque sight. All guided tours of the area add a stop to this industrial mausoleum to their itineraries. Most of the trains in the 'graveyard' date back to the end of the nineteenth century and were imported by a then imperial and corporate Britain to establish Uyuni as an important transportation hub. Engineers invited to Bolivia by the British-sponsored Antofagasta and Bolivia Railway Companies built the rail lines between 1888 and 1892 to assist with the transport of minerals from the Andes to the Pacific Ocean ports. The trains are not only a reminder of the bygone age of steam power, but of Bolivia's much longer history as an exporter of raw materials to the world.

Slowly becoming the skeletons of once-great machines, the trains are a reminder of the periods of both boom and bust that have excited and plagued the country's economic and political development (Contreras 1993). The Spanish, in common with the outlaws Butch Cassidy and the Sundance Kid, were drawn to Bolivia because gold and silver, but other minerals have also had their economic magnetism. From the nineteenth century onwards, the mining industry also focused on the extraction and export of tin. Individuals made vast fortunes – Simón Patiño, a Bolivian industrialist, became one of the world's richest men in the resource-hungry period of the Second World

War, yet the prices would not only rise but also fall and little wealth remained for the benefit of most people in the country. In the 1940s, mineral markets in Bolivia suffered one of their moments of collapse (other severe periods of 'bust' were experienced in the 1910s and the 1980s, only to be overcome by new mineral discoveries and new mining technologies). At that time, many trains were abandoned outside Uyuni, forming the start of this collection of mortal engines.

However, the train cemetery, despite its aesthetic and historical interest, is not the main attraction that draws visitors to the region. Uyuni is now less known as an important highland transport hub and more so as the nearest town to the world's largest area of salt flats, the Salar de Uyuni. The Salar de Uyuni is a vast salt flat spanning almost 11,000 square km in the department of Potosí and at an altitude of 3,656 metres (11,995 feet) above sea level. Here, a thick crust of salt extends to the horizon, covered by quilted, polygonal patterns of salt rising from the ground. Some 40,000 years ago, it was part of a lake that covered a large swath of the Andean highlands. The moon-like landscapes of the salt desert are part of what was left when it dried up. At certain times of the year, nearby lakes overflow and a thin layer of water transforms the flats into a stunning reflection of the sky. 'It's as if you're on a white ocean with no waves', Adrian Borsa, a geophysicist, told *Nature* (Hand 2007): 'You see the horizon, the curvature of Earth. It's absolutely featureless.'

Stretched between distant Andean peaks like a shimmering white carpet, the Salar de Uyuni is also home to pink flamingos, 1,000-year-old cacti, rare hummingbirds and hotels built entirely from blocks of salt. Billed by many travel guides as a must-see wonder of the world, the Salar de Uyuni now attracts 60,000 tourists a year to the area. In the nearby town of Uyuni, residents and local officials have ambitious plans for its future as a hub for tourism. Tourism has fast overtaken the rail transport of minerals, llama herding, quinoa farming and salt production by the local indigenous Aymara population as the impoverished region's main economic activity.

Tourists arriving in Uyuni find themselves in a boomtown atmosphere. Few roads are paved, rubbish blows across streets, and the hot water and electricity supply in local hotels is intermittent and unreliable. At the same time, WiFi is available and local cafes sell stone-baked pizza, vegan options and artisanal coffee and beer in competition with more traditional local offerings of *ch'arki* (dried llama meat), *chuño* (freeze dried potatoes), quinoa and *api morado* (a spiced corn drink). Tourists commonly enjoy these amenities for only a day or two before heading out with guided tours of three to four days. During these tours, they pass by the graveyard of trains on their way to cross the Salar and stop at various vantage points, sights and experiences (including thermal baths) before looping back to Uyuni or leaving the tour at the Chilean border.

On their way to the Salar, the tour commonly stops for an hour to give passing interest to one of traditional foundations of the local economy, i.e. the production and manufacture of blocks of salt taken from the Salar itself. For hundreds of years, the natural process of salt accumulation in the area has provided local people with an important product for trade. Although trucks have now largely replaced llamas and alpacas as the beasts of burden, loads of salt blocks wrapped in pampas grass continue to be transported along ancient routes to marketplaces across the Andean highlands, valleys and lowlands.

The boom in tourism focused on the Salar has been important for Uyuni in recent years. Hopes of economic revitalization and development are currently geared towards catering for the curiosity of foreigners. However, whilst tourism captures the present, future dreams – along with renewed fears of a repeat of earlier economic patterns – have been stoked by the arrival of lithium mining. Under the white lunar-like expanse of the Salar, there is not only salt, but the world's largest brine deposit of lithium, a light metal increasingly sought-after for use in batteries that power everything from mobile phones to electric vehicles (Eichner 2012). Because of their high storage capacity, lithium-ion batteries are expected to make electric vehicles and renewable sources of energy, like solar and wind power, feasible and increasingly affordable (Tran et al. 2012).

Recognizing the increasing value of lithium as an extractive commodity, the Bolivian government has viewed its industrialization as a part of a new era of prosperity. 'With the exploitation of lithium in a 400 sq. km area, we'll have enough to maintain ourselves for a century', Bolivia's President Evo Morales boasted of the rare metal (Sagárnaga López 2016). In 2008, the industrialization of lithium was incorporated into larger development plans that formally prioritize state control over natural resources, expand social programmes and express a rejection of neoliberalism (Revette 2017). The start-up of lithium production in 2009 meant that the Salar ceased to be a confine exclusively for ecologists, tourists and salt sellers.

Lithium is the reason why I arrived in Uyuni in 2011. It is also a vehicle to discuss another aspect of popular sovereignty not fully explored in the previous chapter. In this chapter, I emphasize that claims and contests for resource sovereignty are not only generated by economic and material claims, but often concurrently result from differing perspectives of the value and significance of the landscape, and of the possible impacts of resource development. In this chapter we witness that this is true not only of fossil fuels, but also of resources that despite their 'green' credentials result in similar social and environmental impacts to what are traditionally considered to be non-renewable resources. Whilst recognizing common concerns with economic gain and employment, the chapter highlights through its focus on the politics of the establishment of lithium production in the Highlands of Bolivia that contrasting foundations for knowledge and ontology and changing political pacts and alliances result in dynamic expressions of resource sovereignty.

Charting the establishment of a nascent lithium industry in Salar de Uyuni and its contested significance, I show the manner in which material claims are embedded in long-established cultural and moral relationships with the landscape. Reference and discussion are made here of developments in social theory (principally in science and technology studies and social anthropology) that argue for recognition of political ontology, i.e. the re-activation of different understandings of reality, and especially about the relationship between humans and nature, in politics. This is shown not to be a simple manner of easily distinguishable ontological positions, but rather a complex interaction in which alignments and misalignments take place over time. As well as debating and questioning the terms under which the lithium industry is being established, it is clearly evident that local people, communities, the Bolivian state and private sector interests are locked into a wider discussion and negotiation of sovereignty. As I demonstrate below, this is not only serious in the sense of the dynamics of tensions and contestation at the local level, but also evidently of much wider impacts, which are seen here playing a key role in the dramatic dynamics surrounding the recent departure of President Morales from office.

Warning Signs

Whilst I had always wanted to visit the salt flats for touristic reasons, the cause that brought me to the Uyuni and its surrounding region was the nascent discussion and development of a lithium industry. At that point in time, I was starting research for a project funded by the Norwegian Research Council focused on the politics of energy in Latin America, i.e. 'Contested Powers: The Politics and Anthropology of Energy. In the project, my colleagues and I were interested to not only further capture the complex dynamics of non-renewable resource and fossil-fuel energy expansion in an era of booming commodity prices, but to also comparatively extend our focus to rapidly expanding developments in Latin America in the renewable development field (McNeish, Borchgrevink and Logan 2015).

My research in Uyuni was not a lengthy affair. I had barely spent two weeks in Uyuni when the drama that was to become the TIPNIS crisis – mentioned in earlier chapters – drew my attention away to the Bolivian Lowlands and led to what I thought at the time was a necessary change of empirical focus. However, whilst admittedly only present in Uyuni for a short time, I was able to carry out interviews with people in local government, representatives of COMIBOL (the national mining company), local labour unions and local civil society organizations. I also visited the newly established complex of laboratories, prospecting wells and settling pools set up by the government to break ground for the new national lithium industry located at Llipi. The Bolivian Vice-Ministry of Mines granted me formal assistance in arranging this visit following an interview that focused on the new lithium industry with its then director, Hector Cordova. I also managed to fulfil my touristic ambitions and join a three-day tour of the salt flats themselves. In the course of these experiences, it was already evident that the stage was set in the region for a series of significant disagreements and confrontations between the different economic and social actors within or drawn into tension with the newly established lithium industry.

In the interviews I conducted with union leaders and local members of civil society, concerns were voiced regarding the significance of the new industry for both jobs and the local environment. Despite the national government's claims of sovereign control over the industry, local representatives of the Central Obrera Boliviana (COB) were worried that estimates of national income and job creation were being exaggerated, and little thought was given to how the new industry would impact on the existing foundations of the local economy. They also questioned whether Bolivia was really in a position on its own to draw together the investment and new technology needed to get the new industry off the ground. Local NGOs emphasized the possible environmental impact that lithium production would have on the Salar and how this might negatively affect the tourist and salt industries in the region.

I did not know it at the time, but in the following years, these worries and positions on the pros, cons, costs and value of the industry have only become ever more sharply defined. With this, a deep revision has been made of ideas regarding the relationship between natural resource extraction and sovereignty. The problem of boom and bust remains a focus, but there are now added characteristics to the debate. To wealth creation and political power, important new considerations are added: conflicting local and national political ontologies, and the significance of global discussions regarding green growth and climate change policy.

Recharging Sovereignty

The global demand for lithium is expected to more than double by 2025. The global market's annual consumption of lithium was approximately 40,000 metric tons in 2017, representing a roughly 10% increase year by year since 2015 ('The Global Lithium-ion Battery Market Is Set to Grow on Increasing Battery Applications' 2018). Between 2015 and last year, lithium prices nearly tripled (selling at an average of US$15,700 per ton in May–June

2018), a clear reflection of how fast the demand is rising. This spike in the activity of the market for lithium is expected to climb rapidly in the coming years, largely as a result of political decision-making and changing consumer patterns responding to climate change and questions of energy security. Examples of this include the decision of several European countries to phase out, as part of their strategies for green growth, the use of fossil fuel-driven vehicles over the next decade (Kovács 2019). This shift is also further stimulated by the provision of government subsidies (the reduction of purchase taxes, etc.) to consumers looking to buy a new car, such as in my adopted home country of Norway. Many European countries are also already in the process of diversifying their energy matrix away from fossil fuels through the creation and expansion of hydroelectric and wind power energy projects. Consumers are also interested in the increasingly affordable, and sometimes subsidized, possibilities of home solar and thermal domestic power production and storage. All of these changes, in addition to the continuance of the existing demand for electronic goods, are predicted to encourage a rapid increase in the global demand for lithium-based batteries and the extraction of their raw materials around the world.

Though lithium-mining operations exist on every continent except Antarctica, up to three-quarters of the known lithium reserves are in the Altiplano-Puna Plateau, a 1,100 mile-long stretch in the Andes. The salt bed deposits are concentrated in Chile, Argentina and Bolivia, known as the 'Lithium Triangle'. Since the 1980s, Chile has produced lithium from brine, and its Salar de Atacama is now the pre-eminent source of the chemical in Latin America. Argentina also began extracting lithium from brine in the late 1990s, exploiting its Salar del Hombre Muerto. Bolivia's lithium reserves match those of Chile's highly productive Salar de Atacama, but until recently, its potential had gone untapped. The Bolivian government has estimated its own lithium store to be 70% of the world's lithium reserve, some 100 million tons. The US geological survey puts the figure at a more modest 9 million tons.

In South America, lithium is found mixed in salty mud sitting beneath salt flats high in the mountains. To extract lithium, miners pump the brine into massive ponds, where it is left to evaporate for months (see Figure 4.1). This concentrated liquid is then brought into the labs of an industrial chemical facility for processing where, through filtration and the addition of chemicals, it is turned into lithium carbonate or lithium hydroxide.

In 2008, then President Morales of Bolivia announced that his government would invest US$995 million (until 2019) in the development of the national lithium industry (Sagárnaga López 2015). This was at the time the second-largest investment after the natural gas sector in the country (US$1 billion). Morales placed the lithium industry under the control of a new division of the state-run mining corporation (COMIBOL), i.e. the

Gerencia Nacional de Recursos Evaporiticos (GNRe) and he has repeatedly emphasized how the lithium industry is critical to the growth, development and sovereignty of Bolivia (Revette 2017: 150). As such, lithium became part of a wider ostensible strategy for the nationalization of natural resource production. Morales vowed that along with hydrocarbons, raw lithium would not be exploited by foreign corporations, but would instead be processed by state-controlled entities in Bolivia.

Alvaro García-Linera, then Vice-President (and a well-known public intellectual), echoed the President's link between lithium and national prosperity in even stronger terms in a *National Geographic* article (Draper 2019). He suggested that within a mere four years lithium will be 'the engine of our economy'. All Bolivians will benefit, he continued, 'taking them out of poverty, guaranteeing their stability in the middle class, and training them in scientific and technological fields so that they become part of the intelligentsia in the global economy'. He also stated: 'Throughout our history, we have not created a culture that combines our raw assets with intelligent thinking. This has produced a country which is rich in natural resources and socially very poor.'

Although earlier governments knew about the lithium reserves and supported resource extraction, García Linera observed that 'what they wanted to do was reproduce the whole scheme of a colonial extraction economy'. He suggested the election of his government demonstrates that the Bolivian people do not want this and, as a result, under the Morales government they started from scratch. 'We decided', said García Linera, 'that we Bolivians are going to occupy the Salar, invent our own lithium extraction method, and then partner with foreign firms that can bring us a global market.' Lithium, together with other resource wealth, was seen by the Morales government and its supporters as a means to recharge sovereignty and prosperity. In conjunction with a new constitution and National Development Plan, the Morales government prioritized following its election in 2005 the nationalization of strategic resources, with a particular focus on natural resources (Revette 2017: 150).

This Time It's Different?

The Bolivian government claimed that through its strategy for national support for the lithium industry, it could avoid the instabilities and intervention of past extractive enterprises and be able to sustainably become the 'Saudi Arabia of lithium' at time of necessary energy transition (COHA 2009). However, analysts and Bolivian citizens observing the government efforts to establish the industry over the last few years question the veracity of these claims. They point to a number of factors that instead suggest that other than a renewed rhetoric of sovereignty and serving the global green economy, the development and impact of the lithium industry is not so different from earlier cycles of boom and bust extraction.

Similar to the past, a number of analysts highlight the gap between Bolivia's ambitions, available investment and the country's technical capacity (Lombrana 2018). These were issues that have also limited the competitiveness of Bolivia's other mineral industries. Producing battery-grade lithium from brine involves separating out sodium chloride, potassium chloride and magnesium chloride. This last contaminant is particularly expensive to remove and requires the development of a downstream industry for cathodes (Draper 2019). The Salar receives significantly more rain than its counterparts in the lower altitudes of Argentina and Chile, which can slow the evaporation process. Its lithium deposits also have a higher magnesium content. Bolivia does not currently have a solution to these problems. Aside from a tiny pilot plant that makes batteries in the mining town of Potosí, the multimillion-dollar Llipi plant, which started producing lithium in January 2013, is all the Morales government had to show for its decade-long pursuit of lithium-fuelled prosperity.

In an attempt to address these issues, the Bolivian government approached a number of foreign companies it thought it could trust to develop newer and cheaper technology. However, a number of companies pulled out of contractual talks with Bolivia because of what they saw as a hard line on sovereign control over all elements of the industry. Analysts were also been critical of the signing of a joint venture deal with the German ACI Group in 2018.[1] According to some commentators, this undermined the government's claims of sovereign control (Verdades Ocultas Radio Podcast 2019). To other analysts and observers, the contract is problematic given the limited experience and expertise of the company. Based in a rural village in Germany's Black Forest, the company currently provides project management support to the photovoltaic, battery and automotive industries. ACI Systems Alemania, the section of ACI responsible for the Bolivian contract, employs just twenty people and was created solely to focus on building lithium production in Bolivia. For some industry analysts, this gamble on an inexperienced company is too little too late, especially given the head start and significant private investment that the industries in Chile and Argentina have had. Some analysts also suggest that Bolivia has taken too long to set up its own production facilities and will not be able to catch up with established lithium producers. In a recent Bloomberg article, a prominent analyst argued: 'Producing lithium to a certain level of purity for cathode production can take a great deal of time. For this project to get to where other players are globally, it's going to take years' (Lombrana 2018).

The promise of the employment and economic prosperity that formed part of the Bolivian government's argument for sovereign control over the lithium industry has also largely failed to appear. The Llipi plant has an all-Bolivian workforce of about 250 employees, but the majority of these – requiring high levels of technical and scientific competence – do not originate from nearby Aymara villages, but from the cities of La Paz and Potosí. So far, there has also been next to no effort to ensure that local communities share in the benefits of the new industry through social, economic and infrastructural investment. Responding to this issue in a recent *Washington Post* article focused on Bolivian lithium, a local community leader is quoted as stating: 'We know the lithium companies are taking millions of dollars from our lands. The companies are conscious of this. And we know they ought to give something back. But they're not' (Frankel and Whoriskey 2016). Similarly, in a recent article published in *National Geographic*, another community representative commented:

> We understand that once the plant is fully up and running, it will be a multimillion-dollar business. The scepticism is whether we'll get any of that. Those who should benefit first are the ones where the production is taking place . . . And it's not just cash benefits. There should be a faculty of chemical science established here, or scholarships, so young people can have a future. For three years we've been asking for this. (Draper 2019)

The lack of local-level community-level consultation is yet another feature of the current context that appears to repeat the failures of other extractive enterprises. In current Bolivian jurisprudence, Article 352 explicitly states that all communities are guaranteed to be consulted prior to the exploitation of non-renewable natural resources in their territory. The constitutional recognition of the rights of the population codifies the expectations that the people of Bolivia have a legitimate and legal voice in political decisions. In commenting on this, Revette (2017: 15) writes that whilst most 'communities, representatives and organizations do appear to be in agreement with the need to industrialize lithium production, I was struck by the immediate contrast between the "open door policy expressed to me . . ." by government representatives ". . . and the actual experiences of the surrounding communities"'. Various town representatives spoke of the continued lack of transparency and unfulfilled promise of consultation.

These failed meetings of expectations match the fears that were expressed to me in interviews I conducted with local people and organizations in 2011. Also similar are the growing concerns regarding the environmental impacts of lithium production in the region. Recent research carried out by the Centre for the Study of Labour and Agrarian Development (CEDLA 2018) in Bolivia highlighted the risk of widespread pollution, including the calcination of the soil that would put the Salar's unusual flora and fauna at risk. In a reported exchange between Luis Echazú of the National Evaporate Resource Authority (GNRe) and Ricardo Calla, a CEDLA researcher (and former Minister for Indigenous Affairs), the public servant admitted that the possible use of lime-based production methods in Bolivia would not just create small amounts of waste, but 'mountains of residual sludge' (Sagárnaga López 2015). In more recent comments, these problems have been said by representatives of the GNRe to have their solution in the adoption of other methods reliant on calcimine, not lime. According to the GNRe, this process would have minimum impact on the environment because 'sulfate is a fertilizer and insoluble', allowing for the possible sale of its residues in the future. According to CEDLA, this is not a guarantee of a better result and less pollution.

Analysts have warned that there have been no studies of the environmental impacts of sulfate technologies and that experimental work is now being carried out in Bolivia with inexperienced personnel (Sagárnaga López 2015). They have also observed that none of the technicians have postgraduate-level studies and the majority of them are in their twenties. They also point to an incomplete study by the now-dissolved Salar Scientific Committee in which draft conclusions stated that there was no scientific certainty about the consequences of industrial-scale production with sulfate technology. While further information is still needed on this issue in Bolivia, critics of the industry point to the experience of their neighbours. According to recent reports (Katwala 2018), in Argentina's Salar de Hombre Muerto, locals claim that lithium operations have contaminated streams used by humans and livestock, and for crop irrigation. In Chile, there have been clashes between mining companies and local communities, who say that lithium mining is leaving the landscape marred by mountains of discarded salt and canals filled with contaminated water with an unnatural blue hue.

Whereas there might be some doubt regarding the toxic impacts of the processing chemicals used in Bolivian lithium production, there is no doubt regarding the impact it will have on local water reserves. Lithium production requires enormous volumes of water. To concentrate the brine, which only contains traces of lithium, requires the evaporation of lots of water, and even more is needed to wash the finished product. A ton of lithium generally requires as much as 50,000 gallons of water. As Daniel Galli, an Argentine professor of thermodynamics, commented during a scientific meeting: 'Lithium mining, is really mining mountains of water' (Frankel and Whoriskey 2016). Many of the people in the surrounding communities are now worried that the lithium plants will deepen the existing shortages in the region, which receives less than four inches of rain per year.

A Moral Landscape

Back in 2015, local respondents to my interviews were already worried about the possible consequences of lithium production for the local water supply. In the high Andes, the effects of climate change have been visible for some time, as have the consequences of mining in terms of the contamination and desertification of local rivers and aquifers (Perrault 2012). With its requirements, it was evident to people in both the local tourist and agricultural sectors that lithium production would have serious consequences for already overstretched water resources. However, whilst the consequences that lithium production might have on the physical basis of the local economy was of deep concern, in rural areas this was rarely separated from an equally serious emphasis on the imbalance this would further cause to their relationship with spiritual forces in the local landscape.

As Lynn Sikkink (1997) has emphasized, in the Andes water is not only essential to human life, but is also a powerful metaphor for the ritual of community. Every year during the period of Carnival (February), Aymaran/Quechuan communities across the Bolivian altiplano celebrate *yaku cambio* (the exchange or change of waters). Through the annual ritual of mixing, joining and exchanging water from different sources across the landscape of the *ayllu* (community), community members re-create their ties to each other and strengthen their bonds to the land the spiritual forces within it (Sikkink 1997: 170). The main purpose of the ritual (i.e. to bring rain) highlights water's importance as an essential force that not only makes plants and animals grow, but also helps to retain the balance of land and cosmos, and the fertility and health of the human community. The ritual assists the re-integration of all parts of the community and its understanding as a common. In addition to seeking rain, Andean communities seek the ordered tension of community segments (land and people) that are both brought together through the medium of water and inextricably linked to it as the base of their livelihood and as the system through which water continuously circulates. In other words, they redistribute their commons through this ritual (Sikkink 1997).

Here it becomes clear that water is one of the elements of life that makes up the rural Andean ontological universe – one that emphasizes a balance of forces and model of community. Whilst it cannot be said that all Andean communities exactly share this conceptualization of the links between landscape and community, it is important to note that water, and fears of its loss and contamination, resulting from extractive processes has similar dimensions elsewhere in Bolivia and throughout the Andean-Amazonian region. I personally participated in the ritual of *yuku cambio* when I lived and carried out research for my Ph.D. in Santuario de Quillacas, a short distance north of the Salar in the Department of Oruro. The ritual and the importance of water to the community and its constitution of moral universe were highly visible there. These interactions are also visible at higher levels of political debate and scale.

In Bolivia, the wider significance of water to national-level debates and confrontations became highly visible in the 'Water Wars' in 2000 (this can be historically regarded as one of the foundations of the 2003 Bolivian 'Gas Wars' mentioned earlier in this book). The privatization of drinking water and the tripling of prices for its delivery to homes in the peri-urban areas sparked off a series of protests. To the surprise of the national authorities of the time, this local rejection of the changing conditions of access to water would not only lead to months of street blockades and confrontations between local people and the police in Cochabamba, but would also spread to other major cities in the country, including the capital La Paz. The police and the government retaliated through the use of force, including the use of snipers firing live rounds to kill and confuse protesters. These events were retold as fiction in the 2010 film *Even the Rain*.

Eventually, the private corporation Aguas de Tunari – a subsidiary of the Bechtel Corporation – was expelled from the country. Control over the local water company in Cochabamba (i.e. SEMAPA) was transferred by the national government to representatives of the local municipality, the trade union and the Coordinadora (a body formed by the leadership of the protests to coordinate their actions). Although there is still disgruntlement in the city regarding the water supply, the statutes of SEMAPA were rewritten in a challenging participatory process. The national pro-privatization Law 2029 was also cancelled and rewritten as the Drinking Water and Sanitation Law (2066). The Law recognizes marginalized communities' rights to use water and differentiates them from profit-making activities, now to be authorized and subject to fees. In 2004, similar principles were applied to the irrigation sector (Law 2878), which recognized decentralized irrigation governance. Both laws support indigenous people and farm labourers from being dispossessed of water. In 2009, the Bolivian Constitution was rewritten. The new constitution states that water is a basic right of life and bans the typical methods of privatization and leasing of water services for profit activities. In 2010, the Bolivian Plurinational Legislative Assembly introduced the Law of the Rights of Mother Earth (071). This law defines Mother Earth (known in Andean cosmology as Pachamama) as a 'collective subject of public interest' and declares Mother Earth and Earth's life-systems (human communities and ecosystems) as titleholders of inherent rights specified in law.

This history of protest and of legal reform underlines that a distinct moral landscape exists throughout Bolivia and is not only restricted to rural areas of the Andes and the Altiplano. It is also through the lens of this moral landscape that the Bolivian government's efforts to establish a lithium industry are seen as deeply contradictory. It should be noted that the actions of the Bolivian government also reflect internal struggles on what this moral landscape is within the Morales administration. In 2012, a heavily revised version of the Law of Mother Earth was introduced – the Framework Law of Mother Earth and Integral Development for Living Well (Law 300). The new version of the law was said by the government to give fuller treatment to the necessary nuances of the legal status and protections of Mother Earth. However, according to Hindery (2014), the ratified law 'clearly reflects both the more environmentally progressive ideals pushed by the Unity Pact (an alliance of grassroots organization is support of the MAS government) and the extractivist agenda of the Morales administration'.

In line with Andreucci (2018), it is also important to acknowledge that the position of the Morales administration changed over time. As Andreucci (2018: 18) notes, popular struggles and imaginaries were initially important to push through a progressive institutional restructuring of natural resource industries. However, once the new popular power bloc was stabilized, indigenous demands for emancipatory socio-environmental change began to be perceived as a threat to resource-based accumulation on which the government considered their economic survival relied. Writing on this same political shift, Postero writes:

> Indigeneity and the decolonization were the rallying cries for the Morales revolution, serving as what the French political philosopher Jacques Rancière . . . terms an emancipatory 'politics'. Yet as the MAS government consolidated its control and defeated its political adversaries on the right, its support for indigenous self-determination waned. Morales continues to invoke indigenous history and culture, but he does so in performances of a state-controlled version of indigeneity that legitimizes state power. (Postero 2017: 4)

The current disagreements and concerns voiced by local community representatives regarding lithium production reflect this 'ideological deterioration' (Andreucci 2018), the contradictions it has placed into the existing moral landscape and the efforts of the local population to question the terms of sovereignty.

Moral Landscapes Elsewhere

As earlier chapters in this volume have indicated, the politics of sovereignty and resource extraction is intimately entwined with contrasting, sometimes overlapping, social and political positions and perspectives. Here it is also important to stress that the expression of these positions is furthermore a reflection of complex moral landscapes and the mobilization of these ideas and senses into both daily life and political action. Indeed, the idea that contrasting moral landscapes provides an underlying rationale for conflict and contestation over natural resources is replicated in an expanding academic literature focused on the extractive frontiers of the Andean-Amazonian region.

Since the start of the extractive boom in the late 1990s, a growing number of scholars have attempted to study its characteristics and impacts in different contexts throughout Latin America (e.g. Haarstad 2012; Bebbington and Bury 2013; Veltamayer and Petras 2014; McNeish, Borchgrevink and Logan 2015; Deonandan and Dougherty 2016; Gordon and Webber 2016). Although much fewer in number, some texts also go beyond a detailed description of the historical political economy and contemporary political ecology of this extractive frontier. A series of ethnographies detail the underlying epistemological differences and moral landscapes of communities – in which water is repeatedly implicated as not only a resource but also a spiritual force – and make explicit their role in contemporary struggles over resources, sovereignty and the state in the region (e.g. Sawyer 2004; Hindery 2014; Ulloa 2013; Li 2015; Rasmussen 2015; Anthias 2018; Cepek 2018). Indeed, as a number of anthropologists have emphasized, many contemporary environmental conflicts are conflicts over different realities or worlds (Blaser 2009; de la Cadena 2010). The conflicts do not simply concern competing interpretations of nature, but struggles over the enactment, stabilization and protection of multiple socionatural worlds (Li 2015: 110). Li's (2015) work on a Peruvian Andean mining conflict and Cepek's (2018) work on life and struggle in the oil fields of the Ecuadorian Amazon are highly illustrative examples of writing of this kind. They are also important in that instead of simple polarization or incommensurability, they highlight that moral landscapes frequently overlap with each other in history and political practice.

Writing about the struggle of local people to defend the Cerro Quilish mountain in Peru from the mining company Minera Yanacocha, Li (2015) details how protesters worked to bring together different epistemological concerns to challenge a singular representation of the mountain only as a mineral deposit. In anti-mining campaign materials, the mountain was presented as an aquifer – the source of the main rivers and tributaries that supply water to the city and rural communities (Li 2015: 109). Activists argued that mining activity would compromise the quality of the water and would reduce the quantity of water available in an already drought-prone region. Protesters also argued that the mine should not be built because *campesinos* living in the region considered Cerro Quilish to be an Apu, a Quechuan term commonly translated as 'mountain spirit' or 'sacred mountain' (Li 2015: 109). The campaigns in defence of Cerro Quilish therefore evoked an animate landscape that was part of *campesinos'* experience of the

Cajamarca countryside. Li (2015: 142) therefore suggests that contemporary conflicts such as Cerro Quilish can thus be understood as an ongoing process of contestation over socionatural worlds.

Cepek (2018), writing about a very different context (i.e. the enduring effects of oil extraction on the Cofán indigenous community in the Ecuadorian Amazon), tells of a similarly rich and complex history of socionatural contestation. As he notes, the local experience of 'life in oil' is a slow, confusing violence that manifests itself as a radical transformation of people's understanding and experience of the material world:

> Oil has many other manifestations in Dureño. One of its most important consequences was a radical transformation of people's understanding and experience of the material world . . . Oil became a strange set of things: a swarm of visible and invisible substances that killed not because they were sent by supernaturally empowered enemies but because of their basic physical properties. In complex and confusing ways, the materials transformed rivers, forests, rains, skies, fish and game. The natural world became a hostile force . . . Shamans could injure people with mysterious objects, but oil wastes were a different kind of weapon . . . Illness and death became truly material phenomena. (2018: 236)

In considering the complex formation of socionatural worlds, Li and Cepek are the inheritors of an earlier political anthropology that sought to explain the relationships between cosmology and social organization in Andean society (e.g. Murra 1975; Urton 1981; Harris 2000), and how these provide the basis for a lived critique and accommodation of mining and resource extraction as central expressions of capitalism (e.g. Taussig 1980; Nash 1993). They are also the inheritors of a series of writings concerned with the study and proposal of indigenous or alternative development in the Andean area (e.g. Andolina, Laurie and Radcliffe 2009; Quijano 2010).

Linked to differing extractive projects, Li and Cepek can also be linked in terms of their intellectual inspiration to anthropological and sociological writing recognizing that extractive resources always operate in a matrix of social, natural and conceptual conditions that shape their power and form. The matrix of conditions is recognized to also operate with different temporalities and spatial logics. For example, Coronil (1997) describes how the promise of oil-wealth shaped public fantasies, myths of progress and the national identity of the Venezuelan state itself. Gledhill (2008) argues that similar effects can also be seen in countries where oil accounts for a smaller fraction of national production. He argues that oil is also at the centre of 'popular imaginaries' in countries such as Brazil and Mexico, being closely tied to particular forms of nationalism and claims to national sovereignty against perceived US imperialism (Gledhill 2011: 166). Recognizing the geopolitical importance of oil, Mitchell (2011) suggests through historical sociology that whereas coal power offered workers numerous opportunities to paralyse the economy and press their claims, the shift to oil sustained a less promising infrastructure for the pursuit of democratic politics. Several writers focused on the practice of recent large-scale open-pit mining efforts have similarly commented on changes in technology and the need for labour having similar impacts in reducing the space for union negotiation and the negotiation of benefits and mitigation of social and environmental impacts (Bebbington and Bury 2013; Conde and Le Billon 2017).

With regard to broader debates in social theory, further important links can be made with proposals for what are variously referred to as quasi- or boundary objects. To understand the place of material resources such as oil and minerals in people's everyday lives, authors such as Li and Cepek make reference to Latour's conceptualization of substances as 'quasi-objects', i.e. things that are simultaneously 'real as Nature, narrated as Discourse, collective as Society, existential as Being' (Latour 1993: 90). Quasi-objects are objects that are *neither* quite natural *nor* quite social. Monies, technologies, animals, microbes and natural resources can all come and do come to function as quasi-objects. These quasi-objects all bend human practices in a variety of ways, and constantly configure and reconfigure human relations amongst one another.

Writing about oil, Cepek notes that:

> Although oil is definitely a material thing; it exists in other ways too. It is wrapped up with people's words, thoughts, and actions as they envision its underground existence, enable its rise to the earth's surface, and ensure its movement through pipelines, tankers, refineries, and retail outlets to support the daily lives of billions of people. As it passes between, around, and through them, it composes the bonds that tie people together and force them apart. (2018: 234)

Also inspired in part by Latour, Li (2015) suggests that as an Apu (sacred spirit), the Cerro Quilish mountain represents a kind of 'boundary object' (Star and Griesemer 1989). Like quasi-objects, a boundary object is able to travel across borders and inhabit various communities of practice while maintaining a constant identity. As such a boundary object, Li (2015: 111) suggests:

> The multiplicity of Cerro Quilish proliferated the relations and material connections that were crucial to the success of the campaign. Water springs, canals and rivers that have their origins at Cerro Quilish gave people from various communities a direct connection to the struggle; and the mountain itself – not merely its economic potential, but the force of its physical presence – renewed people's sense of connection to a landscape that mining would permanently transform.

For de la Cadena (2010) quasi- and boundary objects represent elements of a much broader *equivocation* between the competing epistemologies of indigenous peoples and the modern state, or rather indigeneity and modernity – i.e. situations in which interlocutors appear to be speaking of the same thing when they are actually referring to different ones (Viveiros de Castro 2004). In their recognition and promotion of 'earth beings' (such as the Apus or other nature spirits) in their current struggles against mining and extractive operations, indigenous peoples not only put into question the separation of nature and culture that underpins the prevalent notion of politics and its according social contract, but also conjure up new actors in the political arena (de la Cadena 2010: 364). As she recognizes, mining as an economic activity has been part of Andean peasants and indigenous people's lives since the Conquest. However, whereas earlier mining technologies in which tunnels were bored into the land allowed for the continuation of relations with earth beings, the new open-pit mining and mountaintop-removal technologies literally destroy earth beings (de la Cadena 2015). Corporate mining ventures do not just encroach on peasant land and pollute the environment; by destroying earth beings, they erase an entire socio-natural world.

Confronted by heightening levels of destruction, peasant and indigenous communities have responded to this threat in diverse contexts in the Highlands and Lowlands of Latin America. Their actions not only draw attention to different political practice and ideas of rights. They commonly dumfound actors of the state, the private sector and the established left-wing opposition by 'making public' (Latour 2005) the central role of 'things'[2] in their campaigns that are understood not simply as nonhuman, but as sentient entities. For de la Cadena, indigenous peoples understand their landscapes not only as part of a moral universe, but as partly constitutive of it.

Multinaturalism

Although working with a focus on the Andean-Amazonian region, de la Cadena (2010) recognizes that the public presence of 'earth beings' in politics is part of a broader scholarly discussion about 'emergent forms of life' (Fischer 2003) and the actions of 'global assemblages' (Ong and Collier 2005) – as well as Latour's (1993, 2004, 2005) questioning of the boundaries between society and nature, people and objects. In anthropology, this has taken the form of the debate on the ontological turn. Anthropology has long been concerned with social and cultural difference, that societies and their practices may reflect other ways of seeing the world, but that they still see the same world. Proponents of the ontological turn argue that it is this notion – that they still see the same world – that needs to be overturned. The ontological turn instead proposes that worlds, as well as worldviews, may vary (Heywood 2017).

Ontological anthropology is inspired by the premise that a totalizing Western metaphysics of multiculturalism has been, and remains, one of the most insidious forms of modernist power (Bessire and Bond 2014). This critique of Western metaphysics is premised largely on the rediscovery of a 'nonmodern' Amerindian cosmology within indigenous mythology. Known as 'Amerindian perspectivism', this narrative is particularly associated with the pioneering work of Viveiros de Castro (1998, 2003, 2010, 2012), who has provided a foundational charter for many strands of ontological anthropology. It is argued by Viveiros de Castro and others that Amerindian ontology is the opposite of modern, Western, European 'mononaturalist' philosophy and the binaries of nature-culture on which the modern ontology has been based. A commonly cited summary of this perspective is that Amerindian *multinaturalism* may inspire us to invert the entire edifice of modernity by imagining not one world, but multiple worlds, not one nature and multiple cultures, but 'one single culture, multiple natures . . . one epistemology, multiple ontologies' (Viveiros de Castro 1998: 478; cited in Bessire and Bond 2014: 442).

By 'multinaturalist', Viveros de Castro means to make us aware that 'humans' share the same culture, soul or perspective, but differ across the bodies they possess and the worlds they perceive. Amerindians, he suggests, are not culturally relative, for to them all humans share the same culture and view of the world; they are naturally relative, for not all humans share the same body and same world (Heywood 2017: 3). All subjects, in other words, share the same point of view, but the difference lies in what they perceive to be reality:

> if I am in possession of a certain sort of body . . . I will see the same things you see when you see manioc, rice and beer and houses. However, if my body is different to yours – if it is that of a jaguar, for example – I will see beer where you see blood, a house where you see a den, and rice where you see animal remains. Furthermore, bodies can with some effort, be exchanged, put on and discarded like clothing, much as we think of ourselves as being able to exchange viewpoints. (Heywood 2017: 3)

Amerindian perspectivism holds that the point of view creates not the known object, but the relational subject and in doing so demands a comparative approach to comparison. This attention to 'alterity' or 'equivocations' (Viveiros de Castro 2004) is held by ontological anthropology to represent the opportunity of new research of nonmodernities and 'a new New World' (Hage 2012: 303). A fine example of this is Blaser's (2018) application of a sophisticated ontological perspectivism in a critique of the 'cosmopolitics' – the politics of cosmology, originally proposed by Stengers (1997, 2005) –

of caribou hunting in Labrador, Canada. Local wildlife managers in the provincial government think that hunting in present conditions will mean the disappearance of the caribou. This is disputed by local indigenous Innu hunters and elders, who argue that being prevented from hunting according to traditional protocols will mean the disappearance of *atiku* (at first sight, the word used by Inuu to refer to what Euro-Canadians call caribou). Blaser argues that the concept of cosmopolitics makes it possible to avoid the trap of 'reasonable politics', making evident that in this context, there are articulations between 'different reals' rather than between different perspectives on the 'same real' (Blaser 2018: 48). Blaser uses this context to emphasize the idea of 'equivocations', i.e. situations in which interlocuters appear to be speaking of the same thing when they are actually referring to different ones. He demonstrates that the term 'atiku' not only alludes to different understandings of the caribou, but of a simultaneous expression by the Inuu of multiplicity in meaning and significance. Making reference to the trick image that fools the eye to see both a duck and a rabbit at the same time (2018: 56), Blaser points to the possible co-occurrence of things. In a similar fashion, he suggests, 'the material-semiotic assemblages and practices, from which the more than one less than many atiku/caribou emerges, partially co-occur (most evidently in bodily presence) but they remain distinct' (2018: 57). Multiplicity, he stresses, 'refers to mutually entangled but divergent worldings' (2018: 57).

It is evident that the ontological turn in anthropology has gathered a significant momentum over the last decade or so and has inspired a series of high-profile projects and publications, seen by some as the salvation of anthropology as a discipline. In the foreword to Phillipe Descola's volume *Beyond Nature and Culture*, Marshall Sahlins commented that: 'Just when many thought that anthropology was losing its focus along came a Neo-Copernican claim that other people's worlds do not revolve around ours' (2013: xiii). The ontological turn has sparked into life a new wave of writing, drawing together disparate elements of anthropology's post-humanist avant garde. With the removal of the nature-culture distinction, the figure of ontology has been used to voice and valorize disparate concerns about the potentialities and contemporary entanglements, including multi-species ethnography (Kohn 2007; Kirsey and Helmreich 2010; Tsing 2012; Paxson and Helmreich 2014). It has also been used to further experimental scientific realism forming a connection between science and technology studies, actor–network theory (ANT) and anthropology (Law and Hassard 1999; Mol 2002). Leading on from the work of Viveiros de Castro a series of ethnographies have been made to reconsider indigenous cosmologies from Amazonia to Melanesia, Mongolia and Canada (Londoño 2005; Uzendoski 2005; Blaser 2009; Costa and Fausto 2010; Villaça 2010; Kapferer 2011;

Pedersen 2011). A series of phenomenological inflected accounts of dwelling and material vitality have also been produced (Ingold 2000; Henare, Holbraad and Wastell 2007; Bennett 2010; Ishili 2012).

The ontological turn has also importantly redirected the progressive orientation of anthropology, arguing that the discipline's merit lies not in engaging with the details of present problems, but in depicting their alternatives. According to the critical assessment of Bessire and Bond (2014: 441), the 'ontological turn shifts the insurgent front lines of ethnography from located descriptions of resistance, suffering and governance to anticipatory evocations of heterogeneous assemblages'. This is a significant reorientation of political anthropology. Here politics becomes a principal assertion of how things could be. The political purchase of writing on ontologies 'resides not only in the ways in which it may help promote certain futures, but also in the way it figurates the future in its enactment' (Viveiros de Castro, Pedersen and Holbraad 2014). In the opinion of Viveiros de Castro (2003: 18), this 'tactical reason' is more disruptive than dulled critiques of empire, capitalism or the state because it is capable of 'indefinitely sustaining the possible, they could be'. In such ways, ontological anthropology seeks to provincialize forms of power within the modern project while co-creating vital alternatives. It is suggested that 'to be radical, contra Marx, is not to grasp the thing by the root but to tend to a different plant altogether' (Bessire and Bond 2014: 441).

It is suggested by Viveiros de Castro and other ontological anthropologists that 'at the outer edge of modernity, a more contentiously intertwined modality of living has survived, one that does not just recognize the vibrancy of materiality but helps to hold it together' (Bessire and Bond 2014: 445). Here, shamanic revelations of a natural world can come to enact both the placement of local ecologies and the redemptive future we – facing environmental degradation and climate change – should also seize upon. Animism is offered anew as a form of redemption because it recognizes how the natural world is composed of proliferating and discontinuous subjects (Descola 2013).

The Return of the Primitive?

The ontological turn in anthropology has without doubt inspired an important reconsideration of a series of key issues, and interactions, that are of persisting significance in current politics and society: culture, nature, knowledge, cosmology, politics, etc. However, whilst consuming a large part of anthropological thought in recent years, it is also evident that not all anthropologists and social theorists have equally been convinced by its insights and proposals. Although ontological anthropology appears to act as a mechanism to promote 'ontological self-determination of peoples' by 'giving the ontological back to the people' (Viveiros de Castro 2004), it also makes a series of reductive assumptions about the standardization of alterity – that only the 'other' or indigenous authentically experiences alterity. It also assumes that a multinaturalist ontology can be taken as a general description of existing Amerindian and indigenous being without being caught in empirical contradictions.

Drawing on his own ethnographic work with the Kayapó people, Turner (2009) claims that the model of Amerindian multinaturalism re-inscribes the terms it claims to overturn. Turner argues that the figure of a multinaturalist ontology is predicated on the misinterpretation of Amazonian myths and self-understandings. Kayapó myths do not simply invert the nature-culture divide; rather, he argues, 'the whole point' of their myths is to describe how animals (nature) and humans (culture) became fully differentiated from one another. These details exceed and contradict the ontological script, which assumes that indigenous peoples perceive the nature-culture divide in modernist terms 'as a privative binary of mutually exclusive classificatory categories defined through the contrastive presence or absence of traits' (Turner 2009: 2). In other words, 'the explanatory power of the one major strand of the ontological turn depends in large part on an Amerindian ontology figures in ways that do not contradict but constitute the terms of the modern, Western, European ontology it is invoked to disapprove' (Bessire and Bond 2014: 443).

Ontological interpretations of multiplicity also tend to ignore ethnographic evidence that does not fit its standardization of alterity. Indigenous multiplicity may 'be misrepresented when the ontologist discovers that some . . . versions of indigenous worlding take up modern binaries and their memetic opposites as meaningful coordinates for self-fashioning' (Bessire and Bond 2014: 443). Here avoidance is made of more subtle insights and approaches developed in the earlier history of political anthropology, such as the 'hermeneutic violence' Taussig (1992, 1993) observed in historic academic fictions that 'flatten contradiction and systematize chaos' (1987: 132).

In contrast to the ontologists, other anthropologists have documented the complex and at times surprising articulated nature of indigenous ontological alterity (Nietzen 2003; Rodriguez-Piñero 2005; Gordillo 2004; Hale 2006; Bacigalupo 2007; Dennison 2012; Jackson 1995; Ramos 1998; Blackhawk 2006; Kauanui 2008). As I have also indicated in the earlier chapters of this volume, there are also multiple writers (e.g. Engle 2010; Simpson 2014) who, far from denying difference or reducing it to second-order effects of political economies, take its force seriously by examining how claims of sovereignty and its gradations emerge through tensions of accommodation and resistance. Indeed, there is a strong strain within European political philosophy (Nietzche, Bataille, Benjamin, Fanon, Foucault, etc.) that resisted the easy binary of the Enlightenment vs. enchantment. Indeed, we would be wise to remember, at a time when sharp contrasts between Western and non-Western modes of thought are being popularized anew, that Marxist theorists such as Wolf (1982) and poststructuralist thinkers such as Said (1978), Fabian (1983) and Clifford (1986) had been equally wary of such distinctions. For all their differences, these thinkers were keen to stress that the rhetorical construction of an absolute separation between West and non-Western culture might itself be a way in which the non-Western world was kept outside of history in the 'ethnic slot' (Martin 2019: 3).

In the rush to reclaim difference, ontologists end up reifying its boundaries. This is avoided by other anthropologists' approaches to indigeneity. In *Pathways of Memory and Power* (1988), Abercrombie, for example, convincingly demonstrates by drawing on historical archives and ethnography the manner in which Andean communities worked (and work) to standardize their own alterity as a means to exaggerate their indigeneity and survive the colonial state. Abercrombie (1988) painstakingly chronicles how tensions between creative Andean heterodoxies and colonial drives to remove heresies produced a newly bifurcated cosmos and forms of social memories in which colonial binaries were reproduced, reconciled and unravelled. Abercrombie critiques both the romanticist tendency to regard Andean culture as still separate from and resistant to European influences, and the melodramatic view that all indigenous practices have been obliterated by colonial and national elites. He also reveals how the apparent fusion of nature and culture attributed to indigenous people is itself a form of conceit whose genealogy can be traced to the colonial property regimes in which the commons was assigned to the Indians while private property was reserved for the Spanish (Bessire and Bond 2014: 444).

To rediscover a bounded, radical alterity, the ontologist 'at times must misrepresent indigenous actualities and erase the vital tensions' (Bessire and Bond 2014: 444) experienced, and the different fora and scales at which native peoples negotiate their identity and existence. Worryingly, through its creation of sharp boundaries, ontological anthropology may be in danger of not challenging but sustaining the hierarchies of life they are aimed against. It is important to recognize that the turn to ontology coincides with concurrent political economic interests and governmental projects focused on ranking the value of life in general and indigenous life in particular (Franklin and Locke 2003; Bessire and Bond 2014: 444). As Povinelli (2002) warns, the figure of radical alterity may organize new regimes of inequality or create the conditions for the hyper marginality of supposedly insufficient or 'decultured' indigenous populations (Bessire and Bond 2014). Similarly, with regard to the kinds of sacred earth beings now celebrated by de la Cadena and other ontologists in Bolivia and the Andean region, Canessa (2014; quoted in Martin 2019:22) comments that their legal recognition in new laws and constitutional reforms recognizing the rights of nature 'are the all-too-familiar struggles for power amongst humans that often work to further marginalize other groups already excluded and marginalized by capitalist modernity who do not win the battle to claim a political link with those non-human actors'.

Lithium Citizenship?

In emphasizing alterity, political ontologists suggest that indigenous people not only see the world differently, but also, in line with wider academic poststructuralist and post-development theories, reject any variation of development theory and practice. By emphasizing the role of earth beings in everyday politics, indigenous people defy the bounded modernist expectations of states and academics regarding economic growth, the capitalist market and the importance of technocratic solutions. The problem with this is that whilst the actions of indigenous communities in defence of their environment suggest an interest in breaking with the expectations of development, the critiques outlined above also suggest their defiance of ontological expectations. Ontologies are political, but, out of conditioned necessity, they do not always fit expected patterns of a turn away and a rejection of state and corporate actors and structures. This has been empirically explored in different contexts, including indigenous people's negotiation with the state regarding the terms of hydrocarbons extraction.

In her recent book *Limits to Decolonization* Anthias (2018: 12) challenges accounts that construct state extractivism and indigenous territorial projects in Bolivia in purely oppositional terms, revealing how indigenous peoples participate in struggles over the distribution of gas rents under the Morales government. Whereas many other writers have highlighted the intimate relationship between hydrocarbons and nation in Morales' Bolivia (Perrault and Valdivia 2010; Gustafson 2011; Perrault 2014), Anthias demonstrated how local actors in the Guarani territory of Itika Guasu (bordering the departments of Tarija and Chuquisaca in the hydrocarbon-rich Bolivian lowlands) articulate hydrocarbons and citizenship 'from the ground up'. Indigenous engagements in *hydrocarbon citizenship* 'are fraught with ambivalence and disagreement and produce new inequalities' (Humphreys Bebbington and Bebbington 2011). Yet, as Anthias comments, 'these engagements also represent a bold attempt to recapture the political content of 'territory' and its longstanding association with indigenous political autonomy' (2018: 13). Rather than imagining indigenous movements and leftist governments as natural allies in a challenge to neoliberalism 'from below', Anthias highlights 'the shifting alignments of sovereignty – as well as the conflicts – that have emerged between capital, the state, indigenous peoples and other territorial actors under the Morales government' (2018: 13).

Here I emphasize the relevance of Anthias writing on hydrocarbon citizenship as a relevant signpost for further thinking about the complex expression of citizenship observed in Uyuni (citizens of lithium and salt), and to further capture the intricacy of *resource sovereignty* more widely. Returning to Uyuni and Potosí, it is important to note that ontological considerations of a moral and cultural landscape are intertwined with economic and political considerations. Indeed, in recent times, this has been mobilized even further than what was evident in 2011, to the point where it has now become clear that the intricate local question of the industrial development of lithium has played a significant role in the downfall of the Morales government. Evidence of 'shifting alignments of sovereignty' is very clear in this case.

In November 2019, the fourteen-year-long presidency of Evo Morales Ayma came to an end with his and Vice-President Alvaro Garcia Linera's retreat into exile in Mexico (and Argentina more recently). The events surrounding his resignation from the presidency and flight are complicated. Key elements of this include reports of election fraud in the national election of 2019. This includes Morales' refusal to abide by the decision of a referendum in 2016 to deny him the legal right to stand for a third term. And it also includes the head of the armed forces' advice to Morales to stand down, and the eventual positioning of an interim government under the opposition leadership of Janine Añez. Most of the international media coverage of and academic commentary on these events has been focused on either evidencing that what occurred was a coup d'état (Mora 2019) or, in contrast, arguing that what occurred was a rightful end to undemocratic rule ('Bolivian Leader Evo Morales Steps Down' 2019). These are undoubtedly interesting and important debates, but what has largely been ignored in the writing on Morales' departure from power are the lines of fragmentation in the basis of his political and social support in the years leading up to 2019. These splits are related to Morales' refusal to abide by the 2016 referendum, but also growing signs of contradictions in his government's policy and political practice. A political drift away from support for the government was under way following the *gasolinzo* and TIPNIS protests (see Chapter 2). Indeed, at least in relation to the department of Potosí, one of the important steps in the removal of support for the Morales government came about in the reaction to the recent contract signed between the Morales government and the German company ACI. This has nothing to do with claims in the media of the existence of a conspiracy of international interests aimed at accessing Bolivia's rich lithium deposits (Beaulieu 2019).

Having repeatedly asked for a process of consultation and dialogue with the government regarding the terms of the contract signed with the German corporation and supported by Supreme Decree 3738, a series of militant actions were taken by the municipal authorities of Uyuni and the Department of Potosí. Local authorities questioned the setting of a rent on the concession given to the company at an annual rate of 3%. This was much lower that what had been promised and there was no clarity as to the amounts to be paid to the local region or of how their wider concerns regarding both employment possibilities and the social and environmental consequences of lithium production were to be addressed. The Civic Committee in Potosí argued that the agreement should have secured a 11–13% return on resource rents. Having failed to deliver a general strike in line with local expectations, a series of protests and an eleven-day hunger strike were supported in 2019 by the local authorities of the regional government and by the town council of Uyuni. According to Marco Antonio Pumari, President of the Civic Committee in Potosí, these actions paralysed the free movement of transport related to the lithium industry in the department over a period of six months (Verdades Ocultas Radio Podcast 2019). As these actions started to be noticed nationally, the local councils of the cities of La Paz and Cochabamba made a series of public statements formally supporting these actions.

Already in severe disagreement with the government regarding the terms of the industrialization and the profits of lithium production, regional divisions of national cooperative and state mining union organizations and local indigenous associations in the department of Potosí were quick to issue formal statements demanding the resignation of Morales following the reports of election fraud in November 2019. A protest march in the city of Potosí by the cooperative miners and local indigenous farmers further marked this position. On the border between the departments of Oruro and Potosí, a series of blockades were put in place by organizations still loyal to the MAS government as means to stop the spread of this march towards the capital and a possible coup ('Existen cuatro puntos de bloqueo campesino en caminos potosinos' 2019). Whereas violence did occur at these points and several other locations in Bolivia as protest for and against Morales took hold following his departure from office, broad agreement in the department of Potosí regarding opposition to the MAS government meant that civil order remained ('Ejemplo de Paz entre Bolivianos se Refleja en Potosí' 2019). These divergences of support by organizations in Potosí – organizations that had initially been essential to create the robust democratic foundations of the Morales government – added significantly to the wider splits and clamour for political change being expressed elsewhere in the country. Bringing with them both cultural and material concerns, they are also clear expressions of a form of 'lithium citizenship', or resource sovereignty being further articulated with a concrete political impact.

It should be evident in what is written above that the case of lithium politics and citizenship in Uyuni is an example that demonstrates how the idea of resource sovereignty stretches to contexts of 'green energy' production. It is clear from the conditions described above that whereas lithium production is formally characterized as a green energy resource, being linked to lower emissions forms of transport, in reality the consequences of its extraction do not match the expectations of it being renewable or of its representing a more sustainable energy resource in a social sense either. The dividing lines between renewable and non-renewable are evidently blurred here. Indeed, it is important to highlight that the same complexities surrounding lithium production may surround other forms of green energy production. Detailed qualitative and ethnographic study of wind power or hydroelectric development reveal similarly layered forms of socioenvironmental contestation to that of lithium (Millikan 2014; Howe, Boyer and Berrera 2015; Dunlap 2019). Indeed, although not expressed as such, it is clear from the details of these other political mobilizations and territorial claims that resource sovereignty is also a relevant concern and helpful direction in their explanation.

Conclusions

As is revealed in detail above, the expression of resource sovereignty represents a complex expression of concerns not only regarding the economic value and environmental costs of resource use, but also ontological and moral understandings of the landscape in which they are found and seen to belong. In previous chapters in this volume, I demonstrated the links between socioenvironmental contestation at different scales and popular expressions of sovereignty. In this chapter, I have emphasized that an underlying dynamic of conflict and contestation are different interpretations of our natural reality. However, this is shown to not be a marking out of completely contrasting ontological positions. Whereas distinct positions, ideas and beliefs can be identified, these frequently overlap and periodically align with each other as claims regarding sovereignty develop through history and individuals and their communities encounter contradictions, threats and need to compromise. Equally, disagreements over the use of resources and landscapes can lead to breaches in previous agreements on sovereignty and to contrasting positions and disagreement. In this, local politics can be tied to national politics. As I have demonstrated above, changing expressions of 'lithium citizenship' surrounding the development of lithium resources in Bolivia not only led to militancy and a breakdown in community–state relations in the

Department of Potosí, but also contributed significantly to the downfall of the national government.

Of equal importance, in this chapter I have emphasized that expressions of resource sovereignty surround resources seen as vital in the 'green transformation' (Brockington 2012). Indeed, similar ontological concerns, moral conflicts and expressions of resource sovereignty do not only take place with regard to extracted resources with significant environmental contamination and physically invasive footprints such as lithium. Whereas the environmental consequences of wind, solar, tidal or other renewable energy projects might be more limited, by extension it should be evident that similar questions of economic, environmental and social impacts, and ontological concerns, can similarly be relevant. Indeed, given the growing role that these resources are likely to play in the global economy in the near future, it is likely that similarly disruptive clashes over their meaning and impact will occur. Indeed, as the next chapter will reveal, the bracketing together of material and social claims (economy-territory-identity-ontology) has already led to significant legal and political changes to the structure of environmental governance in the region. What is lacking is a more formal acknowledgement of these connections and the value of a more conscious reflection on the importance of resource sovereignty.

Notes

1. Following the departure of Morales from the presidency, the interim government cancelled this contract ('Bolivia Scraps Joint Lithium Project with German Company' 2019).
2. E.g. mountains, rivers, seeds, sheep, alpacas, llamas, pastures, plots and rocks.

References

Abercrombie, Thomas. 1988. *Pathways of Memory and Power: Ethnography and History among an Andean People*. Madison: University of Wisconsin Press.

Andolina, Robert, Nina Laurie and Sarah Radcliffe. 2009. *Indigenous Development in the Andes: Culture, Power and Transnationalism*. Durham, NC: Duke University Press.

Andreucci, Diego. 2018. 'Populism, Hegemony and the Politics of Natural Resource Extraction in Evo Morales's Bolivia'. *Antipode* 50(4): 825–45.

Anthias, Penelope. 2018. *Limits to Decolonization: Indigeneity, Territory and Hydrocarbon Politics in the Bolivian Chaco*. Ithaca: Cornell University Press.

Bacigalupo, Ana. 2007. *Shamans of the Foye Tree: Gender, Power and Healing among the Chilean Mapuche*. Austin: University of Texas Press.

Beaulieu, Devin. 2019. 'The Bolivian Lithium Conspiracy'. *Medium.com*, 25 November. Retrieved 17 November 2020 from https://medium.com/@devin.beaulieu/the-bolivian-lithium-conspiracy-a39e37e9e2a1.

Bebbington, Anthony, and Jeffrey Bury. 2013. *Subterranean Struggles: New Dynamics of Mining, Oil and Gas in Latin America*. Austin: University of Texas Press.

Bennett, Jane. 2010. *Vibrant Matter: A Political Ecology of Things*. Durham, NC: Duke University Press.

Bessire, Lucas, and David Bond. 2014. 'Ontological Anthropology and the Deferral of Critique'. *American Ethnologist* 41(3): 440–56.

Blackhawk, Ned. 2006. *Violence over Land: Indians and Empires in the Early American West*. Cambridge: Harvard University Press.

Blaser, Mario. 2009. 'The Threat of the Yrmo: The Political Ontology of a Sustainable Hunting Program'. *American Anthropologist* 111(1): 10–20.

———. 2018. 'Doing and Undoing Caribou/Atiku: Diffractive and Divergent Multiplicities and Their Cosmological Orientations'. *Tupuya: Latin American Science, Technology and Science* 1: 65–82.

'Bolivia Scraps Joint Lithium Project with German Company'. 2019. *DW.com*, 4 November. Retrieved 17 November 2020 from https://www.dw.com/en/bolivia-scraps-joint-lithium-project-with-german-company/a-51100873.

'Bolivian Leader Evo Morales Steps Down'. 2019. *New York Times*, 10 November. Retrieved 17 November 2020 from https://www.nytimes.com/2019/11/10/world/americas/evo-morales-bolivia.html.

Brockington, Dan. 2012. 'A Radically Conservative Vision? The Challenge of UNEP's Towards a Green Economy'. *Development and Change* 43(1): 409–22.

Canessa, Andrew. 2014. 'Conflict, Claim and Contradiction in the New "Indigenous" State of Bolivia'. *Critique of Anthropology* 34(2): 153–73.

CEDLA. 2018. 'Litio: Cambios en la industria y suspenso en torno a su industrialización en Bolivia'. *Cuadernos de Coyuntura 18. Centro de Estudios para el desarrollo laboral y agrarian*, April. Retrieved 17 November 2020 from https://cedla.org/publicacions/ieye/cuadernos-de-coyuntura-18-litio-cambios-en-la-industria-y-suspenso-en-torno-a-su-industrializacion-en-bolivia.

Cepek, Michael. 2018. *Life in Oil: Cofán Survival in the Petroleum Fields of Amazonia*. Austin: University of Texas Press.

Clifford, James. 1986. *Writing Culture: The Poetics and Politics of Ethnography*. Berkeley: University of California Press.

COHA. 2009. 'Bolivia: The Myth of the Saudi Arabia of Lithium' *Council on Hemispheric Affairs*, 28 October. Retrieved 17 November 2020 from https://www.coha.org/Bolivia-the-Myth-of-the-Saudi-Arabia-of-Lithium/.

Conde, Marta and Phillipe Le Billon. 2017. 'Why Do Some Communities Resist Mining Projects While Others Do Not?' *The Extractive Industries and Society*. http://dx.doi.org/10.1016/j.exis.2017.04.009.

Contreras, Manuel. 1993. *The Bolivian Tin Mining Industry in the First Half of the 20th Century*. London: ILAS.

Coronil, Fernando. 1997. *The Magical State: Nature, Money and Modernity in Venezuela*. Chicago: University of Chicago Press.

Costa, Luiz, and Carlos Fausto. 2010. 'The Return of the Animists: Recent Studies of Amazonian Ontologies'. *Religion and Society* 1(1): 89–109.

de la Cadena, Marisol. 2010. 'Indigenous Cosmopolitics in the Andes: Conceptual Reflections beyond "Politics"'. *Cultural Anthropology* 25(2): 334–70.

———. 2015. *Earth Beings: Ecologies of Practice Across Andean Worlds*. Durham, NC: Duke University Press.

Dennison, Jean. 2012. *Colonial Entanglements. Constituting a 21st Century Osage Nation*. Chapel Hill: University of North Carolina Press.

Deonandan, Kalowatie, and Michael Dougherty. 2016. *Mining in Latin America: Critical Approaches to the New Extraction*. London and New York: Routledge.

Descola, Philippe. 2013. *Beyond Nature and Culture*. Chicago: University of Chicago Press.

Draper, Robert. 2019. 'This Metal is Powering Today's Technology – at What Price?'. *National Geographic Magazine*, February. Retrieved 17 November 2020 from https://www.nation algeographic.com/magazine/2019/02/lithium-is-fueling-technology-today-at-what-cost.

Dunlap, Alexander. 2019. *Renewing Destruction: Wind Energy Development, Conflict and Resistance in a Latin American Context*. London and New York: Rowman & Littlefield.

Eichner, Andrew. 2012. 'More Precious than Gold: Limited Access to Rare Elements and Implications for Clean Energy in the United States'. *Journal of Law, Technology and Policy* 2012: 258–87.

'Ejemplo de Paz entre Bolivianos se Refleja en Potosí'. 2019. *Red Uno Sur*, 16 November. Retrieved 17 November 2020 from https://www.youtube.com/watch?v=iM9D0HxW8eU.

Engle, Karen. 2010. *The Elusive Promise of Indigenous Development*. Durham, NC: Duke University Press.

'Existen cuatro puntos de bloqueo campesino en caminos potosinos'. 2019. *El Potosí*, 15 November. Retrieved 17 November 2020 from https://elpotosi.net/local/20191115_existen-cuatro-puntos-de-bloqueo-campesino-en-caminos-potosinos.html.

Fabian, Johannes. 1983. *Time and the Other*. New York: Columbia University Press.

Fischer, Michael. 2003. *Emergent Forms of Life and the Anthropological Voice*. Durham, NC: Duke University Press.

Frankel, Todd, and Peter Whoriskey. 2016. 'Tossed Aside in the White Gold Rush'. *Washington Post*, 19 December. Retrieved 17 November 2020 from https://www.washingtonpost .com/graphics/business/batteries/tossed-aside-in-the-lithium-rush.

Franklin, Sarah, and Margaret Locke. 2003. *Remaking Life and Death: Toward an Anthropology of the Biosciences*. Santa Fe, NM: School of American Research Press.

Gordillo, Gastón. 2004. *Landscapes of Devils: Tensions of Place and Memory in the Argentinean Chaco*. Durham, NC: Duke University Press.

Gordon, Todd, and Jeffrey Webber. 2016. *Blood of Extraction*. Fernwood Publishing.

Gledhill, John. 2008. 'The People's Oil: Nationalism, Globalization and the Possibility of Another Country in Brazil, Mexico and Venezuela'. *Focaal* 52: 57–74.

———. 2011. 'The Persistent Imaginary of "the People's Oil": Nationalism, Globalization and the Possibility of Another Country in Brazil, Mexico and Venezuela', in Andrea Behrends, Stephen Reyna and Günther Schlee (eds), *Crude Domination: An Anthropology of Oil*. New York: Berghahn Books.

Gustafson, Brett. 2011. 'Flashpoints of Sovereignty: Natural Gas and Spatial Politics in Eastern Bolivia', in Andrea Behrends, Stephen Reyna and Günther Schlee (eds), *Crude Domination: An Anthropology of Oil*. New York: Berghahn Books.

Haarstad, Haavard. 2012. *New Political Spaces in Latin American Resource Governance*. London: Palgrave Macmillan.

Hage, Ghassan. 2012. 'Critical Anthropological Thought and the Radical Political Imaginary Today'. *Critique of Anthropology* 32(3): 285–308.

Hale, Charles. 2006. 'Activist Research vs Cultural Critique: Indigenous Land Rights and the Contradictions of Politically Engaged Anthropology'. *Cultural Anthropology* 21(1): 96–120.

Hand, Eric. 2007. 'The Salt Flat with Curious Curves'. *Nature*, 30 November. Retrieved 17 November 2020 from https://www.nature.com/news/2007/071130/full/news.2007.315 .html.

Harris, Olivia. 2000. *To Make the Earth Bear Fruit: Ethnographic Essays on Fertility, Work, and Gender in Highland Bolivia*. London: ILAS.

Henare, Amiria, Martin Holbraad and Sari Wastell (eds). 2007. *Thinking through Things: Theorizing Artefacts in Ethnographic Perspective*. New York: Taylor & Francis.

Heywood, Paolo. 2017. 'Ontological Turn'. *The Cambridge Encyclopedia of Anthropology*, 19 May. Retrieved 17 November 2020 from http://doi.org/10.29164/17ontology.

Hindery, Derick. 2014. *From Enron to Evo: Pipeline Politics, Global Environmentalism and Indigenous Rights in Bolivia*. Tuscon: University of Arizona Press.

Howe, Cymene, Dominic Boyer and Edith Barerra. 2015. 'Wind at the Margins of the State: Autonomy and Renewable Energy Development in Southern Mexico', in John-Andrew McNeish, Axel Borchgrevink and Owen Logan (eds), *Contested Powers: The Politics of Energy and Development in Latin America*. London and New York: Zed Books.

Humphreys Bebbington, Denise, and Antony Bebbington. 2011. 'An Andean Avatar: Post-Neoliberal and Neoliberal Strategies for Securing the Unobtainable'. *New Political Economy* 16(1): 131–45.

Ingold, Timothy. 2000. *The Perception of the Environment. Essays on Livelihood, Dwelling and Skill*. London and New York: Routledge.

Ishili, Miho. 2012. 'Acting on Things: Self-Poiesis, Actuality and Contingency in the Formation of Divine Worlds'. *HAU: Journal of Ethnographic Theory* 2(2): 371–88.

Jackson, Jean. 1995. 'Culture, Genuine and Spurious: The Politics of Indianness in the Vaupés, Colombia'. *American Ethnologist* 22(1): 3–27.

Kauanui, Kehaulani. 2008. *Hawaiian Blood: Colonialism and the Politics of Sovereignty and Indigeneity*. Durham, NC: Duke University Press.

Kapferer, Bruce. 2011. *Legends of People, Myths and State: Violence, Intolerance, and Political Culture in Sri Lanka and Australia*. New York: Berghahn Books.

Katwala, Amit. 2018. 'The Spiralling Environmental Cost of Our Lithium Battery Addiction'. *Wired*, 5 August. Retrieved 17 November 2020 from https://www.wired.co.uk/article/lithium-batteries-environment-impact.

Kirsey, Eben, and Stefan Helmreich, 2010. 'The Emergence of Multispecies Ethnography'. *Cultural Anthropology* 25(4): 545–76.

Kohn, Eduardo. 2007. 'How Dogs Dream: Amazonian Natures and the Politics of Transspecies Engagement'. *American Ethnologist* 34(1): 3–24.

Kovács, Zsigmond. 2019. 'The End of the Fossil Fuel Car is on the EU Agenda'. *Transport & Environment*, 31 October. Retrieved 17 November 2020 from https://www.transportenvironment.org/news/end-fossil-fuel-car-eu-agenda.

Latour, Bruno. 1993. *We Have Never Been Modern*. Cambridge, MA: Harvard University Press.

———. 2004. *Politics of Nature: How to Bring the Sciences into Democracy*. Cambridge, MA: MIT Press.

———. 2005. 'From Realpolitik to Dingpolitic or How to Make Things Public', in Bruno Latour and Peter Weibel (eds), *Making Things Public: Atmospheres of Democracy*. Cambridge, MA: MIT Press.

Law, John, and John Hassard. 1999. *Actor Network Theory and After*. Oxford: Blackwell.

Li, Fabiana. 2015. *Unearthing Conflict: Corporate Mining, Activism and Expertise in Peru*. Durham, NC: Duke University Press.

Lombrana, Laura. 2018. 'Bolivia's Almost Impossible Lithium Dream'. *Bloomberg*, 3 December. Retrieved 17 November 2020 from https://www.bloomberg.com/news/features/2018-12-03/bolivia-s-almost-impossible-lithium-dream.

Londoño, Carlos. 2005. 'Inhuman Beings: Morality and Perspectivism among Muinane People (Colombian Amazon)'. *Ethnos* 70(1): 1–24.

Martin, Keir. 2019. 'Subaltern Perspectives in Post-human Theory'. *Anthropological Theory* 20(3): 357–82.

McNeish, John-Andrew, Axel Borchgrevink and Owen Logan. 2015. *Contested Powers: The Politics of Energy and Development in Latin America*. London: Zed Books.

Millikan, Brent. 2014. 'The Amazon: Dirty Dams, Dirty Politics and the Myth of Clean Energy'. *Tipití: Journal of the Society of Lowland South America* 12(2): 134–37.

Mitchell, Timothy. 2011. *Carbon Democracy: Political Power in the Age of Oil*. London: Verso.

Mol, Anne-Marie. 2002. *The Body Multiple: Ontology in Medical Practice*. Durham, NC: Duke University Press.

Mora, María. 2019. 'Bolivia's Unravelling'. *NACLA Reporting on the Americas*, 25 November. Retrieved 17 November 2020 from https://nacla.org/news/2019/11/25/bolivia-un raveling?fbclid=IwAR0opPUa1nQqHWkqYUjgyc4GiMzuf-K3wzNdPwIKNeza9ZR Pv24Zc-vLyCU.

Murra, John. 1975. 'El control vertical de un máximo de pisos ecológicos en la economía de las sociedades andinas'. *Formaciones Económicas y Políticas del Mundo Andino* 59–115.

Nash, June. 1993. *We Eat the Mines and the Mines Eat Us: Dependency and Exploitation in Bolivian Tin Mines*. New York: Columbia University Press.

Nietzen, Ronald. 2003. *The Origins of Indigenism: Human Rights and the Politics of Identity*. Berkeley: University of California Press.

Ong, Aihwa, and Stephan Collier. 2005. *Global Assemblages: Technology, Politics and Ethics as Anthropological Problems*. Oxford: Blackwell.

Paxson, Heather, and Stefan Helmreich. 2014. 'The Perils and Promises of Microbial Abundance: Novel Natures and Model Ecosystems – from Artisanal Cheese to Alien Seas'. *Social Studies of Science* 44(2): 165–93.

Pedersen, Morten. 2011. *Not Quite Shamans: Spirit Worlds and Political Lives in Northern Mongolia*. Ithaca, NY: Cornell University Press.

Perrault, Tom. 2012. 'Extracting Justice: Natural Gas, Indigenous Mobilization, and the Bolivian State', in Suzannah Sawyer and Edmund Terenz Gomez (eds). *The Politics of Resource Extraction: Indigenous Peoples, Multinational Corporations and the State*. Springer IPES Series.

———. 2014. 'Nature and Nation: The Territorial Logics of Hydrocarbon Governance in Bolivia', in Anthony Bebbington and Jeffrey Bury (eds), *Subterranean Struggles: New Geographies of Extractive Industries in Latin America*. Austin: University of Texas Press.

Perrault, Tom, and Gabriela Valdivia. 2010. 'Hydrocarbons, Popular Protest and National Imaginaries: Ecuador and Bolivia in Comparative Context'. *Geoforum* 41: 689–99.

Postero, Nancy. 2017. *The Indigenous State: Race, Politics and Performance in Pluri-national Bolivia*. Berkeley: University of California Press.

Povinelli, Elizabeth. 2002. *The Cunning of Recognition: Indigenous Alterities and the Making of Australian Multi-culturalism*. Durham, NC: Duke University Press.

Quijano, Anibal. 2010. 'Coloniality and Modernity/Rationality', in Walter Mignolo and Arturo Escobar (eds), *Globalization and the Decolonial Option*. New York: Routledge.

Ramos, Alcida. 1998. *Indigenism: Ethnic Politics in Brazil*. Madison: University of Wisconsin Press.

Rasmussen, Mattias. 2015. *Andean Waterways: Resource Politics in Highland Peru*. Seattle: University of Washington Press.

Revette, Anna. 2017. 'This Time It's Different: Lithium Extraction, Cultural Politics and Development in Bolivia'. *Third World Quarterly* 38(1): 149–68.

Rodriguez-Piñero, Luis. 2005. *Indigenous Peoples, Postcolonialism and International Law: The ILO Regime*. Oxford: Oxford University Press.

Sagárnaga López, Rafael. 2015. 'Bolivia's Lithium Boom: Dream or Nightmare?' *Open Democracy*, 21 December. Retrieved 17 November 2020 from https://www.opendemocracy.net/ en/democraciaabierta/bolivia-s-lithium-boom-dream-or-nightmare.

―――. 2016. 'Bolivia's Coming Lithium Boom: Economic Miracle or Environmental Nightmare'. *Ecologist*, 1 January. Retrieved 17 November 2020 from https://theecologist.org/2016/jan/01/bolivias-coming-lithium-boom-economic-miracle-or-environmental-nightmare.

Sahlins, Marshall. 2013. 'Foreword', in Philippe Descola, *Beyond Nature and Culture*. Chicago: University of Chicago Press.

Said, Edward. 1978. *Orientalism*. London: Pantheon Books.

Sawyer, Suzannah. 2004. *Crude Chronicles: Indigenous Politics, Multinational Oil and Neoliberalism in Ecuador*. Durham, NC: Duke University Press.

Sikkink, Lynn. 1997. 'Water and Exchange: The Ritual of Yaku Cambio as Communal and Competitive Encounter'. *American Ethnologist* 24(1): 170–89.

Simpson, Audrey. 2014. *Mohawk Interruptus: Political Life across the Borders of Settler States*. Durham, NC: Duke University Press.

Star, Susan, and James Griesemer. 1989. 'Institutional Ecology, Translations and Boundary Objects: Amateurs and Professionals in Berkeley's Museum of Vertebrate Zoology 1907–39'. *Social Studies of Science* 19(3): 387–420.

Stengers, Isabelle. 1997. 'Pour en finir avec la tolérance'. *Cosmopolitiques 7*. La Découverte: Paris.

―――. 2005. 'The Cosmopolitical Proposal', in Bruno Latour and Peter Weibel (eds), *Making Things Public: Atmospheres of Democracy*. Cambridge, MA: MIT Press.

Taussig, Michael. 1980. *The Devil and Commodity Fetishism in South America*. Chapel Hill: University of Carolina Press.

―――. 1987. *Shamanism, Colonialism and the Wild Man*. Chicago: University of Chicago Press.

―――. 1992. *The Nervous System*. London: Routledge.

―――. 1993. *Memisis and Alterity. A Particular History of the Senses*. London: Taylor and Francis.

'The Global Lithium-ion Battery Market Is Set to Grow on Increasing Battery Applications'. 2018. *PR Newswire*, 31 October. Retrieved 17 November 2020 from https://www.prnewswire.com/news-releases/the-global-lithium-ion-battery-market-is-set-to-grow-on-increasing-battery-applications-887538016.html.

Tran, Martino, David Banister, Justin Bishop and Malcom McCulloch. 2012. 'Realizing the Electric-Vehicle Revolution'. *Nature Climate Change* 2: 328–33.

Tsing, Anna. 2012. 'Unruly Edges: Mushrooms as Companion Species'. *Environmental Humanities* 1: 141–54.

Turner, Victor. 2009. 'The Crisis of Late Structuralism, Perspectivism and Animism: Rethinking Culture, Nature, Spirit and Bodiliness'. *Tipiti* 7(1): 3–42.

Ulloa, Aastrid. 2013. *The Ecological Native: Indigenous Peoples' Movements and Eco-governmentality in Colombia*. London: Routledge.

Urton, Gary. 1981. *At the Crossroads of the Earth and the Sky: An Andean Cosmology*. Austin: University of Texas Press.

Uzendoski, Michael. 2005. 'The Phenomenology of Perspectivism: Aesthetics, Sound and Power in Women's Songs from Amazonian Ecuador'. *Current Anthropology* 46(4): 656–62.

Veltamayer, Henry, and James Petras. 2014. *The New Extractivism: A Post-development Model or Imperialism of the 21st Century*. London: Zed Books.

Verdades Ocultas Radio Podcast. 2019. 'El Conflicto del Litio. Fundación Solón', 13 October. Retrieved 17 November 2020 from https://www.youtube.com/watch?v=L66h7J87glk&feature=youtu.be&fbclid=IwAR0jxVckQaSNI1_rjri5HX_fVHKLYX0Xqs78eG_SPDunDMynICgTtdZA21lA.

Villaça, Aparecida. 2010. *Strange Enemies: Indigenous Agency and Scenes of Encounters in Amazonia*. Durham, NC: Duke University Press.

Viveiros de Castro, Eduardo. 2012. 'Cosmological Perspectivism in Amazonia and Elsewhere'. *Masterclass Series 1. HAU Network of Ethnographic Theory*. Manchester UK.

Viveiros de Castro, Eduardo. 1998. 'Cosmological Deixis and Amerindian Perspectivism'. *Journal of the Royal Anthropological Institute* 4: 469–88.

———. 2003. *and: After Dinner Speech Given at 5th Decennial Conferences of the Association of Social Anthropologists of the UK and Commonwealth*. Manchester: Manchester University Press.

———. 2004. 'Perspectival Anthropology and the Method of Controlled Equivocation'. *Tipití: Journal of the Society for the Anthropology of Lowland South America* 2(1): 3–22.

———. 2010. 'Introduction: The Untimely Again', in Pierre Clastres (ed), *Archeology of Violence*. Los Angeles: Semiotext.

Viveiros de Castro, Eduardo, Max Pedersen and Martin Holbrand. 2014. 'The Politics of Ontology: Anthropological Positions'. *Cultural Anthropology*. https://culanth.org/fieldsights/the-politics-of-ontology-anthropological-positions.

Wolf, Erik. 1982. *Europe and the People without History*. Berkeley: University of California Press.

Figure 5.1 Staves carried by Territorial Guardians, Resguardo Cañamomo Lomaprieta, Caldas. Colombia. Published with the Permission of Hector Jaime Vinasco

Chapter 5

No Negotiation with
a Gun to Your Head?

This judgement is a great opportunity to resolve issues caused by the lack of land titling, including exercising authority over our lands, applying our laws, thinking about economic development and opposing projects that affect our survival as indigenous peoples
> —Ex-Governor of the Resguerdo Cañamomo Lomaprieta, in ('Landmark Decision for Indigenous Peoples in Colombia and Globally' 2017)

[S]tate law is begat of violence, of states made possible by the ongoing raw economy- which in the case of Colombia, grew from the hard labour of Afro-descendent and indigenous slaves mining for the Spaniards. From this perspective, 'raw law' is a precursor to, or embedded within, state law from its very origins. And the 'rule of law' is interpreted as 'fundamentally illegal' in and of itself, a mere camouflage enabling concepts such as terra nullius (empty lands that are not empty) to justify plunder, and in engaging in 'lawless or criminal operations.
> —Viviane Weitzer, 'Nosotros Somos Estado'

In 2017, the Colombian Constitutional Court concluded a legal judgment finding in favour of the protection of the land rights of the Embera Chamí[1] community of Cañamomo Lomaprieta Resguardo, an indigenous reserve[2] in western Colombia. The judgment was widely seen as a major win for both indigenous rights and environmental governance in the country, and one that, as the first quote above makes clear, appeared to set the scene for a major improvement in conditions of peace and development for the indigenous community.

In its ruling, the court ordered that the reserves' land must be delimited and titled within one year, during which time all further permits, or formalization of mining activities would be suspended. Any subsequent mining activities proposed on the delimited territories were only to proceed on the basis of the effective participation of the inhabitants of the reserve. The court also ordered that the map produced by the reserve of its land be registered provisionally until it was officially demarcated. Also, in what appeared to be a legal first internationally, the court gave explicit protection to ancestral mining activities carried out by the thirty-two communities within the reserve. The court recognized that this form of mining conformed to the reserve's own laws and that the state had an obligation 'not to criminalize this type of ancestral activity'.

Whilst undoubtedly offering a significant tightening of conditions for the protection of the community, community leaders and researchers who had worked with the community were not convinced that the case was proof of the strength of the Colombian legal system. Having worked with the reserve in the capacity as a representative of both the Canadian Research Centre and the Forest Peoples Programme, Weitzer commented that whilst assisting the protection of indigenous territorial rights, she and her colleagues remained concerned that the court decision 'may increase risks to Resguerdo leaders, some of whom have already suffered a number of credible death threats' ('Landmark Decision for Indigenous Peoples in Colombia and Globally' 2017). As well as tying to the example of a death threat at the start of this volume, in April 2015 Fernando Salazar, an indigenous leader from the community, was brutally assassinated ('Three Years on from His Murder, Colombian Indigenous Leader's Killers Remain Unpunished' 2018). Weitzer goes on to stress the need for the state to further ensure the safety of land and human rights defenders involved in the case. In doing so, she recognizes that whereas Colombia has a well-founded reputation for a strong legal system and legal innovation, it also has an apparently contradictory history in which the formal 'rule of law' is beholden to the shady connections between formal politics and illegal actors. This makes court rulings on land rights and protections little more than 'state effects' that hide the violent reality of Colombia's internal political economy.

Importantly, as an academic, Weitzer proposes that we understand the nature of this contradiction in terms of what she calls 'raw law' (Weitzer 2017: 1198–99). Weitzer comments that although Colombia has some of the most advanced legislation, jurisprudence and practice with regard to ethnic rights, an enormous implementation gap exists. Drawing on Mbembe's (2012) work on 'raw economy' and Nader (2012), Weitzer further outlines the idea of raw law with the second of the quotes given at the start of this chapter.

With the conception of 'raw law', earlier distinctions of legal pluralism, of a division between state law and customary law, or even of interlegality (de Sousa Santos 1987) are further complicated by the recognition of the merging of the illegal with the illegal. Here Weitzer makes an important link to the work of Comaroff and Comaroff (2009) in the context of Africa and the ethnographic evidence of criminal gangs developing their own constitutions. They suggest that that this evinces a 'will to sovereignty', expressed through the exercise of control over lives, deaths and conditions of existence of those who fall within its purview- and the extension over them of the jurisdiction of some kind of law (Weitzer 2017: 1207).

(Weitzer 2017:1207) argues that to not make visible the raw law of armed actors involved in the extractive sector in Colombia is to ignore the realities constraining the agency of a variety of actors, and their abilities to enforce their own laws, and sovereignties. It is the particular history leading up to judgement and fear of what would happen in its aftermath that is suggestive of the Embera Chamí case belonging to this wider Colombian history of raw law – and therefore of a need to treat its win with caution. The court judgment was the culmination of a legal struggle by the reserve to secure official recognition of its land and of the even longer history of the Embera Chamí to defend their indigenous land and identity.

Although one of the oldest recognized indigenous reserves in Colombia with formal legal recognition by the Spanish Crown dating part to the 1500s following forays into the area to look for precious metals, and by national decree (Article 21, Law 2164) and Articles 63 and 329 of the 1995 National Constitution, the reserve had suffered for years from territorial encroachment from surrounding colonization and further incursions for resource extraction because of a lack of a formal land title. For decades, the leaders of the reserve had been seeking official delimitation of its territories through various administrative authorities ('Ground-breaking Win for Indigenous People's Land Rights in Colombia' 2017). In the absence of formal land titles, the National Mining Agency had been able to grant permits and licences for gold mining with the reserve without consulting or seeking the consent of the traditional authorities or Cabildo (the reserve's governing body). These actions had undermined the reserve's regulations related to mining in their lands and threatened the livelihoods of the communities for whom mining is an ancestral activity.

In 2015, the reserve submitted a 'tutela' (a writ of constitutional protection) to the Administrative Court of the Province of Caldas, claiming, among other things, violation of the community's fundamental collective rights to their territory and natural resources, to self-determination and self-governance, and of their right to effective participation (referring to the terms of free, prior and informed consent) in relation to any and all activities proposed within their territory. The writ was rejected in the first instance and on appeal, requiring the leaders of the reserve to request assistance from the Constitutional Court ('Ground-breaking Win for Indigenous People's Land Rights in Colombia' 2017).

It is also important to note that following the court decision in 2017, the threats to members of the community and efforts to illegally enter reserve lands for extractive purposes have not stopped; indeed, members of the community's leadership have been forced into exile. According to a recent report from the Forest Peoples Programme, 'the situation of violence, discrimination and hate discourses against indigenous, Afro-descendant and campesino partners in Colombia has taken a drastic turn for the worse in recent months, despite the 2016 Peace Accords that won then president Santos a Nobel Peace Prize' ('Colombian Communities Face New Wave of Violence, Discrimination Despite Peace Accords' 2019). The article also mentions the pushback coming from landowners and others with interests in the reserve's lands, including former President Uribe. Through videos that have gone viral, he had been rallying the elite to fight against what is perversely being construed as 'land-grabbing' by the reserve. This is leading to a new wave of hate discourse against the reserve and its leaders. Uribe's Democratic Centre Party had also attempted to use the country's legal framework to erode the Constitutional Court win through a proposed Law 354 that would interfere with the present delimitation process ('Colombian Communities Face New Wave of Violence, Discrimination Despite Peace Accords' 2019).

I start this chapter with an account of the Embera Chamí case as a means to emphasize a series of key points that are important in terms of moving this book towards its conclusions. At the start of the book, I gave a short account of the growing problem of the threat and assassination of indigenous leaders and other 'land defenders' in this community. I also characterized the links that exist between these violent dynamics and the claims of sovereignty being newly expressed in the context of expanding extractive frontiers. This was my inroad into setting up the foundational argument for the volume, i.e. that sovereignty is not an outdated matter of politics and academic discussion, but a vital matter that continues to have deep implications. The link between the formation of sovereignty and different aspects and scenarios of environmental governance has been explored through multiple contemporary and historical reflections in previous chapters.

As well as reinforcing these intentions, I suggest here that the outline of the Embera Chamí case above is indicative of a need to integrate the analysis of resource sovereignty into the scientific fields and application of environmental governance and environmental peace-building. The above case underlines the fact that sovereignty is already an issue being navigated by current governance and law, but – as is made visible in this case and others like it – this is done by government authorities and corporate interests without full acceptance or in cynical denial of the seriousness and historical basis of the issue. Indeed, as is alluded to in the story of this case, whilst the state is forced to respond to legal claims and demands for consultation with the community (in compliance with formal commitments to law, democratic participation and the recognition of rights), it turns a blind eye to the full significance of local expressions of sovereignty in the interests of power and profit. Indeed, it becomes visible that states – as in the case of Colombia – share histories of collusion and the directly enablement of the illegal circumvention and abuse of these rights. Whereas governance mechanisms claim to be means to create cooperation and legitimate agreements on the access, use and ownership of resources, we see here that the same governance mechanisms can become means to reinforce existing insecurities.

Colombia has a history of violence and legal innovation that is not shared by other countries in Latin America. As other authors have highlighted, this is a result of a particular history of state-formation into which its topography, the formation of regional elites, severely unequal patterns of land owner-ship, armed militias and paramilitaries, and armed conflict and all contribute (Baquero-Melo 2015; Gutiérrez-Sanín and Vargas 2017; Peña-Huertas et al. 2017). However, observation of the collusion between state, corporations and illegal armed actors and their illegal circumvention or direct abuse of citizens' rights throughout the region is not unusual. There is also a common picture of anger and resentment amongst indigenous and peasant peoples regarding the way in which states have attempted to manage their interests and terri-tory without a true response to local concerns and beliefs (see Chapters 2–4). Although mechanisms for consultation have become widespread, without true opportunities for democratic deliberation, there is an expanding pic-ture – as research frontiers grow – in which the governance of land and ter-ritories is fraught with frustration and violence. Indeed, it is argued by some authors that the creation of managed and therefore disingenuous spaces of participation and consultation regarding territory and resources has actively invited expressions of outrage and reaction (Conde and Le Billon 2017).

In connection with this widespread picture, I intend to outline in depth in the following pages an intertwined and parallel history[3] to the Embera Chamí case, and perhaps one of the most commonly cited examples of the Janus-faced treatment of sovereignty, i.e. the application of prior consulta-tion. Whilst prior consultation and its connection to international conven-tions (ILO160, UNDRIP) have been touched upon earlier in the book, I consider it important to unfold more of the history of its establishment as a standard mechanism of territorial and resource governance. Further description of the politics of prior consultation expands the backstory to the Embera Chamí case above and places into high relief the contradictory and problematic manner in which sovereignty is treated by Latin American states. In particular, it reveals a technocratic avoidance of certain features of contested sovereignty that require attention if environmental governance is to deliver on its commonly agreed aims of setting 'the regulatory processes, mechanisms and organizations through which political actors influence environmental actions and outcomes' (Lemos and Agrawal 2006: 298) and of using these to achieve the goals of preventing, mitigating and adapting to environmental change (Biermann et al. 2012). I also suggest that confrontation with resource sovereignty is of central importance to resolving conflicts over environmental resources (Paavola 2007: 97). In this chapter, I link this technocratic avoidance to the broader juridification of ethnic claims and the application of a procedural logic of neoliberal global governance that Rodríguez-Gavarito (2010) has termed 'ethnicity.gov'.

An exploration of the politics of prior consultation is also a segue to a necessary reflection on environmental governance and environmental peace-building as academic fields. Ultimately, the results of these closely related fields of study have the potential to influence the logics of policy formation and can provide both rationale and excuses for the actions of states and the corporate sector. Connecting to the earlier empirical examples, I intend to demonstrate later in this chapter that there is reason to critique and further develop currently dominant approaches to environmental governance and environmental peace-building. In the following pages, I will demonstrate that there is a clear correspondence to be formed between my concern with and argument for resource sovereignty with the current critical institutionalist turn (Cleaver 2012; Cleaver and de Koning 2015; Cleaver and Whaley 2018). Indeed, I argue that the observations I have made regarding resource sovereignty in previous chapters have a significant contribution to the critical institutionalist approach. This correspondence also points to a series of key factors (outlined below) that are not only of analytic but also practical importance. I argue that they demand a reworking of current governance mechanisms and peace-building approaches such that more conscious consideration is given of the significance of contested sovereignty. Sovereignty is, as will be argued throughout this volume, both a catalyst for conflict and a signpost to the resolution of disagreements regarding territory and resources.

Prior Consultation in Colombia

Between 2013 and 2015, I participated in the Norwegian Ministry of Foreign Affairs-financed research project 'Everyday Manoeuvres: Military-Civilian Relations in Latin America and the Middle East'.[4] Against a background and inspiration from the pro-democracy uprisings of the Arab Spring, the project sought to map out and understand the historical, cultural and political universes in which military actors and civilians make sense of their country and their place within it in the Middle East and Latin America. Amongst other forms of research for the project, I worked with colleagues in the project to study the historical formation and reformulation over time of civil–military relations in Colombia. With these goals in mind, the research in Colombia required us to carry out a large number of semi-structured interviews with representatives of different sectors of its political and military establishments, as well as with prominent voices in civil society. At this time, peace talks between the Colombian government and the FARC guerrilla forces had started, and a significant expansion of infrastructure and resource extraction was taking place in the country, which was sparking off a wave of related consultation exercises between the state and local communities (see Chapter 5). Wishing to capture the impacts of these contemporary dynamics on societal relations, we carried out interviews with commanders of military units and the police, with leaders of prominent indigenous organizations and with state bureaucrats in two of the government ministries most tightly connected to prior consultations exercises (the Ministry of Mines and Energy and the Ministry of the Interior). After more than fifty-five years of civil war, the picture of civil–military relations we captured was a fraught and complicated one (McNeish, Rojas Andrade and Vallejo 2015). Our interviews also clearly revealed a contradiction between the de jure and de facto realities of the country's international reputation for the progressive treatment of indigenous and Afro-descendant rights. Indigenous and Afro-descendant organizations – along with human rights organizations – were deeply frustrated with the state of their dialogue with state actors, despite the existence and formal application of legal mechanisms for consultation and impact assessment in the country. Indeed, a commonly repeated response from indigenous representatives was that these mechanisms represented for them a kind of 'consultitis' (a play on the Spanish word for 'consultation' and the suffix for 'infection'). In their view, there was too much of this 'consultitis' around and it was not helping anyone.

Since 1991, the Colombian government has carried out approximately 1,300 prior consultations with 8,550 different indigenous and Afro-descendant communities (Held 2018). Of these, 900 consultations started between 2010 and 2013, and the vast majority of these were completed by mid-2014 (Jaskoski 2020). Colombia is one of the fifteen countries in Latin America and the Caribbean (and one of twenty-two worldwide) that ratified the International Labour Organization's Indigenous and Tribal People's Convention (ILO 169).[5] Signatories to ILO 169 are required to consult native people affected by major development plans before approving them. The right to *free, prior and informed consent/consultation[6]* (FPIC) (or *consentamiento/consulta previa* in Spanish) allows indigenous and 'tribal' peoples to participate in decision-making on all administrative and legal measures that affect their way of life and, in particular, their traditional lands, territories and resources (Anaya 2005).

Importantly for the governance of extractive sector operating in indigenous territories in Latin America and Colombia, ILO 169 was backed up by developments in international case law. The Inter-American Court of Human Rights (IACtHR) consecrated the right to consultation of indigenous peoples in the well-known cases of *Saramaka People v Suriname* (2007) and *Kichwa Indigenous People of Sarayaku v Ecuador* (2012). The IACtHR established that three safeguards apply if large-scale projects affect indigenous people, i.e. (1) their effective participation in the project plans; (2) a reasonable benefit from such plans; and (3) no issuing of concessions or licences until an independent body carries out and environmental and social impact assessment (IACtHR 2007, para. 129). The Court also ruled that states are responsible for the correct application of the right to and the processes of consultation with indigenous peoples, and not the companies that are working in the concerned area (IACtHR 2012, para. 187), and states not the affected indigenous peoples, bear the duty to demonstrate in an effective way that the consultation process was guaranteed fairly (IACtHR 2012, para. 179). In addition, the Court defined that due processes of consultation require the acceptance and dissemination of appropriate information, including environmental and health risks, continuous communication between parties, good faith, culturally appropriate procedures aimed at reaching an agreement, fair timing at the early stages of development and investment, and the use of traditional methods of decision-making (IACtHR 2012). The Court lastly affirmed that the right of consultation is a 'general principle of international law' (IACtHR 2012, para. 164). These precedents and their significance for practical governance have been reiterated in several cases, including *Garífuna Community of Punta Piedra and Its Members v Honduras* and *Kaliña and Lokono Peoples v Suriname* (Wright and Tomaselli 2019: 616).

Colombia's minority ethnic communities – indigenous, Afro-descendant and Roma gypsy – have had access to an institutionalized, national prior consultation framework since the constitutional reforms of 1991. Article 15 of ILO 169 refers to prior consultation in the context of mining. In its application to address an expanding mining, energy and infrastructure sector in Colombia, communities have in law the opportunity to participate in an open, timely and honest process in planning for future resource development. The 1993 Environment Law also makes direct reference to the requirement of prior consultation. As has been made clear in the previous chapters, Colombia is a highly relevant setting for the application and testing of prior consultation due to its long history of resource extraction and recent expansion of mining, energy production and infrastructural development, including Santos' *locomatora minera-energética*.[7]

Although it was one of the first countries in Latin America to ratify ILO 169, Colombia's legal measures fell short of translating the right (principle) of prior consultation into specific legislation detailing its application. While the first mention of the right to consultation was in the environmental legislation of 1993, it was not until 1998 that the details of the application of prior consultation became embodied in a decree (i.e. Decree 1320). From the outset, this legislation attracted a great deal of criticism from indigenous organizations and international NGOs ('Free, Prior and Informed Consultation in Colombia: The Case of the Expansion of the Cerrejón Project' 2012: 6). The government omitted to consult representatives of indigenous peoples about the wording of the decree prior to its enactment, contrary to the stated requirements of ILO 169. The decree also made no provision for the participation or consultation of affected local communities in the preparation and execution of the environmental impact assessment (EIA) and creation of the Environmental Management Plan. Furthermore, civil society and indigenous organizations pointed out that the corresponding legislation takes insufficient account of indigenous customs, traditions and representative institutions ('Free, Prior and Informed Consultation in Colombia: The Case of the Expansion of the Cerrejón Project' 2012: 6).

Other important arguments have also been made for the amendment of the prior consultation legislation, including its failure to specifically refer to consultation in the exploration and exploitation of non-renewable resources, such as minerals and fossil fuels ('Free, Prior and Informed Consultation in Colombia: The Case of the Expansion of the Cerrejón Project' 2012: 7). It also fails to comprehensively regulate the right to consultation as it is not concerned with decisions in other domains that affect the cultural practices of indigenous and Afro-descendant communities (e.g. education, healthcare provision and rural development). The right to consultation should apply without differentiation to all legislative and administrative measures that may affect them directly (Article 6.1 of ILO 169). It has also been argued that Decree 1320 creates confusion about the right to consultation of indigenous and Afro-descendant communities that do not hold formal ownership titles to their lands.

In an attempt to address some of these concerns, but to also make the existing law and regulation easier to navigate for business, new regulations were introduced by the Duque government and changes were made to the internal organization of the Colombian Ministry of the Interior in 2019. With Decrees 2354 and 2353, modifications were made, renaming the Directorate for Prior Consultation the National Authority for Prior Consultation and providing it with an increased level of both financial and administrative independence. The number of staff in the institution was also increased from fifteen to seventy-five. Adjustments were also made to the processing routines of the institution to both comply with legal commitments and to further speed up the treatment of individual cases. These changes also further reflect the moves that began under the Santos administration towards what the national media ('Consulta previa, ¿sigue el cuello de botella?' 2020) termed *licencias ambientales exprés* (express licences), i.e. a speeding-up of the licensing process.[8]

As has been noted in recent press coverage, these changes may also have been motivated by the growing success of the Constitutional Court in applying its rulings over *tutela* to stop extractive projects ('Consulta previa, ¿sigue el cuello de botella?' 2020). This was a position it fortified with Sentence SU1 2018, in which it called on the national government and Congress, based on the judgments made in the sentence and in line with ILO 169, to adopt the appropriate means to regulate the certification process and its impact on ethnic communities. Responding to 11 different *tutela* presented by indigenous communities, the Constitutional Court legally suspended nine projects with this sentence due to the lack of correctly applied prior consultation. Through its decisions, the Constitutional Court has contributed significantly to the design of consultation procedures. The Ministry of the Interior applies Constitutional Court case law when interpreting the prior consultation regulations. According to Jaskoski (2020: 14), this practice commonly occurs when the Ministry decides whether a project affects native communities and thus whether prior consultation is required. Based on individual *tutela* decisions, Ministry officials not only consider the possible overlap between the land on which the community resides and a project's area of impact, but also other types of indigenous presence, e.g. areas of particular cultural or spiritual significance, or the need to transit territory to reach a river on which a community depends.

The Limits of Consultation in Colombia

Overall, Colombian prior consultations are said to have been orderly and expeditious (Jaskoski 2020). However, it is also evident from the histories of individual consultation cases that things have often not gone entirely to plan. As has been revealed in a recent article by Jaskoski (2020), community responses to the requirements for prior consultation in Colombia have resulted in enduring conflicts. These conflicts can also be characterized as representing different forms of strategies to hinder extraction in indigenous territories, i.e. declining participation in mandatory prior consultation (the U'wa and

Samoré case and the Wayúy legal case); securing environmental protections in the affected area to pre-empt extractive projects (Cosigo Frontier legal case), to challenge the legitimacy of prior consultation from which they were excluded (Mandé Norte legal case) and to contest the omission of prior consultation (the Putamayo oil fields legal case) (Jaskoski 2020:4). Of these, the U'wa and Samoré case has received the widest international attention because of the support and solidarity efforts it inspired. Whilst other cases are of equal importance in indicating the problems of prior consultation, the U'wa and Samoré case is perhaps also the most highly emblematic in revealing the gulf between contrasting values regarding resources and territory – and with this of resource sovereignty – expressed by states, companies and communities in each case. Connecting back to the experience of the Embera, the experience of the Mandé Norte case is also highly significant in the context of this chapter in terms of laying some of the groundwork and background for the case and ruling described in the introduction. It is a case to which people in the nearby Embera Chamí community of the Resguardo Cañamomo Lomaprieta compared their own case.[9]

In the early 1990s, Occidental Petroleum applied for an environmental licence for exploration in the Samoré, a region straddling the northern Colombian Departments of Arauca, Boyacá and Northern Santander. Early on, Occidental's public relations efforts divided the local U'wa indigenous community, some of whom participated in the 1995 discussions. During a time when the 1993 Environmental Law was in place but still unregulated, state and company officials claimed that the meeting qualified as prior consultation (Jaskoski 2020: 9). The U'wa disagreed, to the extent that – as the media readily broadcasted – they threatened collective suicide should oil exploration occur in their territory. The Human Rights Ombudsmen (Defensoría del Pueblo) filed a *tutela* on their behalf to contest the lack of prior consultation and in 1997, the Constitutional Court reached its first ruling in favour of the U'wa. The ruling received wide international attention as one of the first of its kind. However, a parallel administrative-legal ruling by the Council of State (Consejo de Estado) contradicted this by giving legitimacy to the original environmental licence issued to Occidental. An investigation into the U'wa case by the Organization of American States (OEA) resulted in a set of recommendations and proposals, including that the state should properly consult with the U'wa.

As Jaskoski (2020) highlights, it is significant that at this time the U'wa loudly rebuffed the suggestion towards prior consultation. Their communiqué expressed a 'rejection of the Court's ruling' and reiterated that their goal was not that the oil project be the subject of consultation or negotiation, but rather 'that it simply be cancelled for attacking their most profound cultural convictions' (Jaskoski 2020: 9). Despite their continued protests, Occidental was awarded with a new environmental licence in 1999 to explore for oil without consulting the U'wa, who the state suggested did not have a permanent presence in the area. The licence was held up in court, despite another *tutela* action by the U'wa. Also starting in 2002, after Occidental failed to find oil, Ecopetrol was granted exploration rights in the area. It invited the U'wa to participate in prior consultation, only for this to be rejected. This allowed the Council of State to decide in 2006 that the 'state's earnest, multi-year endeavour had satisfied the prior consultation requirement' (Jaskoski 2020: 9). Having exhausted the tactic of prior consultation, the U'wa resorted to physical obstruction, such as in the case of the Magallenes project. The U'wa learned about the environmental licence issued to Ecopetrol in 2013. In response, they blockaded all access to the territory for forty days and physically thwarted all attempts to repair the Caño Limón pipeline, which the FARC – also active in the area – had sabotaged.

By taking such militant action, the U'wa succeeded in getting the state's attention. Ecopetrol removed its equipment from the region and a team of high-level government officials was formed to negotiate a resolution to the stand-off. The talks delivered several agreements, i.e. permission for pipeline repairs, the subterranean construction of a section of the pipeline, a commitment by the state to finance a review of the EIA for the project, and the promise of carrying out the titling of the entire U'wa territory. In recent years, the U'wa have created the Guardia Indigena, a cadre of over 400 U'wa youth from throughout the vast territory, many of them sons and daughters of U'wa leaders and elders ('Colombia's U'wa Still Teaching Us How to Resist' 2017). Dressed in blue vests, the U'wa Indigenous Guard carry only a ceremonial walking stick and it is their task to protect the U'wa territory from various threats and engage in nonviolent actions when necessary. To establish what the U'wa call 'territorial control', in June and July 2016, the U'wa indigenous guard organized a further series of peaceful actions occupying the Gibraltar 3 well site for two months. These actions resulted in further commitments from the government regarding territorial titling, but also a refusal by the state to close the drilling complex. An uneasy stand-off now exists, in which the procedural mechanism of prior consultation is rejected, and communication between the state and the U'wa community has failed to overcome an impasse between the different way in which territory is valued by them. Indeed, while 'state officials and company representatives seek to limit discussion to immediate procedural topics (e.g., operationalizing agreements, certifying the list of participants, and navigating the intricacies of compensation payments), the indigenous representatives . . . in the U'wa case, constantly return to the subjects of the sacredness of the earth and its resources and the collective history and denouncement of the violence that engulfs them' (Rodríguez-Garavito 2010: 35).

In the initial stages of the Mandé Norte copper and gold mine, the state 'consulted' only pro-extraction individuals within the Embera and the Afro-Colombian community of Jiguamiando. The Embera and Afro-Colombian communities that opposed the plan for an open pit mine in the bordering municipalities of Murindó, in the Department of Antioquia and Carmen del Darién in Chocó, denounced these efforts during consultation as a sham and contested their exclusion from the process. Despite these complaints, Ingeominas, the Colombian state agency that granted mining titles, issued a title to the Denver-based Muriel Mining Company. Subsequently, in 2006 and 2007, members of affected communities and officials of Ingeominas, the Ministry of the Interior and the Ministry of Mines orchestrated a series of gatherings to inform the community about the Mandé Norte project (Jaskoski 2020: 11). These meetings did not allay community fears, and conflict erupted in January 2009 when helicopters transporting Muriel Mining geologists arrived in Carmen del Darién to deliver a group of geologists who were intent on carrying out exploratory drilling. Upon arriving in the community, the geologists presented community members with a document that described the intended exploration and had been signed by Embera individuals who had posed as community leaders in the 2006–7 conversations (Jaskoski 2020: 11). Days later, project employees set up a camp on the Cerre Careperro, the proposed focus of exploration and a sacred site and essential water source for local people. The company's arrival sparked a month of strategizing by the community, assisted by representatives of a number of international NGOs. As a result of the meetings, the Embera decided to pursue two routes to confront the mining company: a popular consultation, which generated the momentum for demonstrations, and the filing of a *tutela*.

In February 2009, the Embera held a vote on mining that was framed by them as an exercise of the right to consultation that the state had ignored. The vote was unanimous in its opposition to the mining project. Community members then ascended the Cerre Careperro to camp outside the mining installation for a month and to hold demonstrations that involved dances and prayers (Jaskoski 2020: 11). In the first weeks of March, the community activists warned Muriel Mining – via the local military battalion – that if it did not leave within two days, the community would occupy the company infrastructure by force. As a result, Muriel Mining departed the area. Activists also turned to the courts, a measure that brought an end to the project. In April 2009, with backing from the Human Rights Ombudsman and the Inter-ecclesiastic Commission for Justice and Peace (Comisión Intereclesial de Justicia y Paz), a Colombian NGO, the members of the Embera community filed a *tutela* denouncing the lack of a true process of prior consultation. In a landmark decision, the Constitutional Court pronounced not only that the state had failed to consult affected communities, but also that due to the mine's anticipated high level of harm to the communities, prior consultation was judged to be an inefficient mechanism. The state would need to obtain the communities' consent before authorizing the mine.

Negotiation with a Gun to Your Head

Both of these cases reveal the problematic manner in which prior consultation has been employed, and sometimes abused, by states and corporations. They demonstrate the ambiguity of prior consultation as a mechanism to solve disagreements over territory and resources, and of the ostensibly incommensurable values and expressions of sovereignty at play in efforts to apply prior consultation. Demonstrating the coercive conditions in which prior consultation commonly takes place in Colombia, the cases also remind us of the discussion of *raw law* and violence with which this chapter started. It is evident here that prior consultation does not take place as a neat technical exercise or in a power vacuum. Indeed, keeping in mind that these attempts to carry out prior consultation are taking place in the midst of persisting armed conflict, it is perhaps not surprising that things have not followed the official plan.

Emphasizing the pressured and unequal nature into which prior consultation is supposed to work in Colombia, Rodríguez-Garavito (2010: 37) quotes a leader of the National Indigenous Organization of Colombia (ONIC): 'There is no negotiation when you have a gun to your head.' In highlighting this quote, Rodríguez-Garavito captures a sense of the violent dynamics and inequalities that lay in the background of the Urrá dam project, a project that was constructed in the 1990s against the will of the local Embera-Katío (another Embera subgroup) community. In the case of the Urrá dam project, he highlights that consultations took place in the midst of battles between the FARC and the national armed forces, and in close proximity to an area of paramilitary activity in which hundreds had been killed and as a result of which thousands had been displaced. He draws on this observation to argue that 'contrary to the neo(liberal) premise of equality between parties, the legal battle is actually highly asymmetric' (Rodríguez-Garavito 2010: 36). Instead of the ideal conditions for communication postulated by governance theorists – that all parties enter negotiations with the same level of power and influence, experience, information and knowledge – the reality of consultation is that it 'reproduces and legitimates structural power differences among the parties' (Rodríguez-Garavito 2010: 36) i.e. it reinforces the dominant relations among companies, states and indigenous peoples. Rodríguez-

Garavito claims that this reinforcement is an example of the 'domination effect' of prior consultation.

Even when there is not physical coercion involved, the relations of domination among parties are present due to profound economic inequalities that consultations leave intact (Rodríguez-Garavito 2010: 37). However, he suggests that the domination effect has a particularly violent face in contexts of armed conflict such as Colombia, in which company or extractive operation depend in some way or another on protection provided by legal or illegal groups. In the Urrá case, the company had the enthusiastic support of right-wing paramilitary groups, who considered the dam to be essential for the interests of the large landowners they represented (Rodríguez-Garavito 2010: 36). In other cases, reports suggest that paramilitary organizations and Bacrim (criminal bands) not only supported the actions of extractive enterprises, but either directly taxed their operations through protection rackets or even worked as security guards within local company operations (McNeish 2017). In yet other contexts, the FARC and ELN guerrilla forces have also conducted similar methods of taxation and protection.

The domination effect observed by Rodríguez-Garavito is one of five effects he observes taking place in what he otherwise terms 'social minefields' (2010: 5). Working off the back of David Harvey's (2003) analysis of contemporary capitalism and his observations of both renewed importance of export-oriented extractive industries laying the ground 'accumulation by dispossession' and an explosion of socioenvironmental conflicts, the term 'social minefields' aims to capture the particular dynamics of politics and law this has also made ubiquitous. He suggests that prior consultation processes are social minefields in both the sociological and the economic sense:

> In sociological terms, they are true social *fields*, characterized by the features of enclave, extractive economies, which include grossly unequal power relations between companies and communities, and a limited state presence. They are *mine*fields because they are highly risky; within this terrain, social relations are fraught with violence, suspicion dominates, and any false step can bring lethal consequences. (Rodríguez-Garavito 2010: 5)I call them minefields because they are also frequently minefields in the economic sense. In many cases, they revolve around a mine's exploitation of some valuable resource (Rodríguez-Garavito 2010: 6).

Reflecting back on the particular context of Colombia, he also observes that these fields of negotiation are also minefields in a very literal sense, given that they correspond to territories that are in dispute and that are plagued by anti-personal mines planted by illegal, armed groups as a strategy of war and for obtaining territorial control (Rodríguez-Garavito 2010: 6).

In addition to the domination effect, Rodríguez-Garavito (2010) importantly characterizes the following effects: the displacement effect, the miscommunication effect and the emancipation effect. In simple terms, the displacement effect refers to the way in which prior consultation displaces, replaces or postpones more substantive and longer-lasting conflict and discussions between states, corporations and communities. The miscommunication effect refers to a manner in which consultations embody a discursive in which different epistemological and ontological perspectives and positions get crossed. The result of this crossing may in some instances be a direct clash and breakdown in communication, as in the case of the U'wa. Alternatively, not all misunderstandings are involuntary. Companies, state agencies and indigenous peoples may in some instances use laws, judicial decisions and legal resources to defend their substantive interests. Rodríguez-Garavito (2010) also acknowledges that prior consultations also demonstrate the opposite of a domination effect, i.e. emancipatory possibilities. Consultation is simultaneously a means to both perpetuate and challenge profound inequalities among actors situated in social minefields. Although the procedural norms of prior consultation may dilute indigenous demands, these norms may also represent the only ones available for halting the cultural and environmental harm of extractive projects and for reinvigorating processes of collective mobilization. Here Rodríguez-Garavito links back to the regional and international levels recognizing that:

> In societies such as those of Latin America, where the wave of multicultural constitutionalism of the 1990s arrived precisely when indigenous peoples were experiencing both organizational revitalization and collective extermination, the norms enshrined in Convention 169 and other legal instruments opened up additional paths of resistance and political mobilization. In these circumstances, consultation has been embraced as an instrument for slowing down the avalanche of mining and other extractive projects engulfing indigenous communities situated in economies bent on the exploitation of natural resources. (2010: 41)

Rodríguez-Garavito's observations regarding social minefields and these effects are important not only because of what they reveal about prior consultation, but also because they are also seated in and contribute to a wider critique of the practice of neoliberal governance. The idea of prior consultation, ushered in by ILO 169, precipitated an explosion of hard and soft law norms at both the international and national levels, and entailed a new neoliberal approach to ethnic rights and multiculturalism that replaced earlier integrationist approaches that had previously prevailed in international and domestic legal frameworks (Rodríguez-Garavito 2010: 6). Prior consultation here represents only the tip of the iceberg of a wider process of juridification, and part of a zeitgeist of neoliberal globalization starting at the end of the twentieth century. An essential aspect of this era, Rodríguez-Garavito (2020: 12) and Comaroff and Comaroff (2001) acknowledge, is the 'centrality of law, or 'the fetishism of the law': the global faith in 'the capacity of constitutionalism and contract, rights and legal remedies, to accomplish order, civility, justice, empowerment'.

The extension of this process into the domain of ethnicity is what Rodríguez-Garavito terms 'ethnicity.gov', i.e. the juridification of collective claims of cultural identity, self-determination and control over territories and resources. He uses the suffix '.gov' to denote governance, not government, and emphasizes that the juridification of ethnicity occurs not only through hard law that is created by governments (and states in general), but also through a wide range of soft law rules, such as the operational policies that multilateral and private banks impose on companies that work in indigenous territories and the codes of conduct that pertain to mining companies that operate in these territories. Consequently, 'ethnicity.gov' is marked by the phenomenon of legal pluralism and comprises multiple manifestations of governance without government. Crucially, in line with the liberal fiction embedded in the institutions of freedom of contract and due process, in the process of prior consultation, the ethnic collective subject (e.g. an indigenous people) is also characterized as being on a level playing field with the other subjects that participate in the consultations and negotiations (e.g. TNCs and the state entities interested in economically exploiting indigenous territory).

The Problematics of Prior Consultation Elsewhere

Rodríguez-Garavito's (2010) analysis helps to situate the problems of prior consultation in Colombia within wider observations of the difficulties of consultation in the region and further afield. A vast and growing volume of literature now documents the deficiencies of prior consultation exercises across the globe (Grugel, Nem Singh and Fontana 2017; Leifsen et al. 2017; Wright and Tomaselli 2019). Many of these writings take as their inspiration the observation of a 'implementation gap' first observed by Rodolfo Stavenhagen, the first Special Rapporteur on Indigenous Rights, to refer to the formal and informal impediments and inconsistencies between legislation for prior consultation and its practice.

Existing publications document the deficiencies of prior consultation processes such as their narrow project specific logic, the pro-extraction bias of the distributed information and a lack of ownership of these processes by local populations, despite the apparent requirements of international case law (Hipwell et al. 2002; O'Faircheallaigh 2010, 2013; Bebbington 2012;

Pellegrini and Ribera 2012). Echoing Rodríguez-Garavito, scholars also commonly argue that FPIC or prior consultation is frequently reduced to a system of legal procedures, which dilute and bracket substantial claims such as control over territories and earlier claims for self-determination, as well as jeopardizing the viability of livelihoods and alternative visions of development and wellbeing (Leifsen et al. 2017: 1045).

Research on public participation in EIAs, a mandated part of prior consultation processes, has shown that they commonly result in 'invited spaces' (Cornwall and Brock 2005), wherein local actors have no opportunity to veto decisions and little leeway to do anything other than legitimize decisions that have already been taken. This echoes the critical perspective that has circulated for some time in critical development research regarding the commonly 'managed' outcomes of participatory mechanisms and institutions (Cooke and Kothari 2001; McNeish 2001). It also corresponds with the critique of studies that have narrowly considered the operation of participatory institutions during 'normal times'. Jaskoski (2020: 3) highlights research on extractive conflicts, which recognizes that organizing may occur outside of stipulated participatory structures and that there are enormous power asymmetries intrinsic to hydrocarbons and mining. Other authors have examined how EIAs and other 'participatory' instruments work to establish the validity of some forms of authority and knowledge over others, limiting the political possibilities and influence of local spokespersons (Leifsen, Sánchez-Vásquez and Reyes 2017).

As several authors (Kirsch 2014; Sawyer 2015) have shown in detail, in the context of prior consultation and EIAS, scientific technical knowledge, 'corporate science' and local experiential knowledge are required to compete with each other. EIAs create a discourse of accountability parallel to a discourse of science-based management of risk. These instruments, even when successfully including affected populations, also often narrowly define the spatial, social and temporal effects of extraction (Leifsen et al. 2017: 7). The effectiveness of EIAs to reduce the inevitable socioenvironmental impacts of extractive and large-scale development projects is also influenced by the fact that because of limited government financing, corporations themselves end up financing these studies (Devlin and Yap 2008; Kirsch 2014; Aguilar-Støen and Hirsch 2015).

Several authors (e.g. Schilling-Vacaflor 2017) have also acknowledged that as indigenous communities are faced by these difficulties and are increasingly aware of their causes, they have searched for and tested – with varying levels of success – new ways to contest, circumvent and pragmatically engage with the terms of consultation and participation offered to them. This has frequently been done recognizing – in line with Rodríguez-Garavito (2010) – that they have no option other than to take part in these dynamics. As in Colombia, indigenous peoples elsewhere in Latin America have questioned the terms of EIAs and consultations, and with the assistance of international NGOs and contacts in academia have produced alternative knowledge and data to countervail pro-extraction impact assessment studies (see also Chapter 5). As well as providing solid evidence of an 'implementation gap' with regards to prior consultation gap, Schilling-Vacaflor (2017, 2019) has detailed the manner in which the Guaraní in Bolivia have operated to rework the terms and contents of the EIA carried out in their territory. Costanza (2015) writes describing the use by indigenous communities in Guatemala of 'good faith community consultations' as a means to express their right to prior consultation. Faced with the limits of the domestic regime for prior consultation in Canada, Papillon and Rodon (2019) also describe the current efforts made by indigenous peoples in the country to mobilize in order to assert their own interpretations of FPIC. Lawrence and Larsen (2017) have also examined a community-based impact assessment (CBIA) undertaken by a Swedish Sami community together with the authors. O'Faircheallaigh (2017) also describes how participatory processes in Australia have provided an opportunity for local aboriginal populations to draft more realistic, comprehensive and context-sensitive EIAs to reshape extraction projects.

Environmental Governance and Peace-Building

Importantly, the histories and experiences of prior consultation and the insights of Rodríguez-Garavito (2010) outlined above also help to support a critique and expansion of the theoretical assumptions of environmental governance and its connection to sovereignty. Recognizing the common background and history of the fields, by extension I also demonstrate a similar connection to thinking and that concerns the field of environmental peace-building. Reading across these works, it is also evident that mechanisms for prior consultation and the difficulties that surround it are also particularly relevant in thinking anew about the practice of resource governance and of the until now poor consideration of the violence and contestation that surround expressions of sovereignty. Indeed, a useful connection can be made to the recent efforts of a number of scholars to rethink institutions for natural resource management and, with it, both the theoretical and practical bases of environmental governance.

In this part of the chapter, I suggest that the experiences and problematics of prior consultation help to exemplify the need for 'critical institutionalism' (Cleaver 2012) to go further in its consideration of complex expressions of sovereignty and of resource sovereignty in particular. The previous chapters have revealed, in line with this chapter, the connections between sovereignty and natural resources. They have also revealed the complex material and social nature of claims to sovereignty, and of their impact on state–community relations. They have revealed the manner in which claims to sovereignty express contrasting demands and ideas regarding the use of territory and resources, and that, as such, can engender differing levels of contestation, instability and violence. As we have also seen, these claims have deep roots linking them to complex and differentiated histories of colonialism and colonization, state-formation, social and ethnic relations, and political and economic development. All of these elements are visible in the treatment of prior consultation above. In this chapter, it is important to emphasize that an acknowledgement of this should also have practical significance, both as the basis of a critique of still-influential theoretical assumptions and as a guide towards possible improvements in the conduct of environmental governance and peace-building initiatives. A short background to the environmental governance and environmental peace-building will now be described, before the text moves on to discuss the meaning and significance of critical institutionalism.

In the course of the late 1990s and early 2000s, a new policy agenda focusing on a more selective allocation of aid based on the quality of governance in recipient countries became regarded by governments and international development institutions as a key to aid effectiveness (Smith 2007). This had largely been a result of the post-Washington Consensus and a focus on institutions and public sector management (a continued result of structural adjustment and decentralization policies that began in the 1980s). In this new era of the 'good governance agenda', getting institutions right became central to development policy across the world, including Latin America. As part of this agenda, policy ideas linked market reforms and the individualization of property rights to decentralization and community-based development (Peters 2004). The agenda also carried the assumption that institutions were channels through which individuals and collective actions were shaped, social capital was built, and the weaknesses of the state and the market could be redressed (Merrey et al. 2007; Osei-Kufour 2010). From this perspective, institutions were seen to represent clear structures of roles, rules and lines of accountability that could help to shape the desirable governance arrangements of transparency, accountability and probity (McGranahan and Satterwaite 2006; Cleaver 2012). As part of the unfolding of this policy agenda, participatory mechanisms and institutions were proposed as ways of creating an improved basis for the community-based management of development funds and of local natural resources. It was asserted that communities could most effectively manage natural resources as they were best placed to monitor resource use and to deal with the 'open access' problems of overuse (countering earlier thinking regarding the 'tragedy of the commons'). It was argued that communities have an advantage in efficient resource and use and allocation, being able to draw on their local knowledge and resources, environmental conditions and technology (Ostrom 2008; Cinner et al. 2011).

Pro-poor planning at the national and regional levels was seen as a complementary outcome at a time during which Poverty Reduction Strategy Papers (PRSPs) – a national accounting of socioeconomic conditions and plans to reduce poverty – had become a standardized part of international development planning. With post-conflict democratization and establishment of the rights agenda, the community management of natural resources was thought to be pro-poor, allowing local institutions to specify a place for marginalized people in their decision-making, an assertion of living for all and the possible generation of economic benefit from resource management activities. Community – taken as a general notion – was also seen as contributing to a virtuous 'cycle of good governance' helping to mitigate and to hold historic state failures to account (Cleaver 2012: 2). It was assumed that local traditions of cooperation provided the building blocks of good resource management, but lacked robustness due to informality and a lack of clarity in rights incentives and authority structures (Cleaver 2012: 2). Policy approaches to rectify this 'institutional deficit' included processes of formalization and the codification of property rights and governance arrangements (Sturgeon and Sikor 2004). At this time, de Soto's (1986, 2000) arguments for large-scale land tenure regularization programmes to transform 'dead capital' into active economic assets became popularized and were given widespread support in implementation efforts by many national development agencies and international organizations.

As Cleaver puts it, 'mainstream policy discourse' became optimistic about the possibilities of designing local institutions that shaped good community-based governance of natural resources (2012: 7). This was also reflected in the growing academic field of environmental governance, in which many scholars in support of the ideas of New Institutional Economics (North 1990; Ostrom 1990) viewed the role of institutions to be the provision of information and assurance regarding the behaviour of others, to offer incentives to behave for the collective good and to monitor and sanction opportunistic behaviour (Cleaver 2012: 6). The work of Ostrom (1990, 2005) has been particularly influential in establishing the common acceptance of the idea that institutions for common property resource management can be deliberately crafted. The numerous case studies carried out by Ostrom and her colleagues demonstrate that such resources are in fact 'owned' as common property through institutional agreements, and through publicly designed and administered rules of access and distribution.

Key to the new institutional or 'mainstream institutionalist' approach (Cleaver 2012: 10) is a specification of 'design principles', i.e. conditions that are central to the functioning of robust and enduring institutions for common property resource management (Blaikie 2006; Wong 2009; Ostrom 2009). Here emphasis is placed on the formalization of institutional arrangements, the delineation of clear boundaries for resource use and jurisdiction, the specification of inclusive decision-making arrangements, and the codification of rule and regulations. Within this school of thought, institutions are essentially arrangements of rules and regulations used to repeatedly shape individual actions (Cleaver 2012: 11). Whilst the focus of this approach is primarily on formal and public institutions, recognition is made of the role played by norms, as they are seen as concepts of appropriate actions or outcomes on particular situations. The focus of common property scholarship is largely on interactions between individuals and community-level institutions. Biophysical variables, community attributes and rules are conceived of as 'exogenous variables' that are effectively external to the local institutions.

Mainstream institutionalism does not recognize that resource management issues that cross scales require specific attention and coordination and have developed the concepts of 'nesting' and 'polycentricity' to accommodate this (Ostrom 1990; Cleaver 2012: 11). Local arrangements can be 'scaled up' and linked to other levels of management without losing the advantage of local 'fit' because institutions are nested in polycentric systems and 'at each level – from small to medium and large scale – entities govern the complex and dynamic eco-system based on the most relevant information and with respect to the specific socio-cultural and ecological context' (Andersson and Ostrom 2008; 'Shaping Institutions for Natural Resources Management' 2010: 6–7). It is evident in that in its expression of the functioning of polycentricity, mainstream institutionalism is strongly influenced through its links to wider economic theory by rational choice assumptions about human behaviour. Individuals act purposefully to maximize their own interests. As Ostrom suggests, 'institutional rule is often self-consciously crafted by individuals to change the structure of repetitive situations that they themselves face in an attempt to improve the outcomes they achieve' (2005: 19). In this way, institutions are thought to help reduce the transaction costs of the repeated calculative interactions between individuals. Despite the efforts to refine the theoretical 'public choice' principles that underpin this school of thought (Vatn 2009, 2016; Aligica and Boettke 2011), the underlying rational action of institutions and their interactions remain.

Whilst emphasizing that a debt is due to mainstream institutionalism for its theoretical and empirical demonstration that the management of common property through collective action is possible, an increasing number of authors have in recent years questioned the reductionist assumptions attached to 'design principles' and suggest that the faith 'that small is always beautiful' in international policy is misguided (Cleaver 2012). Several authors claim that there is considerable promise in attempts to find complementary perspectives that link mainstream and newer critical perspectives (Bruns 2009; Komakech and van der Zaag 2011; Ingram, Ros-Tonen and Dietz 2015). Cleaver highlights, for example, that writers advocating the mainstream approach (van Laerhoven and Ostrom 2007: 5) actively elaborated a need to find ways 'to deal more explicitly with complexity, uncertainty and institutional dynamics' (Cleaver 2012: 2). There is also recognition that the focus on power-sharing arrangements that developed out of the mainstream common's literature gave rise to the new fields of adaptive management and adaptive governance (and its managerial counterpart, adaptive co-management (Folke et al. 2005; Armitage et al. 2009). Adaptive governance gained considerable purchase in academic and policy worlds (e.g. Stockholm Resilience Centre 2012). However, in the analysis of some scholars, these developments did not deal sufficiently with the need for 'thicker' contextualized and power-sensitive approaches to adaptive governance. The proposal for a critical institutionalist approach has been one effort to better enhance adaptive governance theory in this direction (Cleaver and Whaley 2018).

Similar trends, albeit to a lesser extent, have taken place in the development of the field of environmental peace-building. Environmental peace-building shares its origins with environmental governance, having also been primarily born out of the good governance agenda. In the 1990s, Lederarch (1995, 1997) refined Galtung's (1975) original emphasis on addressing the root causes of conflict and eliciting indigenous capacities for peaceful management and resolution of conflict by stressing a need to engage with grassroots, local, NGO, international and other actors in order to create sustainable peace processes. The concept was pushed into international policy by the 1992 UN Report *An Agenda for Peace* and the creation of several international peace-building institutions following the 2005 World Summit. It would also pick up significant influence in relation to international debates regarding efforts to end the conflict of a series of the 'new wars'[10] involving international interests in the 1990s and 2000s, including Iraq, Afghanistan and Colombia. Environmental peace-building was a further development of this initial peace-building field and, more specifically, a reaction to a growing literature in resource politics and peace-building that claimed the need for a securitized response to conflicts sparked by resource scarcity (Homer Dixon 1991). Environmental peace-building represented an important paradigm shift away from a nexus of environmental scarcity to one of environmental peace. Environmental peace-building rests on the assumption that the biophysical environment's inherent characteristics can act as incentives for cooperation and peace rather than violence and competition (Dresse et al. 2019). Instead of only stressing the role of natural resources as a catalyst for conflict and violence, scholars contributing to the environmental peace-building field stress that natural resources represent critical assets that are the foundations for rebuilding livelihoods and economies that have been affected by conflict. Inheriting an optimism about the possibilities of designing local institutions, in this case to shape legitimate governance following conflict, environmental governance aimed to examine the proposition that coopera-tion can generate synergies for peace and begin to identify the conditions and institutional forms through which those benefits might be realized (Conca and Debalko 2002: 4).

Also, somewhat in parallel to environmental governance, recent trends in the field of environmental peace-building have questioned its underlying rationalism and reduction of both study and practice to a series of techni-cal steps that ignore particular biophysical and socio-political conditions. Because of this critical reflection within the field, it has been highlighted that feedback loops between changes in the environment, conflict and peace conditions are still not yet well understood. It is now argued that without rigorously examining this feedback, any claims that environmental peace-building yields both peace-building and environmental improvement within a self-sustaining virtuous cycle cannot be substantiated (Dresse et al. 2019). Furthermore, feedback loops between top-down (e.g. advocacy) and bottom-up (e.g. community engagement) strategies have also not been sufficiently examined due to a general focus that generically relies on creating dialogue. Improved dialogue between parties is now recognized as a limited measure of success because dialogue alone may not lead to policy changes that hold sway over geopolitical relations and environmental conditions. Indeed, en-vironmental improvements achieved through dialogue is also no guarantee of a positive outcome of peace-building. In relation to the wider context above, it has been demonstrated, for example, that the 2016 Peace Accords in Colombia paved the way for widespread deforestation that put indig-enous communities and their long-term livelihoods and wellbeing at risk (Murillo-Sandoval et al. 2020). Such post conflict environmental destruction in turn has the potential to undermine recovery from violence and transi-tion to peace, and to contribute to a vicious cycle of renewed conflict and environmental degradation. Ide (2020) emphasizes a potential 'dark side' to environmental peace-building efforts if the focus is too narrowly on achiev-ing an outcome without explicit consideration of the driving mechanisms. As a result of these growing concerns, some authors now suggest the need for a 'local turn' (Leonardsson and Rudd 2015) and more *adaptive* forms of environmental peace building (Swain and Öjendal 2020).

Critical Institutionalism

Cleaver (2012) suggests that it is possible to distil the outline of a new 'critical institutionalist' approach from the various alternative ways of thinking about the collective management of natural resources. This approach 'reflects a debt to critical realist thinking which recognizes diversity in social phenomenon, the potentially creative effects of individual agency and highlights the enduring influence of social structures in shaping individual behaviour and the patterning of outcomes' (Cleaver 2012: 13; see also Archer 2000; Sayer 2000). She also suggests that the critical label is justified given that the insights are variously drawn from grounded empirical research in critical social justice theory, socio-history, social-anthropology, political ecology and post-structural perspectives (Cleaver 2012: 13; Cleaver and de Koning 2015). These perspectives do not focus exclusively on a rational and focused improvement of the outcomes of particular institutional processes. Critical institutionalism is cautious instead in assuming that local governance will lead to 'good governance' and is concerned with the limits to decentralization and unpacking over-romantic myths of community (Agrawal and Gibson 1999; Campbell et al. 2001; Wong 2010). These perspectives acknowledge the particularities of power relations in different societies and the manner in which they imbue and constrain the spaces of collective action and participation in governance. They also emphasize the effects of broader societal governance arrangements of local institutions (Blaikie 2006) and query the idea that institutions can be crafted to be efficient (Boelens 2009; de Koning 2011; Chowns 2014). I argue that for the purposes of this chapter and volume, Cleaver's critique of mainstream institutionalism provides an important insight into the dynamics of environmental governance that more closely approximates the contextual, political and socioenvironmental complexities I have explored.

In providing a thumbnail sketch, Cleaver and de Koning (2015) suggest that the critical institutionalist approach questions the underlying rational choice assumptions of standard institutionalist thinking. Instead, the insights of these writers emphasize 'the multi-scalar complexity of institutions entwined in everyday social life; their historic formation dynamically shaped by creative human actions; and the interplay between the traditional and the modern, formal and informal arrangement' (Cleaver and de Koning 2015: 4). From this perspective, institutions are not necessarily designed for a particular purpose such as environmental or resource governance, but are borrowed or adapted from other working arrangements that are crucial for society. Reflecting complex social identities, unequal power relations and wider political and geographical factors, the rules, boundaries and processes of these institutions are also commonly not clearly defined or static in nature.

Cleaver and de Koning (2015: 4) suggest that people's 'motivations to cooperate in collective arrangements are a mix of economic, emotional, moral and social rationalities informed by differing logics and world-views'. Institutions are dynamic because they respond to and operationalize human actions, making the relationship between institutional form and outcome anything but simple or automatic.

Working to capture the critical realist perspective of critical institutionalism, proponents (Cleaver 2012; Cleaver and de Koning 2015) suggest the employment of the term 'institutional bricolage'. This concept draws heavily on Lévi-Strauss' (2004) formulation of *intellectual bricolage* (people's creative use of heterogeneous but socially structured repertoires in their thinking and social invention) and, more centrally, on Douglas' (1986) further development of this idea as a critique of rational choice assumptions about collective action in the form of *institutional bricolage*. Here institutional bricolage is held to represent the process through which 'people, consciously and non-consciously, assemble or reshape institutional arrangements, drawing on whatever materials and resources are available, regardless of their original purpose' (Cleaver and de Koning 2015: 4). In contrast to mainstream approaches, institutions not only operationalize public choice, but are formed by it. These refurbished arrangements are necessary responses to everyday challenges and are embedded in daily practice. Actors innovate, but they do so within the limits of their resources, social circumstances and what is perceived as legitimate. Institutions are naturalized (Douglas 1987) through a number of processes ranging from calls on tradition (invented and re-invented), on symbols, discourses and power relationships borrowed from other settings, and by analogy to accepted ways of doing things, to the social order and to ideas of rightness in relation to social, natural or spiritual worlds (Douglas 1987).

Observations regarding time and scale are also important additions made by critical institutionalists. Critical institutionalists view historical trajectories as important because they shape contemporary institutions. The concept of path dependence has some traction here – not in a deterministic way, but in the sense that institutions are formed in sedimented layers of governance arrangements (van der Heijden 2011; Peters et al. 2012). Commons scholarship has often focused on community-based institutions, but a promising direction for critical institutionalism is in explaining how change occurs at the messy middle – the meso-level of institutions (Peters et al. 2012). The messy middle consists of a number of interfaces (Berkes 1989; Long 2001) between scales of organizations, sets of values, professional and lay knowledge, and individual, community and state action. It is at these interfaces that much bricolage work is done to navigate between different interests. Importantly, however, critical institutionalists also recognize that path dependence, power relations, and national and international governance frameworks can constrain attempts to innovate and negotiate (Cleaver and de Koning 2015: 7). Indeed, contemporary practices are located in social, political and environmental histories and in the rich layering of resource arrangements, which may provide opportunity or constraint for innovation and adaptation (Page 2005; de Koning 2014).

Things (relationships, resources, material goods, land and social order) are observed in critical institutionalism as having meaning to people beyond their mere instrumental functionality, i.e. they have emotional, symbolic or moral dimensions as well as more pragmatic or strategic ones (Sayer 2011). In their efforts to secure or defend access to resources and services, people are also concerned with wider ends (relating to order and meaning, identity and citizenship, and wellbeing). This means that practical arrangements for managing resources are imbued with wider social significance and can be traced back to the generative principles of the social field (Bourdieu 1977). Understanding people's actions and the ways in which these affect institutions goes further than merely tracking practices and social relationships – there is a need to uncover meanings, worldviews, forms of legitimation and authority, all of which are aspects that may or may not be visible in public decision-making (Cleaver and de Koning 2015:9). Worldviews or cosmologies provide a way of ordering the social and natural world, of accommodating unpredictability and of defining proper responses. It is also recognized that these expressions of knowledge may not completely align with professional or state representations of rights and resource management as embodied in legislation, regulation and bureaucratic institutions (Cleaver and de Koning 2015: 9).

Critical Institutionalism and Resource Sovereignty

There is a significant complementarity between critical institutionalism and the explorations of governance dynamics and resource sovereignty that I have undertaken earlier in this and other chapters. Indeed, critical institutionalism not only helps to capture and represent some of what I have been alluding to throughout, but also provides a suitable conceptual and applied paradigm to which this work can critically contribute. In short, critical institutionalism aligns well with my empirical and normative intent. However, whereas there are a series of direct matches between observations and thinking, I argue here that critical institutionalism could be positively expanded through the integration of a better understanding of the complex nature of sovereignty and its impacts on environmental and resource governance. Indeed, as is the intent of this book, it is also through this combination that resource sovereignty can be better exposed as an issue that cannot be ignored or unduly treated in the practice of environmental governance.

Critical Institutionalism and Prior Consultation

Many of the logics and assumptions of mainstream forms of environmental governance (and peace-building) are visible in the design and application of prior consultation. Prior consultation, in line with other mechanisms of governance, was intended to create a regime of fair conduct in which historical grievances could be addressed and compensated, rights and opportunities could be given to local indigenous communities to participate in and influence decision-making regarding development in the present, and age-old conflicts over land and resources could be solved. Good governance was to be secured by the implementation of a standardized set of norms and practices in which all stakeholders (indigenous peoples, states and corporations) had equal opportunity to secure their interests according to both law and procedure. Recognition was made of contrasting practices of land tenure, including cultural practices of holding land in common, but these differences were to be harmonized through democratic practice, i.e. the delineation of clear boundaries for resource use and jurisdiction, the specification of inclusive decision-making arrangements, and the codification of rules and regulations. Prior consultation has also been understood to be polycentrically nested within a wider system of national and international law and convention that further acts to bolster its legitimacy and the requirement for all stakeholders to respect its requirements and process.

The histories of prior consultation given above reveal that, whilst perhaps with good intentions, these logics and assumptions have been deeply flawed. Rather than showing a level playing field, the empirical research and the accounts provided by indigenous peoples and supporting organizations frequently reveal deep imbalances of power, influence and knowledge at play in settings of prior consultation (e.g. the first four effects highlighted by Rodríguez-Garavito and their echoes in other research and reports cited above). These accounts suggest the need for a more critical institutionalist account of prior consultation and efforts towards its implementation. In line with this approach, it is important to highlight its questioning of the 'good governance agenda' and its claims that 'small is always beautiful' given these power imbalances. Multiple cases of prior consultation in Colombia and elsewhere starkly demonstrate the manner in which these dynamics for participation are purposely abused by states and corporations.

Other elements of the critical institutionalist approach expressed above also appear to have strong significance in interpreting the dynamics of prior consultation. The experience of prior consultations and the dealings of indigenous peoples with the Colombian state are suggestive of critical institutionalism's arguments questioning rational choice assumptions regarding institutional design and in favour of a critical realist perspective. Although prior consultation represents a standardized global mechanism for governance, it needs to operate in Colombia within a very particular historical and formal institutional environment – and one that borrows from other legal and political arrangements, including those made because of the country's armed conflict (including the enforcement of decisions on territorial ownership by the military). The motivations and interests of people in participating in prior consultation exercises are clearly a mix of economic, emotional, moral and social rationalities informed by differing logics and worldviews. Prior consultation is also meant to be dynamic because of its need to respond to and operationalize human actions and competing claims with very different historical, ideological and ontological points of departure. However, as the examples given above suggest, these kinds of complex variables are often overlooked in the drive towards securing results.

As the cases of prior consultation above also reveal, biophysical variables, community attributes and rules are not 'exogenous variables'. Relationships, resources, material goods, land and the local social order are all partly determinant of responses to prior consultation – so much so that, as we have seen above, some communities (such as the U'wa) refuse to participate in prior consultation, recognizing the manner in which it would immediately undermine relationships and the balance of their cosmology, and furthermore lock communities into an endless cycle of negotiation with external actors they would struggle to comprehend. In their efforts to secure or defend territory and resources through prior consultations, indigenous communities are expressly concerned with wider ends than boundaries and economic livelihoods (i.e. order and meaning, identity and citizenship, and a culturally defined understanding of wellbeing).

In line with critical institutionalist observations, prior consultation exercises are also a significant example of how governance (and peace-building) not only takes place through institutions at the local and national levels, but also through institutions and interactions of governance at the meso-level. We see in fact that prior consultation exercises consist of organizations, sets of values, professional and lay knowledge, and individual, community and state action that are made to interface and operate at different scales. Indeed, both in the manner in which they are understood and employed by state and corporations, and in the manner in which they are understood and employed by indigenous communities, prior consultations could be said to represent forms of institutional bricolage. Prior consultations are forced to bend towards and be 'refurbished' in response to everyday challenges and embedded daily practices. Indeed, as we have seen above, in some contexts where indigenous communities are unsatisfied with the process of prior consultation offered by the state, they have organized alternative consultations or 'people's' referenda. Participants in prior consultation are able to innovate, circumvent, contest and block its progression, but it is also evident that they can only do so within the limits of their resources (including financial, intellectual and legal support from outside actors), social circumstances (and perhaps geographical positioning with regard to perceived strategic resources) and what is perceived as legitimate (by the state or customary law). Ultimately, it is the outcome of this dynamic that will determine which effects – domination, emancipation or otherwise – the consultation will produce.

Bringing Resource Sovereignty into Critical Institutionalism

Critical institutionalism cannot only assist the academic study of prior consultation, but has significance as a means to further frame and draw out the practical significance of the other governance dynamics and empirical contexts covered in this book – whether it be differences over the governance of renewable resources, disputes over popular consultations, the smuggling of resources across borders or national-level contestations of territory and national sovereignty. Many of these share significant features to the contexts of prior consultation discussed above. Critical institutionalism is sensitive and flexible enough to address and help to make further sense of the issues of power, scale, legality, identity, ontology and territoriality evident in the previous chapters. Whereas I therefore argue that critical institutionalism is a suitable theoretical frame to apply to the empirical cases in this book, I think that it is also important to observe that taken together, these cases provide insights that critically and constructively contribute to its further development.

Critical institutionalism pays attention to the complex dynamics of power, and its historical and social settings. Yet despite its critique of mainstream institutionalism's limited focus on the local and discovery of the importance of the 'middle', it is itself far from attentive to the institutional formation of environmental governance within both a national and an international setting. Critical institutionalists (Cleaver and de Koning 2015) claim that they embrace plurality and recognize that the governance of resources occurs through a variety of scales with no very clear boundary between the domains of the local and the global. However, other than emphasizing the 'leakage of' meaning' between scales in the form of legitimized discourses, arrangements, symbolic authority and values (Douglas 1987), little is said about the constitution of international political economy and its impact on the structure of national and subnational governance structures from top to bottom. Whilst there is an expressed interest in history, there is no focused consideration of state-formation, or of sovereignty, within existing critical institutionalist writing. Here a connection should perhaps be made to the resource politics literature that contains such a consideration, but largely lacks qualitative contextual detail. Indeed, I suggest here that the contested claims to sovereignty and to popular and resource sovereignty explored earlier in this book are strong empirical examples of the complex and problematic constitution and operation of environmental governance both as meaning and structure across scales. Prior consultation (as detailed above) and popular referenda (as detailed earlier in the book) demonstrate very clearly the manner in which mechanisms for environmental governance come into tension with competing claims and perspectives of sovereignty, and of the weaknesses and prejudices of the state and the private sector to fairly deal with this.

With all of the dynamism, complexity and contradictions I have described in the earlier chapters, resource sovereignty can easily be seen as a process of both intellectual and institutional bricolage. Claims to land and resources are formed and reformed both in response to new political and legal opportunities, and on the basis and constraints of existing governance structures, cultural vernacular, identity and ontology, and forms of outside technical and professional expertise. As I have claimed, in this way resource sovereignty brackets together both the material and the social. Indeed, in line with critical institutionalism, my understanding of resource sovereignty recognizes that things (including land and resources) have deep meaning. However, it also recognizes that claims to sovereignty capture the dynamic internal dialogue amongst individuals and within communities that express deep-seated emotional, symbolic or moral concerns and a pragmatism to secure what is needed through adoption and innovation – to the point that this defies external expectations of indigenous peoples. Critical institutionalism recognizes that power shapes institutional functioning, but that it is often invisible. As such, existing and problematic hierarchies of power (both external and internal to a community) may in the process of bricolage be reinforced rather than progressively questioned. Observations of these problematics are reinforced by the explorations of popular sovereignty and resource sovereignty made in earlier chapters. As I have shown, there is no guarantee that expressions of resource sovereignty will be emancipatory. Despite this, resource sovereignty – with parallels to institutional bricolage – is a dynamic that has to be reckoned with in environmental governance (and environmental peace-building).

Whereas critical institutionalism demonstrates a keen sense of the workings of power, it tends to set its critical realist gaze away from a treatment of the conditions of violence and crime that frequently surround the practices and mechanisms of environmental governance. These conditions are evident in the context of prior consultation and of the other contexts of environmental governance explored in this book. Indeed, I suggest here that a concern with sovereignty, and with claims for resource sovereignty, can add significantly to the scope and reach of critical institutionalism. If we are to truly understand the complexity of institutional formation, these conditions must be reckoned with wherever empirical research is conducted.

Critical institutionalism, with its empirical experience firmly oriented towards forest governance and community-led development in Africa, picks up on the significance of legal pluralism and competing systems of legal norms and values to the outcome of governance efforts. However, so far, it has given little attention to the fact that this might not only engender discursive and ideational disagreements but also forms and different scales of violence and contestation. Critical institutionalism is certainly more subtle in its treatment of clashes between state and community over natural resource management compared to those applying the resource curse, but it does not address the seriousness of the physical violence and abuse expressed in these contexts and processes – or of their connection to ongoing civil war or armed conflict (where Colombia's social minefields are perhaps exceptional examples that prove a rule). Indeed, as was indicated at the start of this chapter, the complications of competing systems of law are not simply reduced to those of state versus customary law, but by conditions of 'raw law' (Weitzer 2017) in which there is evidence of corruption and collusion between legal and illegal actors in their application of law and regulation. These are aspects that I argue on the basis of past explorations are unavoidable in an exploration of resource sovereignty.

Exposing Resource Sovereignty in Environmental Governance and Peacebuilding

Recognition of the complexity of the dynamics of institutional formation and operation assists improved study and understanding of the challenges and problems in environmental governance. However, as critical scholars are also aware, it also opens up questions regarding the extent to which this new awareness can lead to a greater opportunity for the actors involved to form more sustainable and democratic institutions. An awareness of the workings of bricolage helps us to understand institutional dynamics, but it is not clear whether this is a dynamic that can be facilitated to secure positive social, economic and environmental change (Nunan 2006; Merrey and Cook 2012). It is important to note here Cleaver and de Koning's (2015: 1) observation that 'analyses emphasizing complexity can be relatively illegible to policy-makers, a fact which lessons their reach'. A critical institutional analysis might highlight both the intended and unintended consequences of bricolage, but this leads to serious questions about how to judge and encourage the success or effectiveness of such arrangements. A key concern of recent development and governance-related literature has been to identify 'arrangements that work', which are conceptualized as the practical hybrid mechanisms that people create to get a job done and ensure meaning and social fit (Jones 2015). In common with many 'wicked problems', resource management issues and the fairness of institutional arrangements commonly depend on contrasting viewpoints. Institutional plurality suggests that arrangements for natural resource management are multistranded, overlapping and imbued with a variety of meanings and interests. It is therefore unlikely that a single institutional solution will represent all users and livelihood interests (Cleaver and de Koning 2015: 8).

Cleaver (2012) and Cleaver and de Koning (2015) do not attempt to provide a simple answer to these problems. Whilst she (2012: 211) highlights different scenarios that can help us to think about how processes of change may take place in 'institutional corridors', she agrees with de Koning (2011) that institutions 'partially elude design – there is no guarantee that designed arrangements will work out as intended'. In a later work, Cleaver and Whaley (2018: 49) suggest a possible alliance with more prescriptive adaptive governance theory, but also an abiding critical realist critique of a 'recipe of ingredients' or generalized lists of criteria necessary in order for governance to function. This lack of a recipe is viewed as critical institutionalism's strength, not its weakness, in the sense of allowing solutions to be revealed not by prescription, but by revealing from complexity the possibilities for transformation in development practices. Here the plurality and plasticity of institutional dynamics is perceived to offer multiple entry points for facilitated change (Merrey and Cook 2012).

My work on resource sovereignty aligns with critical institutionalism again in these observations. Resource sovereignty, as should hopefully now be obvious from the previous chapters, is not a prescriptive solution to major challenges of environmental governance and peace-building, or a fix to governance mechanisms such as prior consultation. Rather, it is an analytic device, expressing the same possibilities as institutional bricolage, i.e. helping to reveal the complex (social, political, economic and biophysical) machinery of environmental governance and possibilities for peace-building. Where my exploration of resource sovereignty can add to the important observations of critical institutionalism is in its highlighting the requirement for an evidence-based response. By laying bare the threat and violence of state–community relations, of the social minefields in which governance and peace-building are carried out, peace is brokered and sovereign claims are made, it obviates more intensely the need for a substantive reworking of institutions and law. This is a process in which local communities and the private sector play important roles through their own sovereign claims, but – as should be evident reflecting on the case of the Embera Chamí given at the start of this chapter – where state–community relations ultimately still set the terms for how genuine a process this will be in its delivery of possibilities and protections.

Notes

1. The Embera Chamí is a language grouping within the nation of the Embera indigenous peoples who inhabit several clusters of territory straddling the Colombian and Panamanian border.
2. About 30% of Colombia's land is occupied by 768 indigenous reserves, while an estimated 343,303 hectares of mining concessions in the country overlap with reserve lands ('Groundbreaking Win for Indigenous People's Land Rights in Colombia' 2017).
3. The Embera Chamí case was only considered necessary by the community leaders and their international supporters because of the previous failure of the state and corporate actors to respect local rights to free, prior and informed consent.
4. Financing was provided by the Department for Peace and Reconciliation, Norwegian Ministry of Foreign Affairs.
5. It has endorsed the UN Declaration on the Rights of Indigenous Peoples (UNDRIP 2007) in 2012. Unlike ILO 169, the Declaration is not legally binding.
6. While the written text of ILO 169 specifies *consultation*, there remains both a tension and debate regarding the more radical original proposal for *consent*. Whilst indigenous organizations have pushed for terminology and interpretations that express their historic claims for self-determination, states and employers' organizations have feared the implications of the adoption of consent (and with it the implicit veto right of indigenous peoples) to national governance and sovereignty. As a result of the intense debates regarding the idea of consent in the late 1980s, the ILO Office modified its proposal for the convention in favour of the more *consensual* idea of consultation.
7. Mining and Energy Locomotive. For more details, see Chapter 5.
8. In September 2014, President Santos introduced a decree (2820) to allow companies to pay more in order to reduce the standard processing time of environmental impact studies.
9. Personal communication with the leadership of the reserve, 2018.
10. 'New wars' is a term advanced by British academic Mary Kaldor (2013) to characterize warfare in the post-Cold War era. This form of warfare is characterized by violence between varying combinations of state and nonstate networks and fighting in the name of identity politics as opposed to ideology.

References

Agrawal, Arun, and Clark Gibson. 1999. 'Enchantment and Disenchantment: The Role of Community in Natural Resource Conservation'. *World Development* 24(4): 629–49.
Aguilar-Støen, Mariel, and Cecilie Hirsch. 2015. 'Environmental Impact Assessments, Local Power and Self-Determination: The Case of Mining and Hydropower Development in Guatemala'. *The Extractive Industries and Society* 2(3): 472–79.
Aligica, Paul, and Peter Boettke. 2011. 'The Two Social Philosophies of Ostrom's Institutionalism'. *Policy Studies Journal* 39(1): 9–49.

Anaya, James. 2005. 'Indigenous Peoples' Participatory Rights in Relation to Decisions about Natural Resource Extraction: The More Fundamental Issue of What Rights Indigenous Peoples Have in Lands and Resources'. *Arizona Journal of International & Comparative Law* 22(1): 7–17.

———. 2009. 'Indigenous Law and Its Contributions to Global Pluralism'. *Indigenous Law Journal* 6: 3–12.

Andersson, Krister, and Ellinor Ostrom. 2008. 'Analysing Decentralized Resource Regimes from a Polycentric Perspective'. *Policy Sciences* 41(1): 71–93.

Archer, Margaret. 2000. *Being Human: The Problem of Agency*. Cambridge: Cambridge University Press.

Armitage, Derek et al. 2009. 'Adaptive Co-management for Social – Ecological Complexity'. *Frontiers in Ecology and the Environment* 7(2): 95–102.

Baquero-Melo, Jairo. 2015. 'Regional Challenges to Land Restitution and Peace in Colombia: The Case of the Lower Atrato'. *Journal of Peacebuilding and Development* 10(2): 36–51.

Bebbington, Anthony. 2012. 'Extractive Industries, Socio-environmental Conflicts and Political Economic Transformations in Andean America', in Anthony Bebbington (ed.), *Social Conflict, Economic Development and Extractive Industry: Evidence from South America*. London: Routledge.

Berkes, Fikret. 1989. *Common Property Resources: Ecology and Community-Based Sustainable Development*. London: Belhaven Press.

Biermann, Frank, Kenneth Abbott, Steinar Andresen, Karen Bäkstrand, Steven Bernstein and Michelle Betsill. 2012. 'Navigating the Anthropocene: Improving Earth System Governance'. *Science* 335(6074): 1306–7.

Blaikie, Piers. 2006. 'Is Small Really Beautiful? Community-Based Natural Resource Management in Malawi and Botswana'. *World Development* 34(11): 1942–57.

Boelens, Rutgerd. 2009. 'The Politics of Disciplining Water Rights'. *Development and Change* 40(2): 307–31.

Bourdieu, Pierre. 1977. *Outline of a Theory of Practice*. Cambridge: Cambridge University Press.

Bruns, Bryan. 2009. 'Metaphors and Methods for Institutional Synthesis'. Paper presented at the Water Resource Governance and Design Principles. Workshop in Political Theory and Policy Analysis. Bloomington: Indiana University Press.

Campbell, Bruce, Alois Mandondo, Nontokozo Nemarandwe, Bevlyne Sithole, Wil de Jong, Marty Luckert and Frank Matorse. 2001. 'Challenges to Proponents of Common Property Resource Systems: Despairing Voices from the Social Forests of Zimbabwe'. *World Development* 29(4): 589–600.

Chowns, Eleanor. 2014. 'The Political Economy of Community Management: A Study of Factors Influencing Sustainability in Malawi's Rural Water Supply Sector'. Ph.D. thesis. Birmingham: University of Birmingham.

Cinner, J.E., Xavier Basurto, Pedro Fidelman, John Kuange, Rachael Lahari and Ahmad Mukminin. 2011. 'Institutional Designs of Customary Fisheries Management Arrangements in Indonesia, Papua New Guinea and Mexico'. *Marine Policy* 36(1): 278–85.

Cleaver, Francis. 2012. *Development through Bricolage: Rethinking Institutions for Natural Resource Management*. New York: Routledge.

Cleaver, Francis, and Jessica de Koning. 2015. 'Furthering Critical Institutionalism'. *International Journal of the Commons* 9(1): 1–18.

Cleaver, Francis, and Luke Whaley. 2018. 'Understanding Process, Power and Meaning in Adaptive Governance: A Critical Institutional Reading'. *Ecology and Society* 23(2): 49.

'Colombia's U'wa Still Teaching Us How to Resist'. 2017. *Amazon Watch*, 30 January. Retrieved 22 November 2020 from https://amazonwatch.org/news/2017/0130-colombias-uwa-still-teaching-us-how-to-resist.

'Colombian Communities Face New Wave of Violence, Discrimination Despite Peace Accords'. 2019. *Forest Peoples Programme*, 20 September. Retrieved 22 November 2020 from https://www.forestpeoples.org/en/node/50454.

Comaroff, John, and Jean Comaroff. 2009. 'Reflections on the Anthropology of Law, Governance and Sovereignty', in Franz Benda-Beckmann, Keebet Benda-Beckmann and Julia Eckert (eds), *Rules of Law and Laws of Ruling: On Governance of Law*. Farnham: Ashgate.

———. 2001. 'On Personhood: An Anthropological Perspective from Africa'. *Social Identities*. 7(2): 267–83.

Conca, Ken, and Geoffrey Debalko. 2002. *Environmental Peacemaking*. Washington and Baltimore: Woodrow Wilson Centre Press and John Hopkins University Press.

Conde, Marte, and Phillippe Le Billon. 2017. 'Why Do Some Communities Resist Mining Projects While Others Do Not?' *The Extractive Industries and Society* 4(3): 681–97.

'Consulta previa, ¿sigue el cuello de botella?'. *El Nuevo Siglo*, 13 January. Retrieved 22 November 2020 from https://www.elnuevosiglo.com.co/articulos/01-2020-consulta-previa-sigue-el-cuello-de-botella.

Cooke, Bill, and Uma Kothari. 2001. *Participation: The New Tyranny*. London: Zed Books.

Cornwall, Andrea, and Karen Brock. 2005. 'What Do Buzzwords Do for Development Policy? A Critical Look at "Participation", "Empowerment" and "Poverty Reduction"'. *Third World Quarterly* 26(7): 1043–60.

Costanza, Julia. 2015. 'Indigenous Peoples' Right to Prior Consultation: Transforming Human Rights from the Grassroots in Guatemala'. *Journal of Human Rights* 14(2): 260–85.

De Koning, Jessica. 2011. 'Reshaping Institutions: Bricolage Processes in Smallholder Forestry in the Amazon'. Ph.D. thesis. Wageningen: Wageningen University.

———. 2014. 'Unpredictable Outcomes in Forestry: Governance Institutions in Practice'. *Society and Natural Resources* 27(4): 358–71.

De Soto, Hernando. 1986. *The Other Path*. New York: Basic Books.

———. 2000. *El Misterio de Capital: Por que el Capitalismo Triunfa en Occidente y Fracasa en el Resto del Mundo*. Peru: El Commercio.

Devlin, John, and Nonita Yap. 2008. 'Contentious Politics in Environmental Assessment. Blocked Projects and Winning Coalitions'. *Impact Assessment and Project Appraisal* 26(1): 17–27.

Douglas, Mary. 1986. *How Institutions Think*. Syracuse, NY: Syracuse University Press.

Dresse, Anaïs, Itay Fischhendler, Jonas Nielsen and Demitrios Zikos. 2019. 'Environmental Peacebuilding: Toward a Theoretical Framework'. *Cooperation and Conflict* 54(1): 99–119.

Economic and Social Council. 2006. 'Human Rights and Indigenous Issues Report of the Special Rapporteur on the Situation of Human Rights and Fundamental Freedoms of Indigenous People'. Mr Rodolfo Stavenhagen. UN Doc. E/CN.4/2006/78.

Folke, Carl, Thomas Hahn, Per Olsson and Jon Norberg. 2005. 'Adaptive Governance of Social-Ecological Systems'. *Annual Review of Environment and Resources* 30(1): 441–73.

'Free, Prior and Informed Consultation in Colombia: The Case of the Expansion of the Cerrejón Project'. 2012. *IKV Pax Kristi*, January. Retrieved 22 November 2020 from https://www.google.com/url?sa=t&rct=j&q=&esrc=s&source=web&cd=1&ved=2ahUKEwiC15KgkszoAhXKo4sKHQcoCAUQFjAAegQIBBAB&url=https%3A%2F%2Fwww.paxforpeace.nl%2Fmedia%2Ffiles%2Ffree-prior-and-informed-consultation-colombia.pdf&usg=AOvVaw0pD0HSl-g_sGEnCrZXsKP_.

Galtung, Johan. 1975. *Peace: Research-Education-Action*. Copenhagen: Chr. Ejlers Forlag.

Gutiérrez-Sanín, Francisco, and Jennifer Vargas. 2017. 'Agrarian Elite Participation in Colombia's Civil War'. *Journal of Agrarian Change* 17(4): 739–48.

'Ground-breaking Win for Indigenous People's Land Rights in Colombia'. 2017. *Forest Peoples Programme*, 8 February. Retrieved 22 November 2020 from https://www.for

estpeoples.org/en/rights-land-natural-resources-extractive-industries/press-release/2017/groundbreaking-win.

Grugel, Jeanne, Jewellord Nem Singh and Lorenza Fontana (eds). 2017. *Demanding Justice in the Global South: Claiming Rights*. New York and Shanghai: Palgrave Macmillan.

Hardin, Garret. 1968. 'The Tragedy of the Commons'. *Science* 280(5365): 1243–48.

Harvey, David. 2003. *The New Imperialism*. Oxford: Oxford University Press.

Held, Sergio. 2018 'Diecisiete años de consultas previas'. *Semana*, 11 November. Retrieved 22 November 2020 from https://www.semana.com/contenidos-editoriales/hidrocarburos-son-el-futuro/articulo/diecisiete-anos-de-consultas-previas/590034.

Hipwell, William, Katy Mamen, Vivianne Weitzner and Gail Whiteman. 2002. *Aboriginal Peoples and Mining in Canada: Consultation, Participation and Prospects for Change*. Ottawa: North-South Institute.

Homer-Dixon, Thomas. 1991. 'On the Threshold: Environmental as Causes of Acute Conflict'. *International Security* 16(2): 76–116.

Ingram, Verina, Mirjam Ros-Tonen and Ton Dietz. 2015. 'A Fine Mess: Bricolaged Forest Governance in Cameroon'. *International Journal of the Commons* 9(1): 41–64.

ILO (International Labour Organization). 1989. *Indigenous and Tribal Peoples Convention 169*. Retrieved 22 November 2020 from: https://www.ilo.org/dyn/normlex/en/f?p=NORMLEXPUB:12100:0::NO::P12100_ILO_CODE:C169.

IACtHR (Inter-American Court of Human Rights). 2007. *Saramaka People v Suriname*, Judgment of 28 November 2007 (Preliminary Objections, Merits, Reparations and Costs), Ser C. No 172.

———. 2012. *Kichwa Indigenous People of Sarayaku v Ecuador*.

Ide, Tobias. 2020. 'The Dark Side of Environmental Peacebuilding'. *World Development* 127(104777): 1–9.

Jaskoski, Maiah. 2020. 'Participatory Institutions as a Focal Point for Mobilizing: Prior Consultation and Indigenous Conflict in Colombia's Extractive Industries'. *Comparative Politics*. Retrieved 22 November 2020 from https://doi.org/10.5129/001041520X15757670821639.

Jones, Stephan. 2015. 'Bridging Political Economy Analysis and Critical Institutionalism: An Approach to Help Analyse Institutional Change for Rural Water Services'. *International Journal of the Commons* 9(1): 65–86.

Kaldor, Mary. 2013. 'In Defence of New Wars'. *Stability: International Journal of Security and Development* 2(1): 1–16.

Kirsch, Stuart. 2014. *Mining Capitalism: The Relationship between Corporations and their Critics*. Durham, NC: Duke University Press.

Komakech, Hans, and Pieter van der Zaag. 2011. 'Understanding the Emergence and Functioning of River Committees in a Catchment of the Pangani Basin, Tanzania'. *Water Alternatives* 4(2): 197–222.

'Landmark Decision for Indigenous Peoples in Colombia and Globally'. 2017. *Land Rights Now*, 10 February. Retrieved 22 November 2020 from https://www.landrightsnow.org/landmark-decision-for-indigenous-peoples-in-colombia-and-globally.

Lawrence, Rebecca, and Rasmus Larsen. 2017. 'The Politics of Planning: Assessing the Impacts of Mining on Sami Lands'. *Third World Quarterly* 38(5): 1164–80.

Lederarch, John. 1995. *Preparing for Peace: Conflict Transformation Across Cultures*. Syracuse: Syracuse University Press.

———. 1997. *Building Peace: Sustainable Reconciliation in Divided Societies*. Washington, DC: United States Institute of Peace.

Leifsen, Esben, Marie-Therese Gustafsson, Maria Guzmán-Gallegos and Almut Schilling Vacaflor. 2017. 'New Mechanisms of Participation in Extractive Governance: Between Technologies of Governance and Resistance Work'. *Third World Quarterly* 38(5): 1043–57.

Leifsen, Esben, Luis Sánchez-Vásquez and Maleny Gabriela Reyes. 2017. 'Claiming Prior Consultation, Monitoring Environmental Impact: Counterwork by the Use of Formal Instruments of Participatory Governance in Ecuador's Emerging Mining Sector'. *Third World Quarterly* 38(5): 1092–109.

Lemos, Maria, and Arun Agrawal. 2006. 'Environmental Governance and Political Science', in Magali Delmas and Oran Young, (eds) *Governance for the Environment: New Perspectives*. Cambridge: Cambridge University Press.

Leonardsson, Hanna, and Gustav Rudd. 2015. 'The "Local Turn" in Peacebuilding: A Literature Review of Effective and Emancipatory Local Peacebuilding'. *Third World Quarterly* 36(5): 825–39.

Lévi-Strauss, Claude. 2004. *The Savage Mind: Nature of Human Society*. Oxford: Oxford University Press.

Long, Norman. 2001. *Development Sociology: Actor Perspectives*. London: Routledge.

Mbembe, Achille. 2012. 'Theory from the Antipodes: Notes on Jean and John Comaroffs' TFS'. *Fieldsights: Theorizing the Contemporary, Cultural Anthropology Online*. Retrieved 22 November 2020 from https://culanth.org/fieldsights/theory-from-the-antipodes-notes-on-jean-john-comaroffs-tfs.

McGranahan, Gordon, and David Satterwaite. 2006. *Governance and Getting the Private Sector to Provide Better Water and Sanitations Services to the Urban Poor*. IIED Human Settlements Working Paper.

McNeish, John-Andrew. 2001. 'Globalization and the Politics of Participation'. Unpublished Ph.D. thesis. University of London.

———. 2017. 'A Vote to Derail Extraction: Popular Consultation and Resource Sovereignty in Tolima, Colombia'. *Third World Quarterly* 38(5): 1128–45.

McNeish, John-Andrew, Gabriel Rojas Andrade and Catalina Vallejo. 2015. *Striking a New Balance? Exploring Civil–Military Relations in Colombia in a Time of Hope*. Bergen: CMI Working Paper.

Merrey, Douglas, and Simon Cook. 2012. 'Fostering Institutional Creativity at Multiple Levels: Towards Facilitated Institutional Bricolage'. *Water Alternatives* 5(1): 1–19.

Merrey, Douglas, Ruth Meinzen-Dick, Peter Mollinga and Eiman Karar. 2007. 'Policy and Institutional Reform: The Art of the Possible', in David Molden (ed.), *Water for Food, Water for Life: A Comprehensive Assessment of Water Management in Agriculture*. London: Earthscan.

Murillo-Sandoval, Paolo, Kristina Van Dexter, Jamon Van de Hoek, David Wrathall and Robert Kennedy. 2020. 'The End of Gunpoint Conservation: Forest Disturbance after the Colombian Peace Agreement'. Environmental Research Letter 15(034033). Retrieved 7 January 2021 from https://iopscience.iop.org/1748-9326/15/3/034033/media/ERL_15_3_034033_suppdata.pdf.

Nader, Laura. 2012. 'Law and the Frontiers of Illegalities', in Franz von Benda-Beckmann, Keebet von Benda-Beckmann, and Anee Griffiths (eds), *The Power of Law in a Transnational World: Anthropological Enquiries*. New York and Oxford: Berghahn Books.

North, Douglass. 1990. *Institutions, Institutional Change and Economic Performance*. Cambridge: Cambridge University Press.

Nunan, Foina. 2006. 'Empowerment and Institutions: Managing Fisheries in Uganda'. *World Development* 34(7): 1316–32.

O'Faircheallaigh. Ciaran. 2010. 'Aboriginal-Mining Company Contractual Agreements in Australia and Canada: Implications for Political Autonomy and Community Development.' *Canadian Journal of Development Studies/Revue Canadienne D'études du Développement* 30(1–2): 69–86.

———. 2013. 'Extractive Industries and Indigenous Peoples: A Changing Dynamic?' *Journal of Rural Studies* 30: 20–30.

———. 2017. 'Shaping Projects, Shaping Impacts: Community-Controlled Impact Assessments and Negotiated Agreements'. *Third World Quarterly* 38(5): 1181–97.

Osei-Kufour, Patrick. 2010. 'Does Institutionalizing Decentralization Work? Rethinking Agency, Institutions and Authority in Local Governance: A Case Study of Ntonaboma in Kwahu-North District, Ghana'. Unpublished Ph.D. thesis. University of Bradford.

Ostrom, Ellinor. 1990. *Governing the Commons: The Evolution of Institutions for Collective Action*. Cambridge: Cambridge University Press.

———. 2005. *Understanding Institutional Diversity*. Princeton: Princeton University Press.

———. 2008. 'Design Principles of Robust Property-Rights Institutions: What Have We Learned?' Paper presented at Land Policies and Property Rights, Lincoln Institute of Land Policy, Cambridge, MA, 2–3 June.

———. 2009. 'Beyond Markets and States: Polycentric Governance of Complex Governance Systems'. Nobel Lecture, 8 December.

Paavola, Jouni. 2007. 'Institutions in Environmental Governance: A Reconceptualization'. *Ecological Economics* 63(1): 93–103.

Papillon, Martin, and Thierry Rodon. 2019. 'The Transformative Potential of Indigenous Driven Approaches to Implementing Free, Prior and Informed Consent: Lessons from Two Canadian Cases'. *International Journal on Minority and Group Rights* 27(2): 314–35.

Page, Ben. 2005. 'Naked Power: Women and the Social Production of Water in Anglophone Cameroon', in Anna Coles and Tina Wallace (eds), *Gender, Water and Development*. Oxford: Berg.

Pellegrini, Lorenzo, and Marco Ribera Arismendi. 2012. 'Consultation, Compensation and Extraction in Bolivia after the "Left Turn": The Case of Oil Exploration in the North of La Paz Department'. *Journal of Latin American Geography* 11(2): 103–20.

Peña-Huertas, Rocío, Luis Enrique Ruiz, María Parada, Santiago Zuleta and Ricardo Álvare. 2017. 'Legal Dispossession and Civil War in Colombia'. *Journal of Agrarian Change* 17(4): 759–69.

Peters, Ida, Ian Christoplos, Mikkel Funder, Esbern Friis-Hansen and Adam Pain. 2012. 'Understanding Institutional Change: A Review of Selected Literature for the Climate Change and Rural Institutions Research Programme'. *DIIS Working Paper* 2012: 12.

Peters, Pauline. 2004. 'Inequality and Social Conflict Over Land in Africa'. *Journal of Agrarian Change* 4(3): 269–314.

Rodríguez-Garavito, César. 2010. 'Ethnicity.gov: Global Governance, Indigenous Peoples and the Right to Prior Consultation in Social Minefields'. *Indiana Journal of Global Legal Studies* 18(1): 263–305.

De Sousa Santos, Boaventura. 1987. 'Law: A Map of Misreading. Toward a Postmodern Conception of Law'. *Journal of Law and Society* 14(3): 279–302.

Sayer, Andrew. 2000. *Realism and Social Science*. London: Sage Publications.

———. 2011. *Why Things Matter to People: Social Science, Values and Ethical Life*. Cambridge: Cambridge University Press.

Sawyer, Suzannah. 2015. *Crude Chronicles: Indigenous Politics, Multinational Oil and Neoliberalism in Ecuador*. Durham, NC: Duke University Press.

Schilling-Vacaflor, Almut. 2017. 'Who Controls the Territory and the Resources? Free, Prior and Informed Consent (FPIC) as a Contested Human Rights Practices in Bolivia'. *Third World Quarterly* 38(5): 1058–74.

———. 2019. 'The Coupling of Prior Consultation and Environmental Impact Assessment in Bolivia: Corporate Appropriation and Knowledge Gaps', in Claire Wright and Alexandra Tomaselli (eds), *The Prior Consultation of Indigenous Peoples in Latin America: Inside the Implementation Gap*. London: Routledge.

Schilling-Vacaflor, Almut, and Riccarda Flemming. 2015. 'Conflict Transformation through Prior Consultation'. *Journal of Latin American Studies* 47(5): 811–39.

'Shaping Institutions for Natural Resources Management'. 2010. *InfoResources Focus 3/08*. Swiss Agency for Development and Cooperation. Retrieved 22 November 2020 from https://boris.unibe.ch/70310/7/focus08_3_e.pdf.

Smith, Brian. 2007. *Good Governance and Development*. Basingstoke: Palgrave Macmillan.

Stockholm Resilience Centre. 2012. 'Insight #3 Adaptive Governance'. Research Insights, Stockholm University, Sweden. Retrieved 22 November 2020 from https://www.stock holmresilience.org/download/18.3e9bddec1373daf16fa439/1459560363382/Insights_ adaptive_governance_120111-2.pdf.

Sturgeon, Janet, and Thomas Sikor. 2004. 'Post-socialist Property in Asia and Europe: Variations on "Fuzziness"'. *Conservation and Society* 2(1): 21–38.

Swain, Ashok, and Joakhim Öjendal. 2020. *Routledge Handbook of Environmental Conflict and Peacebuilding*. London: Routledge.

'Three Years on from His Murder, Colombian Indigenous Leader's Killers Remain Unpunished'. 2018. *Forest Peoples Programme*, 7 April. Retrieved 22 November 2020 from https://www.forestpeoples.org/en/safeguard-accountablility-issues/news-article/2018/ three-years-later-colombian-embera-Cham%C3%AD.

Van der Heijden, Jeroen. 2011. 'Institutional Layering: A Review of the Use of the Concept'. *Politics* 31(1): 9–18.

Van Laerhoven, Frank, and Ellinor Ostrom. 2007. 'Traditions and Trends in the Study of the Commons'. *International Journal of the Commons* 1(1): 3–28.

Vatn, Arild. 2009. Cooperative Behaviour and Institutions. *Journal of Socio-economics* 38(1): 188–96.

———. 2016. *Environmental Governance: Institutions, Policies and Actions*. Edward Elgar.

Weitzer, Viviane. 2017. 'Nosotros Somos Estado: Contested Legalities in Decision-Making about Extractives Affecting Ancestral Territories in Colombia'. *Third World Quarterly* 38(5): 1198–214.

Wong, Sam. 2009. 'Lessons from a Participatory Transboundary Water Governance Project in West Africa', in *Participatory Learning and Action Vol. 60: Community Based Adaptation to Climate Change*. International Institute for Environment and Development.

———. 2010. 'Elite Capture or Capture Elites? Lessons from the "Counter-elite" and "Co-opt Elite" Approaches in Bangladesh and Ghana'. *UNA-WIDER*, 82.

Wright, Claire, and Alexandra Tomaselli. 2019. *The Prior Consultation of Indigenous Peoples in Latin America*. London: Routledge.

Figure 6.1 Symbolic contest, Petare, Venezuela. Digital photomontage
by Owen Logan, 2013

Conclusion

MAKING USE OF SOVEREIGN FORCES?

A man lifts a gold framed painting of Simon Bolivar aloft in the middle of a highway running through the centre of Caracas, Venezuela. To the left in the background, on a billboard a scantily clad woman is used as part of an advert for fine brandy, and the apartment blocks of one of the city's wealthier districts are visible further back at the foot of the surrounding mountains. To the right, in the background, a contrasting scene of a clearly much less economically well-off neighbourhood stretches over nearby hills.

Years ago, my colleague and friend the photographer Owen Logan showed me this photo montage. This was a montage he had made in 2013 shortly after visiting the country and one that he had intended to depict what he termed 'competing expressions of sovereignty'. We had discussed the possibility of using the image on the front cover of a book, but the publisher had other ideas, so the picture was set to one side. Now completing this new volume, the obvious relevance of this image comes back to mind as a means to help sum up one of its central arguments, i.e. the role of competing expressions of sovereignty in natural resource politics. In its content, the picture cleverly captures what photographers and researchers commonly ignore in the study of resource politics, i.e. that there is a temporal, scalar, social, political and economic layering to these competitions. Indeed, the picture is indicative that there is not only direct violence and conflict, but also a structuring of differences and socioeconomic divisions into the physical environment. Furthermore, these are not only visible dynamics, but also expressions of competing but frequently overlapping values and epistemologies.

To enter into discussion of another context beyond those covered in earlier chapters would be a mistake at such a late stage in this volume and especially given my complete lack of research experience in this location. Nonetheless, it worth noting that Owen's intention with the picture – to depict a competition for sovereignty in Venezuela – is now far more relevant now than at the time when the image was captured. In the interim between the taking of the picture and the present moment, Venezuela has been consumed by a series of contests over sovereignty and natural resources. This is visible in a timeline stretching from the Bolivarian Revolution led by President Chavez and its promise to sow the petroleum wealth, through to his death and replacement by the Maduro administration and its initiation of a mining boom to waylay the effects of an economic crisis caused by mismanagement and the falling price of oil. A series of colleagues have captured these developments and other related controversies in their writing (Strønen 2007, 2020; Bull and Rosales 2020). These dynamics in Venezuela are interesting in their own right, but in the context of this book, they also reinforce the wider significance of my argument regarding resource sovereignty and the detailing of its application to other Latin American contexts.

It is of course also of significance that it is Simon Bolivar, one of the leading figures (together with San Martín, O'Higgins and Hidalgo) of the Latin American Wars of Independence (circa 1808–83) that is placed at the centre of the photograph. As well as a muse to Chavez in Venezuela, the image of Bolivar can be found in almost every classroom and public building the length and breadth of South America. It is the quintessential image of both Latin American regionalism and nationalism – his history being linked not only to liberation from the Spanish Crown, but also the establishment of a series of new republics (Bolivia being a name that directly paying homage to Bolivar). Importantly, Bolivar was also well acquainted with the divisiveness of the issue of sovereignty. His grand vision of a new country, Gran Colombia, and of a regional union of Latin American nations quickly fell apart following the Wars of Independence as regional leaders squabbled over access to land, resources and boundaries. Bolivar, like many of his contemporaries also recognized and worried about the ethnic make-up of Latin America as a region. As Stavenhagen[1] (1992) reminds us, Bolivar acknowledged early on the difficulty of creating unified nations out of heterogeneous populations. Bolivar warned in 1819:

> We must keep in mind that our people are neither European nor North American: rather, they are a mixture of Africans and Americans who originated in Europe . . . It is impossible to determine with any degree of accuracy where we belong in the human family. The greater portion of the native Indians have been annihilated; Spaniards have mixed with Americans and Africans, and Africans with Indians and Spaniards.[2]

Bolivar, himself of mixed origin, and many of the region's elites throughout its history positively expected that these various population groups would either disappear or eventually mesh into a new amalgam. Whilst Latin American leaders were at first concerned about the negative consequences of racial mixing, in time nineteenth-century concerns would be replaced by twentieth-century government efforts in many parts of the region to promote a process of ethnic mixing or *mestizaje*. This would in part result in the indigenous communities being retitled peasant (*campesino*) communities. However, although mixing did occur, it did not occur to the extent or manner that early proponents had foreseen. Integration either only took place to the degree that changes in the socioeconomic structure and national elites allowed (Stavenhagen 1992: 423) or it followed paths that were not expected at all. The expansion of the *mestizo* population did not result in the disappearance of indigenous peoples. Despite the political, economic and cultural aggressions that they suffered at the hands of colonizers and their descendants, and later the ruling classes of independent states, a deeply rooted 'culture of resistance' (Stavenhagen 1992: 424) ensured their survival. However, this survival has been hard won.

Successive waves of development, and the logics of developmentalism, have made it difficult for indigenous peoples to retain their territories, lifestyles and cultural beliefs. From the 1970s onwards, various organizations began to express claims about indigenous rights and autonomy that had only been stated occasionally and unsystematically beforehand. Developments in international rights and law would assist these movements and would lead to important recognitions and political openings, enabling the size and number of indigenous organizations to grow in the 1990s. However, this would not remove the issue of relationship between indigenous and national identity, or the *indian problem* (Stavenhagen 1992: 429) particularly when indigenous movements started to renew claims to autonomy, gained international support for consent (and more commonly consultation) and every more vehemently contested the sovereign right of national government to expand its extractive frontiers into their lands.

The difficulty of navigating these complex *sovereign forces* is evidently covered in the earlier chapters of this book. These chapters provide an account of the recent state of play of the competing expression of and claims to sovereignty in Latin America. They are also an account of how these are intimately connected to questions of natural resource use and governance. However, they also reveal that history does not necessarily leave behind easily differentiated categories and positions; rather, what is visible in previous chapters is a complex and at times overlapping dynamic, and not only of race or ethnicity. Several of the previous chapters demonstrate in detail the different temporal, spatial, scalar and ontological nature of contests over sovereignty and natural resources. However, they also point not only to division and contestation, but also to pragmatism and common interests in terms of securing legitimate governance and economic livelihoods. In conclusion, I argue that the strength of the idea of resource sovereignty is in its acknowledgement of this multiplicity of scenarios, some leading towards contestation and others at least indicating the possibility for conflict avoidance if not possible cooperation. As I have stated since the start of this book, resource sovereignty improves our analytic understanding of resource conflict and may be suggestive of directions to improve practice in environmental governance and peace-building.

Resource Sovereignty and Conflict

The earlier chapters of this book have aimed to qualify in rich empirical detail and theoretical discussion my initial claims regarding the concept of resource sovereignty, i.e. that it represents a valuable hybrid concept that recognizes the manner in which different social sectors bracket material interests and social claims together to form political claims for land and territory. Research experience from Bolivia, Guatemala and Colombia is used here to demonstrate the manner in which questions of resource politics and sovereignty in Latin America have become (and continue to be) closely intertwined.

The individual chapters focus on the way in which claims to territory and natural resources are also expressions of popular sovereignty and the contestation not only of state plans and visions for development, but of the very idea of what the state represents. At times, the focus of these contests is national in nature, while at other times they are much more localized, and throughout the influences of global political economy are apparent. At times, the expression of popular sovereignty takes place at the margins of the state and aims to circumvent state geographical and legal limits. At other times, the expressions of popular sovereignty, or of indigenous sovereignty, do not aim to attack the state but seeks to engage with it through the use and reworking of existing law, regulations and government institutional responsibilities.

These expressions of sovereignty are shown to connect to natural resources and territories that are considered vital to economic development and energy provision, and to the governance of the environment in a time of recognized climate change and need for environmental protection. This is not only a politics of non-renewable resources, but also of renewable and supposedly 'green' resources. They are also shown to express not only the material concerns of territorial control, economic value, and physical impacts and limits, but the deep-seated cultural, ontological and spiritual concerns of the communities and individuals involved.

Responses to claims to popular and indigenous sovereignty by states and other interests (the private sector, international community, etc.) are also visibly multiple in nature. There are clear instances of direct and structural violence, even collusion with illegal armed actors. However, as a result of the changing historical and legal circumstances that have evolved in the region and internationally, governments and corporations have also commonly accepted the need to attempt to respond to these claims through institutionalized forms of dialogue, regulation and consultation. I have also outlined evidence that they have also frequently done so somewhat half-heartedly or with other agendas in mind.

Wrapped together with these global ethnographic investigations of resource sovereignty, there are a series of important theoretical and historical discussions. These include a necessary exploration of the meaning and historical development of the idea of sovereignty. I have shown how the idea has been interpreted differently and has transformed over time, including its revalorization in the context of colonial and postcolonial settler societies. I have discussed in previous pages its recent reconsideration within social theory and particularly within social anthropology. Sovereignty has moved a long way from a strict stereotype of 'supreme authority within a territory' to an understanding of the distributed nature of sovereignty produced in everyday encounters with power.

In this book I have joined these theoretical reflections with a historical anthropology that demonstrates the manner in which indigenous and peasant peoples have not only been the victims of colonization and state-building, but also agents who through everyday encounters with the state, the market, and politics and conscription into exceptional events of revolution and rebellion have left their mark on the maps and idea of Latin American states. I also sadly note that it is also sometimes their annihilation that has left a shadowy stain on these maps and ideas. I further form connections between the revalorization of sovereignty and a discussion of the meaning of indigeneity, and its complex place within recent claims to rights and territorial autonomy. Campaigns for food and energy sovereignty are explicit expressions of these claims, as are what might analytically termed hydrocarbon or lithium citizenship.

The previous chapters also further test ideas and theories directly relating to the relationship between natural resources, sovereignty and conflict. In line with earlier work I have carried out with colleagues, in this book I question again the value of the resource curse thesis and related explanations for resource-related conflict. I argue that the analytical lens of resource sovereignty adds a much richer understanding of these conflicts. Drawing on new empirical information and reflection, I further show that whilst there are openly violent conflicts over natural resources, democratic contestation is far more common. Indeed, in line with others (Conde and Le Billon 2017), I demonstrate that the opening of new spaces and mechanisms of resource governance can act as an invitation for contestation. I also demonstrate throughout the volume that whilst economic rent-seeking may in some instances be a relevant dynamic, indigenous and peasant contestation of natural resource extraction and governance is driven primarily by a desire for historic and contemporary grievances to be addressed. This is clearly observed as the primary driving force for renewed calls for sovereignty and territorial autonomy. These contestations are described in detail as taking place at different scales of interaction, whether this be with the state, the private sector or the international community. It is also evident that these claims for sovereignty are not only driven by material interests, but by particular claims to identity and at times the defence of culture, ontology and distinct systems of value. However, this is acknowledged, with the proviso that these differences can often be overstated as entirely distinct states of alterity.

It is of interest to note that whilst analysts who are supportive of the resource curse stress the high risk of conflict in the context of resource abundance, there are other writers who sustain an argument for environmental securitization because of the high risk of conflict in the context of resource scarcity. It is to this last perspective that the literature of environmental peace-building critically responds, emphasizing (as expressed in the previous chapter) that resources can also represent a possible basis for cooperation. On the basis of the empirical and ethnographic explorations made throughout this book, it should now be clear that these schools of writing have operated with models that are overly reductionist in their form and delimitation. Indeed, as noted in the previous chapter, recent trends in environmental governance and environmental peace-building emphasize new directions that question assumptions of rational choice and can adapt to distinct biophysical and socio-political conditions. I have suggested that the analytical frame of resource sovereignty could be of particular relevance to this shift and, in particular, could assist proposals for a critical institutionalist turn in environmental governance. In some contexts (e.g. Colombia and Guatemala), this may also be of significance to peace-building initiatives.

Resource Sovereignty and Peace

Ultimately, what people from the communities I mention in this volume are looking for in claiming sovereignty over territory and resources is the possibility of living in peace. These claims and efforts may result in conflict, violence and contestation, but the eventual goal of all of their efforts is not to live in a constant state of insecurity as they often do, but a future in which they determine the terms and meaning of their own security (as individuals, communities and peoples). As I have described in earlier chapters, at times this might mean that they attempt to circumvent and ignore the restrictions of the state and its laws and borders. As in other parts of the world, there is also an 'art to not being governed' (Scott 2009) in Latin American indigenous and peasant communities. However, more often, these communities do not avoid the state, but rather look for formal and informal mechanisms through which to either confront, negotiate or *counterwork* (Leifsen et al. 2017) the state through its own institutions, laws and regulation. As I have argued, a number of these strategies may be employed in parallel by different communities. Engagement and dialogue are also observed to take place with other governance actors, including the private sector and the international community, when legal and governance rules require it (in cases of popular and prior consultation, environmental impact assessment, etc.). It is evident from these observations that whilst resource sovereignty is meant to approach the dynamics of conflict, it is also indicative of points of connection and of meaningful cooperation (where cooperation is, as I have described, not the same as acquiescence).

As the Chapter 5 has posited, these signs of cooperation, even when tense and fraught with contradiction, are significant in terms of possible signposts towards improved environmental governance and peace-building. I have also suggested that they indicate that a significant match can be made between resource sovereignty and critical institutionalism in both an analytical and an applied sense. Critical institutionalism's recognition that institutions are not just acts of design and singular foundation but are the outcome of long-term acts of bricolage in which previous experiences from socioecology and beyond are repeatedly combined with local systems of value to create new institutional arrangements and actions matches the ethnographic detail I have provided in earlier chapters. It also matches my emphasis on an anthropological history that recognizes the everyday interactions of indigenous and peasant communities with the state, and their ability to write themselves back into the history of state-formation. As I have highlighted earlier in the book, the actions of these communities not only leave traces on law and regulation and sometimes the rise and fall of political leaders; put bluntly, their engagement and institutional transformation has a direct impact on the success and failure of environmental governance.

In proposing the addition of resource sovereignty to critical institutionalism, I also acknowledge the perspective's careful attention to complex social identities, competing rationalities, unequal power relations, and wider political and geographical factors. Institutions are seen to be dynamic because they respond to and make human interests operational, allowing for institutional form to change and to take different forms and achieve different results. They also respond to local cultural ideas, ontologies and contrasting systems of epistemology that may contrast significantly with dominant liberal ideologies. Critical institutionalism also recognizes that there are both points of alignment and nonalignment between individuals, communities and governing bodies in these processes. These dynamics are recognized to take place over long periods of time and in response to both ordinary and extraordinary events. I suggest that the addition of resource sovereignty to critical institutionalism helps to reinforce its significance by enabling an understanding of vernacular state-building. Although it makes an important critique of mainstream institutionalism's limited focus on the local and correctly emphasizes the importance of the 'middle', critical institutionalism has done little to study the institutional formation of environmental governance within both a national and international setting. Indeed, whilst there is an expressed interest in history, there is no focused consideration of state-formation, or of sovereignty, within existing critical institutionalist writing. As well as pointing to inroads in relation to these important issues, resource sovereignty can also add significantly to critical institutionalism's attention to the workings of power and, in particular, to the conditions of informality, war and crime that frequently surround the formal practices and mechanisms of environmental governance. It also helps to point out the particular importance of legal pluralism and competing systems of legal norms and values to the outcome of governance efforts. Systems of law are also visibly not simply reduced to those of state versus customary law, but in some contexts are defined by conditions of 'raw law' (Weitzer 2017). My conclusions here complement the recent and rich description provided by Ballvé (2020), which demonstrates that areas described as existing in a condition of statelessness in earlier writing have in fact long been part of state-building projects, despite their violence.

As I have also suggested in the previous chapter, recognition of the complexity of the dynamics of institutional formation and operation assists improved study and understanding of the challenges and problems in environmental governance. In this regard, the combination of resource sovereignty and critical institutionalism may have significance in both everyday settings and in exceptional conflict and post-conflict settings. However, in stating this, I concur with critical institutionalists that this is not a simple process of designing blueprints for peace-building, but rather a consideration of tailor-made solutions that respond to the particularities of context, history and peoples. Rather than a weakness, this emphasis on plurality and complexity should be seen as a strength. Although requiring more time and sensitivity, I have suggested that in line with the expressed desire of peace-building efforts, this approach opens up more entry points for identifying not only the causes of conflict, but also the possibilities for cooperation. Despite their apparent chaos and violence, the pragmatism of local communities in negotiating with authorities and working with existing law, regulation and governance mechanisms suggests that sites of extraction 'can also be territories enabling social orders and forms of development' (Le Billon, Roa-García and López-Granada 2020: 3). Indeed, it opens up the opportunity for cooperation between qualitative research and quantitative research that questions standard logics and assumptions of prescriptive development. Importantly, I argue here that this is not out of step with good practice, but rather is in line with contemporary policy concerns of the possibilities of 'working with the grain' to support local hybrid institutional arrangements that work (Booth 2012; Cleaver and Whaley 2018).

With this in mind, I hasten to add in conclusion that the proposed combination of resource sovereignty with critical institutionalism also makes sense in the light of current legal, political and intellectual developments in Latin America and further afield. Although currently suffering from the spread of COVID-19 and a virus of renewed and persisting right-wing politics that respects neither indigenous and peasant claims for sovereignty nor the damage caused by expanding extractive frontiers, other more positive trends are also taking hold. Whilst the *pink tide* and, with it, the political left is largely at low ebb, innovative ideas for peace and improved governance have not stopped being generated in the region. Here the importance of resource sovereignty and critical institutionalism should again be strongly evident. In recent years, the debates regarding decolonization have transformed academic debates and, whilst still controversial, entered the standard discourse and action of politics in many parts of the region. As part of the rejection of the intervention of US or European influence, emphasis is increasingly being placed on the need for reconciliation with the past and a new consideration of the value of truly Latin American, or indigenous, ideas.

This process is in part encouraged by a recognition of climate change and a scientifically founded call to find new ways of living in a new time, the *Anthropocene*. In an era in which the global community is facing climate change and struggling to hold in check the increasing degradation of the planet, indigenous peoples, pastoralists and forest-dwelling communities have been singled out by academics and international policy-makers as essential contributors to the practical rethinking of human–nature relations. Multiple international organizations now suggest that answers to the problems of climate change and environmental destruction can be found in indigenous beliefs, knowledge and practice. For instance, the Intergovernmental Panel on Climate Change (IPCC) recognizes that the world has much to learn from local communities and indigenous peoples, whose knowledge and practices constitute a 'major resource for adapting to climate change'. Similarly, the UN has repeatedly emphasized that without the protection of indigenous territories, it will not be possible to achieve the Sustainable Development Goals (SDGs). A Local Communities and Indigenous Peoples Platform was established by the UNFCCC in 2018 with the aim of giving indigenous peoples an active role in climate action and multistakeholder dialogue. This increasing valuation of indigenous peoples' environmental knowledge has taken place in parallel to an unprecedented recognition of human rights principles and the opening of global environmental governance to the participation of nonstate actors (Kuyper, Linnér and Schroeder 2018). In the natural and environmental sciences, there has also been an expressed interest in 'bridging indigenous and scientific knowledge' and, in particular, learning from indigenous land-use practices in order to control deforestation, to monitor environmental changes and to reduce carbon dioxide emission (Weiss, Hamann and Marsh 2013). These efforts suggest that in order to be legitimate and effective, the governance of global environmental challenges must incorporate diverse knowledge systems and practices (Armitage 2008).

In contrast to other regions of the world, all Latin American governments have (with the current exception of Brazil) accepted the impact of climate change and need for its mitigation through strategies for environmental protections, albeit to different degrees. Limiting and excluding communities from territorial access, these strategies have in some instances been criticized for hampering local communities' own efforts at protections in practice. However, despite these problems, international and national policies have together helped to stimulate increasingly mainstream discussion of the contradictions of modernist anthropocentric proposals for development and its historic failures on both the right and the left of the political spectrum. Scholarship throughout the region expresses a range of radical new ecocentric theoretical tendencies that importantly draw decolonization and the environment into new conversations with one another (political ecology,[3] environmental justice,[4] ecological justice,[5] post-extraction,[6] the pluriverse).[7] Indeed, going beyond ecocentric imaginings, a series of recent court cases in the region have sought to implement a sensitivity to *socionature* in practice.

In May 2016, the Constitutional Court of Colombia released its decision (T-622/16) recognizing the Atrato River as an *entidad sujeto de derechos* (entity of subject rights), which formally granted it rights as a legal person. It is important to stress that despite providing protection in this manner to the river system, the decision of the Court was first and foremost meant as a means to address a writ (*tutela*) for the protection of the constitutional rights of indigenous and Afro-descendant communities who are reliant on the river. In 2018, the Colombian Supreme Court also recognized the Colombian Amazon as a subject of rights (STC4360-2018) with a similar goal of protecting both the local environment and dependent communities. The

Atrato and Amazon rulings by two Colombian High Courts signalled to other Colombian courts that legally recognizing ecosystems as rights-holders is an appropriate remedy for environmental conflicts, where local stakeholders were to act as legal 'guardians'. As a result, there are currently fourteen Colombian ecoregions (Richardson 2020) recognized as rights-holders, making Colombia the country with the most distinct rights-bearing ecoregions recognized at some level of governance. The court rulings are widely cited as setting an innovative precedent for changing the basis of environmental governance elsewhere in the region and beyond (Macpherson 2019).

Each of these trends strengthens the claim that a more subtle understanding of sovereignty and claims to the improved governance of natural resources remains relevant and necessary. Whilst more research on each of these new developments in the region is needed, it is clear that their successful outcome is dependent on careful attention to complex sovereign forces. Indeed, they are indicative of the acute necessity of a much more nuanced approach to analysis and governance than has been acknowledged in mainstream environmental governance and peace-building before. In this light, I propose that resource sovereignty, and its application in connection with critical institutionalism as explained in this book, represents a very real means to address vital matters. These sovereign forces are revealed here as determinant of Latin America's environmental *everyday*, both present and future.

Notes

1. UN Special Rapporteur on Indigenous Rights 2001–8.
2. Quoted in Stavenhagen (1992).
3. See e.g. Martinez Alier (2013).
4. See e.g. Curruthers (2008).
5. See e.g. Washington et al. (2018).
6. See e.g. Acosta (2017).
7. See e.g. Escobar (2020).

References

Acosta, Alberto. 2017. 'Post-extractivism: From Discourse to Practice – Reflections for Action', in *Alternative Pathways to Sustainable Development: Lessons from Latin America*, International Development Policy Series No. 9. Geneva/Boston: Graduate Institute Publications, Brill-Nijhoff.

Armitage, Derek. 2008. 'Governance and the Commons in a Multilevel World'. *International Journal of the Commons* 2(1): 7–32.

Ballvé, Teo. 2020. *The Frontier Effect: State Formation and Violence in Colombia*. Ithaca: Cornell University Press.

Booth, David. 2012. *Development as a Collective Action Problem: Addressing the Real Challenge of African Governance, Africa Power and Politics Programme, Synthesis Report*. London: Overseas Development Institute.

Bull, Benedicte, and Antulio Rosales. 2020. 'Into the Shadows: Sanctions, Rentirism, and Economic Informalization in Venezuela'. *European Review of Latin American and Caribbean Studies* 109: 107–33.

Cleaver, Francis, and Luke Whaley. 2018. 'Understanding Process, Power and Meaning in Adaptive Governance: A Critical Institutional Reading'. *Ecology and Society* 23(2): 49.

Conde, Marta, and Philippe Le Billon. 2017. 'Why Some Communities Resist Mining While Others Do Not?' *The Extractive Industries and Society* 4(3): 681–97.

Curruthers, David. 2008. *Environmental Justice in Latin America: Problems, Promise and Practice*. Cambridge: MIT Press.

Escobar, Arturo. 2020. *Pluriversal Politics: The Real and the Possible*. Duke University Press.

Kuyper, Jonathan, Bjørn Ole Linnér and Heike Schroeder. 2018. 'Non-state Actors in Hybrid Global Climate Governance: Justice, Legitimacy and Effectiveness in a Post-Paris Era'. WIRES Climate Change, 9:e497. DOI: 10.1002/wcc.497.

Le Billon, Philippe; María Cecilie Roa-García and Angelica López-Granada. 2020. 'Territorial Peace and Gold Mining in Colombia: Local Peacebuilding, Bottom-up Development and the Defence of Territories'. *Conflict, Security and Development* 303–33.

Leifsen, Esben, Marie-Therese Gustafsson, María Guzmán-Gallegos and Almut Schilling-Vacaflor. 2017. 'New Mechanisms of Participation in Extractive Governance: Between Technologies of Governance and Resistance Work'. *Third World Quarterly* 38(5): 1043–57.

Macpherson, Elizabeth. 2019. *Indigenous Water Rights in Law and Regulation: Lessons from Comparative Experience*. Cambridge University Press.

Martinez Alier, Joan. 2013. 'The Environmentalism of the Poor.' *Geoforum* 54: 239–41.

Richardson, Whitney. 2020. 'Nature's Rights in Colombia: An Exploration of Legal Efforts to Secure Justice for Humans and Nature'. Unpublished Master's thesis. Faculty of Landscape and Society, Norwegian University of Life Sciences.

Scott, James. 2009. *The Art of Not Being Governed: An Anarchist History of Upland South East Asia*. London: Yale University Press.

Strønen, Iselin. 2007. *Grassroots Politics and Oil Culture in Venezuela: The Revolutionary Petro State*. London: Palgrave Macmillan.

———. 2020. 'Venezuela's Oil Spectre: Contextualizing and Historicizing the Bolivarian Attempt to Sow the Oil'. *History and Anthropology*. DOI: 10.1080/02757206.2020.1762588.

Stavenhagen, Rodolfo.1992. 'Challenging the Nation-State in Latin America'. *Journal of International Affairs* 45(2): 421–40.

Washington, Haydn, Guillaume Chapron, Helen Kopnina, Patrick Curry, Joe Gray and John Piccolo. 2018. 'Foregrounding Ecojustice in Conservation'. *Biological Conservation* 228: 367–74. DOI: 10.1016/j.biocon.2018.09.011.

Weiss, Kristen, Mark Hamann and Helene Marsh. 2012. 'Bridging Knowledge: Understanding and Applying Indigenous and Western Scientific Knowledge for Marine Wildlife Management'. *Society and Natural Resources* 26: 285–302.

Weitzer, Viviane. 2017. 'Nosotros Somos Estado: Contested Legalities in Decision-Making about Extractives Affecting Ancestral Territories in Colombia'. *Third World Quarterly* 38(5): 1198–214.

INDEX